The Almost
Everything I know about Astrology
Astrology Dictionary

by Terry Nazon

Accidental Ascendant - A device employed by Evangeline Adams whereby to draw Horary interpretations from a natal Figure. In applying this method one determines the Ascendant for the moment the question is propounded, and rotates the Figure until this degree occupies the East point.

Accidental Dignity: Conditions of placement wherein a planet's influence is strengthened are termed Dignities; if weakened they are termed Debilities. These are of two varieties: Essential and Accidental.

Acronycal: Said of the rising after sunset, or setting before sunrise, of a planet that is in opposition to the Sun, hence in a favorable position for astronomical observation.
Acronycal place: The degree the planet will occupy when it is in opposition to the Sun.

Active Influence: That which results from an aspect between two or more astrological factors or sensitive points, thereby producing the action that can materialize in an event.

Adept: One who has attained to proficiency in any art or science. It may be said of a skilled astrologer who, through spiritual development, has attained to superior powers and transcendental knowledge concerning the origins and destiny of mankind. Formerly said of an alchemist who had attained the 'great secret' - presumably that concerning the 'transmutation of metals'. Its modern application is to the transmutation of unfavorable cosmic stimuli and the baser emotions into nobler impulses - thereby achieving the triumph of mind over matter, and of the spiritual over the carnal.

Adjusted Calculation Date: A term used in reference to a directed or progressed horoscope, indicating the date on which the planet culminates. Also termed Limiting Date. See 'Directions'.

Advantage, Line of: A term sometimes used with reference to the position of the Moon's Ascending Node in a Geocentric Figure. The line of advantage runs between the cusps of the third decanates of the Third and Ninth Houses. A position of the Node East of this line is judged to be favorable.
Related to it are the Arcs of Increased and Dwarfed Stature. From the middle of the First House, clockwise to the middle of the Eighth House, is the arc of Increased Stature, with its peak at cusp of the Twelfth House; and from the middle of the Seventh House, clockwise to the middle of the Second House, is the Arc of Dwarfed Stature, with its peak at the cusp of the Sixth House. *See Nodes, Moon's.*

Affinity: A binding by mutual attraction. The Sun is said to have an affinity with all the planets; Mars with Venus, in a magnetic or physical sense; Venus with Jupiter, in a philanthropic sense as one who loves his fellowman; Venus with Mercury, in an artistic sense.

Afflicted: (Afflicted by / in affliction with): Unfavorably aspected planets, points of house cusps. Loosely applied to: any inharmonious aspect to a planet, or to any aspect, particularly conjunction, parallel, square or opposition, to a malefic planet. Also by some applied to a mundane or zodiacal parallel with, or when, besieged by both in fortunes (q.v.). Some authorities consider that the sensitive degree on any House cusp can be afflicted, though any such consideration must be confined to instances where the birth-moment is known to a certainty.

Astrological Ages: As anciently
Air Signs: The mental or intellectual signs: Gemini, Libra, And Aquarius. Considered collectively, sometimes termed the Air asterism.

Albedo: Literally, whiteness. A measure of the reflecting power of a planet, in ration to its absorptive capacity; expressed in a figure which represents the amount of light reflected from an unpolished surface in proportion to the total amount of light falling upon it.
The albedo of the Moon and Mercury is 7; Venus 59; Earth 44; and Mars 15. Thus, the changeable character manifested by Moon and Mercury is seen to be connected in some way with their low reflective capacity.
An entirely different set of Lunar characteristics comes of the fact that as the Moon approaches an opposition to the Sun its surface temperature rises some 70-odd degrees above boiling point, and in consequence it emits a wide band of infra-red frequencies that are several times more powerful than any of the rays it reflects from the Sun. During the first few minutes of a lunar eclipse, the surface temperature falls to a sub-zero level and the infra-red emanation ceases.
The dimly-lit surface of the Moon at the Lunation is due to light reflected back from the Earth, which with its high albedo would appear to the Moon-dweller as four times larger and many times brighter than the Moon as seen from Earth.
There are some indications that Jupiter emits a ray of its own in addition to its reflected ray, but astrophysicists are not as yet in accord on that point.

Almanac: A book or table containing a calendar of days, weeks and months, to which are added astronomical or other data. Its use dates back at least to the Alexandrian Greeks. The Roman almanac was the fasti - days on which business could be transacted.
The earliest of which we have concise record is that of Solomon Jarchus, 1150 A.D. Purbach published one from 1450-6. His pupil Regiomontanus issues the first printed almanac in 1475. The most outstanding almanac maker of the Middle Ages was Nostradamus.
All English almanacs were prophetic until the year 1828; and until 1834 the stamp duty was 1s.3d. Per copy. The first almanac in the U.S. was issued in 1639 by William Pierce. It was exceeded in popularity by Poor Richard's Almanac (1732-57) issued by Benjamin Franklin. Watkins Almanac, issued since 1868, has an annual circulation of upward of two million copies. The chief Astrological Almanacs of the present epoch are 'Raphael's', first published in 1820, and Zadkiel's first published in 1830. All governments now issue an Ephemeris and a nautical almanac. *See 'Ephemeris'*.

Almuten: The planet of chief influence in a Nativity by virtue of essential and accidental dignities. Its strength is estimated from: its intrinsic character; its Sign position where posited, its own Sign, or the Sign in which it is in exaltation; its harmonious aspects from favoring planets; and its elevated position in a geo arc Figure. A term of Arabian origin, seldom employed by present day astrologers.

Altitude: Elevation above the horizon, measured by the arc of a vertical circle. A planet is at meridian altitude when it is at the Midheaven, the cusp of the Tenth House.

Ambient: That which moves. A term loosely applied to the heavens. Milton speaks of the ambient air; Pope of ambient clouds. Ptolemy used it to describe the tenth sphere that by its compelling force moved all other spheres with it from the East across the heavens. Since Copernicus exploded this concept, the modern astrologer is free to apply this excellent term to the Earth's surrounding magnetic field as varyingly charged by virtue of the cycles of the planets, the Sunspot cycle, and other cosmic phenomena.

Anahibazon: Arabic term for Caput Draconis *(q.v.)*.

Anareta, *n.*, **anaretic**, *a.* (destroyer). The planet which destroys form; that which kills, if such a term may be applied to a planet that unfavorably aspects the hyleg (q.v.). Last degree for example 29* also referred to as the "Karmic degree" of the "fated degree". The last degree of a sign before moving onto a new sign, or experience.
Anaretic Point. Anaretic Place. The degree occupied by the Anareta. The 29th degree of any sign.

Androgyny, *n.*, androgynous, *a.*: Hermaphroditic; having characteristics of both sexes. Said of the planet Mercury, which is both dry and moist.

Angels: The angels which were associated with the different planets. Some texts refer to angels being created by our thoughts for good or bad. *v. Planetary angels.*

Angle: (L., a corner). Any one of the four cardinal points in a Figure, or map, of the heavens; variously referring to the Zenith, or South Vertical; the Nadir, or North Vertical; and the East and West horizons: the cusps of the Tenth, Fourth, First and Seventh Houses, or the Medium Coeli, Immum Coeli, Oriens (Ascendant) and Occident (Descendant) of a Solar or, indeed, of any Celestial Figure. Usually identified as the Southern, Northern, Eastern and Western angles. They are the most powerful and important arcs in Astrology. Planets therein become immensely potent for good or ill, according to the nature of the planets and their aspects. The term may refer to the shape and position of the House as placed on the square maps employed by the ancient astrologers.
Many depose that the Ascendant is the most powerful angle in any Figure, though Ptolemy gives preference to the Midheaven, or Zenith, since the celestial bodies are uniformly more potent in their effects at their meridian altitude than when rising.

Angstrom: A ten-billionth of a meter. Employed as a unit for measuring the wave lengths of light. Ten angstrom equal one milli micron. *v. Wave Length.*

Angular: said of a planet in an angle *(q.v.)* or in an angular House. The angular Houses bear a correspondence to the Cardinal Signs, and planets therein posited are materially strengthened, though whether beneficially or adversely depends upon the nature of the planet itself as also upon the nature of the aspects it receives from other planets in the Scheme.

Angular Velocity: The angle through which a planet sweeps in a unit of time. Technically, the daily motion of a planet, expressed in degrees and minutes of arc, is its Angular Velocity.

Anomaly: The angular distance of a planet from its perihelion or aphelion.

Antipathies: The unaccountable aversions and antagonisms people feel toward each other when positions in their Nativities are in conflict. Among the causes of such conflict are the luminaries in dissociate Signs, or in inharmonious aspect to one another; the Ascendants in opposition Signs; the unfortunate conjunct or in inharmonious aspect to the luminaries, or to each other, or in opposition from angular Houses. Sometimes loosely applied to planets seen in an inharmonious relationship through an adverse aspect, whereat they are considered to bear an anipathy to one another.

Antipathy: Disharmony of two bodies, usually planets, which rule or are exalted in opposite Signs. For example, Saturn ruling Capricorn has an antipathy for the Moon, ruling Cancer.

Antiscia: Solstice Point
Gemini-Cancer
Leo-Taurus
Virgo-Aries
Libra-Pisces
Scorpio-Aquarius
Sagittarius-Capricorn
find the Antiscia of your Sun by subtracting your Sun sign degree from ees 29 degrees 60 minutes to arrive at your Antiscia. From the list above, we find that the Antiscia of the sign Virgo is always Aries.

Antiscion: or solstice point As modernly used in the so-called Uranian Astrology, it is the reflex position of a planet's birth position, in that degree on the opposite side of the Cancer-Capricorn axis, of which either 0º Cancer or 0º Capricorn is the midpoint. For example, the antiscion of a planet at 14º Capricorn is at 16º Sagittarius, which point becomes effective when occupied by another planet, or one in transit or by direction. As first used by Ptolemy the term is applied to two planets which have the same declination on the same side of the equator. One in the same declination on the opposite side was termed a contra antiscion. *v. Parallel.*

Antisedentia: An older term descriptive of retrograde motion.

Aphelion: *v. Orbit.*

Apheta: Prorogator. The planet or place that exercises an influence over the life and death of the native. *v. Hyleg.*

Aphorism: A short, pithy statement of a truth, presumably based on experience; the dictum of a wise man. Applied in Astrology to considerations involved in the summing-up or synthesis of the various testimonies contained in the Figure. In interpreting a figure, or chart, consider the Signs as static forces; the planets as driving forces. The planets in the Signs show capacities that make for character, but the aspects, like verbs, denote action.
Neptune gives the answer to 'Who is he?'; Uranus to 'Why is he and what is his purpose?'; and the rest of the planets answer the question 'How will he fare?'

Apogee: *v. Orbit.*

Apparent Motion: In describing motions it is traditional to speak of them in terms of what they appear to be rather than what they are. The west wind personifies the wind that comes out of the west but which actually blows in an easterly direction. Because of the axial rotation of the Earth, the planets appear to rise over the Ascendant and travel across the meridian to the west, while they actually travel in the opposite direction. The Signs likewise appear to travel in a westerly direction while actually they do not travel at all. When we say the Sun is in Taurus, we are not actually speaking of the Sun's travel or of its position, but of the Earth's position and travel as measured by the Sun.

Application: *n.* Applying to; to apply. Said of a body in motion toward a point whence it will aspect another body. *(v. Aspect.).*
Applying, Retrograde: When the applying body is in retrograde motion. *(v. Motion.)*
Some authorities have used the term 'approach' as synonymous with 'apply'. The faster-moving body is said to be applying to an aspect of the slower-moving one. Precision in this regard might indicate, for example, that Saturn in direct motion could be applying to an aspect of Uranus, Neptune or Pluto only. Aspects are more powerful when forming than when separating. If planet be retrograde, the influence is said to be injurious, or the promised result so subject to delay that it is of little value when it materializes.

Appulse: The near approach of one orbital body to another - a conjunction; the culmination at or crossing of the meridian. Applied particularly to the appulse of the Moon near to the Earth's shadow. *v. Penumbral Eclipse.*

Apsis, *n.* (pl., apsides). The points of greatest and least distance of a heavenly body from its centre of attraction. *v. Orbit.*

Aquarius. The eleventh sign of the zodiac. *v. Signs.*

Arabian Points, or **Parts.** Of the so-called Arabian Points, Fortuna, or the Part of Fortune, is the best known to modern astrologers, although its full significance is not generally realized. These Points tend to show that the Arabians understood the value of the Solar Houses -- those based upon the Sun's degree as the Ascendant, erecting twelve Houses consisting of successive thirty-degree arcs.

Arc. A portion or segment of a curved line, such as a circle, or ellipse. Hence the orbital distance separating two bodies, or between two points.

Arc of Vision. The least distance from the Sun at which a planet is visible when the Sun is below the horizon. ***Diurnal Arc.*** The arc through which the Sun passes from sunrise to sunset. At the Equinox this arc is 180°, or 12 hours of right ascension. With increased latitude (distance away from the Equator) and nearness to the Solstices it becomes larger or smaller. ***Nocturnal Arc.*** That portion of 360°, or 24 hours, which remains after subtracting the Diurnal Arc. ***Semi Arc.*** Diurnal and Nocturnal, Half of either the Nocturnal or Diurnal Arc, measured from the Midheaven or Imum Coeli to the horizon. ***Arc of Direction.*** The distance between a significator and the point where it forms an aspect with a promittor, measured in degrees and minutes of the Equator; distance from the place of a planet to the body of same, or to a point where an aspect will be formed thereto. It may be measured either in Sidereal Time according to Tables of Ascension, or in Right Ascension as computed by spherical trigonometry. In primary directions this Arc is translated into time in the proportion of one degree of arc to a year of time, or five minutes of arc to one month of time. *(v. Directions.)*

Ares. The Greek god of War and Pestilence: Son of Zeus and Hera, consort of Aphrodite. The Romans associated him with Mars, the enemy of tyrants and defender of the just.

Aries. The first sign of the zodiac. *v. Signs.*

Armillary Sphere. A skeleton sphere suggested by concentric rings which represent the relative positions of the celestial circles of the equator and the ecliptic revolving within a horizon and meridian divided into degrees of longitude and latitude. It was invented by Eratosthenes *(q.v.)*, who by this means computed the size of the Earth, and inclination of the ecliptic to the equator; also the latitude of the city of Alexandria. The armillary sphere is frequently used as a decoration, such as the beautiful specimen cast in bronze and supported on the shoulders of Atlas, which adorns the entrance to Rockefeller Plaza in New York.

Ascendant. The degree of the Zodiac, which appeared on the eastern horizon at the moment for which a Figure is to be cast. It is often loosely applied to the whole of the Rising Sign and to the entire First House as well as specifically to the exact degree on the horizon. With reference to a Birth Figure it signifies properly the east point of the same, placed at the *left* thereof *(v. Map of the Heavens)*; hence the Sign and the degree thereof are distinguished as the Rising Sign *(q.v.)* and the Rising Degree. A planet between the lower meridian and the eastern horizon is ascending by virtue of the Earth's rotation, but it does not arrive at the Ascendant until it reaches the last degree of the nocturnal semi-arc.
Old authority speaks of the Ascendant as the Horoscope, and of all planets in the eastern segment of the Figure as Ascendant planets since all are actually rising, but in course of time this term has become obsolete. Only those planets that are within orbs of a conjunction with the Rising Degree, or that are in the First House, are said to be in the Ascendant. Some authorities deem that a planet in the last 12 degrees of the Twelfth House should be interpreted as a First House planet.

Ascending. A term Loand Tosely applied to any planet on the eastward side of the line between the cusps of the Fourth enth Houses, which by the diurnal motion of the Earth is rising in the heavens. More precisely it applies to a planet on, or near, the eastern horizon, or in the First House. A planet oriental and matutine to the Sun is said to ascend to the Sun. One that is occidental and vespertine to the Moon is said to ascend to the Moon. Ptolemy describes the luminaries, when so placed, as guarded.
A. Latitude. The increasing latitude of a planet moving toward the north pole of the Ecliptic.
A. Signs. v. Signs.

Ascension. The vertical rising of a planet above the Ecliptic, equator or horizon. *Right Ascension*, the circle of declination reckoned toward the east from 0° Aries, measured in the plane of the Equator. *Oblique Ascension*, measured on the Prime Vertical. The Midheaven is directed by Right Ascension; the Ascendant by Oblique Ascension.
Ascension, Signs of Long. Cancer, Leo, Virgo, Libra, Scorpio, Sagittarius. *(v. Signs.)*
Ascension, Signs of Short. Capricorn to Gemini inclusive.

Ascensional Difference. The difference between the Right Ascension of any body and its Oblique Ascension: used chiefly as expressing the difference in time between the rising or setting of a celestial body, and six o'clock; or, six hours from the meridian passage. To find this, add the log. tangent of the declination of the planet, to the log. tangent of the latitude of the place. The sum will be the log. sine of the Accessional Difference. This added to the planet's Right Ascension, when in South declination (or subtracted, when in North declination), gives the Oblique Ascension of the planet. The reverse process yields the Oblique Descension.

Aspect. Anciently termed Familiarities or Configurations (Q.V.). Certain angular relationships between the rays which reach the Earth from two celestial bodies, or between one ray and a given point: such as -- the horizon; the degree that was on the horizon at a given moment, or that represents the position of a planet at a given moment; the point on which an Eclipse or other celestial phenomenon occurred; the places of the Moon's Nodes; or the cusps of the Houses, particularly the First and Tenth.

Many factors enter into the delineation of the effect of an aspect: such as -- the nature of the aspect; the character of the planets involved, their latitude, character and rate of motion; their strength by virtue of their sign position; the measure of harmony that exists between the signs in which are posited, and between the signs they rule; and sundry other considerations. Various terms are employed to describe these factors.

Generally speaking, the term Aspect is applicable to any blending of rays that results in their interactivity. The body, which has the faster mean motion, is said to aspect the slower. As speed in orbit is relative to the size of the orbit, the inner planet aspects the one farthest removed from the Sun. Thus Venus aspects Saturn, not vice versa. There are exceptions, but only when other factors are involved. Transiting Saturn cannot pass over Venus, but Saturn can pass over the degree, which Venus occupied on some former occasion, at which time its influence was sufficiently augmented to create a sensitive degree -- a Venus sensitivity. Thus when Saturn transits this degree, you receive a Saturn impulse through a Venus expectancy. This illustrates the two principal types of aspects: (a) mutual aspects -- those which occurred between two moving bodies on some specified date; and (b) directional, progressed or transitory aspects -- between a moving body, and a fixed point, usually the degree a planet occupied on a specified day of birth, when it became a sensitive point in a life pattern of daily expectancy and receptivity. The planet, which "burned" its mark into, your pattern, has moved away -- but the expectancy and receptivity lingers on.

FORMING, is said of the conditions of motion, which are bringing two bodies within each other's sphere of influence, whereby an exact aspect will result. After the aspect has become exact, the receding motion is termed SEPARATING. Also, the faster planet may be spoken of as APPLYING TO or SEPARATING FROM an aspect or a CONTACT with the other. When sufficiently within each other's ORBS of influence to be deemed operative - within half the sum of their two orbs - it is a **wide** or PLATIC aspect, which CULMINATES in an EXACT or PARTILE aspect. An aspect computed forward in the order of signs, or counter-clockwise on the map, is a SINISTER or left-hand aspect; in the reverse direction, a DEXTER or right-hand aspect. There is lack of agreement as to which are the stronger, but ancient texts favor the dexter aspects.

ZODIACAL ASPECTS, those most widely considered, are measured in degrees along the Ecliptic. They are based upon fractional divisions of the 360-degree circle of the ecliptic - as measured in arc from the point of an observer on the Earth.

Conjunction. Said of two planets occupying the same degree of Longitude along the Ecliptic. It is often classed as a position rather than an aspect.

Dividing the circle by one-half, results in the OPPOSITION, a 180° separation, the reverse of a conjunction.

Dividing the circle by one-third, results in the TRINE, or 120° separation.

Subdividing the one-half aspect, there results the square, quadrate or quartile (90°), Semi-square, semi-quadrate or semi-quartile (45°), and the sesquiquadrate (135°) - square plus semi-square - the inversion of the semi-square.

Subdividing the one-third aspect, yields the Sextile or Hexagon (60°), Semi-sextile (30°), and the Quincunx (150°) - the inversion of the Semi-sextile.

The matter of Orbs is one that has never been settled. The figures given are merely an average of opinion:

NAME	*Signs*	*Degrees* WHEN EXACT	*Operative From*	*To*
Conjunction	0	0	-10°	+6°
Semi-Sextile	1	30	28°	31°
Semi-Square	1½	45	42°	49°
Sextile	2	60	56°	63°
Square	3	90	84°	94°
Trine	4	120	113°	125°
Sesquiquadrate	4½	135	132°	137°
Quincunx	5	150	148°	151°
Opposition	6	180	170°	186°

Names have been given to these Aspects, as follows: 0°, Prominence; 30°, Growth; 45°, Friction; 60°, Opportunity, 90°, Obstacle; 120°, Luck; 135°, Agitation; 150°, Expansion; 180°, Separation.

QUINTILE. A group of aspects, introduced by Kepler, based on a division of one-fifth of the circle. They have had limited adoption, and their value is chiefly in directions. They are:

   Bi-Quintile........................ 144°
   Tridecile........................... 108°
   Quintile (one-fifth of 360°)....... 72°
   Decile or Semi-Quintile............ 36°
   Quindecile......................... 24°
   Semi-Decile, or Vigintile.......... 18°

COMBUST. Said of a planet closer than 5° to the Sun. It introduces factors that considerably alter the interpretation of the conjunction.

CAZIMI. A planet within 0°17' of the Sun's longitude is said to be "in the heart of the Sun" - or Cazimi. Ancient authorities deemed that it fortified the planet as much as a Combust position debilitated it; but modern authorities generally ignore the distinction and classify it as combust, imparting to the nature a one-track viewpoint on all matters appertaining to the planet so placed.

ABSCISSION, or FRUSTRATION. When a planet is simultaneously forming an aspect to two other planets, the one that culminates first may produce an abscission of light that will frustrate the influence of the second aspect. The term was much used by ancient writers, but unfortunately has been neglected by modern astrologers -- other than those who practice Horary astrology. v. **FRUSTRATION**.

BENEFIC. The aspects based on 3 are said to be benefic in their influence, though much depends upon the character of the planets involved. The Trine joins harmonious signs; the Sextile, those reasonably congenial.

MALEFIC. Those based on 2, combine signs that are less congenial, and operate generally at cross-purposes, hence are termed malefic. Modern astrologers tend to prefer malefic aspects between harmonious planets, to benefic aspects between malefic planets - but this enters into the realm of interpretation where mathematics yields to psychology. A planet thus aspected, particularly if by a malefic planet, is said to be afflicted.

LATITUDE, Parallels of. Latitude is measured in degrees of arc N. or S. of the Ecliptic. It is reasonable to assume that planets conjoined in latitude as well as longitude will impart a stronger accent than when at different distances above the ecliptic. The Zodiacal **Parallel** is a latitudinal aspect. Older authorities considered a Parallel effective between one planet in North and another in South Latitude, but modern authorities largely agree that both bodies must be on the same side of the Ecliptic. Within orbs of 1° it is a powerful influence, greatly intensifying the effect of a conjunction. On rare occasions, when planets are close to their nodes of intersection with the ecliptic, a parallel may result in an eclipse between planets. The eclipse of a planet by the Moon is of more frequent occurrence, and is termed an **Occultation** (q.v.).

DECLINATION, Parallel of. This is the same phenomenon as a Parallel of Latitude, except that longitudinal position is measured along the Equator in terms of Right Ascension, while latitudinal position is computed in terms of declination, measured in degrees N. or S. of the Equator instead of along the Ecliptic.

MUNDANE ASPECTS are those reckoned along the Equator, and measured in subdivisions of the nocturnal or diurnal semi-arc. For example: Any two planets that have a separation of two houses are in mundane Sextile; of four houses, in mundane Trine. Thus it is possible for two planets to be simultaneously in the mutual relationship of a mundane Trine and a zodiacal Square. Mundane aspects can be computed only on a map erected for a birth moment. They represent a computation of coincidental influences on a basis of time, in subdivisions of the Earth's period of rotation; instead of on a basis of degrees of arc, in subdivisions of the orbits of the bodies involved. Zodiacal Aspects, based on the degree of longitudinal separation along the ecliptic, are computed without reference to an hour of birth, and are the ones commonly employed in delineation.

Because of the alternation of signs of long and short ascension throughout the daily rotation of the Earth, equal units of arc rise over the horizon of an individual on the Earth's periphery, in disproportionate units of time; and vice versa. This affords one explanation of the phenomenon of the ***Orbs*** in reference to Aspects, and suggests that consideration should be given to the seasons at which a wide zodiacal aspect may become an exact mundane aspect.

Mundane Parallel. Parallel in Mundo. This has to do with a similarity of relationship between two planets on opposite sides of, and the same distance, measured along the Equator, from any one of the four angles of the horoscope. Mundane parallels bear no analogy to zodiacal parallels. A RAPT PARALLEL is a mundane parallel by direction, formed after birth, as a result of the Earth's rotation (axial), whereby the places of the planets are carried from East to West to the point where the two planets are equidistant from, and on opposite sides of the same angle. Another variety of mundane parallel by direction, is that formed when one planet advances to the same distance from an angle as that held by another planet at birth. These parallels are the invention of Placidus de Titus who held them in high esteem. Yet it appears that time tempered his judgment, for in his collection of Nativities he frequently employs zodiacal directions as taught by Ptolemy.

Strength of Aspects. The relative strength of aspects is a debatable factor, for so much depends on the intrinsic character of the rays. If you consider the rays as energy, each altered in character by virtue of the sign position of the planet from which it is emitted, the aspect determines the direction of the influence upon you as an individual. It is in the synthesis of qualitative, quantitative and directional factors that the practice of Astrology becomes both an art and a science.

FORMING Aspects are considered more powerful than SEPARATING Aspects; or at least the orb of influence is wider when forming. Some authorities make an exception in the case of the Sun and Moon, to the extent of placing the point of maximum influence from 2 to 5 degrees beyond the Degree in which the aspect becomes exact. There is the theory that separating aspects in the birth map represent influences which have already been made manifest; while forming aspects, particularly in the progressed map, represent influences which are yet to be experienced. Sepharial, in his Dictionary, has this to say regarding Separating Aspects: "When two bodies have been in exact aspect, the one which by its swifter motion moves away from the aspect, is said to separate from the other. When one of two bodies in aspect turns retrograde, it separates. When both bodies turn retrograde, doubtless a mutual separation is effected. In Horary Astrology these relations have distinct significations: the party representing the separating planet will decline the proposition, back out of the agreement, or annul the contract; the party represented by the retrograde planet will default in his agreement or contract; and when both turn retrograde there will be an annulment by mutual consent. Similar effects have been noted in regard to marriage."

CONJUNCTION. This is classified as a constructive influence, though much depends on the nature of the planets. Modern authorities tend to reject the classification of aspects as good or bad, since a so-called bad aspect has constructive possibilities to an individual who has the strength of resolve to put it to constructive use.

PARALLEL. The same nature as a conjunction. Since it is usually coincident with a conjunction it serves to give it an added accent. This accent is helpful if it involves other aspects from favorable planets. The effect of a parallel is generally considered to be of longer duration than that of a conjunction.

SEMI-SEXTILE (30°). An aspect of mixed quality, rhythmically favorable but involving planets in inharmonious signs.

SEMI-SQUARE OR SEMI-QUARTILE (45°). Generally termed a malefic aspect; somewhat mitigated, in case the aspecting planet is a benefic.

SEXTILE, Hexagon (60°). A favoring aspect, involving planets in congenial signs of the same polarity (q.v.). Alan Leo says of the Sextile aspect: that it partakes of the nature of Moon and Neptune; that it is more combining than any other aspect, and is often more potent and favorable than the trine; that its color largely depends on the nature of the planets involved, and of the Signs they occupy; and that while the trine may be said to denote negative goodness such as a reward for past deeds, the sextile denotes positive good in that it generates the activity that produces change and thus possesses greater potentiality for the future.

SQUARE. QUARTILE (90°). Generally deemed unfavorable, since it represents the struggle of two forces at cross-purposes. It imposes severe tasks to be accomplished only through much concentration and self-denial -- often interpreted by the individual in terms of ambition.

TRINE (120°). Supposedly the most favoring of aspects, joining planets in congenial signs of the same element. Trines are like having "a silver spoon in your mouth" - luck becoming "happy-go-lucky" for lack of the ambition that is born of challenge.

SESQUIQUADRATE (135°) Inversion of a Semi-square, and deemed equally unfortunate but less powerful.

QUINCUNX (150°). The inversion of a Semi-Sextile. Ptolemy called it inconjunct, practically rejecting it as an aspect of appreciable force. Modern statistics appear to indicate, however, that it has unrealized possibilities. It is presumed to be mildly favorable, but as it operates through inharmonious signs the resulting influence must be somewhat contradictory.

OPPOSITION (180°). Proper interpretation must give consideration to the psychological stimulus resulting from whatever planetary influences are then in operation, *from* a sign and *through* a house.

BIQUINTILE (144°). Classed as a harmonizing influence.

QUINTILE (72°). A mildly benefic aspect, but ineffectual when directed to malefic.

SEMI-QUINTILE OR DECILE (36°). Kepler deemed it a good influence, but mild.

SEMI-DECILE (18°). Harmonious, but weak.

INCONJUNCT, DISSOCIATE. These are terms sometimes applied to the Semisextile and the Quincunx aspects, as indicative that no relationship can exist between adjacent signs and houses, or between those which are one sign or house less than an opposition.

The aspects were anciently classified as benefic and malefic:
The **benefic aspects** are the Trine and Sextile. The conjunction is generally classed as a benefic aspect. In them the relationship is harmonious, between congenial signs, even though the influences related are often inharmonious -- because of the intrinsic nature of the rays so combined. They are deemed conducive of harmony, in that cosmic energy is released without obstruction.
The MALEFIC ASPECTS were the square and semi square. The opposition is generally classed as malefic, even though it combines signs that are moderately congenial. These are generally deemed conducive of friction, in that two opposing forces challenge the individual's capacity for adjustment. There follows a condensed interpretation of the aspects:

According to the ancient philosophers two systems of force are in operation, whereby Nature is maintained in a state of balance, and life enabled to manifest itself in physical form: These are the positive and the negative, the inflow and the outflow, the centrifugal and the centripetal, construction as opposed to destruction, expansion versus contraction. The result is a continual cycle of birth, maturity, decay and dissolution. Since these forces are equal, each complements the other.

All organic structures are built of cells, which in their simplest form are hexagonic spheroids, similar to those of the honeycomb. Therefore, the hexagon is the primary structural pattern of beneficence. When light enters at the external angle of 60°, and the internal angle of 120°, it necessarily illuminates all parts of the structure in equal lines of influence. The light that pours in at either of these angles, imparts exhilarating and harmonious vibrations, which stimulate its continuous growth. Opposed to this is the process of crystallization, recognized in magnetism and electricity, wherein the two forces operate at right angles to each other - a geometrical relationship that is destructive to organic form. As a result, side by side through Nature two mutually antagonistic forces exist, which, despite their antipathy to each other, work together toward the ordered disposition of the whole: one based upon the quadrature, the other upon the hexagon - the square and the trine.

Astrology postulates: that the quadrate relationship between energy sources is destructive to form, through releasing the energy that is locked up in the various structures Nature has built; and that the trine aspects constitute the constructive side of Nature, whereby organic forms are created, nourished and perpetuated, to be released when subsequent destructive configurations are encountered.

Ancient astrologers who looked upon the Zodiac as representing the soul of Nature, divided it into four parts, making the beginning point of each part the apex of an equilateral triangle. Thus it obtained the twelve signs of the Zodiac and their corresponding Houses.

To establish a relationship between the physical body and these two systems of partitioning a sphere, one considers first that portion of the heavens which, like the physical body born into this world, is at that moment emerging from darkness into light; the eastern horizon - otherwise known as the Ascendant, the cusp of the First House; or as anciently termed, the Horoscope.

Aspectarian. A chronological list of all aspects formed during a specified period. Most astrology magazines carry an Aspectarian for the concurrent month; and one for the year is now usually appended to the Ephemeris.

Asterism. A constellation. Sometimes misleadingly applied to a zodiacal Sign, but can be applied to the three signs of the same element, considered collectively.

Asteroids. v. Solar System.

Astral Body. In occult terminology a replica of the physical body, but more subtle and tenuous. It penetrates every nerve, fiber and cell of the physical organism and is constantly in a supersensitive state of oscillation and pulsation. The psychic faculty within the astral body is impressionable to extra-sensory vibrations. The astrological concept is that of a magnetic field wherein the individual does most of his thinking, and from which he draws impressions by way of interpreting changes in the field due to cosmic radiation.

Astral Light. In occult terminology, the invisible region that surrounds the Earth, perceived by those who are psychically developed. Within its realm is recorded every condition, event or circumstance - past, present and future. It is called the "great terrestrial crucible," in which everything is resolved and perpetuated. The psychically gifted behold there, in panoramic detail, the histories of nations and individuals, and are able to reveal coming events by what they see mirrored on the astral screen. It has been spoken of as the Mercury of Nature.

Astral projection. In occult terminology, the partial or complete separation of the astral body from the physical body, and visiting another locality, near or far. This occurs in sleep - though, as a general rule, one does not recall the experience on waking. The adept can command his astral body to go any place he desires in order to make observations and investigations, and acquire essential information. Some dreams are the result of such travel episodes.

Astrolabe. A mechanical device, predecessor to the sextant, whereby mariners determined the time of day by the Sun, of the night by the stars, and the height and depth of mountains and valleys. The astrolabe of Christopher Columbus was on display at the Philadelphia Sesquicentennial. The oldest known example, called "The Mathematical Jewel," is of Persian origin. It was made by Ahmad and Mahud, sons of Abraham *(q.v.)* the Astrologer of Isfahan, and is in the Lewis Evans collection in the Old Ashmolean Museum at Oxford, England. The invention is attributed by some to Hipparchus *(q.v.)* but others credit it to the Arabs, some 400 years prior.

considered, a period of roughly 2150 years during which the point of the Spring Equinox recedes through one sign of the Zodiac of Constellations. Since the constellations have no precise boundaries, the points of beginning and ending are mere approximations.

However, it is an absurdity to date the beginning of the processional cycle, of presumably 25,800 years, from the particular time in history when it was decided no longer to treat the Equinox as a moving point, but instead to freeze it at 0º Aries. It is probably that midway between the Equinoctial points are the Earth's Nodes, where the plane of its orbit intersects that of the Sun, at an inclination of approx. 50º; but since the Equinoctial Point is now considered as a fixed point and the motion takes place only within its frame of reference, it appears that a study of the circle which the celestial pole describes around the pole of the Ecliptic will be required in order to determine when it passes an East point, to mark the time of beginning of the first of twelve astrological ages of 2150 years each, into which the precessional cycle is subdivided. On this manner of reckoning the Earth might now be in the Capricorn Age, as well as any other. At least there is no justification for us to consider mankind as now in the Aquarian age, even though a recent astronomical treatise speaks of the Signs of the Zodiac as 'now precessed some 25º west of the constellations of the same name'. Historical records show the Equinox as having once began in Taurus, at which time Taurus was considered to be the first Sign of the Zodiac. *See 'Precession'.*

Astrology. The science, which treats of the influence upon human character of cosmic, forces emanating from celestial bodies. It has been spoken of as the soul of astronomy. Its antiquity places it among the earliest records of human learning. To these ancient astrologers we owe the modern Science of Astronomy. According to Hindu lore Astrology reached its zenith some two hundred thousand years ago, and is presumed to have been first taught by the Manu who had charge of the fourth root race. In ancient times it enjoyed general acceptance, and was practiced by the Chaldeans, Egyptians, Greeks, Romans, and Arabs. It flourished in Europe during the 14th and 15th centuries. It is charged that the Spanish Inquisition was a cloak to disguise a secret purpose to stamp out Astrology. It was once termed Astromancy - divination by the stars.

Geocentric vs. Heliocentric Astrology. As practiced by various authorities in various countries there are two fundamentally different methods, or approaches, of Astrology: the Geocentric and the Heliocentric. Geocentric Astrology is based upon calculations of the planetary positions as seen by the observer on the Earth, i.e, using the Earth as a center. Heliocentric Astrology bases its interpretations upon positions within the solar system with reference to the Sun as the center. While it is true that the Sun is the center, the effect of the motion as manifest on the Earth is the basis of most astrological interpretation. Therefore the vast majority of astrologers employ the geocentric calculations of the planets' positions. However, these terms are used by many astrologers in a different sense, i.e., heliocentric when considering changes of position by virtue of the body's motion in orbit, and geocentric when considering changes of position with reference to the observer, by reason of the observer's personal orbit around the Earth -- the revolution of the periphery of the Earth around the Earth's center. Thus considered the Signs are heliocentric divisions, or Heliarcs, while the Houses are geocentric divisions, or Geo arcs.

There are several distinct branches of Astrology:

Natal*, or *Genethliacal - having to do with the birth figure and the subsequent transits of the bodies and their Progressed, or average net progress. *v. Directions, Progressions.*

Horary: fundamentally a horoscope cast for the birth-moment of an idea, a question, or an event. Practitioners of this branch of Astrology usually take the moment when the question is propounded.

Electional: an application of Horary art whereby to choose the most propitious moment for initiating a new enterprise, or commencing a journey, etc.

Mundane, also termed Judicial Astrology: a consideration of the current positions of the planets with respect to their influence upon entire populations, or portions thereof, by countries, cities or localities, at Ingresses, eclipses, ordinary Lunations and Full Moons, and major transits or conjunctions.

Medical: the application of the science to questions of health, chiefly as a diagnostic aid when confronted with baffling symptoms of disease and obscure ailments.

Meteorological, also known as Astro-Meteorology: the application of the science to the forecasting of weather conditions, earthquakes and severe storms.
Agricultural: an application of Astrology to the planting and the harvesting of crops.

Astromancy. A system of divination by means of the stars, the practice of which had much to do with the popular connotation of Astrology with fortune telling, which modern scientific Astrology has had to live down.

Astrometeorology. Investigation of the relation between the Solar system bodies and the weather.

Astronomical unit. Mean distance of Earth to Sun, or 92,900,000 miles; employed as a unit for indicating intra-solar system distances.

Astronomos. The title given by the priests to the Initiate in the seventh degree of the reception of the mysteries in the Initiation at Thebes in Egypt.

Astronomy. The science that deals with the heavenly bodies: their positions, motions, magnitudes and conditions.

Astrotheology. A system of theology founded on what is known of the heavenly bodies, and of the laws, which regulate their movements.

Aten. The solar disk, or more specifically the light that proceeds from the sun, as defined by Akhenaten, or Amenhotep IV (obit. circa 1397 B.C.), father-in-law of King Tutankamen, who promulgated a religion largely based on astrological teachings.

Athazer. An ancient term applied to the Moon when in conjunction with the Sun, or separated from it by an arc of 12°, 45°, 90° 150°, 160°, or 180°.

Aura. In occult terminology, a psychic effluvium that emanates from human and animal bodies and inanimate objects. It is composed of electro-vital and electro-mental magnetism; an envelope surrounding that of which it partakes - visible only to the psychic. The aura is multi-colored and brilliant, or dull, according to the character or quality of the person or thing. To the seer, the aura of a person is an index to his hidden propensities.

Aurora Borealis, Northern Lights. Scientists associate the phenomena with unusual sunspot activity, and astronomers are working on the theory that the sunspot cycles, generally recognized as having some connection with economic trends, are the result of planetary movements. The most brilliant display of the Aurora Borealis in fifty years occurred on January 25, 1938. Transatlantic radio was interrupted and crowds in Holland, awaiting the birth of Princess Juliana's baby, cheered the display as a lucky omen for the little Princess Beatrix, who was born January 31, 1938, with 15° Aries on the Asc., and 6° Capricorn on the M.C. At this time Venus and the Sun were forming conjunctions with Jupiter, and Mars was forming a conjunction with Saturn.

Axis, Inclination of. The equators of rotating bodies appear never to parallel their orbits. Hence there is an inclination of the axis when considered in reference to the plane of the orbit. Within the solar system these inclinations are, at this epoch, as follows: Mercury 72°, Venus 60°, the Earth 23½°, Mars 25°, Jupiter 3°, Saturn 26°, Uranus 102°, Neptune 155°, Pluto unknown. The inclination of the Sun's axis to the plane of the Earth's orbit is about 7°. Its inclination to the plane of its own orbit is unknown, because the Sun's orbit is itself unknown. It is claimed by some that there is an additional motion of the Earth's axis amounting to 50" a century, making an orbit of about 2½ million years, in the course of which the North Pole and the South Pole successively point to the Sun instead of as at present to the Pole Star. This theory is advanced by way of explanation for successive Ice Ages.

Axial rotation: The diurnal motion of the Earth around its axis; also similar motion on the part of any other celestial body. *v. Solar System.*

Azimene. Said of a planet posited in certain weak or lame degrees or arcs, which, if ascending at birth, were supposed to make the native blind, or lame, or otherwise physically afflicted.

Azimuth. A point of the horizon and a circle extending to it from the zenith; or an arc of the horizon measured clockwise between the south-point of the horizon and a vertical circle passing through the center of any object.

Baal. (Lord). Among the Phoenicians the chief male divinity who appears to have symbolized the Sun, more particularly the Sun in Taurus. Baal was worshipped in agricultural festivals as the god of fertility of soil and increase of flocks. In successive periods of the history of the ancient Semitic races, the name was assigned to innumerable local deities. The Baal of Tyre was introduced among the Israelite settlers by Ahab. Hannibal was so named because he was supposed to be in favor with Baal.

Babel, Tower of. A temple dedicated to the study of the planets, which were supposed to divulge the secrets of life and guide human destiny.

Babylon. An ancient Semitic city in the Euphrates valley, which after 2250 B.C., as the capital of Babylonia, became a center of world commerce and of the arts and sciences, its life marked by luxury and magnificence. The city in which they built the Tower of Babel, its location coincides approximately with that of the modern city of Baghdad - now the center of a vast agricultural community. The Babylonians attached great importance to the motions of the planets, accurately fixed their orbits and worked out tables of the phases of the Moon, whereby eclipses could be correctly predicted. Their great astrological work, "The Illumination of Bel," was compiled within the period of 2100-1900 B.C.. From fragments of the tablets of another astrological work, which has been preserved, it is found that their calendar began with March 21; and its twelve divisions, and their names, give evidence of astrological significance. Their story of the deluge closely parallels that of the Bible, and the location of their Mount Nisir (Mount of Refuge) is seemingly that of Mt. Ararat, where the ark stranded. Their Hanging Gardens were one of the Seven Wonders of the Ancient World. From what remains of their literature, it appears that with the rise of astrology there arose a wave of fatalism that, however, later gave way to a doctrine of self-determination

- the belief that the stars impel but do not compel. Babylon is generally conceded to have been the cradle of astrology. It was overthrown in 539 A.D., by Xerxes, the Persian.

Babylonian. An astrologer: so-called because the Babylonians were famed for their knowledge of Astrology.

Barren Signs. Gemini, Leo and Virgo. The Moon in Sagittarius, and Aquarius is also said to signify a tendency toward barrenness. *v. Signs: Barren and Fertile.*

Beholding Signs. Those which have the same declination; i.e., at equal distances from the Tropics; as Aries and Virgo, Taurus and Leo, Gemini and Cancer, Libra and Pisces, Scorpio and Aquarius, Sagittarius and Capricorn. Because such pairs of Signs were either both Northern, or both Southern, they were by Ptolemy deemed to be "of equal power." This consideration, however, applied only when two such Signs were joined by a body in each, mutually configured.

Bel. (Lord). The Babylonian form of Baal. He was a member of the supreme triad of deities: Anu, god of the heavens; Bel, god of the Earth; and Ea, god of the waters.

Belts of Jupiter. A varying number of dusky belt-like bands or zones encircling the planet Jupiter, parallel to its equator. It suggests the existence of an atmosphere, the clouds forced into a series of parallels through the rapidity of rotation, the dark body of the planet showing through relatively clear spaces between.

Benefic Aspects. Planetary relations, or familiarities, which permit the unobstructed release of cosmic energy, hence conducive to harmony. (*v. Aspects: Benefic, Malefic.*) *B. Influences.* Those produced by benefic planets and aspects, either in the Nativity or by transits. *B. Planets.* The so-called benefics: Venus and Jupiter, by some the Sun. *(v. Planets.)*

Besieged. A benefic planet situated between two malefics, within orbs of each, is said to be besieged and therefore unfortunately placed. Some authorities restrict its application to a Significator when between and within orbs of two benefics. Older authorities, which applied the term to a planet situated between any two planets, considered a planet between Venus and Jupiter to be favorably besieged, but if between Mars and Saturn it was in an extremely unfavorable position.

Bestial signs: Those, which have been symbolized by beasts, or animals: Aries, Taurus, Leo, and Scorpio, the last half of Sagittarius, Capricorn and Pisces. v. Signs.

Bicorporeal: Said of double-bodied Signs: Gemini, Sagittarius and Pisces. As originally employed by Ptolemy, bicorporeal was the only term by which he characterized the signs that are now designated as Mutable, or Deductive. Thus it is apparent that he classified Virgo also as bicorporeal. *v. Signs.*

Bi-Quintile *v. Aspect*

Birth Moment: What is generally accepted as the true moment of birth is the moment of the first inspiration of breath after ligation of the umbilical cord. At that moment the infant ceases to receive blood conditioned through the mother's receptivity, and in response to the law of adaptability must grow channels of receptivity to cosmic frequencies that accord with those present in the Earth's magnetic field, and through these receptivities it begins to condition its own blood. This moment must be reduced to Standard Time, adjusted to Greenwich world-time for calculating the planets' places, thence readjusted to Local Mean Time at the birth place to determine the Ascendant and the Midheaven degrees and the House-cusps.

Birth Stones:

By her who in January was born
No gem save **garnets** shall be worn
They will ensure her constancy
True friendship and fidelity.

The February born shall find
Sincerity and peace of mind,
Freedom from passion and from care,
If they, the **amethyst** will wear.

By her who in March was born
No gem save **bloodstone** shall be worn
They will ensure her constancy
True friendship and fidelity.

She who from April dates her years,
diamonds shall wear,
lest bitter tears
For vain repentance flow.

Who first beholds the light of day
In spring's sweet, flower month of May
And wears an **emerald** all her life
Shall be a loved and a loving wife.

By her who in June was born
No gem save **pearls** shall be worn
They will ensure her constancy

The gleaming **Ruby** should adorn,
All those who in July are born,
For thus they'll be exempt and free,
From lover's doubts and anxiety.

Wear a **peridot** or for thee,
No conjugal fidelity,
The August born without this stone,
'Tis said, must live unloved; alone.

A maiden born when autumn leaves
Are rustling in September's breeze,
A **sapphire** on her brow should bind;
To bring her joy and peace of mind.

October's child is born for woe,
And life's vicissitudes must know,
But lay an **opal** on her breast,
And hope will lull those woes to rest.

Who first comes to this world below
In dreary November's fog and snow,
Should prize the **topaz** amber hue,
Emblem of friends and lovers true.

If cold December gave you birth
The month of snow and ice and mirth
Place on your hand a **turquoise** blue;

True friendship and fidelity.   Success will bless whate'er you do.

—Gregorian Birthstone Poems

Bitter Signs. A term applied by older authorities to the Fire Signs Aries, Leo and Sagittarius, which were said to be hot, fiery and bitter. v. *Signs.*

Blend: A term employed by Maurice Weymss to indicate a relationship between zodiacal degrees (1) when the ruler of one degree is in or in close aspect to the other degree; (2) when one degree is closely aspecting or in the same degree as the ruler of the other degrees; or (3) when the rulers of each degree are in close aspect to each other.

Brahmanaspati. Hindu name for the planet Jupiter. A deity in the Rig-Veda. Known in Vedic mythology as Brihaspati, signifying the power of prayer. His wife Tara was carried away by Soma (the Moon).

Broken Signs. v. *Signs.*

Brutish signs v. *Signs*

Buddha. (1) Gautama Siddhartha, founder of Buddhism in the 6th century B.C., was classed by his followers as the perfect example of a divine godly man. His religion taught tolerance, universal compassion, charity, love, self-sacrifice, poverty, and contentment with one's lot. His faith was never enforced by fire and sword. (2) Esoterically connected with the planet Mercury, as the enlightened and wise one who has attained perfect wisdom.

Cadent houses: These are the 3rd, 6th, 9th and 12th houses of the horoscope.

Cardinal signs: Aries, Cancer, Libra and Capricorn. These are signs which are initiating.

Celestial equator: The earth's equator projected into space.

Chart: A horoscope drawn up for a individual's birth date or for an event date.

Combust: A planet is said to be combust when it is in close conjunction with the sun.

Constellation: A grouping of stars which form a pattern in the sky. For example: The 12 zodiac constellations which are found on the ecliptical belt share identical names, although they are not found in the same locations as the 12 signs of the zodiac.

Culmination: When a planet is positioned on or near the Midheaven in a horoscope chart, it is said to be culminating.

Cusps: In astrology the word cusp refers to the lines which divide the houses or signs in a natal horoscope chart.

Day. The interval of time between two successive passages of a star over the meridian is a Sidereal day 23h, 56m of mean solar time). The interval between two successive passages of the Sun's center over the same meridian is a solar day (24 hours); of the Moon's center a lunar day (24h, 50m). In old astrological texts the Lunar Day refers to the day of the Full Moon. Because of the Earth's motion in orbit the mean solar day is 4 minutes longer than the sidereal day and because of the Moon's daily motion in orbit the lunar day is 50 minutes longer than the solar day. The term natural day is a misnomer, loosely applied to the 24-hour period of the Earth's rotation. The mean solar day becomes the civil day when reckoned from the hour affixed by law. In most countries this is from midnight to midnight. With the Hindus and Babylonians it was from sunrise to sunrise; with the Athenians and Jews from sunset to sunset; with the ancient Egyptians and Romans at midnight. This is divided into 24 hourly divisions from 1 to 12 noon, and 1 to 12 midnight.

Army and Navy time during recent years has been largely superseded by numbering the hours straight through from 0h at midnight to 24h of the next midnight; which also is 0h of the next day.

Astronomical Day. Until January 1, 1925, this day was reckoned as beginning 12 hours later than the civil day. Now all calendars and almanacs begin the day at midnight.

Julian Day. On January 1, 1925, the astronomical day was superseded by the Julian day, numbered consecutively beginning from 4713 B.C. To avoid confusion in the comparison of ancient and modern dates the Julian day was made to begin at noon, twelve hours later than the civil day. January 1, 1934, was J.D. 2,427,439.

Civil Day. The civil day begins at midnight at 180 east or west from Greenwich. It then continues one hour later with every 15° of the Sun's westward travel. Thus when one passes this International Date Line he begins a day that will not end until 24 hours later, with the result that when it becomes Tuesday to the west of the Line it has just become Monday to the east thereof, and circumnavigating travelers gain or lose a day according to their direction of travel; losing a day if westbound, gaining it when eastbound. Loosely speaking, a day is the period of light between sunrise and sunset, the period of daylight or sunshine. In the Far East it is the distance that can be traveled in 24 hours.

In astrological parlance a Day Horoscope is one cast for a birth moment in which the Sun was above the horizon, hence in one of the Houses numbered from 7 to 12; a Night Horoscope one in which the Sun is below the horizon, in a House numbered between 1 and 6.

Day House. *v. Ruler.*

Day of Week, to determine *v. Dominical Letter.*

Daylight Saving Time. *v. Time, Daylight-saving.*

Day Triplicity. Older authorities deemed that in the daytime some planets are stronger when posited in Signs of a certain element; i.e. Saturn in an Air-Sign, the Sun in a Fire Sign, Mars in a Water Sign, and Venus in an Earth Sign.

Debility. An embracive term, preferably applied to any planet disadvantageously placed by virtue of its House position, but frequently employed loosely as a synonym of Detriment.

Decade. Ten consecutive years; any grouping of ten.

Decanate, Decan. A term applied to a subdivision of Sign into 10° arcs, referred to as the first, second and third decanates or decans. The interpretation of Decans is based upon a system of ruler ships, of which there are two in common use. One method ascribed Mars to the first Decan of Aries and thence carried a fixed series throughout the 36 Decans, ending again with Mars ruling the third Decan of Pisces. The series is Mars, Sun, Venus, Mercury, Moon, Saturn, Jupiter; as follows:

............First Decan..Second Decan..Third Decan
...**Aries**........ Mars .... Sun .... Venus
...**Taurus**....... Mercury ..... Moon ...... Saturn
...**Gemini**....... Jupiter ..... Mars ...... Sun
...**Cancer**....... Venus .... Mercury ... Moon
...**Leo**.......... Saturn ...... Jupiter ... Mars
...**Virgo**........ Sun .... Venus ..... Mercury
...**Libra**........ Moon .... Saturn .... Jupiter
...**Scorpio**...... Mars .... Sun .... Venus
...**Sagittarius**.. Mercury ..... Moon ...... Saturn
...**Capricorn**.... Jupiter ..... Mars ...... Sun
...**Aquarius**..... Venus .... Mercury ... Moon
...**Pisces**....... Saturn ...... Jupiter ... Mars

The other method employs the Ruler of the Sign as specifically the Ruler of the First Decan, with the Second and Third Decans associated with the Rulers of the other two Signs of the same Triplicity. Thus the First or Aries Decan of Aries is ruled by Mars; the Second or Leo Decan, by the Sun; and the Third or Sagittarian Decan, by Jupiter. This gives this series:-

....................1.............2...........3
...**Aries**..........Mars..........Sun.........Jupiter
...**Taurus**.........Venus.........Mercury.....Saturn

and so on.

Decatom: a Dichotome *(q.v.).*

Decile: *v. Quintile.*

Declination. The manner of indicating distance N. or S. of the Celestial Equator. The maximum possible declination of the Sun is 23° 28', which occurs at the Solstices, when the Sun passes the Tropics (0°) of Cancer and Capricorn, the limit of the pole's greatest inclination from the plane of the Earth's orbit. The first degrees of Aries and Libra have no declination, since at these points the ecliptic intersects the equator. However, planets at this longitude may have declination. *(v. Celestial Sphere.)*

The declination of a body whose longitude and latitude are known is found by this formula:

1. Radius (10,000): Tangent of Ecliptic (23° 27')∷ sine of longitudinal distance from equinox: tangent of Angle A.

2. Cosine of Angle A: cosine (latitude plus/minus 90°- minus Angle A)∷ cosine of Ecliptic Obliquity (23° 27'): sine of the Declination. (In this equation the latitude is taken from go, if the latitude and longitude are of different denomination; but when of the same denomination they are added, and from this sum Angle A is subtracted.)

The Moon, Mercury, and Mars reach a declination of 27° north, and on rare occasions Venus reaches 28°. Jupiter, Saturn, Uranus and Neptune have practically the same declination as the Sun.

Decreasing or Increasing in Light. From the New to the Full Moon the Moon is increasing in light, and from the Full to the next lunation it is decreasing in light. In a Figure measured from the Sun position, if the Moon is less than 180° counterclockwise from the Sun it was waxing, or increasing in light; if less than 180° clockwise from the Sun it was waning or decreasing in light. Although generally applied to the Moon, it is also applicable to any planet when passing from an opposition to a conjunction with the Sun. It usually occurs when approaching the Sun in the order of the signs; but Mercury and Venus, after they have reached their greatest elongation East or West and are retrograding toward the Sun, decrease in light against the order of the signs. It is generally accepted as weakening the planet's influence.

Decumbiture. Literally, a "lying down." A horary figure erected for the moment when a person is taken ill, wherefrom to judge as to the possible nature, prognosis and duration of the illness.

Deductive Type. Referring to a certain quality or habit of mind that characterizes those born when the Sun was in a Mutable sign: Gemini, Virgo, Sagittarius or Pisces. *v. Signs.*

Deferent. In Ptolemaic astronomy, an imaginary orbit pursued by a celestial body, around which another body moved in an epicycle *(q.v.)*. A deferent was employed in conditions wherein the natural motion of the body was not involved. The term reflects the fact that Ptolemy was ignorant of the Earth's motion.

Degree. One 360th part of the circumference of a circle. The rough measure of an angle of one degree is the apparent diameter of a dime held at arm's length from the eye. The apparent diameter of the Sun and Moon is about 0.5°. The longest dimension of the bowl of the Big Dipper is about 10°. A degree is divided into 60 equal parts called minutes of arc. The length of a degree of latitude on the Earth's surface increases from 68.71 miles at the equator to 69.41 miles at 90°. The length of a degree of longitude on the Earth's surface varies from 69.65 miles at the Equator to 53.43 at 40°. Degrees are equally applicable to the Zodiac or the Ecliptic. As a time unit it is applicable to the Equator thus:

Degrees of Arc......Hours and minutes of time

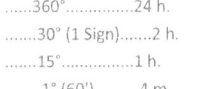

......360°...............24 h.
.......30° (1 Sign).......2 h.
.......15°................1 h.
.........1° (60')..........4 m.

........1' (60").........4 s.

Degree Rising. The degree of the zodiacal Sign posited on the Ascendant (Q.V.), or cusp of the First House at birth, and generally considered the most important in the Nativity. The rising degree is based upon the exact moment of birth, or of the event for which the Figure is cast, and the correct geographical latitude and longitude. Should either factor be unknown the Figure is usually cast for sunrise, which places the Sun's degree upon the horizon, resulting in what is termed a Solar Figure. As it is based only on the Earth's apparent motion around the Sun some authorities term it a Heliard Figure.

Degrees, Individual. Several works, symbolical, speculative and statistical, treat of influences presumed to repose in certain individual degrees. Maurice Wemyss in the four volumes of his "Wheel of Life" even introduces some hypothetical and as yet undiscovered planets to account for certain qualities and effects. It is probable that many of the qualities ascribed to individual degrees have to do with sensitive points created by Eclipses, major conjunctions, or a close conjunction in both longitude and latitude between a solar system body and a fixed star, which points are accented by the transit of another planet at a later date. For ready reference a list of such points is arranged in a zodiacal sequence, which includes: (1) the degrees created by important stars, nebulae and clusters; (2) the planets' Nodes; (3) the points of the planets' Exaltation and Fall; (4) the major planetary conjunctions from 1940 to 1946 inclusive; to which others can be added at will from the Ephemerides; (5) Solar Eclipses, from 1940 to 1946, inclusive; and (6) such other degrees which from experience appear to exert a decisive influence.

Individual Degree Tables (in following articles)

The stars listed in these tables of Individual Degrees are located as of 1925. To adjust them to other dates add 50 1/3" of longitude for each year later, or subtract for each year earlier. (APOLLO'S NOTE: FOR 2003, 78 YEARS LATER, THIS GIVES AN ADDITION TO MAKE OF 65.4333', IE 1°5', OR APPROX. 1.1°.)

The ancients ascribed names to the various stars, and many of these names are still in use. In 1603 Bayer devised a more scientific system whereby the stars in a constellation are known by the name of the constellation to which they belong, the individual stars within the constellation known by Greek letter prefixes, according to size, beginning with the largest as Alpha, and continuing downward to Omega. The system is still in use, except for the telescopic stars, of which a million have been classified, and these are identified by a catalogue number.

The sequence of the data on the Fixed Stars, supplied in the following lists, is as follows:

Longitude, Latitude (magnitude) (WHERE SPECIFIED - FOR THE FIXED STARS ETC.), popular name, astronomical designation, description (NATURE ACCORDING TO PTOLEMY - WITH ADDITIONS BY ALVIDAS - AND OTHERS) and its astrological significance.

The interpretations given are mostly from ancient authorities, which apparently were inclined to place undue stress upon the direful.

To see these tables, v. Degrees, Individual, Aries; Degrees, Individual, Taurus, etc. etc.....

Degrees, Individual, Aries (accurate 1925; add 1° 5' for 2002 positions of fixed stars etc.)
(Abbreviations: neb, nebulae; cl, cluster; v, variable.)

Aries

0°.....A positive nature that creates its own destiny. Cusp of First Lunar Mansion, a so-called Critical Degree.
1°.....Degree of the Surgeon; an organizer.
1°14', 20° 48'S (2) Diphda, Beta Ceti. A yellow star in the Whale's Tail. (Saturn - Mercury Mars) Sickness, misfortune, compulsory changes, self-destruction by brute force.
1° 50'.Mars-Jupiter conj.: January 6, 1940.
2°.....Degree of abscesses; literary and poetic.
3°.....Birds and aviators; collisions; goitre.
4°.....Cruelty.
5°.....Unsatisfied ambitions.
6°.....Jaundice.
7°.....Degree of life and death
7°51', 12° 36'N (3) Algenib. Gamma Pegasi. A white star at the top of the wing of Pegasus. (Mars Mercury)Notoriety, violence, the pro- fessional beggar.
8°.....Degree of courage; immorality.
9°.....Triumph; great generals
10°....Spiritual triumph; scientific interests; a degree of electricity.
11"....Spiritual intuitions.
12°....Cusp of Second Lunar Mansion.
13°....Degree of the Physician; of food and drink.
13°24' 25° 41'N (2) Alpheratz, alpha Andromedae. A double star, purple-hued white, in the hair of Andromeda; often called Andromeda's head. Its name, from Al Surrat Al Faras, or The Horse's Navel, indicates it was formerly listed in the constellation Pegasus. (Jupiter Venus - Mars) Riches, horrors, independence and a keen intellect.
14°....Degree of apoplexy or suicide.
15°....Persuasive oratory; public life.
16°....Children.
17°....Oratory.
18°....Mental fertility and physical passionateness.
19°....Exaltation of Sun: Fall of Saturn; a Fortunate Degree.
20°....Abscesses; accidents; electricity.
20°50' 20° 20'S (3 1/2) Baten Kaitos, Zeta Ceti, the Whale's Belly. A topaz-yellow star. (Saturn) Enforced migration, accidents; shipwreck, with rescue.
21°....Hope; artistic.
22°....Music.
23°....Philosophy.

24°....Literature; travel.
25°....Cusp of Third Lunar Mansion; exploration and discovery.
25°42' 5° 22' N (4) Al Pharg, Eta Piscium, associated with the Greek Head of Typhon. A double star near the tail of the Northern Fish. (Saturn Jupiter) Determination, preparedness, and eventual success.
26°....Degree of tuberculosis of the lungs; of opposition and strife; militant leaders. Great soldiers are found on this Aries- Libra axis.
26°15'.Mars-Saturn conj.: February 11, 1940.
26°43' 33° 21'N (Neb.) Vertex, 31m Andromedae, the great nebula N. of Andromeda's head. (Mars Moon) Eye weakness or blindness, violent death.
27°....Tenacity of purpose; hair; Mars in this degree indicates red hair.
28°....Power to realize a lofty ideal.
29°....A prophet of a new order.
29°17' 25° 56'N (2) Mirach, Beta Andromedae. A yellow star in the Zona (girdle) of Andromeda. (Venus - Mars Moon) Beauty, love of home, brilliant mind, fortunate marriage, renowned for benevolence.

Degrees, Individual, Taurus (ACCURATE 1925; ADD 1º 5' FOR 2002 POSITIONS OF FIXED STARS ETC.)
(ABBREVIATIONS: NEB, NEBULAE; CL, CLUSTER; V, VARIABLE.)

Taurus
0°.....Powerful in combining old principles in new applications.
1º.....Magic.
2°.....Degree of plot and strategy. Important degree in nativities of great military generals.
2°5' 8° 29'N (3) Sharatan, beta Arietis. A pearly white star on the Ram's North Horn. (Mars Saturn) Unscrupulous; defeat; destruction by war, fire or earthquake.
3°.....Exaltation of the Moon; a fortunate degree. One accustomed to the exercise of authority.
4°.....Founder of a sect; the seat of law.
5°.....Occultist, healer; hermit.
6°.....Degree of many enemies.
6°32' 9° 58'N (2) Hamal. Alpha Arictis. A yellow star in the Ram's forehead -- the "following horn." (Mars Saturn - Venus Saturn) Cruelty; premeditated crime.
7°.....Determined and resourceful.
8°.....Cusp of Fourth Lunar Mansion. A critical degree.
9°.....Neurasthenia.
9°6'...Jupiter-Saturn conj.; February 15, 1941.
10°....Architecture (10° - 12°).
11°....Experimental scientist.
12°....Air pressure and gravitation.
12°30'.Jupiter-Saturn conj.: October 20, 1941.
13°....Circulation of money: unfortunate for marriage.
13°7' 27° 48'N (2) Almach, Gamma Andromedae. An orange, emerald and blue binary or ternary star in left foot of Andromeda. (Venus) Eminence; artistic ability.
13°12' 12°35'S (2V2) Menkar, alpha Ceti. An orange star in the Whale's jaw. (Saturn - Venus Moon - Mars) Injury from wild beasts; loss of fortune.

14°....First point of stabilization; a fortunate degree; religious nature.
14°27'.Jupiter-Saturn conj.: August 8, 1940.
15°....Growth; music.
16°....Painting; influential in organizations.
17°....Appendicitis.
17°14'.Mercury North Node.
18°....Leader of a party.
19°....Self-made man.
19°8'..Mars North Node.
20°....Cusp of Fifth Lunar Mansion; a critical degree; oratorical.
21°....Water travel.
22°....Success at any cost.
22°18'.Mars-Saturn conj.: February 22, 1942.
23°....Patient in toil.
23°5' 40° 22'N (cl) Capulus, 33 Uranus vi Persei. A double cluster in the sword-hand of Perseus. (Mars Mercury) Defective eyesight.
24°....Poet and recluse.
25°....Autocratic and unscrupulous; death of partner; a bad reputation.
25°3' 22° 25'N (v) Algol, Beta Persei. A white binary and variable star, marking the Medusa's head held in the hand of Perseus. (Saturn) Said to be of a violent nature, the M.C. directed to this position arousing mob violence and murderous tendencies, which dispose toward a tragic end. It is reputed to be the most malefic of the stars. Conjunct the Sun, Moon or Jupiter it gives victory in war.
25°34'.Jupiter-Uranus conj.: May 8, 1941.
26°....Fortune by marriage.
26°38'.Mars-Uranus conj.: March 1, 1942.
27°....A fortunate degree; steadfast; fortune through employment
28°....Literature; powerful will, and organizing ability.
28°52° 4° 2'N (3) Alcyone, Eta Tauri. A greenish yellow star; the brightest of the Pleiades, representing one of the seven daughters of the nymph Pleione, by Atlas, who by Neptune became the mother of Hyreus. The names of the other six are Maia, Electra, Taygeta, Sterope (or Asterope), Celano, and the invisible, or "lost" one, Merope, who concealed herself from shame at having loved a mortal. That Alcyone was at one time presumed to be the center of the Milky Way Galaxy indicates that the ancients may have visualized Atlas as resting on this point while supporting the Earth on his shoulders. (Mars Moon) Eminence; if conjoining Sun or Moon - accidents to face, or blindness from smallpox; a strong love nature.
29°....Degree of fate; favored by fortune; a dramatic area; a famous actors' degree.
29°19'.Saturn-Uranus conj.: May 3, 1942.

Degrees, Individual, Gemini (ACCURATE 1925; ADD 1º 5' FOR 2002 POSITIONS OF FIXED STARS ETC.)
(ABBREVIATIONS: NEB, NEBULAE; CL, CLUSTER; V, VARIABLE.)

Gemini.
0°.....Degree of draftsmanship (also 1° and 2°).
2°.....An ambassadorial degree.

3°.....Exaltation of Moon's North Node: a point of spiritual illumination. Cusp of Sixth Lunar Mansion: a critical degree.
4°.....Degree of aviation; of mental stability.
4°41' 5° 44'S (4) First of the Hyades, Gamma Tauri (Saturn Mercury - Mercury Mars) Contradiction of fortunes; injuries to the head by instruments; impaired eyesight.
5°.....Degree of quiet fortunes.
5°8'...Mars-Uranus conj.: January 16, 1944.
6°.....A degree of brilliant intellectuality; of expression in language.
7°.....Degree of cantankerous irritability.
8°.....Ascendant and Uranus in U.S. horoscope.
8°40' 5° 28'S (i) Aldebaran, Alpha Tauri. The Watcher of the East; the Bull's Eye. A red star, the brightest of the Hyades, a group of seven stars called "Weepers" because when they rise or set heliacally they were anciently supposed to bring rain. The Sun conjoins them during the latter days of May and the beginning of June. (Mars - Mercury Mars Jupiter) Said to have ruler ship over hands and fingers, and when afflicted to be conducive to pneumonia. In conjunction with Mars or Saturn, or either luminary, it was said by the older astrologers to presage a violent death. It is rendered increasingly malefic by the opposition of Antares in 8°39' Sagittarius.
9°.....Degree of homicide; elevation through partnership or marriage.
10°....A Fortunate degree.
12°....A degree of hope realized.
13°....Degree of accidents to wheeled vehicles; of imitation and acting.
13° 43'Uranus North Node.
14°....Degree of dumbness from impaired speech organs.
15°....Inheritor of a home.
15°43' 31° 8'S (1) Rigel, Beta Orionis. Orion's left foot. (Jupiter Mars) Preferment, riches, great and lasting honors. If culminating: great military or ecclesiastical preferment.
16°....Cusp of Seventh Lunar Mansion; a critical degree. A degree of sleep and trance.
16°11'.Venus North Node.
16°20'.Mars-Jupiter conj.: April 3, 1942.
16°53'.Mars-Uranus conj.: August 17, 1945.
17°....A degree of homicide.
19°50' 16° 50' S (2) Bellatrix, Gamma Orionis. (Mars Mercury) Said to confer military and other honors that end in disaster. Conjoining Sun or Moon, blindness. If culminating: a forger or swindler.
19°54'.Mars-Saturn conj.: March 7, 1944.
20°44' 22° 55'N (1) Capella, Alpha Aurigae; Hircus, the Goat. (Mars Mercury) When culminating: said to confer martial or ecclesiastical honors and riches, attended by waste and dissipation. It is too far north to conjunct Sun or Moon, or to rise or set.
21°16' 23° 37'S (2) Mintaka, Delta Orionis. Slightly variable double star, brilliant white and pale violet, in Orion's belt. (Saturn Mercury - Mercury Saturn Jupiter) Good fortune.
21°27' 5° 23'N (2) El Nath, Beta Tauri. (Mars) Eminence.
21°55' 28° 42'S (Neb) Ensis, 42m Orionis. (Mars Moon) Blindness or defective sight; illness; violent death.
22°....Degree of Literature.

22°22' 24° 32'S (2) Alnilam, Epsilon Orionis. Bright white star in the center of Orion's belt. (Jupiter Saturn - Mercury Saturn) Confers fleeting public honors. The three stars in Orion's belt, when in the Midheaven of a nativity are said to confer signal honors.
23°....Faith: a military degree; also affecting the spine.
23°40' 2° 12' S (3) Al Hecka, Zeta Tauri. (Mars - Mercury Saturn) Violence, malevolence, accidents.
25°....Degree of neurasthenia.
27°27' 66° 5N (2) Polaris, Alpha Ursae Minoris. A topaz-yellow and pale white double star, in the tail of the Little Bear, and marking the celestial pole. It is now 1°14' distant from North Pole, but in 2095 it will reach the nearest distance, 26'30". The pole has been successively marked by Alpha Lyrae (Wega), c. 12,200 B.C.; Tau Draconis, c. 4500 B.C.; and Alpha Draconis, c. 2700 B.C. It will be marked by Gamma Cepheis, c. 4500 A.D., Alpha Cephei, c. 7500 A.D.; Delta Cygni, c. 11,300 A.D.; and again Wega, c. 13,500 A.D. (Saturn Venus) Sickness and affliction; legacies attended by evil effects.
27°38' 16° 2'S (1) Betelgeuze, Alpha Orionis. Irregularly variable orange star in right shoulder of Orion. (Mars Mercury - Mercury Saturn Jupiter) When in opposition, said to cause accidents; but in conjunction, to bring honors. A military star.
28°....Degree of tuberculosis of lungs.
28°48' 21 ° 30'N (2) Menkalinan, beta Aurigae. (Mars Mercury) Ruin, disgrace.
29°....Degree of imitation and acting.

Degrees, Individual, Cancer (ACCURATE 1925; ADD 1º 5' FOR 2002 POSITIONS OF FIXED STARS ETC.)
(ABBREVIATIONS: NEB, NEBULAE; CL, CLUSTER; V, VARIABLE.)

Cancer.
0°.....Cusp of Eighth Lunar Mansion; a critical degree;
(1°-3°)Fortunate degrees;
(1°-2°)Degrees of sight.
2°19' 0° 54'S (3) Tejat, Eta Geminorum. A binary and variable star. (Mercury Venus) Pride, overconfidence, shamelessness, and violence.
4°.....A medical degree.
4°11' 0° 50'S (3) Dirah, Mu Geminorum. A yellow and blue double star. (Mercury Venus) Energy, power, protection.
5°.....Degree of sleep and trance (5°- 6°)
7°59' 6° 45'S (2) Alhena, Gamma Geminorum. A brilliant white star; called the wound in the Achilles' heel. (Mercury Venus - Moon Venus) Eminence in art; accidents to the feet.
9°54'..Jupiter North Node.
10°....Historical degree.
11°....Degree of retentive memory; of cancer and alcoholism.
12°....Cusp of Ninth Lunar Mansion; a critical degree.
12°59' 39° 39'S (1) Sirius, Alpha Canis Majoris. A yellow star; known as Orion's big dog - the dog star. (Jupiter Mars - Moon Jupiter Mars) Honor, renown; custodians, guardians, curators; high offices in the government. When rising, said to confer great dignity; often associated with dog bites.
13°....Degree of business; also 12°, 14°, 15°, 16°.
14°....A fortunate degree.

15°....Exaltation of Jupiter. A suicide degree.
16°....Degree of duty.
16°57'.Solar Eclipse: July 10, 1945.
17°57'.Mars-Saturn conj.: March 20, 1946.
17°24' 0° 11'S (3) Wasat, Delta Geminorum. A pale white and purple double star in the right arm of the Northern Twin. (Saturn) Malevolence, violence and destructiveness; associated with poisons and gases.
17°50° 5° 45'N (4) Propus, Tau Geminorum. (Mercury Venus) Eminence, strength, success.
19°8' 10° 5'N (2) Castor, Alpha Geminorum. The mortal one of the heavenly twins; associated with Apollo. (Mercury - Mars Venus Saturn - Moon Mars Uranus) Violence; sudden fame; honors, followed by disgrace or imprisonment. Rising: weakness, sometimes blindness; injuries to face.
19°34'.Pluto North Node.
20°....Degree of limitation and hindrance.
20°46'.Mars-Saturn conj.: January 20, 1946.
22°7'..16° 0'S (1) Pollux, Beta Geminorum. The immortal one of the twins, son of Jupiter and Leda; associated with Hercules. (Mars - Moon Mars Uranus) Connected with poisons; the art of self-defense; subtle, crafty, rash, cruel. If rising, eye weakness, sometimes blindness; injuries to face; wounds, imprisonment. If culminating, honor, preferment, followed by disgrace.
23°....Degree of forethought.
23°11'.Saturn North Node.
24°....Degree of music.
24°41' 16° 0'S (1) Procyon, Alpha Canis Minoris. (Mercury Mars -- Moon Jupiter Uranus) Sudden preferment, the result of individual exertion; yet eventually the activity it promotes brings sudden misfortune. Afflictions threaten trouble with and danger through liquids, water, gas, poisons, or dog bites. When rising, said to inspire admiration for the canine species.
24°47'.Mars-Saturn conj.: October 20, 1945.
25°....Cusp of Tenth Lunar Mansion: a critical degree.
27°....Degree of farming.
28°....Fall of Mars. Has to do with the hair.
29°....Degree of the avid collector.

Degrees, Individual, Leo (ACCURATE 1925; ADD 1º 5' FOR 2002 POSITIONS OF FIXED STARS ETC.)
(ABBREVIATIONS: NEB, NEBULAE; CL, CLUSTER; V, VARIABLE.)

Leo.
0°.....Homicide.
3°.....Biliousness.
5°.....Homicide, aviation accidents.
6°.....Sight.
6°7' 1°33' N (cl) Presaepe, 44m Cancri. The manger of the Aselli: a nebulous cluster. (Mars Moon) Adventure, wantonness, brutality; at other times fortunate, though liable to loss through others; industry, order and fecundity; large business. Rising, or conjunction an afflicted Moon: blindness, especially of left eye; ophthalmia; facial injuries; fevers, wounds. If Sun oppose Mars or Asc.: violent death. If culminating: disgrace, ruin, violent death.

6°25' 3°11'N (5) North Asellus, Gamma Cancri. Identified with Balaam's ass. The Aselli represent the asses ridden by Bacchus and Vulcan in the war between the Gods and the Titans. (Mars Sun - Sun sextile Mars) Patience, beneficence, courage; sometimes marital preferment; heroic and defiant leaders.

7°36' 0°4'N (4) South Asellus, Delta Cancri. (Mars Sun - Sun > Mars) Fevers, quarrels, slander.

8°.....Cusp of Eleventh Lunar Mansion; a critical degree; Anaemia; hearing.

9°.....Bladder afflictions; alcoholism; Army and Navy.

9°31'..Mars-Pluto conj.: May 12, 1946.

11°10'.Neptune North Node.

12°....A degree of beauty.

12°31' 5°5'S (4) Acubens, Alpha Cancri. (Saturn Mercury) Activity, malevolence, prevarication.

13°....Degree of literature.

15°....First point of Affection: The Lion point.

17°....Degree of aviation; of air and gas.

18°....Medical ability (18°-22°).

19°....The back.

19°35' 9°43'N (3) Algenubi, Epsilon Leonis. (Saturn Mars) Cold, heartless, bombastic, destructive; but with artistic perceptions and facility of expression.

20°....Cusp of Twelfth Lunar Mansion; a critical degree. A degree of Faith.

20º-24ºDegrees of homicide.

21°....Comedy.

22°....Appendicitis.

23°....The stage.

25°....Alcoholic (25°-26°); astrology (25°-29°).

26°....Mars-Jupiter conj.: July 5, 1944.

26°10' 22°23'S (2) Alphard, Alpha Hydrae; often called the Heart of the Hydra. (Saturn Venus - Sun sextile Jupiter) Wisdom, artistic appreciation; knowledge of human nature; yet immoral, uncontrolled, and subject to tragedy.

26°27' 11°52' N (3) Adhafera, Zeta Leonis. (Saturn Mercury) Associated with criminal tendencies, poisons, suicide. If rising: military preferment and riches.

26°47' 4°52' N (3) Al Jabhah, Eta Leonis. Violent and intemperate nature; a military officer in danger of mutiny.

28°43' 0°28'N (i) Regulus, Alpha Leonis. A triple star; called the Lion's Heart; one of the Royal stars of the Persians, as Watcher of the North, marking the Summer solstice about 3000 B.C. (Mars Jupiter - Mars - Sun trine Uranus) Destructiveness; military honors, with ultimate failure; magnanimity, liberality, generosity; independent and high-spirited. If rising: honor and wealth, but subject to ill health. If culminating: high office under government; military success. If conj. Sun, Moon or Jupiter: honors and ample fortune.

Degrees, Individual, Virgo (ACCURATE 1925; ADD 1º 5' FOR 2002 POSITIONS OF FIXED STARS ETC.)

(ABBREVIATIONS: NEB, NEBULAE; CL, CLUSTER; V, VARIABLE.)

Virgo.

3°.....Cusp of the Thirteenth Lunar Mansion: a critical degree; appendicitis.

4°.....Asthma.
7°.....Degree of dress (7° - 10°)
8°.....Mixing and blending.
9°.....Homicidal tendencies.
10°....Purifying, cleansing, refining, and reducing to simplest essence. A degree of theology.
10°22' 14°20 N (2) Zosma, Delta Leonis. (Saturn Venus) Egotistical, immoral; fearful of poisoning.
11°....An astrological degree.
12°....Business (12° - 16°).
13°....Stage; feet.
14°....Degree of transformation and versatility (13° - 14°).
15°....Exaltation of Mercury.
16°....Cusp of Fourteenth Lunar Mansion; a critical degree, Christian ministers; a degree of symbolism.
17°....Degree of gliding or flowing.
20°30' 12° 16'N (2) Denebola, Beta Leonis, the Lion's Tail. (Saturn Venus - Mercury Uranus Mars) Said to bring honors and wealth, but leading eventually to disgrace; swift judgments; despair, regrets, misfortunes, through natural forces. If rising: good fortune, attended by dangers and anxieties, because of folly.
22°....A military degree; said to rule appendicitis; hairdressers.
23°58' 50°55'N (Neb) Copula, 51m Canum Ven. (Moon Venus) Blindness, defective vision, hindrances and disappointments.
24°....Degree of painting (24° - 26°).
25°....Cancer.
25°35' 17°34'S (4) Labrum, Delta Crateris. Associated with the Holy Grail. (Venus Mercury) Ideality, spiritual intelligence; salvation through fall from grace.
25°38' Mars-Neptune conj.: September 29, 1940.
26°2' 0°42'N (3½) Zavijava, Beta Virginis. (Mercury Mars) Combative, destructive, but beneficent; strength of character. Near to it was the Solar Eclipse of September 21, 1922, used by physicists in confirming the Einstein theory.
27°....Diabetes.
27°48' 63°43' S (2½) Markeb, Kappa Argus. (Saturn Jupiter) Piety, educational work; voyages.
28°....Solar Eclipse: August 21, 1941.
29°21'.Mars-Neptune conj.: September 16, 1942.

Degrees, Individual, Libra (ACCURATE 1925; ADD 1º 5' FOR 2002 POSITIONS OF FIXED STARS ETC.)
(ABBREVIATIONS: NEB, NEBULAE; CL, CLUSTER; V, VARIABLE.)

Libra.
0°.....Cusp of Fifteenth Lunar Mansion; a sensitive degree.
3°.....Abscesses.
3°4'...Mars-Neptune conj.: August 23, 1944.
3°43' 1°22'N (4) Zaniah, Eta Virginia; a variable star. (Mercury Venus) Congeniality, refinement, order; a lovable nature.
5°.....Homicide.

6°.....Degree of birds; aviation; goiter.
6°53'..Mars-Neptune conj.: August 20, 1946.
7°.....Sudden death; animal life.
8°.....Solar Eclipse: October 1, 1940.
8°50' 16°13'N (3) Vindemiatrix, Epsilon Virginis. So called because it anciently rose at vintage time. (Saturn Mercury) Falsity, sometimes dishonesty; loss of partner. If conj. Uranus: spinal trouble; heart trouble; seclusion.
9°.....Courage, triumph.
9°2' 2°48'N (3½) Caphir, Gamma Virginis. (Mercury Venus - Venus Mars) Refined and lovable character; prophetic instincts.
12°....Cusp of Sixteenth Lunar Mansion; a sensitive degree.
12°20' 12° 11' (3) Algorab, Delta Corvi. (Mars Saturn) Destructive, malevolent; a scavenger.
13°....Food and drink.
15°....Suicide, apoplexy.
16°32' 49°33'N (3) Seginus, Gamma Boötis. (Mercury Saturn) Subtle mind, but suffers through bad company.
17°....Electrical (16°-18°).
19°....Fall of the Sun.
21°....Exaltation of Saturn. The stage, comedy.
21°3' 58°55'S (v) Foramen, Eta Argus. Surrounded by the "Key-hole" nebula. (Saturn Jupiter) Piety; acquisitiveness; danger to eyes. If conj. Sun: shipwreck.
22°....Artistic; hope.
22°43' 2°3'S (1) Spica, Alpha Virginis. (Venus Mars - Venus Jupiter Mercury) Said to be fixed and benefic; offering riches, renown, and a sweet disposition; the most fortunate of stars, when rising or on the Midheaven.
23°....Degree of homosexuality.
23°7' 30° 47'N (1) Arcturus, Alpha Boötis; Arctophilax, the bear watcher. Brightest star in the northern hemisphere (V. JOB 38:32). (Mars Jupiter - Mercury conjunct Venus) Renown through self-determination; prosperity by navigation and voyages.
24°....Musical.
25°....Cusp of Seventeenth Lunar Mansion; a sensitive degree; literature.
26°....Detectives.
27°....Consumption.
28°....Hospitality; hair.

Degrees, Individual, Scorpio (ACCURATE 1925; ADD 1º 5' FOR 2002 POSITIONS OF FIXED STARS ETC.)
(ABBREVIATIONS: NEB, NEBULAE; CL, CLUSTER; V, VARIABLE.)

Scorpio.
0°.....Sensuous and passionate degree.
2°.....Plot.
2°2' 48°59'N (3) Princeps, Delta Boötis. (Mercury Saturn) Profound and studious mind, adapted to research.

3°.....Fall of the Moon.
5°45' 0° 28'N (4) Khambalia, Lambda Virginis. (Mercury Mars) Changeable, unreliable, argumentative.
6°.....Occultist and leader; that which is slippery but soothing.
8°.....Cusp of Eighteenth Lunar Mansion; a critical degree.
10°....Neurasthenia
10°46' 52°52'S (1) Acrux, Alpha Crucis. Brightest star in the Southern Cross. (Jupiter) Ceremonial, benevolent, mystic.
11°10' 44°20'N (2) Alphecca, Alpha Coronae Bor. (Venus Mercury -- Mars Mercury) Dignity; artistic sensibilities, inclined to poetry.
12°....Business (12°-16°)
13°....Air pressure.
13°58' 0°20'N (3) South Scale, Alpha Librae. (Jupiter Mars - Mars Venus Saturn) Unforgiving, untruthful; ill-health.
15°....The Center of Regeneration: the Eagle-point.
16°....Growth; painting.
17°....Music.
17°41'.Mercury South Node.
18°....Appendicitis.
18°15' 8°30'N (2½) North Scale, Beta Librae. (Jupiter Mercury - Mars sextile Jupiter) Good fortune, high ambition.
19°....The degree of avidity, an evil degree; the crucial point in the war between the Ego and the Supreme Will; animal life. 19°8'..Mars South Node.
20°....Cusp of Nineteenth Lunar Mansion; a critical degree.
20°56' 25°25'N (2½) Unukalhai, Alpha Serpentis. (Saturn Mars - Mars Saturn opposition Venus) Immorality, accidents, danger of poison.
21°....Bronchial tubes.
22°43' 44°9'S (1) Agena, Beta Centauri. (Venus Jupiter - Mars conjunct Mercury) Refinement, morality, good health; universally respected.
25°....Dumbness; alcoholic.
27°....Literature; memory.
28°....Brewers.
28°28' 42°34'S (1) Bungula, Alpha Centauri. Often called Proxima, because of its nearness to the Earth: 275,000 astro. units. (Venus Jupiter) Friends; refinement; honor.

Degrees, Individual, Sagittarius (ACCURATE 1925; ADD 1º 5' FOR 2002 POSITIONS OF FIXED STARS ETC.)
(ABBREVIATIONS: NEB, NEBULAE; CL, CLUSTER; V, VARIABLE.)

Sagittarius.
0°.....Degrees of draughtsmanship (0°-3°).
1°11' 17°15'N (3) Yed Prior, Delta Ophiuchi. (Saturn Venus) Shameless immorality; revolutionary.
1°27' 1°58'S (2) Isidis, Delta Scorpii (Mars Saturn - Venus Gemini Moon) Sudden assaults; malevolence; immorality.

2°4' 1°1'N (3) Graffias, Beta Scorpii. (Mars Saturn - Venus Gemini Moon Saturn) Malicious, merciless; susceptible to contagious diseases.

3°.....Exaltation of Moon's South Node: Fall of Moon's North Node. Cusp of Twentieth Lunar Mansion: a critical degree.

4°.....Aviation.

6°.....Degree of expression in language.

7°.....Degree of the heart.

8°7' 11°4'N (3) Han, Zeta Ophiuchi. (Saturn Venus) Harbinger of trouble.

8°39' 4° 34S (1) Antares, Alpha Scorpii; Mars' deputy; the Scorpion's heart. The Watcher of the West. It shows a fluted spectrum in which the reds predominate. (Mars Jupiter) Malevolent, destructive; generous; subject to presentiments of impending tragedy; rash impulses; headstrong obstinacy, chiefly injuring themselves. If rising or culminating: honor, preferment, good fortune.

9°.....Homicide.

10°50' 75°17'N (3) Rastaban, Beta Draconis. (Mars Saturn) Criminal tendencies; property losses; accidents.

12°....Accidents to wheeled vehicles.

13°....Degree of acting.

13°43'.Uranus South Node.

14°....Degree of dumbness; indecision.

16°....Cusp of Twenty-First Lunar Mansion: a critical degree. 16°11'.Venus North Node.

16°51' 7°11'N (2) Sabik, Eta Ophiuchi. (Saturn Venus - Jupiter Venus) Wasteful, inefficient; bad morals, but successful evildoer.

17°....Degree of matter in transition - heat, flame; homicidal. 18°....Royalty.

20°....Faith (20°-23°).

21°....Growth.

21°20' 35°51'N (2) Rasalhague, Alpha Ophiuchi. (Saturn Venus - Jupiter Mercury sextile Mars) Perverted and depraved tastes; misfortunes through women.

22°....A military degree.

22°54' 14°0'S (3) Lesath, Gamma Scorpii. (Mercury Mars) Associated with acids; danger, desperation; immorality.

23°....Faith.

24°39' 8°50'C (cl) Aculeus, 6m Scorpii. (conjunct Moon) If conj. or opposition an afflicted luminary, or its afflicting planet: impaired eyesight, perhaps blindness.

25°....Neuresthania.

27°35' 11°22'S (cl) Acumen, 7m Scorpii. (conjunct Moon) Companion to Aculeus, and of same nature and influence.

28°....Consumption.

28°38' 13°41'N (3) Sinistra, Gamma Ophiuchi. (Saturn Venus) Slovenly, immoral.

29°....Imitation; acting.

29°32' 0°1'N (CNC) Spiculum, 8, 20, 21m Sagittarii. (Mars Moon) Mentioned by Ptolemy in connection with blindness.

Degrees, Individual, Capricorn (ACCURATE 1925; ADD 1º 5' FOR 2002 POSITIONS OF FIXED STARS ETC.)

(ABBREVIATIONS: NEB, NEBULAE; CL, CLUSTER; V, VARIABLE.)

Capricorn.

0°.....The Galactic Center. The most important point in astrology. Cusp of the Twenty-Second Lunar Mansion. An ambitious degree.
2°.....Sight.
2°6' 2°21'N (4) Polis, Mu Sagittarii. (Jupiter Mars) Keen perception, domination; ambition, success; horsemanship.
3°.....Medical.
4°.....Sleep and trance (4°-5°).
6°.....Analogy.
7°.....Unusual ability.
7°12' 0°43'C (cl) Facies, 22m Sagittarii. (Sun Mars) Blindness or defective sight; illness; accidents.
9°.....Degree of history.
9°54'..Jupiter South Node.
10°....Memory.
11°....Religion.
11°16' 3°26'S (2) Pelagus, Sigma Sagittarii. (Jupiter Mercury - Saturn Mercury) Optimism; veracity; a religious tendency.
12°....Cusp of the Twenty-Third Lunar Mansion.
12°31' 7°10'S (3) Ascella, Zeta Sagittarii. (Jupiter Mercury) Happiness, good fortune.
13°52' 0°52'N (4½) Manubrium, Omicron Sagittarii. (Sun Mars) Heroic, courageous, defiant; blindness from fire or explosion.
14°....Suicide.
14°12' 61°44'N (1) Wega, Alpha Lyrae, a pale sapphire star in the lower part of the Lyre. (Venus Mercury - Jupiter trine Saturn in Part of Fortune) Beneficent, idealistic, hopeful, refined, changeable; grave, outwardly pretentious, but usually lascivious.
15°....Fall of Jupiter. A degree of duty.
16°....Degree of solid matter.
17°....Intellectual and governmental.
18°41' 36°12'N (3) Deneb, Zeta Aquilae. (Mars Jupiter) Benevolent, liberal; ability to command; and a successful warrior.
19°34'.Pluto South Node.
21°....A scholarly degree.
23°....Governmental authority; music.
23°11'.Saturn South Node.
24°43' 5°25'S (6) Terebellum, Omega Sagittarii. (Venus Saturn) Cunning, mercenary; a fortune, with a guilty conscience and unsavory reputation.
25°....Cusp of the Twenty-Fourth Lunar Mansion.
26°....Land and farming.
27°....Hair.
28°....Exaltation of Mars.
29°....Degree of collecting.

Degrees, Individual, Aquarius (ACCURATE 1925; ADD 1º 5' FOR 2002 POSITIONS OF FIXED STARS ETC.)
(ABBREVIATIONS: NEB, NEBULAE; CL, CLUSTER; V, VARIABLE.)

Aquarius.

0°.....Homicide (0° - 5°).
0°9' 48°59'N (3) Albirco, Beta Cygni. (Venus Mercury) Beauty; a lovable disposition; resigned to Fate.
0°39' 29°18'N (1) Altair, Alpha Aquilae. (Mars Jupiter - Uranus Mercury sextile Sun) Bold, confident, unyielding, liberal, valiant; sudden, but ephemeral wealth; a position of command; danger from reptiles.
2°42' 6°58'N (4) Giedi, Alpha Capricorni; a multiple star, yellow, ash, lilac. (Venus Mars - Venus sextile Uranus - Venus Mercury) Beneficences; sacrifices; brings strange events into one's life.
2°56' 4°36'N (3) Dabih, Beta Capricorni. (Saturn Venus - Saturn Uranus Gemini Mercury) Suspicion and mistrust; success, but retirement under a cloud.
3°36' 0°54'N (5) Oculus, Pi Capricorni. (Saturn Venus) If conj. Mercury: a clever and penetrating mind.
4°3' 1°12'N (5) Bos, Rho Capricorni. (Saturn Venus) Similar to Oculus.
5°.....Solar Eclipse: January 26, 1944.
8°.....Cusp of Twenty-fifth Lunar Mansion.
9°.....Executive; presidential.
10°....The principle of things.
11°10'.Neptune South Node.
11°37' 2°59'S (5) Armus, Eta Capricorni. (Mars Mercury) Contemptible, nagging, contentious, unstable.
12°....If Mars afflicted here: assassination.
12°43' 0°36'S (5) Dorsum, Theta Capricorni. (Saturn Jupiter) Bites from venomous creatures.
13°....Degree of beauty; literature.
15°0'..The Center of Humanity, the angel point. Solar eclipse, February 5, 1943.
17°....State of air and gases.
18°....Explosiveness.
19°....The back.
19°5' 4°58'S (5) Castra, Epsilon Capricorni. (Saturn Jupiter) Bad reputation; uncontrollable temper.
20°....Cusp of Twenty-Sixth Lunar Mansion; a degree of Faith
20°40' 2°33'S (4) Nashira, Gamma Capricorni. (Saturn Jupiter) Danger from beasts; conflict with evil, but ultimate success.
22°....Astrological area (22°-28°).
22°17' 8°37'N (3) Sadalsund, Beta Aquarii. (Saturn Mercury - Sun sextile Uranus)Trouble, disgrace.
22°25' 2°35'S (3) Deneb Algedi, Delta Capricorni. (Saturn Jupiter) Sorrow and joy, life and death, always hanging in the balance.
23°....Benevolence.
25°....Alcoholism.

Degrees, Individual, Pisces (ACCURATE 1925; ADD 1º 5' FOR 2002 POSITIONS OF FIXED STARS ETC.)
(ABBREVIATIONS: NEB, NEBULAE; CL, CLUSTER; V, VARIABLE.)

Pisces.

2°14' 10°39'N (3) Sadalmelik, Alpha Aquarii. (Saturn Mercury) Persecution, sudden destruction; the death penalty, if afflicted.
2°44' 21°8'S (1) Fomalhaut, Alpha Piscis Aust. The Watcher of the South v. ROYAL STARS. (Venus Mercury - Jupiter square in Pisces - Sagittarius) Supposedly fortunate and powerful, yet a sublime malevolence that fluctuates between material and spiritual expression. If rising, according to Cardan: great learning, and an "immortal name."
3°.....Cusp of Twenty-Seventh Lunar Mansion.
4°14' 59°55'N (1) Deneb Adige, Alpha Cygni. (Venus Mercury) Facile and ingenious mind.
7°45' 8°11'S (3) Skat, Delta Aquarii. (Saturn Jupiter - Uranus Venus sextile Mercury) Good fortune; lasting happiness.
14°10' 59°22'S (1) Achernar, Alpha Eridani; called the Cherub and Sword. (Jupiter) Confers royal honors; success in public office.
15°....Fall of Mercury.
16°....Cusp of Twenty-Eighth Lunar Mansion.
22°22' 19°24'N (2) Markab, Alpha Pegasi. (Mars Mercury) Honors, but danger from fire, fever, cuts and blows.
27°....Exaltation of Venus.
28°15' 31°8'N (2) Scheat, Beta Pegasi. (Mars Mercury) Extreme misfortune; suicide, drowning, perhaps murder.
29°9' 6°32'N (2) Theta Piscium; tail of western fish. (Saturn Mercury) A fatalistic influence.

Delineation. (1) Applied to the generally accepted composite interpretation of specific influences, such as a planet's position in a Sign or House, an aspect between two planets, or a configuration of planets; **(2)** Sometimes applied to the interpretation of the Figure as a whole, but such a summing up is more properly termed a synthesis. (Q.V.)

Depression. Distance of a celestial body below the horizon: its horizontal distance North.

Descendant The opposite point to the Ascendant *(q.v.)*. The cusp of the 7th house. The western angle. Loosely applied to the whole of the seventh house.

Descending. Said of a planet in any house from the Fourth to the Ninth. While one may speak of a body as "setting" when it passes below the Western horizon, it is "descending" from the time it passes the Midheaven until it reaches the opposite point, or Imum Coeli.

Destiny. The end to which all unrestrained forces lead. The aim of most religions, including Astrology, is to help one to become the master of his Destiny. Lacking this mastery, Destiny largely determines the part we play in the scheme of things. Destiny vs. Will adds up to experience, as a result of which we can be said to evolve, and become a developed or remain an undeveloped child of Destiny. The shrinking statue of the character Destiny from scene to scene in Maeterlinck's "Betrothal" was symbolic of the diminishing power of Destiny as man evolves in character through the experience of the will and as the fruit of experience. The Consciousness of Purpose, which is a fundamental of MacDougan's system of Psychology, compares to the Astrological sense of Destiny that is imparted through the sign position of the Sun. The individual feels but fails to identify that Destiny until after a long search he "finds himself" - his place in life. But the demand for self-expression through that Destiny is the driving and sustaining conviction that spurs his search until he does find it. It is well described in Browning's "Childe Roland to the Dark Tower Came." The search for self-expression is hampered or helped: by the desire nature, determined by the Moon position; and by emotional urges conditioned by the positions and aspects of the planets which deliver by reflection an altered solar spectrum, consisting of combinations of energy frequencies. These stimulate the unequal development of the endocrine glands which results in the state of glandular imbalance that is now recognized as the cause of so many mental and emotional complexes and physical ills.

Detriment. Properly employed it applies to the placement of a planet in the opposite Sign from that of which it is said to be the Ruler; although it is frequently applied to Debility by Sign position, which includes the opposite Sign to that in which it is in its Exaltation, as well as to those of which it is Ruler.

Dexter. Applied to an aspect which is computed backward, against the order of the Signs; in which the aspected body is elevated above the aspecting body. If this appears opposite to what you sense it should be, remember that Ptolemy, who originated the term, knew only apparent motion - that of the daily motion of the heavens because of the Earth's rotation; therefore the one ahead, was on the right hand - dexter; and the one behind, was on the left hand - sinister. There is some controversy as to which are the stronger, although the ancients gave preference to the dexter. Today, some differentiation can be had by application of the Doppler effect noted in spectroscopy, wherein the ray from a body whose position is becoming increasingly distant is displaced toward the red end of the spectrum, while with lessening distance the displacement is toward the violet end. Since the dexter aspect is forming as the result of increasing distance it would show a displacement toward the red end, which would tend to introduce into the aspect a measure of Mars energy; while the sinister aspect, forming as the result of decreasing distance, would show a displacement toward the violet end, which would tend to introduce into the aspect a measure of Venus or Jupiter geniality. From this one might infer that the relative desirability of a dexter and sinister aspect is somewhat dependent upon the nature of the planets that are involved.

Dhanus. The ninth. The Hindu name for the sign Sagittarius.

Dichotome, or Dicotome. (Gr. cut in half.) Applied to that phase of the lunar orb, or of an inferior planet, in which only half of its disk appears illuminated, i.e. the First and Third Quarters, in which the body is assuming the shape of a half-moon, and in which the Moon is said to be oriental.

Dignities and Debilities. Conditions of placement wherein a planet's influence is strengthened, are termed Dignities; if weakened they are termed Debilities. These are of two varieties: Essential and Accidental.

Part One OF THIS ARTICLE.

A planet in a Sign in which it is strengthened, is in one of its Essential Dignities; in a House in which it is strengthened, in its Accidental Dignity.

The Essential Dignities are: (1) when a planet is in a Sign of which it is the Ruler, when it is said to be in its own Sign, or in its Domal Dignity. It is ambiguous and confusing to call this its House-position. If the Sign which a planet rules is on the cusp of the House in which the planet is posited, the planet may be described as the Lord of the House: but the strength as such depends upon its Essential Dignity by virtue of its Sign placement. Some authorities deem that placement in any other Sign of the same element as that of which it is the Ruler confers a degree of Dignity; (2) When it is posited in the Sign in which it is said to be Exalted, wherein its strength is augmented and its virtues magnified. A planet in its Exaltation is only slightly less favorably placed than when it is in its own Sign; (3) By ancient precepts, the placement of a planet in the same Triplicity as that of which it is the Ruler, in the same Term, or in the same Face, were deemed to be Essential Dignities of varying degree.

Relative values were computed by points as follows: Sign 5; Mutual reception by house, 5; Exaltation 4; mutual reception by Exaltation 4; Triplicity 3; Term 2; Face 1.

In the opposite Sign to that which it rules, a planet is said to be in its Detriment; which is to say, in opposition to its most congenial environment, hence materially weakened.

In the opposite Sign to that in which it would be in its Exaltation, it is said to be in its Fall.

The scale of Essential Debilities arc: Detriment 5; Fall 4; Peregrine 5.

A planet in its Debility is generally to be interpreted as an indication of weakness in that it increases the bad effects of malefic, and lessens the possibilities for good of a benefic.

Of the Accidental Dignities the strongest is placement in Angular Houses: firstly, the Tenth; then, in order, the First, Seventh and Fourth Houses. The Succedent Houses come next, with the Cadent Houses weakest.

Other Accidental Dignities, according to older authorities, are: favorable aspects to Fortune; freedom from combustion; favorable aspects from benefics; swift in motion and increasing in light; and in a House which corresponds to the Sign of its Essential Dignity - as the Sun in the Fifth House, corresponding to Leo; Moon in the Fourth House, corresponding to Cancer; Mercury in the Third or Sixth House, corresponding to Gemini and Virgo; and so on.

Modern authorities, however, usually confine the use of the term to House placement or Elevation. Accidental Dignities are not necessarily benevolent. The increased strength may result harmfully if expressed through unfavorable aspects. The number of planets which are accidentally dignified is a character - index of importance. A planet so placed as to gain strength by way of Essential or Accidental dignity, does not necessarily confer a benevolent disposition. For example, a significator that is exalted, angular, and not afflicted indicates a person of haughty arrogant nature, assuming more than is his due. Charles E. O. Carter considers that a planet in its own sign benefits quantitatively, but not qualitatively; i.e., its strength is increased, but not necessarily rendered benefic. Point values by which to judge the relative strength of the Accidental Dignities, as listed by Wilson, are:

Ascendant or Midheaven............................5
<NOT DIV 5< Cazimi... 5 Combust..>
Besieged by Jupiter and Venus...................... 6
Partile conj. with Jupiter and Venus................ 5
Conj. Cor Leonis..................................... 6
Conj. Spica.. 5
4th, 7th or 11th House............................. 4
Direct motion.. 4
Partile conj., North Node.......................... 4
Partile trine, Jupiter and Venus................... 4
Partile sextile, Jupiter and Venus................. 3
2nd or 5th House.................................... 2
9th House... 2
Swift of motion...................................... 2
Increasing in light.................................. 2
Saturn, oriental..................................... 2
Jupiter, oriental.................................... 2
Mars, oriental....................................... 2
Moon, occidental.................................... 2
Mercury, occidental................................. 2
Venus, occidental................................... 2
3rd House.. 1
Hayze... 1
In the Term of Jupiter or Venus.................... 1

Point values of the Accidental Debilities are:

Besieged by Mars and Saturn......................... 6
Partile conj., Mars and Saturn...................... 5
Conj. Caput Algol.................................... 6
Combust.. 5
Retrograde... 5
12th House... 5
Under the Sunbeams.................................. 4
6th or 8th House.................................... 4
Partile conj., South Node........................... 4
Partile opposition, Mars or Saturn................. 4
Partile square, Mars or Saturn..................... 3
Decreasing in light................................. 2
Decreasing in motion, or slow...................... 2
Saturn occidental................................... 2
Jupiter occidental.................................. 2
Moon oriental....................................... 2
Mercury oriental.................................... 2

Venus oriental...................................... 2
In term of Mars or Saturn........................... 1

Certain **Dignities** specifically ascribed to **Fortuna** are:

Conj., Cor Leonis................................... 6
Asc. or Midheaven................................... 5
Partile conj., Jupiter or Venus..................... 5
Conj., Spica.. 5
Not Combust... 5
In Taurus or Pisces................................. 5
Besieged by Jupiter and Venus....................... 6
In Cancer, Leo, Libra, or Sagittarius............... 4
4th, 7th, or 11th House............................. 4
Partile trine, Venus or Jupiter..................... 4
Partile conj., North Node........................... 4
In Gemini... 3
2nd or 5th House.................................... 3
Partile sextile, Jupiter or Venus................... 3
In Virgo.. 2
9th House... 2
3rd House... 1
In Term of Venus or Jupiter......................... 1

The **Debilities** ascribed to **Fortuna** are:

Conj., Caput Algol.................................. 6
Besieged by Mars and Saturn......................... 6
12th House.. 5
In Scorpio, Capricorn, or Aquarius.................. 5
Combust... 5
Partile conj., Mars or Saturn....................... 5
6th or 8th House.................................... 4
Opposition, Mars or Jupiter......................... 4
Partile conj., South Node........................... 4
In Aries.. 3
Partile square, Mars or Saturn...................... 3
Term of Mars or Saturn.............................. 1

The totals of the Dignities in comparison to the totals of the Debilities affords a determination of the potential strength of the planet.

According to the strength each assumes in a nativity, will its power to activate become manifest:

Sun......builds
Moon.....nourishes
Mercury..communicates
Venus....allures
Mars.....energizes
Jupiter..expands
Saturn...endures
Uranus...perceives
Neptune..dissolves
Pluto....consolidates

Dignities and Debilities, CONTD. (*Part Two* OF THIS ARTICLE).

A fixed star is in conjunction with a planet when not more distant than 5° of longitude and 2° of latitude.

Of Dignities Calvin in "Scientific Astrology" says:- "A planet in its own Sign, unless retrograde or seriously afflicted by the malefics, is as one who is master of his own house and goods. In its Exaltation it is strong, but less so than were he his own master. In its Detriment it is weak, as one in his neighbor's house and not master thereof. In its Fall it is as one who is poverty-stricken and without power."

Of Mutual Reception he says: "When two planets are in each other's Signs, even though in evil aspect to one another, the effect is beneficial, as of people exchanging courteous social amenities."

As to Accidental Dignities, he says: "A planet is strong if it is in an angle of the Figure, swift in motion, direct, and overwhelmingly in good aspect with other planets."

As to retrograde motion he says: "It tends to bring out the introspective rather than the objective qualities of the native, and is generally synonymous with belated or denied benefits."

Another generalization based upon the Accidental Dignities of the Geocentric Figure stipulates that "When the Moon is higher than the Sun, the personality and sensibilities usually rule. With their positions reversed the character will dominate the career. If both are below the horizon, the life will be correspondingly unfortunate."

James Wilson expressed doubt concerning the efficacy of some of the dignities, and cited the Ptolemy dictum that "Planets are strong IN THE WORLD when they are oriental, swift in motion, direct, and increasing in light; and strong IN THE NATIVITY when angular or succedant, particularly in the south or east angles."

The following Table shows the Essential Dignities and Debilities:

PLANETS	RULER	DETRIMENT	EXALTATION	FALL
Sun	Leo	Aquarius	Aries	Libra
Moon	Cancer	Capricorn	Taurus	Scorpio

Mercury......Gemini-Virgo.......Sagittarius-Pisces..Aquarius#.....Leo#
Venus........Taurus-Libra.......Scorpio-Aries.......Pisces........Virgo
Mars.........Aries-Scorpio......Libra-Taurus........Capricorn#....Cancer#
Jupiter......Pisces-Sagittarius. Virgo-Gemini........Cancer#.......Capricorn#
Saturn.......Capricorn-Aquarius. Cancer-Leo..........Libra.......Aries
Uranus.......Aquarius*..........Leo*.................Scorpio......Taurus
Neptune......Pisces*............Virgo*..............Cancer........Capricorn
Pluto........Scorpio*...........Taurus*.............Aries........Libra

* MODERN AND ARBITRARY ASSIGNMENTS.
\# SOME AUTHORITIES GIVE VIRGO AS THE EXALTATION OF MERCURY - AS WELL AS THE SIGN OF ITS RULER SHIP; HENCE ALSO PISCES AS THE SIGN OF ITS FALL. OTHERS GIVE VIRGO AS THE EXALTATION OF MARS, AND CAPRICORN AS THE EXALTATION OF JUPITER.

A planet that is unfavorably aspected is sometimes loosely characterize as debilitated; also any Sign dissimilar in its nature to the Sign it rules - as Saturn in Pisces. Properly speaking, a planet is said to be in its Dignity solely by virtue of position, in distinction to any strength conferred by a supporting aspect.

The same table arranged in the order of the Signs follows:

SIGNS.......RULER................DETRIMENT.........EXALTATION.........FALL
Aries........d. Mars..............Venus..............Sun...............Saturn
Taurus.......n. Venus..............Mars -Pluto*.......Moon..............Uranus
Gemini.......d. Mercury...........Jupiter............North Node........South Node
Cancer.......Moon.................Saturn............Jupiter -Neptune*..Mars
Leo.........Sun..................Saturn -Uranus*....-.................Mercury
Virgo........n. Mercury...........Jupiter -Neptune*..Mercury...........Venus
Libra........d. Venus.............Mars..............Saturn............Sun
Scorpio......n. Mars -Pluto*.......Venus..............Uranus*...........Moon
Sagittarius..d. Jupiter............Mercury............South Node........North Node
Capricorn....n. Saturn.............Moon...............Mars................Jupiter -Neptune*
Aquarius.....d. Saturn -Uranus*....Sun................Mercury...........-
Pisces.......n. Jupiter -Neptune*..Mercury............Venus..............Mercury

Some authorities limit the Exaltation and Fall to specific degrees:

PLANET.........SUN...........MOON.........MERCURY,........VENUS...........MARS
Exaltation:.....Aries 19º......Taurus 3º....Virgo 15º......Pisces 27º......Capricorn 28º
Fall:..........Libra 19º......Scorpio 3º...Pisces 15º.....Virgo 27º.......Cancer 28º

PLANET.........JUPITER........SATURN........NORTH NODE.....SOUTH NODE
Exaltation:.....Cancer 15º.....Libra 21º....Gemini 3º......Sagittarius 3º
Fall:..........Capricorn 15º..Aries 21º....Sagittarius 3º..Gemini 3º

Wemyss attributes the ruler ship of Pisces to the asteroids; probably fragments of what once was or was intended to be a planet between the Earth and Mars. Thereby he explains the lack of a consciousness of Destiny which is an outstanding feature of the Pisces nature.

Most authorities attribute to an Essential Dignity the force of a harmonious aspect, and to a Debility that of an inharmonious aspect.

Some authorities speak of congeniality of planet in element as a species of Dignity; Moon and Neptune in the Water Signs; Sun and Mars in the Fire Signs; Mercury and Venus in the Air Signs; and Jupiter and Saturn in the Earth Signs.

The basis on which these Exaltations were assigned is lost in antiquity. Certain correspondences are worthy of notice, as bearing on their selection. The Sun as giver of life, finds an important function in Aries, which rules the head. The changeable nature of the Moon is stabilized by the fixity of Taurus - the provider of the home. Venus finds its most ready servitor in the philanthropic Pisces. Mars is stabilized and harnessed in Saturn-ruled Capricorn. Saturn finds a noble outlet in Libra - the purveyor of justice. Jupiter in Cancer, representing the home, is there sublimated into devotion. This supposed dignity seems to have had its origin with the Arabians. Almansor, in his aphorisms, says "Saturn and the Sun have their exaltations opposite, because one loves darkness and the other light; Jupiter and Mars are opposite, because one is a lover of justice and the other of misrule; and Mercury and Venus have opposite places, because one loves learning and science, and the other sensual pleasures - which are mutual enemies to each other."

It can be noted that harmonious aspects join the signs of Ruler ship and Exaltation, as follows:

```
PLANET....RULER.....................EXALTATION
Sun.......Leo...........TRINES........Aries
Moon......Cancer........SEXTILES.....Taurus
Mercury...Gemini........TRINES........Aquarius
Venus.....Taurus........SEXTILES.....Pisces
Mars   ...Scorpio.......SEXTILES.....Capricorn (OR Virgo)
Jupiter...Pisces........TRINES.......Cancer (OR SEXTILES Capricorn)
Saturn....Aquarius......TRINES.......Libra
```

As explained by Ptolemy in the Tetrabiblos, the Moon and the Sun were assigned to the Ruler ship of Cancer and Leo because "these are the most Northerly of all the Signs, and approach nearer than any others to the Zenith of this part of the Earth: the Moon to Cancer because both are feminine, and the Sun to Leo, because both are masculine." This resulted in the division of the zodiac into a Solar semi-circle from Leo forward to Capricorn, and a Lunar Semi-circle from Cancer backward to Aquarius. In order that each planet might rule a Sign in each semi-circle, whereby it could be configurated with both Sun and Moon, Mercury, which is never more than one Sign distant from the Sun, was assigned to the ruler ship of Gemini and Virgo; Venus, which is never more than two Signs distant, to Taurus and Libra; Mars, because it is dry in nature, was assigned to two Signs of a similar nature, Aries and Scorpio, whose square relation to the respective Signs of the luminaries was appropriately discordant; Jupiter, whose fruitful nature deserved a harmonious relationship in which to operate for good, was assigned to the two trine Signs Pisces and Sagittarius; leaving Saturn, a cold planet in an orbit remote from the harmonious, to be assigned to Cancer and Aquarius, and for the added reason that their "configuration by opposition does not cooperate towards the production of good." As the basis on which the Exaltations were assigned is equally arbitrary it is no wonder that Wilson scoffs at and refuses to accept the entire doctrine of Essential Dignities.

To render matters worse confounded some of the moderns have endeavored to upset the scheme by assigning to Uranus the ruler ship of Aquarius, and to Neptune the ruler ship of Pisces, and are now in a battle royal as to whether Pluto shall be assigned to Aries or Scorpio. Looked at from a scientist's viewpoint the entire Doctrine of Dignities appears to be a fortune-teller's device whereby to find at least SOME answer to a question concerning a House which contains no planets, and is thus unable to give positive testimony regarding a question asked. Wilson seemed to think that Placidus side-stepped the doctrine as one with which he could not agree, but regarding which he dared not disagree. Marc Edmund Jones says that few modern practitioners pay much attention to the Essential Dignities and Debilities. **v. PTOLEMAIC ASTROLOGY.**

To distinguish between these dual ruler ships, the positive signs were called Day Houses, and the negative signs, the Night Houses -- although since they are signs not houses, the terms Day Home and Night Home would be preferable.

..DAY HOME.......PLANET.....NIGHT HOME
..Gemini.........Mercury....Virgo
..Libra..........Venus......Taurus
..Aries..........Mars.......Scorpio
..Sagittarius....Jupiter....Pisces
..Aquarius.......Saturn.....Capricorn

A person born by night, with the Sun below the horizon, looks to the Night Homes of the planets to be the stronger; if born with the Sun above the horizon, the Day Homes.

The moderns have thrown this into confusion in an effort to ascribe ruler ships to the newly-discovered planets - Uranus, Neptune and Pluto. Many authorities prefer however to consider these as second-octave planets: Uranus of Mercury, Neptune of Venus, and Pluto of Mars.

Other systems of ruler ship have been variously proposed. **v. RULER SHIP.**

For further observations on the relative strength of the Dignities: **v. SYNTHESIS.**

Triplicity, Rulers of. Another variety of Dignity, used in Mundane and Horary practice, is that of a planet posited in its own Triplicity. The ruler ships of the Triplicities are, however, not always the rulers of the three signs which make up the Triplicity. For example, of the FIRE Trigon, Mars as an enemy of the Sun is dethroned, and the Sun is made the ruler by day, and Jupiter by night. This was the Northern Triplicity, since because Jupiter brought to the Egyptians fruitful showers from out of the North he was said to rule the North; also the Northwest, because the outlawed Mars now and then brought in the West wind; and Southwest, because Mars is feminine, and the South is feminine. Of the *Earth* Trigon Venus was its ruler by day and the Moon by night. This was the Southern Trigon, because "under the petticoat government of Venus and the Moon," as Wilson puts it, "they contrived to exclude Saturn - for what reason we are not informed." It rules the South because Venus brings South winds, and Southeast because Saturn brings East winds. Of the *Air* Trigon Saturn rules by day and Mercury by night. It was the Eastern Trigon because Saturn brings East winds and persuaded Mercury to cooperate; and Northeast because Jupiter claimed a share since both are diurnal planets, hence related. The WATER Trigon was ruled by Mars with the co-rulership of Venus by day and the Moon by night. It was the Western Trigon because Mars liked the West winds for the reason that they scorched the Egyptians; and the Southwest because of the share of Venus in the trigon. Concerning all this Wilson adds: "Its absurdity requires no comment; and since the doctrine that countries and cities are governed by certain signs and planets is solely founded on this folly, it is undeserving of the smallest attention."

In Horary practice a planet in its Triplicity denotes a respectable person who has a sufficiency of everything, hence is quite comfortable.

Dionysian Period. The 28-year cycle of the Sun, on which is based the Dominical Letter, brings the Sun back to the same day of the week. The 19-year Metonic Cycle restores the new moon to the same day of the month. Therefore 28 X 19 = 532 years - the period on which Lunations recur on the same day of the month and the same day of the week. This is the Dionysian Period, so called after Dionysius Exiguus; also called the Victorian period, after Victorius of Aquitain. Its use in determining Easter Sunday was discontinued with the Gregorian reformation of the Julian calendar.

Directions. Progressions. No phase of Astrology is subject to such differences of opinion and practice as that which treats of the changing influences resulting from the various moving bodies of the solar system, as they affect the individual through the sundry sensitive points produced by the impact of planetary rays during his first day of life. Chief among these are three basic systems: Transits, Primary Directions, and Secondary Progressions.

Transits are based upon the actual motions of the various bodies, whereby Saturn, for example, with a revolutionary period of approximately 30 years, will in that time return to the place it occupied on a day of birth; during which period it will transit over each one of the sensitive points of the Birth Figure. Thus when it passes over the radical position of Venus there results a Saturn impulse through a Venus expectancy; and so on for all the moving planets in relation to each of the sensitive points. There is no controversy concerning transits, other than their relative strength and importance as compared to Directions and Progressions.

Directions and Progressions are based on a theory that since each actual day's revolution of the Earth finds the Sun advanced one degree beyond the point where it was on the preceding day, and since the extra four minutes of rotation required to traverse this degree is the equivalent of the day required for the Earth to traverse the degree in its annual revolution, one degree of rotation is equal to one day's revolution. Out of this it is deduced that since a degree is equal to a day, and a day is equal to a year, a degree is equal to a year. There is also biblical authority for some such statement. On this assumption is founded an elaborate system of calculations, all of which come to naught in case the original premise is rejected.

The Primary System, so called, is thus a calculation of the number of four-minute intervals during which a given planet will move from its birth position to the place where it conjoins or aspects a sensitive degree - usually the birth-position of some other planet. Then since each four-minute arc represents a year of life, it is assumed that in a given year there will be in force a directed aspect between these two bodies. Since each of these calculations are separately made and applied, the term "directed" is employed, such as "Jupiter directed to the place of Saturn," and so on. These arcs of Direction must be computed in fractional divisions of the semi-arc, since in various latitudes at different seasons of the year the arc from the horizon to the Midheaven may be variously more or less than go". Instead of calculating a day as 1°, the distance travelled in 4 minutes is calculated at one-ninetieth of the arc which the sunrise degree must traverse in order to reach its Midheaven point on that day; or if below the horizon, for the degree on the Imum Coeli to reach its horizon-point.

Secondary Progressions, much easier to calculate, are based on the theory that the positions of the planets on the third day of life, for example, will represent a correct Progressed horoscope for the third year of life, and so on. In this system one casts a Progressed Figure for the year desired, by casting it for that many days after birth, using the ephemeris of the year of birth. One of the first observations is the evident fact that in ancient times the astrologer did not have the availability of ephemerides for different years, and this was a simple means whereby to secure an approximation. One modern adaptation which combines features of both systems is the so-called Radix System, which assumes an Ascendant degree that is advanced for every year an amount equal to one day's average travel of the Earth around the Sun, which in advancing sweeps the whole scheme of sensitive points along with it. This unit is 0° 59' - or 360° of the circle divided by 365¼ days of the year. Also, as the Ascendant moves downward, carrying the planets to new positions, the original places of the planets move upwards - thereby creating double the number of sensitive points, and allowing for directions to be figured in both direct and converse motion. To these sensitive points the Sun is directed at the rate of its average daily travel - the major arc of 0° 59'; and the Moon at the rate of its average daily travel - the minor arc of 13° 11'.

Another method is the Annual Solar Revolution, a Figure cast for the exact moment in any given year on which the Sun returns to the exact degree, minute and second which it occupied on the day of birth. A derivation of this system is the so-called "Key-Cycle" devised by Wynn.

There are other systems of calculating the supposed accents which are imparted by the changing cosmic conditions that mark successive years, but a detailed discussion of the problems involved in the various systems of Directions and Progressions would make a ponderous volume in itself.

Every system has its exponents, but the chief reason for all of them is found in the effort of the astrologer to foretell future events. The more conservative of the modern scientific astrologers confine themselves largely to known factors, such as transits, interpreting them as subordinate to the Birth Figure, and delineating both of them in terms of psychological tendencies, the control of which is within command of the individual who seeks to rule his destiny rather than to be ruled by it.

To such, the most satisfactory method, other than the transits, on which to base deductions concerning the changing influences of each year, is perhaps the Solar Revolution Figure, on the assumption that since with each successive year the Sun becomes the predominating influence on the unfolding destiny of the individual, the moment of its return to its exact birth position represents an anniversary marked by a sub-conscious recheck of the pattern of receptivity which was stamped at birth, and which has been noted and revised with each annual return of the Sun. On the very first anniversary, the relationship of the Rising Degree and the Solar Degree was found altered; hence, one of them had to be revised. In early life it might be possible to ignore the Sun and to continue to measure from the Ascendant; but with the advance toward the age at which one attains to his majority, it must be apparent that the Sun will have asserted itself as the most compelling of all sources of cosmic stimulation - as regards consciousness of the dictates of destiny, if not emotionally - and thereby will have supplanted the Ascendant degree as the individual point of reference. There is this to be said for the Solar Revolution Figure, that the planetary positions are those the planets actually then occupy, and not some symbolic approximation - hence such a Figure cannot offer a contradiction to transits which will continue from these points throughout the year. It also coincides with the observations of a considerable number of modern astrologers, to the effect that in tracing adult character development the Solar Houses give more reliable testimony than those of Houses based upon either a birth or a Progressed Ascendant.

To make vivid the difference between the Primary and Secondary systems, they can be summarized as follows:

Primary Directions are based on the "first motion," the Primum Mobile of Aristotle, the apparent nightly trek of the planets across the sky from East to West. This means that calculations are made in Right Ascension along the Equator, and that *an error of four minutes* in the actual birth moment *makes a difference of one year* in the timing of a prognosticated condition or event.

Secondary Progressions are based upon the actual motions of the planets along the Ecliptic, on the assumption that the conditions encountered on the second day of life will be those which will govern the second year of life; hence *an error of four minutes* in the actual birth moment *makes a difference of only one day* in the timing of the prognosticated condition or event. The crux of the matter is whether or not you accept the one degree for a year Arc of Direction as having a scientific justification, and if this unit is rejected both the Primary and the Secondary systems go into the discard as far as you are concerned. The Transits in effect in any year of life are the actual positions the planets then occupy, considered in relation to the places they occupied on a given date of birth.

Radix System of Directing. This system refers all Directions to the radical places of the planets. The Midheaven, the Sun and all the planets and bodies are moved forward at a mean rate of diurnal progress, of 59' 08" - the Naibod arc, and the Ascendant is brought up by Oblique Ascension under the latitude, as shown in the Tables of Houses for the birthplace. The Moon is also moved forward in the Zodiac at its mean rate of 13° 11' per year - termed the minor arc. While moving forward in the heavens all the bodies except the Moon preserve their radical relationships, at the same time forming aspects to the radical places of the Significator s, while the latter form aspects to the radical places of the Promittors. By this means the arcs are simultaneously equated to the mean motion of the heavens, the radical relations of the celestial bodies are preserved, and the radical significance of a planet remains undisputed. By this method many events for which neither Primary nor Secondary Directions could be obtained have been clearly indicated and predicted. The method is worth the close attention of all students. All planets act from the Sign and House to which they have attained by direction, but when their radical places are directed they act in terms of their radical positions.

Gustave Lambert-Brahy of Brussels and Henry J. Gouchon of Paris have confirmed the belief that the progressing of the Ascendant "carries with it all the rest of the sky." They propose as a logical procedure that the Ascendant be advanced on the basis of 4' of S.T. per year, adding the same arc to each planet's position. Recessional Directions. A term applied by P. J. Harwood, a British astrologer, to H. S. Green's system of prenatal directions, in which the day prior to birth corresponds to the first year after birth.

Recessional Directions. A term applied by P.J. Harwood, a British astrologer, to H.S. Green's system of pre-natal directions, in which the day prior to birth corresponds to the first year after birth.

Depositor. (to dispose of) The Ruler of the Sign on the cusp of a House disposes of, or is the depositor of, a planet posited in that House. When the depositor of any planet taken as a significator, is itself disposed of by the Ruler of the Ascendant, it is deemed a strongly favorable indication. In a Solar Figure, the Ruler of the Sign is the Depositor of a planet posited therein. The assumption is that when a planet is in a Sign that is ruled by another planet, it is supposed to be so influenced by the planet that rules the Sign in which it is placed, as in effect to alter its nature. Thus, if Saturn is in a Sign ruled by Jupiter, the Jupiterian influence is presumed so to permeate the Saturn influence as to render it more Jupiterian and less Saturnian. This idea is expressed by saying either that "Saturn is disposed of by Jupiter," or that "Jupiter is the depositor of Saturn." Definitions of various authorities are somewhat vague and apparently contradictory, but a study of older texts appears to justify the simple explanation here given. of course the term must not be interpreted too literally, for most authorities argue that a planet actually in-a-House is more potent in its influence over the affairs of that House than is the Ruler of the Sign on its cusp, or of a Sign intercepted within the House. The extent to which the Depositor nullifies the influence of the planet of which it disposes, is a matter of judgment based upon the strength of aspects and the character of the aspecting planets as affecting both the Depositor and the planet of which it disposes.
In his dictionary Alan Leo gives a reverse definition to that offered by Sepharial, but evades the issue by remarking that "it is probably of more importance in Horary Astrology, though it must have some value in Nativities." However, too many ancient texts base judgments on the "depositor of Mercury" to admit of Mercury not having a Depositor - which under Leo's definition that "a planet in the House of another disposes of that planet," would occur if no planets were in Gemini or Virgo. However, since Mercury must always be in some Sign, the designation of the Ruler of that Sign as Mercury's Depositor becomes a logical application of the term. The Ruler of the Sign Mercury posits is thus a determining factor in the qualities of disposition that the fluctuating Mercury will develop.

Dissociate Signs. Adjacent Signs and those that are five Signs apart: those which bear to each other a 12th, 2nd, 6th or 8th House relationship. *v. Inconjunct.*

Distance. in the heavens is measured in Right Ascension or Oblique Ascension, or along the Ecliptic, the Equator, or the Prime Vertical, in (1) Sidereal hours and minutes of Right Ascension along the Equator; (2) degrees and minutes of arc of Oblique Ascension along the Ecliptic, and in degrees and minutes of arc of declination above or below the Equator, or of latitude above or below the Ecliptic.
Polar Distance. The angular distance of a celestial object from the pole: 90° minus the declination.
Actual Intra-solar system distances are expressed in astronomical Units *(q. v.)*: Ultra-solar system distances in Light Years *(q. v.)*.

Diurnal. Of or belonging to the day: as the apparent diurnal motion of the planets resulting from the axial rotation of the Earth *(v. Motion)*.
D. Arc: Measurement, in degrees, of the arc a celestial body traverses from its rising to its setting.
D. Houses. v. Houses, Rulers of.
D. Planets. v. Planets.
D. Ruler, that which rules by day.
D. Triplicities: the Fire Trigon for the Sun; and so on.
v. Dignities: Rulers of the Triplicities.

Dog Days. A forty-day period extending from July 4 to August 11; given by some authorities as from July 20th to August 27. It was considered by the ancients to be the hottest period of the year. They reckoned the commencement from the heliacal rising of Sirius (the Dog Star). Hesiod placed the ending of the period at 50 days after the Summer solstice. Mars, the planet associated with heat, conjoined Sirius during the serious drought and hot spell of mid-July 1937.

Dog Stars. Sirius and Procyon. v. STARS.

Domal Dignity. Said of a planet when it tenants its own Sign (v. RULERS.) A planet so placed was described by the ancients as 'domiciliated'.

Dominical Letter. Literally, the "Sunday" letter. To connect a week day with a day of the year, January 1 is A; 2, B; 3, C; 4, D; 5, E; 6, F; 7, G. Thus 8 becomes A, and so on. However, if one says that the Dominical letter is C then January 1 of that year will fall upon Friday. Its chief use is in connection with an involved system for determining the date upon which will fall the "movable feast" known as Easter, around which the Ecclesiastical calendar is arranged. The letters of successive years rotate in the reverse order: on Leap year the preceding letter applies only to January and February dates, the next preceding letter applying to the remainder of the year. For example, 1929, F; 1930, E; 1931, D; 1932, January-February, C; March-December, B; 1933, A; 1934, G; and so on.

Doryphory. A Ptolemaic term describing a planet which serves as a sort of bodyguard or John the Baptist to the Sun, rising shortly before it - either in the same or the contiguous Sign. The doryphory of the Moon similarly rises after it. The best meaning of the word is spearbearer.

Double-bodied or Bicorporeal Signs. Gemini, Sagittarius and Pisces; and by some authorities, Virgo *(v. Signs)*. So called because their symbols represent two Figures: Gemini, the Twins; Sagittarius, half-man, half-animal; and Pisces, the two fishes. They are presumed to signify a dual nature. On the cusp of the Seventh House it suggests the possibility of more than one marriage; on the cusp of the Fifth, the possibility of twin offspring.

Dragon's Head. Dragon's Tail. v. MOON'S NODES.

Dumb Signs. Mute Signs: Cancer, Scorpio and Pisces, *v. Signs*. One of them on the Ascendant and Mercury afflicted, or Mercury aspected by a malefic posited in one of them, is cited as the possible cause of a speech impediment.

Duration of Life. *v. Hyleg.*

Dwa-da-shamsa. *v. Signs, Subdivisions of.*

Dysis. The western angle or point of setting. v. HOUSES.

Eagle. (1) Aquilla. A small constellation located approx. Capricorn 29°; sometimes called the Vulture. (2) Frequently associated with the sign Scorpio, as seen in the wings of the Sphinx *(qv.)*. The sharp eyes and aquiline nose of the pure Scorpio person thoroughly stress the connotation. (3) By the Greeks and Persians, the Eagle was held sacred to the Sun and Jupiter.

Earth Shine. The dimly lit surface of the Crescent Moon caused by sunlight reflected from the Earth, to the Moon, back to the Earth. It is one of several factors which enter into the astrological significance of the Lunation.

Earth Signs. Those of the Earth Triplicity: Taurus, Virgo, Capricorn. The ancients symbolized these types by the Earth element, because of their predominant "Earthiness" or practicality. *v. Signs*.

East. (1) One of the four cardinal points. (2) The general direction in which the Sun rises, particularly at the equinoxes. (3) The rising degree at the cusp of first house, placed at the midpoint on the left side of the map. (4) Loosely applied to the entire six houses which occupy the left half of the map - the Eastern houses: 10, 11, 12, 1, 2, 3.

Easter. From Eastre, the Anglo-Saxon goddess of light or Spring, in whose honor a festival was celebrated, usually in April - since at that time the Spring Equinox occurred in April. A Festival marking the commencement of Spring has been celebrated among many peoples under a variety of names. By the Christians it was celebrated in commemoration of the resurrection of Jesus. It coincides in general with the Jewish Passover, or Pasch, which the Jews celebrate on that 14th day of a lunar month that falls upon or next follows after the vernal equinox. After some schism over the point, the council of Nicea in 325 A.D., ordained that Easter should take place on the Sunday that immediately follows the full moon that happens upon, or the first full moon after, the day of the vernal equinox; except that if this falls on Sunday, or if Easter and the Passover coincide, then Easter is deferred one week. The reconciling of three such unrelated factors as the week, the lunar month and the solar year is sometimes a complicated matter. The full moon as calculated by the ecclesiastical rule does not always coincide with the astronomical full moon. These rules are based upon the golden number, epact, and Dominical letter *(q.v.)*.

Eccentric. An eccentric orbit is one formed about a centre, which itself is revolving about another centre. Ptolemy first employed the term as descriptive of the orbits of the planets about the Sun, viewed from the Earth as the central point of observation. His supposition was that the orbit was a circle, but that the Sun was not in the center of the orbit. In fact he considered it to be an imaginary circle representing an imaginary orbit, since it had not been discovered that the planets revolved round the Sun. The term is now applied to an elliptical orbit. The eccentricity of an elliptical orbit is defined astronomically as its degree of departure from a circle. It is expressed by the ratio of the major to the minor axis. The orbit of Venus has the least, and that of Mercury the greatest eccentricity of the planets in the solar system.

Eclipse. This phenomenon is one that involves Sun, Moon and Earth. There are two distinct types: (1) that in which the Moon stands between the Sun and Earth, cutting off from our vision not only the light of the Sun, but the Sun itself. This is a *Solar Eclipse*, and occurs only at the time of a new Moon, when the Sun and Moon form a conjunction near one of the Nodes at which the orbits of the Earth and Moon intersect; and (2) that in which the Earth cuts off from the Moon the light of the Sun, depriving it of its illumination but still leaving it in our line of vision as a dark and shadowy object. This is a *Lunar Eclipse*, and occurs only at the time of a Full Moon, when the Sun and Moon are in opposition, close to the Moon's nodes.

An Eclipse of the Sun comes from the West; of the Moon, from the East. An Eclipse can occur between the Sun, the Earth and a planet, but that is of infrequent occurrence; also between the Moon, the Earth and a planet, the Moon coming between the Earth and the planet. The Eclipse of a planet by the Moon is called an occultation *(q.v.)*.

The position of a Solar Eclipse coincides with that of the Sun on that day. The position of a Lunar Eclipse coincides with the opposition point to the Sun's position on that day. Both Solar and Lunar Eclipses can occur at either Node. *(q.v.)*. The magnitude of an eclipse depends upon (1) the relative distances of the luminaries from the Earth; and (2) their distance from the Nodes. The duration of an eclipse depends on the relative rapidity of motion of the bodies.

The ancient rule was that the effects of a Solar eclipse last as long in years as the eclipse lasts in hours; of a Lunar eclipse, a month for every hour. From a Figure cast for the moment of commencement of the eclipse, events were deduced as affecting countries ruled by the ascending Sign, based upon the strength of the planets in the Signs and Houses

Some modern authorities consider that the countries which lie within the eclipse shadow are probably those in which the events signified by the eclipse will be felt. In the Nativity, the eclipse is most powerful when it falls upon the birth position of a planet, luminary, or ascending degree.

Contrary to ancient superstitions, eclipses are not uniformly evil. One man's loss is often another's gain, and an eclipse in good aspect to a benefic under good directions can result favorably. Those on the places of the Sun, Moon, Ascendant, or M.C. and on the malefics are, however, unfavorable influences.

Frequently their effects are not felt until some time thereafter, when another planet, principally Mars, transits over the degree on which the eclipse occurred. Thus an eclipse-degree becomes a sensitive point for several years after the eclipse has passed; in fact, until its consummation is attained with a subsequent transit of Saturn over the eclipse degree. Frequent reference to the following tables in connection with current or past events, will contribute vastly to an understanding of the major trends that are set into motion by the third dimension of the Moon's orbit - that which is vertical to the plane, marked midway by the passing of the Nodes.

The temperature on the Sunlit Full Moon exceeds the boiling point of water, at which time it emits infra-red rays that are several times more intense than the rays it reflects from the Sun. During the first five minutes of a Lunar Eclipse the surface temperature falls far below the freezing point, and the emission of the infra-red rays ceases.

Saros Cycle of Eclipses. The Plane of the Moon's Orbit has an inclination of 5-15 degrees to that of the Earth's orbit. Two opposite points of intersection of these orbits are the North or ascending Node, and the South or descending Node. These Nodes regree from month to month, and in approximately 19 years make a complete circle of the zodiac. In the following tables showing the nineteen Saros series, since each year one or more eclipses occur at each Node, separated roughly by half a year, the entire number of from 2 to 6 are listed as belonging to one Saros Series. Taking as the first of the series the group that follows the passing of the Node over 0° Aries, there result 19 series - after which each group repeats itself slightly altered.

It should be noted that a Solar Eclipse, caused by the passage of the apex of the Moon's shadow in a narrow path across the Earth some 70 miles in width, is visible only to a person located in the path. A Lunar Eclipse, partial or total, caused by the passage of the Moon into the Earth's shadow, is, however, visible all over the hemisphere that is turned toward the Moon.

If the Moon is at such distance from the Earth that the apex of its shadow falls short of the Earth's surface, the Moon's body will not entirely obliterate the Sun and a narrow rim of light will surround the dark body of the Moon. This is termed an Annular Eclipse. Sometimes an eclipse begins as an Annular Eclipse and then becomes total as the apex of the shadow approaches the equatorial* regions. This is called an Annular-Total Eclipse. Both are termed Umbral Eclipses. Where there is an appreciable separation in latitude there results a Partial Eclipse.

*: *Because of its convexity, the circumference of the Earth's surface is some 4,000 miles father from the Moon than its central position.*

Because of the eight-hour fraction of a day, the umbral track of the eclipse shifts some 120° West at each return; hence on every fourth Saros return (54y 1m) it recurs in the same longitude, but somewhat farther North or South.

A complete Lunar cycle consists of 48 or 49 eclipses over a period of about 865 years; a solar cycle of 68 to 75 returns, over a period of about 1260 years. A Saros cycle consists usually of 14 partial, 17 annular and 10 total solar eclipses, and 29 Lunar eclipses - or a total of 70 eclipses.

Eclipse Limits.

When a conjunction of Sun and Moon occurs within 18° 31' from either node, the major solar eclipse limit, a solar eclipse may occur; within 15° 21', the minor solar eclipse unit, a solar eclipse will occur; within 11° 15', the major central solar ecliptic limit, a total or annular eclipse may occur; within 9° 55', the minor central solar ecliptic limit, a total or annular eclipse will occur. When an opposition of Sun and Moon occurs near either node the major lunar ecliptic limit is 12° 15' and the minor 9° 30'; the major total lunar ecliptic limit is 3° 45' and the minor 6° 0'.

The series of Metonic returns bear no relationship to the Saros series. Meton's cycle of 19-year intervals consists of an eclipse in approximately the same degree of the zodiac on the same date 19 years later. Approximately 23% of Solar eclipses have no Metonic returns; 38% have 1 return; 19%, 2 returns; 13%, 3 returns; and 7%, 4 returns. A Metonic return may be of a different phase and nature, and belong to a different Saros series. A Solar Eclipse begins as partial at one or the other poles, and increases in strength as it moves toward the Equator - finally fading away into outer space beyond the opposite pole. Thus an eclipse may be said to have a "birth" and a "death," with a life span of from 865 to 1252 years, or from 48 to 70 appearances.

Looking back to the "birth," or beginning partial (BP) of any series, you can, in delineating its recurring effects, take into consideration the Sign in which it first appeared, and the Ruler of the Sign.

The Solar Eclipse of June 8, 1937 in Gemini 18°, Saros series 11, which lasted for 7m 13s, was of longer duration than any in the last 1,200 years; although those of 1955 and 1973 were to be almost as long. That on July 20, 1963 at 0° 28°, Saros series 1, was to be one of the shortest, lasting 65s.

The Saros Cycle of 223 Lunar months was discovered by the Chaldeans. This is 18y 11d 8h, where 4 leap years are contained; otherwise, if 5 intervene, it is one day shorter; or if 3, one day longer. The series consists of 70 eclipses: 41 Solar, and 29 Lunar.

The Penumbral Eclipses. The Saros cycle is generally stated by astronomers to consist of 29 Solar eclipses in 1260y and 41 Lunar eclipses in 865y, making a total of 70 eclipses, on an average, for one complete series. However, each series of Lunar eclipses is both preceded and followed by about 10 periods of Penumbral eclipses, of some 180y duration. Since the Solar eclipse limit is much wider than that of the Lunar, a Lunar eclipse in the penumbra has an importance, astrologically, about equal to that of the Partial Solar eclipse, in that it embodies both the gravitational effect of a parallel, and the interference with normal radiation, that characterize all eclipses. An eclipse in the penumbra is generally termed an

Appulse, in that the rim of the Moon just touches the Earth's shadow, while the body of the Moon receives the light of the Sun from only one side of the Earth, which during a portion of the time shuts off the light of part of the Sun's disc. By way of illustration, note Saros cycle 4, Lunar eclipse at the North Node: the last Lunar partial eclipse of the series (EP), October 7, 1930, 14" Aries, was to be followed by Penumbral eclipses in 1948, 1966 and 1984. In Saros series 11 is a continuing series at the South Node that follows an eclipse cycle which ended prior to 1800: also in this series the Total Solar eclipse of June 20, 1955 is so close to the node that there is a penumbral eclipse both before and after it. Therefore when making note of the position of a Solar eclipse in any map it is advisable also to note as temporarily sensitized degrees, the Moon's opposition points to the Sun 14 days earlier and later, and check on their strength by reference to the tables of eclipses and the chronological list of Appulses for the years 1871 to 1959. Even if it is on neither list, it represents what is sometimes called "approximate eclipse conditions," and can become an important factor if it falls exactly upon the degree which posits a planet.

The ancients did not have the benefit of the modern Ephemerides. They actually studied the motion of the bodies in the heavens, and thereby discovered the various cycles that would enable them to calculate the intervals between successive recurrences of similar phenomena; therewith to make calculations of the psychological fluctuations that produce events. Among these were the Mercury cycle of 92 years, the Venus cycle of 486 years, the heliacal rising of Sirius in September every 162 years, the Metonic 19-year luni-solar cycle of eclipses, the mutation periods based on the conjunctions of the great chronocrators Jupiter and Saturn, and most important of all the solilunar Saros cycle and its multiples and derivatives. As this cycle brought the recurrence of the same eclipse 18 years and 10 days later, at a point about 10 degrees farther along the ecliptic, it was found that each third return, an interval of 54 years and 1 month, brought a similar return of a visible eclipse at about the same time of day; also that in 12 times that period, or 649 years, the cycle was completed with a Solar eclipse prior to the seventh month after the Autumnal equinox, then the beginning of the ecclesiastical year; and that the lunar eclipse two weeks later began a new 649-year cycle. It was by such means that most of the prophecies and the dates of their fulfillment as recorded in the Bible were arrived at.

The 15-year Solar cycle of the Chaldeans was a slightly different cycle: largely a chronological point of reference, arrived at by dividing the 360 degrees of the circle into 24 hourly segments of 15 degrees. On the basis of 1 degree to a year, it became a method of reckoning occurrences, terrestrial as well as celestial, in fifteen-year intervals. This cycle was adopted by the Romans as the period of reappraisals for taxation, and became known as the Indiction cycle. The Solar cycle of 28 years was the period in which the days of the week reoccurred on the same days of the month.

J. J. Scaliger devised the Julian period from the product of these three cycles: the 28-year Solar cycle, the 19-year Soli-Lunar cycle, and the 15-year Indiction cycle (28 x 19 x 15 = 7980), and made it begin January 1, 4713 B.C., when the three cycles coincided.

About 1896, J. B. Dimbleby began the reconciling of Biblical dates, and arrived at the conclusion that the historical records of the Anti-diluvian Epoch were based upon a 7-year Solar cycle - one fourth of the Solar cycle as it was employed in a later epoch; and that after the deluge, chronology was recorded by the 15-year Solar cycle of the Chaldeans.

His chronology is thus given in successive years, beginning with the Creation year as 0 A.M. - Anno Mundi, "the year of the world" - thus avoiding much of the confusion incident to B.C. and A.D. dates. It begins with the eclipse that fell on the Autumnal Equinox, September 20, 3996 B.C., a year in which its two Solar eclipses fell in April and October, in which the Solar and Lunar years began simultaneously, and which coincides with the command recorded in Leviticus 23:24.

Few astrologers of today take the trouble to study the major cycles through means of which the ancient Biblical porphets were able to foresee the workings of Destiny - that man could stay if he would, but seldom does. It is certain that a study of the Eclipse cycles, and the application of modern adaptations to the study of the various cycles that were successfully used by the early astrologer-astronomers, will be productive of gratifying results.

Eclipse of Thales. May 28, 585 B.C., predicted by Thales of Miletus, and which stopped a battle in the war between the Medes and the Lydians. Other historic eclipses were that which occurred at noon in the first year of the Peloponnesian War, when several stars became visible, presumed to have occurred August 3, 432 B.C.; and that which occurred when Agathocles, King of Syracuse, was sailing with his fleet toward Africa, on Aug. 15, 310 B.C. Saying "The die is cast" Caesar crossed the Rubicon on the day of a Solar Eclipse, March 7, 51 B.C..

Ecliptic; Via Solis, the Sun's path. The Sun's apparent orbit or path around the Earth; or the orbit of the Earth as viewed from the Sun. So named because it is along this path, at the points where it intersects the Equator, that Eclipses occur. Its inclination (23°27') to the plane of the Equator is now decreasing at the rate of 50" per century. A comparison of the calculations of this obliquity by Hipparchus, Ptolemy and Placidus, with those of modern astronomers, shows that the decrease has been continuous for over two thousand years. Discoveries of explorers in the Arctic and Antarctic regions indicate the one-time presence of tropical flora and fauna, suggesting that the poles of the earth were once in the plane of its orbit, and the present equatorial region was a great ice-belt. However, some astronomers figure that the inclination will decrease to a minimum of 22°30' in about the year 11,500. A similar condition is observed in Mars and Uranus. Sometimes termed the Celestial Ecliptic to distinguish it from the path of the Moon's orbit around the Earth - termed the Terrestrial Ecliptic.

Ego. The conscious feeling that "I am Me." In psychology the *ego*, as a system of mental states, is approximately synonymous with the mind. Occult philosophy claims there are two egos: one identified with mortal personality; the other divine and indestructible.

Elections. Electional Astrology is a method by which to choose a suitable time for commencing any honestly conceived and reasonable project or endeavor, such as a marriage, journey, law-suit, building operation, engaging in a new business or profession, the reconciling of opponents, drawing up a will, buying land or house, planting a garden, launching a ship, or moving into a new home.
The theory of Elections is a reverse application of Horary procedure in that the latter begins with a Time and works toward a prognosis, while the former begins with a desired prognosis and works toward the selection of a suitable time. The selection of the day, hour and minute must take into account a number of practical, scientific and theoretical considerations, in order to determine the most propitious birth-moment for the project in prospect, after which the actual initiating of action is deferred so that it may be begun on the selected moment. The Figure thus cast, termed the Electional or Inceptional Figure, thereafter becomes a horary figure for the conception of the project, from which to estimate the probable success or failure of the plan, most of the important particulars connected therewith, the high and low tides that will beset its progress, and in general forecast the eventual outcome of the project

under contemplation. It is presumed to be effective for whatever length of time is required for the carrying out of the project.

To make a reliable Election the following considerations must be observed:

1. The Nativity of the person for whom the Figure is to be cast should, if the data is obtainable, be diligently studied. All authorities agree that this feature is of paramount importance.

2. The radical Ascendant, when used for this purpose, should not be moved *against* the Earth's motion; which is to say, it must be moved clockwise rather than in the order of the Houses. Ptolemy, in the sixth aphorism of his Centiloquy, says: "It is advantageous to make choice of days and of hours at a time well constituted by the Nativity. Should the time be adverse, the choice will in no respect avail, however favorable an issue it may chance to promise."

3. The Directions concurrently at work in the Nativity should be taken into account, to make sure that the proposed project is not beyond the native's capabilities. No useful purpose can be served by making an Election for a project that is foredoomed to failure.

4. Attention must be paid to the Sign positions and aspects of the transiting planets before considering the House positions they will occupy in the Election Scheme, since favorable House positions cannot be expected to offset unfavorable sign positions and adverse aspects. Frequently it is found impossible to cast an Election that is even remotely favorable, in that the planets refuse to arrange themselves harmoniously within the time limits at one's disposal. However, should the project be imperative and impossible to defer but otherwise valid, an Election arranged with the available forces at one's command will usually be found better than none at all. Even so, if the Nativity, or the Directions concurrently in force, promise failure, no Ellection, however astutely conceived, can possibly impart success. Therefore, one should not assume that the electional technique is a master-key to success; wealth and happiness. However, in such cases it will often be found impossible to initiate action at the elected time, one obstacle after another entailing delay, until finally the project can be initiated at a more favorable season, with eventual success.

5. The planet disposing of the project should be free from the adverse rays of the Infortunes - Mars, Saturn, Uranus, Neptune and Pluto; and, when possible, should tenant its chief Dignity.

6. No Infortune, nor any planet that is retrograde, combust or otherwise notably debilitated by Sign, degree or aspect, should hold any Angle of the Figure, unless said Infortune happens to dispose of the affair in question, is well dignified, strong by Sign, well disposed toward the other two signs of its Triplicity, largely unafflicted, and as distant as possible from the Luminaries. If it is less than 8º from the Sun, or 12º from the Moon, the project will suffer many hindrances and delays. The parallel of declination has an influence similar to that of a conjunction, and both of these along with the trine aspects constitute the most powerful adjuncts to success. The sextile is notably weaker, while the square and opposition are notably adverse.

7. By reason of its proximity to the Earth, its reflections of solar light and retransmission of planetary vibrations, and its swiftness as compared to the motions of the planets, the Moon is deemed the most important element in any Electional Figure. Therefore a time must be chosen when the Moon is free from any serious affliction and - in case the matter is desired to be accomplished quickly - swift in motion. The nearer its rate of travel is to 15º17' per day, as at perigee when nearest to the Earth, the quicker will its influence be manifest. Also it should be increasing in light; i.e., from three days after the lunation to three days before the Full Moon. Care should be exercised that the Moon does not tenant a Cadent House, and all things considered it is desirable that it is not in an Angle. When the lunar motion is less than 13°11' - hence near its apogee and thus farthest from Earth - its ray is deemed in many respects similar to that of a

retrograde planet. When possible, place the luminaries, or at least one of them, in trine to the radical Sun, Moon, Ascendant or its Ruler, of the person for whom the Election is cast. It should be free from affliction, and in a close favorable aspect to transiting Venus, Jupiter, Sun, or still better to the planet disposing of the project under contemplation. Under no circumstances begin a new business when the Moon is radiating adverse aspects or when it is past the Full, however propitious the other testimonies may appear to be. When past the Full, hence decreasing in light, the strength of the Moon is diminishing, and as a result the project will be greatly retarded; as also when the Moon conjoins Saturn on its own South Node, or Saturn is rising, or in the Fourth House. Since the Moon rules Cancer, that regulates the inflow and outflow of the life-tides, and is exalted in Taurus, that controls the basic materials of which the Earth is compounded, and since both luminaries govern the tides of Earth and of the waters surrounding, it should be apparent how potent are the configurations of this nearest of the Earth's gravitational and radiating forces in the destiny of all living things. If the Ascendant is in a Sign of short ascension - Capricorn to Gemini inclusive - and Mars afflicts, the elector places himself in no little jeopardy of some untoward accident, or outbreak of temper on the part of himself or another, which could seriously upset the matter in hand.

8. When beginning a project presumed to be reasonably permanent, render it durable by placing the four Fixed Signs, and preferably the 5th degree thereof, on the Angles of the Figure; or at least see that the Moon tenants one of them.

9. See that your Election does not notably stimulate any serious affliction in the Nativity; that the Moon is strong and well placed and that neither the Moon nor the Angles in the Nativity are afflicted by the more important electional positions. The natal House that disposes of the project for which the Election is cast should be well fortified, and care should be exercised to see that its Ruler is strong, well placed and unafflicted.

10. If the project is a financial one, the cusp of the radical Second House and its Ruler should be fortified by good aspects, as also the corresponding position and planet in the Election.

11. It is desirable to place the Lord of the radical Ascendant in an Angle, or at least in a Succedent House, in the Election, and oriental to the Sun, whether the planet be benefic or malefic, thereby avoiding its placement in a cadent House or an occidental position, which would be particularly undesirable if it conjoins the Moon.

12. A malefic that rules the radical Ascendant may be made use of in the Election, since it is not harmful to the person whose Ruler it is.

When the Nativity is unobtainable, the cautions relating thereto must of necessity be disregarded. In the literature of Horary Astrology and Elections are to be found many aphorisms relating to the subject, for which reference may be had to the works of Ptolemy, Guido Bonatus, Cardan, William Lilly, A. J. Pearse and Dr. Broughton, including Ramesey's "Rules for Electing Times for all Manner of Works," contained in his *Astrology Restored* (edition of 1653), to be consulted in a few of the libraries.

To cast thoroughly sound Electional Figures one should first master the rules of Horary Art; then develop it by recurrent practice in casting Electional Schemes for one imaginary project after another. To perform this successfully necessitates the memorization of lists of the various ventures and commodities falling within the province of each planet; such as that: the Sun disposes of business, professional and social preferment, and rules games, hobbies and certain classes of investments; the Moon disposes of those matters in which permanency is not desired, and favors dealings with women and servants, and concerning domestic affairs; Mercury disposes of travel, messages, writing, mail, and the ephemeral type of publications; and so on for the remaining planets, as listed in any good text-book on Electional Astrology.

When an elector lacks a sufficient knowledge of astro-dynamics to enable him accurately to cast the Figure whereby to select a suitable moment, the next best substitute is to consult the aspectarian in any good ephemeris, and begin operations just prior to the formation of a good lunar aspect. Another resort is to refer to a Planetary Hour Table calculated to latitude, and select the middle of a Jupiter hour.
- FREDERIC VAN NORSTRAND.

Electric planets. *v. Planets.*

Elements. The four fundamental natures, symbolized as Fire, Earth, Air and Water. *v. Signs.*

Elevation. Astronomically, the distance of a planet above the horizon; its altitude.

Elevation of the Pole. As this increases as one advances N. or S. from the Equator, it is the equivalent of Latitude, hence is seldom now employed in this sense, to avoid confusion with the use of the term in reference to the relative House positions of the planets.

Elevation by Latitude. Of any two planets, the one that has the more latitude, either N. or S., is said to be "in elevation by latitude." If the latitudes be the same, that which has the least declination is the more elevated.

Eleveation by House Position. That one of the Ascending planets which is nearest to the cusp of the Tenth House, the Midheaven or highest point in the map, is said to be elevated above the others. Loosely applied to any planet that occupies a position above the horizon in a geocentric chart. Elevation is one of the Accidental Dignities. *(v. Dignities.)* A malefic in elevation above the luminaries, especially if in the Midheaven, indicates much adversity - unless mitigated by strong and favoring aspects. If the malefic is anareta, it presages a violent death; if it be elevated above a benefic, the benefic will be powerless to prevent; but if the reverse, the benefic will moderate the anaretic tendency. If either of the luminaries is elevated above the malefics, their power to harm will be greatly lessened.

Elongation. (a) The angular distance of an inferior, or interior, planet from the Sun, as viewed from the Earth. The maximum elongation which Mercury attains is 28 degrees; Venus, 46 degrees. Consequently in a birth map the only aspects Mercury can form to the Sun are a conjunction and semi-sextile; Venus, these and a semi-square. (b) The farthest distance of any planet from the Sun; aphelion.

Embolismic Month. Embolismic Lunation. An intercalary month employed in some ancient calendars, whereby to preserve a seasonal relationship between the Lunar and Solar calendars. *v. Calendar.*

Emerge. Emersion. To come out from a coalescence with the Sun's rays; employed chiefly in reference to eclipses and occultations. Antonym: immersion.

Emotional Natures. Referring to the quality of sensory receptivity and reaction through the sympathetic nervous system that characterizes those born with the Sun in Cancer, Scorpio and Pisces - respectively, the initiative, executive and deductive types of the Emotional group. To classify this group as Emotional, does not imply that other groups are not capable of Emotion; but where those of the Intellectual group experience emotion chiefly through mental processes, of the Inspirational group through a super-consciousness of the Ego, and of the practical group through a capacity for sentiment, the Emotional group appear to be motivated almost entirely through Emotional stimulation apparently generated in their nerve ganglia as reflexes, and which penetrate to the very fibres of their physical being.

Enneatical. The ninth in any series. Said of a climax which occurs on the ninth day of an illness - or every ninth day of its progress; also of the ninth day after birth; the ninth year of life; or every ninth year throughout life. *(v. Climacterical Periods.)*

Epact. A word of Greek origin, applied to a number that indicates the Moon's age on the first day of the year. As the common solar year is 365 d., and the lunar year 354 d., the difference of 11 indicates that if a new moon falls on January 1st in any year, it will be 11 days old on the first day of the next year, and 22 days old on the first of the third year. Hence the epacts of those years are numbers 11 and 22. In a leap year, however, the remainder is 10, which introduces such complexities that the chief and almost sole use of the epact is in determining the date of Easter. A number which represents the number of days of excess of the Solar year over 12 lunar months is the *annual epact*. The number which represents the number of days of excess of a calendar month over a lunar month is the *monthly epact*. The epacts differ from the Golden Numbers, from which they are derived, in that they provide for the adjustment of (1) the solar equation, a correction of the Julian Calendar, and (2) the lunar equation, a correction of the error in the lunar cycle. In its use in determining the date of Easter, apparently more concern was paid to the consideration that it must not coincide with the Passover than to astronomical exactness, for the Tables of Epacts are frequently in error by as much as two days earlier or later.

Ephemeral Map. One erected for the time of an event, to be judged by Horary Astrology.

Ephemeral Motion. The day-to-day motion of the celestial bodies of the solar system in their orbits. Said in contradistinction to directional or progressed motion.

Ephemeris. *pl.* Ephemerides. An almanac listing the ephemeral or rapidly changing position which each of the solar system bodies will occupy on each day of the year: their Longitude, Latitude, Declination, and similar astronomical phenomena. The astronomer's Ephemeris lists these positions in heliocentric terms; that of the astrologer, in geocentric terms. A set of Ephemerides which includes the year of the native's birth, is essential in the erection of a horoscope. Ephemerides were first devised by astrologers to facilitate the erection of a horoscope. Finally, when they became of common use to navigators and astronomers, they were given official recognition by the Government, and issued as the Nautical Almanac. The oldest almanac in the British Museum bears the date 1431. It is said that Columbus navigated by the aid of an Astrologer's Ephemeris.
Some of the notable ephemerides have been: Vincent Wing, 1658-81; John Gadbury, 1682-1702; Edmund Weaver, 1740-46; Thomas White, 1762-1850 (also reappeared in 1883); George Parker, in *Celestial Atlas*, 1780-90; John Partridge, in *Merlinus Liberatus*, 1851-59; E. W. Williams, in the *Celestial Messenger*, 1858; W. J. Simmonite, 1801-61; Raphael, 1820 to date.
The old astronomical day which began at noon was abolished on Jan. 1, 1925, and since then the astronomical day has begun at midnight. Gradually this is reflected in the making of Ephemerides. Therefore it is important to verify whether the ephemeris one is using for any given year since around

1930 shows the planets' places at noon or midnight. This can be determined at a glance by noting the sidereal time on Jan. 1: if it is around 18h the ephemeris is for noon; if around 6h, it is for midnight; if neither of these, it is probably calculated for some longitude other than that of Greenwich.

Epicycle. A term employed by Ptolemy, in whose astronomical system the Earth was regarded as the centre, to indicate a small orbit around a central deferent *(q.v.)*. He assumed that the orbits of all the other planets formed epicycles around the Earth's orbit. It was involved in an attempted solution of the phenomenon of retrograde motion. Assuming that the Sun pursues an orbit, the Earth's orbit is an epicycle, which while pursuing its own orbit is carried forward in the larger orbit of the Sun. The Moon's orbit is an epicycle upon the orbit of the Earth around the Sun. The Sun, which is never retrograde, was the only solar system body which, according to Ptolemy, did not have an epicycle.

Epoch. A point of time with reference to which other dates are calculated. Prenatal Epoch applies to a system of rectification in which the Moon's place ten lunar months previous to the birth moment becames the ascending or descending degree at the moment of birth. v. RECTIFICATION.

Equal Power, Signs of. *v. Beholding Signs.*

Equation of Time. (1) Astron. The difference between mean solar time and apparent solar time. The moment the Sun is exactly on the Midheaven of any place is apparent noon at that place; hence an apparent solar day is the interval between two consecutive passages of the Sun across the Midheaven, or the elapsed time from one apparent noon to the next. However, since the Sun - or more correctly speaking, the Earth - does not move at a uniform speed throughout its orbit, the length of the apparent day varies at different times of the year. To make possible the use of time-keeping mechanisms, there was adopted a standard fixed day of 24 hours, known as a mean day - the length of which is the average of all the apparent days of the year. The result is that mean noon is sometimes earlier and sometimes later than apparent noon. The difference between mean and apparent noon on any particular day, the Equation of Time, may amount to as much as sixteen minutes. (2) Astrol. It is generally considered that in a Figure erected for noon the Sun will be at the cusp of the Tenth House. This is approximately true, although at certain times of the year it will be two or three degrees removed, on one side or the other from the Midheaven. One sometimes hears the suggestion that the Figure should be erected by the Sun and not by the clock, which would involve the application of the Equation of Time as a correction of clock time. This is done when calculating the time of the rising of the Sun or other bodies. Its application to the erecting of the Figure, however, would be utterly unsound, for the time in which the birth is stated and the ephemerides which give the planets' places are both based on mean time. If the Figure were to be erected for apparent time, the birth moment would have to be corrected to apparent time, and the result would be the same. (3) It is unfortunate that this term is incorrectly applied by some authorities to the difference between mean and sidereal time, more properly termed the *correction* employed in reducing to sidereal time the elapsed mean time of a given birth moment before or after noon or midnight. (4) The term has frequently been incorrectly applied to the time equivalent of an Arc of Direction, in years, months and days - of which few points in Astrology have been more debated. The coordination of the 360° of the Equational circle and the 365¼-day year yields a mean value of 3m 56.33s per day, and a mean increment of either Right Ascension or Longitude of 59'8". Some authorities advocate an equation of 1° per year or 5' per month. Others advocate a method wherein the Arc of Direction is added to the R.A. of the Sun at birth - the number of days after birth at which the Sun attains this directional position, reduced to years at the rate of one day for a year or 2 hrs. for a month. Others divide the Arc of Direction by the Sun's mean motion per year (59'8"), the result converted into time at the rate of one degree for a year. *(v. Directions.)*

Equator. The circle that lies midway between the poles of the earth, dividing it into two hemispheres - North and South. Also the projection of the Earth's equator upon the celestial sphere - sometimes called the equinoctial circle.

The celestial equator has also been defined as "the continuation of the plane of the terrestrial equator without limit into celestial spaces."

Equinox. A point in the Earth's annual orbit around the Sun, at which the polar inclination is at right angles to a line drawn between the Earth and the Sun; in consequence of which the length of the day and the night are equal all over the earth. This occurs at two points, called respectively the Vernal Equinox, which the Earth passes on March 21 when it enters Aries, and the Autumnal Equinox, on September 22nd when it enters Libra. Astronomers have not yet charted the Sun's orbit or determined its plane, or the inclination of the orbit of the Earth to that of the Sun, but it is possible that when these have been determined, it will be found that the Equinoctial points are the Earth's Nodes, where the plane of the Earth's orbit intersects that of the Sun. Thus the Zodiac, measured from the Spring Equinox, will be shown to represent a fixed relationship of the Earth and Sun in an orbit around some remote galactic center. *(v. Galaxy.)* This will make the Equinoctial points in reference to the Sun's orbit, analogous to the Moon's Nodes in reference to the Earth's orbit.

The equinoxes are commonly defined as the moment wherein the Sun reaches the point at which the plane of the ecliptic intersects the plane of the equator.

Equinoctial Signs. Aries and Libra. *v. Signs*

Era. Applied to numerous historical epochs, presumably starting on some specific date of constant reference, among them the following:

The Grecian Mundane Era............... Sept. 1, 5598 B.C.
The Civil Era of Constantinople....... Sept. 1, 5508 B.C.
The Alexandrian Era................... Aug. 29, 5502 B.C.
Ecclesiastical Era of Antioch......... Sept. 1, 5492 B.C.
The Julian Period..................... Jan. 1, 4713 B.C.
The Mundane Era....................... October 4008 B.C.
Jewish Mundane Era.................... October 3761 B.C.
Era of Abraham........................ Oct. 1, 2015 B.C.
Era of the Olympiads.................. July 1, 776 B.C.
Roman Era............................. Apr. 24, 753 B.C.
Era of Nabonassar..................... Feb. 26, 747 B.C.
Metonic Cycle......................... July 15, 432 B.C.
Syro-Macedonian, or Grecian, Era...... Sept. 1, 312 B.C.
Tyrian Era............................ Oct. 19, 125 B.C.

Sidonian Era.......................... October 110 B.C.
Caesarean Era of Antioch.............. Sept. 1, 48 B.C.
The Julian Year....................... Jan. 1, 45 B.C.
The Spanish Era....................... Jan. 1, 38 B.C.
Actian Era............................ Jan. 1, 30 B.C.
Augustan Era.......................... Feb. 14, 27 B.C.
The so-called Vulgar Christian Era.... Jan. 1,   1 A.D.
The Destruction of Jerusalem.......... Sept. 1, 69 A.D.
Era of the Maccabees.................. Nov. 24, 166 A.D.
Era of Diocletian..................... Sept.17, 284 A.D.
Era of Ascension...................... Nov. 12, 295 A.D.
Era of the Armenians.................. July 7, 552 A.D.
Mohammedan Era of the Hegira.......... July 16, 622 A.D.
Persian Era of Yezdegird.............. June 16, 632 A.D.
The Gregorian Year.................... Oct. 15, 1582 A.D.
Standard Time zones................... Nov. 18, 1883 A.D.
The Julian Day........................ Jan. 1, 1925 A.D.

Eros. (1) Greek God of Love, Son of Aphrodite. Equivalent of the Latin God Cupid. A divinity of fertility. In Orphism Eros was born of the cosmic egg produced by Night. (2) The 433d asteroid, discovered by DeWitt in 1898. Eros at times comes closer to the Earth than any heavenly body except the Moon. v. HERMES (3).

Erratics. Erratic Stars. A term applied by the ancients to the planets, in distinction to the Fixed Stars.

Esoteric. Secret knowledge not accessible to the uninitiated. When such information is published it ceases to be esoteric and becomes exoteric, which means that the facts have become the property of the rest of humanity. As employed by Leo, exoteric interpretations are those wherein a predicted event is considered to be inescapable, while esoteric interpretations are based upon the assumption that the developed individual is able to exercise self-determination and volition, and to render himself immune to the harmful effects of astrological influences by transmuting them into a source of power.

Essential Dignities. v. *Dignities.*

Eudemon. The good demon. A term anciently applied to the Eleventh House, indicating that it is productive of good, as the Twelfth House is of evil.

Exaltation. v. *Dignity.*

Executive Type. Referring to a quality of unyielding determination liberally possessed by those born when the Sun was in a Fixed Sign: Taurus, Leo, Scorpio or Aquarius. v. *Sign.*

Exoteric. The exposed, the visible. Antithesis of Esoteric. *(q.v.)*

Externalize. Said of the event which transpires when an astrological influence is incited to action by contact with a circumstance of environment. The thought is based upon the theory that astrological influences have to do with the mental and emotional conditioning that determines the nature of the individual's reaction to circumstances, but that they do not of themselves produce events.

Extra-sensory Perceptions. Commonly abbreviated, E.S.P. A phrase coined and defined by Dr. J. B. Rhine of Duke University and applicable to mental phenomena such as telepathy, clairaudience, clairvoyance, precognition and similar supernormal sense capacities. A capacity for receiving extra-sensory impressions is generally associated with a favorable Neptune accent.

Face. There is so much contradictory testimony with reference to this term that the entire subject has been ignored by many modern authorities.
(1) As employed by Ptolemy, a planet in a House that is distant counter-clockwise from the Moon, or clockwise from the Sun by the same number of Houses as the Sign, is in its Face. This means that Mercury is in its Face when in a House preceding that of the Moon, or following that of the Sun; Venus, when two Houses preceding or following; Mars, three Houses; Jupiter, four Houses; or Saturn, five Houses - duplicating in Houses from the actual Sun and Moon positions, the scheme of Sign-Ruler ship from Cancer and Leo, around to Capricorn and Aquarius.
(2) James Wilson gives a series of 10° Faces which are merely the scheme of Decanates with their Rulers according to one of the ancient Systems. Since this is only a distinction of terms without a difference in meaning, the employment of the term Face in this sense is confusing and unnecessary.
(3) Alan Leo defines a Face as one of a series of 5° subdivisions of a Sign. His fondness for symbolism is reflected in the interpretations which he applies to those who have a rising Degree in each of the 72 arcs in this series of what might better be called demi-Decans. *v. Signs, Subdivisions of.*

Fall. A planet in the Sign opposite that in which it is said to be Exalted. *v. Dignity.*

False Angle; False Arc. *v. Directions.*

Familiarity. A term used by Ptolemy to indicate an aspect or parallel between two bodies; or their mutual disposition, as when each is in the other's Sign or House.

Fate. The belief that astrological influences determine Man's fate, that the issues of all events is predetermined, and that no effort can avail him to alter it, is an extreme view to which few modern astrologers subscribe, since it would deprive his active will and effort of mind of any effective part in determining the events of his life. The doctrine of Fate should therefore be regarded as somewhat misleading on the ground that it is in conflict with the modern concept of Man as a free moral agent. *v. Free Will.*

Feminine Signs. The even-numbered signs: Taurus, Cancer, Virgo, Scorpio, Capricorn, and Pisces. *(v. Signs.)*

Feral. A wild or undomesticated animal. A term anciently employed whereby inference was made to the bestial nature of those with an Ascendant in Leo or the latter half of Sagittarius; also those with either Luminary so placed and with the malefics in Angles. The Moon was said to be feral when void of course (q.v.).

Figure. An astrological or Celestial Figure, variously called Geniture, Map, Scheme, Chart, Theme, Mirror of Heaven, Nativity or Horoscope, as cast, erected or drawn by modern astrologers, consists of a circle of the heavens, representing the 360° of the Earth's orbit, divided into twelve arcs - resembling a wheel of twelve spokes. These arcs may represent Signs of 30° each beginning at the Spring equinoctial point, or Houses of an indeterminate number of degrees beginning at an ascending degree. A Solar Figure, used where a specific moment of birth is not known, employs the Sun's degree as the point of beginning, or Ascendant. The Houses or geo-arcs, based upon the degree rising in the east at the specific moment for which the Figure is cast, supposedly represent the number of degrees which pass over the horizon in two hours from that particular longitude and latitude and on that day. The Sign-divisions, or heliarcs, are thus subdivisions of the Earth's annual orbit round the Sun, while the House-divisions, or geo-arcs, are subdivisions of the daily orbit of a particular point on the Earth's surface around the Earth's axis.

Most of the difficulties concerning astrological terminology result from the fact that this circle represents the celestial sphere, subdivided according to three different systems at one and the same time. This paradox ceases to baffle only when the one who employs the map learns to read and interpret it in each of the three ways, consecutively rather than simultaneously.

With the Earth as a center of reference, its annual orbit extends impersonally from the point of the Vernal Equinox, in successive 30° arcs, each corresponding to one sign of the zodiac. Therefore, if for a given day, month and year, the planets are placed in certain degrees of certain signs, this placement remains valid no matter at what point on the earth the observer is located.

If now we confine ourself to a given individual located at a given point on the Earth, and erect a map showing the Sun at the sunrise point, choosing the Sun as the point of commencement of a circle or experience, because it is a permanently powerful center of energy radiation, our twelve 30° arcs will be measured from the degree the Sun occupied on that day. Such a set of arcs would be applicable to any one born with the Sun in the same degree; but when the places of the remaining planets are inserted it will apply only to one born also on the same day of the same year. If the different planetary reflectors of solar energy, as they appear over the horizon at irregular intervals throughout that first day of life, stimulate a certain growth, there must result a cycle of sensitive degrees or points of receptivity. On successive days the actual places of these planets will advance, but the point of receptivity or expectancy remains - resulting in the "human time clock" to which physiologists frequently refer.

If now these twelve divisions of the circle are to be based on the diurnal rotation of the Earth on its axis, the twelve arcs must represent subdivisions of the Equator instead of the Ecliptic. Furthermore, this involves the question of time of day, and Latitude as well as Longitude of place. Such arcs are measured from the degree of the Horizon that is rising at that moment of time from that particular Longitude and Latitude of place; and are measured in two-hour units along the Horizon instead of 30° units along the Ecliptic.

Since the Inclination of the Earth's axis introduces another factor, the degrees of arc that cross the horizon in two hours, vary with the Latitude and with the time of year. This expanding and contracting of the degrees encompassed in two hours throughout the year, is also doubtless involved in the factor of orbs. *(q.v.)*

Therefore, the map of a nativity is a combination of three maps: (1) Of Signs, 30º subdivisions of a horizon, at right angles to a line between a Zenith and a Nadir (v. Celestial Sphere); (2) of Solar House, 30° subdivisions of the Ecliptic, at right angles to a line between the North and South poles of the Ecliptic; and (3) Of Houses, two-hour subdivisions of the Equator, at right angles to a line between the North and South Celestial Poles.

For this reason some modern scientific astrologers utilize the map in a method somewhat altered from the traditional method. The divisions of the printed design are the Signs, with 0° Aries at the left. A colored line is drawn through the Sun position to the opposite point in the orbit, and another at right angles thereto, indicating the solar houses. On the outside of the circle are placed the degrees of the cusps of the Geocentric Houses as measured from the Rising Degree, thus showing at a glance the unequal arcs that pass over the horizon in equal periods of time. In reading such a map, the design is read upright, or successively rotated to place at the left the Sun degree or the Rising Degree.

This explains the use of the terms Midheaven and Ascendant, as indicating the points at the top or at the left of the map, which terms are not synonymous with Zenith or Nadir. *(v. Celestial Sphere.)*

Fire Signs. The inspirational signs: Aries, Leo, Sagittarius. *v. Signs.*

First point. 0º Aries; from which point Longitude is reckoned along the Ecliptic, and right ascension along the Celestial Equator.

Fixed Signs. Taurus, Leo, Scorpio and Aquarius, constituting the Fixed Quadruplicity. *v. Signs, Qualities.*

Fixed Stars. *v. Stars.*

Flexed. An alternate term for the mutable signs, preferred by some modern authorities.

Fortified. Strongly placed; either elevated, in a congenial Sign, or well-aspected.

Fortitude. An ancient term indicating a quality or strength possessed by a planet when posited in its own sign or that of its exaltation.

Fortuna. Pars Fortuna. The Part of Fortune. One of the Arabian Points (Q.V.). A point that bears the same relation to the Rising Degree that the Moon bears to the Sun. It occupies the same House-position in a Figure based on a birth-moment, that the Moon tenants in a Solar Figure. Its symbol, a cross within a circle ⊕, is that utilized by astronomers to represent the Earth. It is the ancient Chinese symbol TIEN, a field; used by the Egyptians to signify territory. It is generally considered that the House position of Fortuna is an indication of the department of life that will most readily contribute to the financial welfare of the native. If so it tends to lend emphasis to the theory that one succeeds best at that which one likes best; that congeniality of occupation is a contributing factor to success therein. v. ARABIAN POINTS.

Fortunate Signs. A positive Sign, especially on the Ascendant, is sometimes so characterized; but, unless the Ruler thereof is well aspected, this ought not to be taken too literally, for too often it is overbalanced by other considerations.

Fortunes. The benefic planets: Jupiter, the 'Greater Fortune"; and Venus, the "Lesser Fortune". The Sun and Mercury, or by some authorities the Moon and Mercury, when well placed and aspected, particularly if by Jupiter or Venus, are sometimes so classed. Simmonite in his "Arcana of Astrology" says: "If Jupiter be with the Part of Fortune in good aspect with the Moon and angular, especially in the First House, the native will become rich".

Four-footed Signs. Aries, Taurus, Leo, Sagittarius and Capricorn, sometimes termed "animal Signs." One whose Ascendant is posited in one of these Signs was anciently presumed to possess some of the qualities of that particular animal; as bold as the Lion, lustful as a goat, and so on.

Fourth Dimension. The interrelationship of space and time, as developed by contemporary physicists, makes Time the Fourth Dimension of Space. The concept has no immediate application to Astrology, but its comprehension makes more understandable the factors upon which all astrological considerations are based. In occult terminology the Fourth Dimension has to do with internal qualities that when seen in the astral light become visible. It is defined as "the sum of the other three" dimensions; also as "Man's expanding sense of time." In another sense Astrology is the Fourth Dimension of Psychology, in that it alone takes cognizance of the added factor of time.

Free-Will. A doctrine that applies to the exercise of the will in overcoming the obstacles of terrestrial environment and cosmic influences, whereby so to control and direct cosmic forces operating at a given time, as to transmute them into power under control. It is opposed to any such yielding to an influence as that which is called Fate. According to this concept the hour and place of birth, and the planets thereby located in the Figure, represent the tools with which the individual is enabled to work out his destiny. How he uses them, how he applies his individual gifts, is in his own hands by virtue of the divine gift of Free Will. This philosophy thus removes from astrological teachings the fatalistic doctrine which is repugnant to all who believe that Man's control of his ultimate destiny is in his own hands.

Friendly planets. Ptolemy appeared to believe that those planets which have ruler ship, exaltation or Triplicity in each other's Signs should be classed as friendly planets. Other authorities class them as follows:
Sun - unfriendly only to Saturn.
Moon - unfriendly only to Mars and Saturn.
Venus - unfriendly only to Saturn.
Mars - friendly with Venus only.
Jupiter - unfriendly only to Mars.
Saturn - friendly only to the Sun, Mercury and Jupiter.
Just how Saturn can be friendly to the Sun when the latter is unfriendly to him is nowhere explained, and James Wilson says the entire concept is nonsense. However, a little thought will discern its basic truth when the qualities of the various vibrations are considered, and as regards the Sun-Saturn objection what Ptolemy probably meant was Saturn's application in beneficent aspect to the solar orb, for no one can

deny that a sextile or trine from Saturn to the Sun mightily strengthens the latter and agrees with its purpose.

Fruitful Signs. Cancer, Scorpio and Pisces. The Water Signs. In Horary Questions the Ascendant, Moon, or Lord of the Ascendant, if strongly placed in any one of these Signs, become symbols of children. Some deem this equally applicable to the Natal Figure, and that the 5th or its Lord in a fruitful Sign is a symbol of children. v. Signs.

Frustration. A term used in Horary Astrology when one planet is applying to an aspect of another, which aspect would tend to signify some event; but before such aspect culminates, a third planet, by its swifter motion, interposes to anticipate the culmination of the forming aspect by completing one of its own. It is said to produce an Abscission of Light that will frustrate the promised effect of the slower-moving aspect, constituting a prohibition (q.v.) against its operation. The indication is that the matter thus subjected to the prohibition will be retarded or utterly prevented, through influences connected with the House of which the frustrating planet is Ruler, or in which it was posited at birth. In his "Arcana of Astrology" Simmonite gives this illustration of its application to an Horary Figure: "If Venus, Lady of the Ascendant, were hastening to the trine of Mars, Lord of the Seventh, in a question of marriage, it might denote that the match would take place; but if Mercury were to form an opposition to Mars before Venus reached her trine of that planet, it would be a frustration and would show that the hopes of the querent would be cut off, and if he were Lord of the Twelfth, it might denote that it would be done by a private enemy; if Lord of the 3rd, by means of relations, and so on."

Gabriel. The angel (q.v.) of the Moon.

Galactic Center. The gravitational center around which the Sun revolves. Astrology has hypothetically placed this at 0° Capricorn, which is exactly confirmed by recently published results of thousands of calculations of spectroscopic radial velocity measurements, and other thousands by the parallax method of determining proper motion, by Charlier, Stromberg, Wilson, Campbell and More, and Smart and Green. In consequence the astronomers have arrived at a position of the center of the Milky Way Galaxy at R.A. 270°, declin. +29.7°. Therefore at the time of the Winter Solstice, the Galactic Center is a few degrees South of the Sun.

The Sun's actual travel is estimated at 200 miles per second in orbit. As it is placed about 30,000 light-years from the center of the Milky Way Galaxy, one complete orbit is estimated to require 200 million years. Its apparent motion toward a point near Wega in the constellation Hercules, as measured by nearby stars, is 12 miles per second - which should not be confused with its computed actual rate of travel.

The plane of the Sun's orbit is presumed to be approximately that of the Galactic Center, which is inclined to the Earth's orbit by about 50 degrees.

Galactic Latitude. The angular distance of a celestial body from the median plane of the Milky Way.

Galaxy. A star-cluster or group of stars. The Sun and its system are a unit in the Milky Way Galaxy, which moves around a gravitational center that must be in the vicinity of 0° Capricorn, as viewed from the Earth, geocentrically considered. In that event, the Sun's path, at right angles to this point, must be along the line between 0° Aries and 0° Libra, which the Earth intersects at the Equinoxes. The inclination of the Earth's axis, that causes this phenomenon, may thus be due to the inclination of the plane of the Earth's orbit, or in response to the attraction from the gravitational center that bends the Sun's travel into an orbit, or a combination of these and other influences.

Gamut, Notes of the. Having to do with what Pythagoras termed "the music of the spheres."
C The Sun
D Saturn
E Mercury
F The Moon
G Mars
A Venus
B Jupiter
Peculiarly, the next two planets discovered have, according to Sepharial, an axial rotation from east to west, contrary to the order of the other bodies. It is in reference to the Gamut that Uranus, Neptune and Pluto are spoken of as belonging to the second octave: Uranus, the octave of Mercury; Neptune, of Venus; and Pluto, of Mars. *(Mark Knights, d. March 20, 1897 fr. asphyxiation, traced references to five of these "notes" in Shakespeare's "Taming of the Shrew" 1623 folio ed.)*

Gemini. The Third Sign of the Zodiac. *v. Signs.*

Gems. *v. Signs; Planetary.*

Genethliacal Astrology. Natal astrology - that which deals with the geniture in a nativity.

Genethlialogy. That department of Astrology which deals with the birth of individuals, whereby one forms a judgment of the characteristics of a person from a map of the heavens cast for his given birth moment.

Geniture. A Birth or Genesis. A term that is approximately synonymous with Nativity, as referring to the subject whose birth horoscope is under consideration. A reasonable discrimination would be to employ Nativity in reference to the person, and Geniture to the configurations which show in his birth map. Ptolemy speaks of Lord of the Geniture in referring to the Ruling planet in a given horoscope of birth.

Geo arc. A term applied by some modern authorities to one of the house divisions of a map erected for a given moment, when there is under consideration the effect upon an individual, at a given point on the Earth's periphery, of his motion around the Earth's center - in the Earth's daily rotation. The same subdivision of the same map is called a heliarc, when there is under consideration effects based on the actual motions in orbit around the Sun, of all the planets - including the Earth. In other words, Geoarc is synonymous with House, and Heliarc with Solar House, emphasizing the character of the motion to which the subdivisions apply. A geoarc considers the Earth as a rotating body, imparting an appar- ent motion to celestial points and objects. A heliarc views the Earth as a fixed point from which one considers the effects of the actual motions of celestial objects. The heliarcs are 30° arcs measured from the Sun's position on the day for which the Figure is erected.

Geo arc Figure. One in which the cusp of the first Geo arc is the degree rising at a given moment. If the Sun's position becomes the first cusp, it is a Heli arc Figure. However, the subdivisions of either map may be considered either as Geo arcs or Heli arcs, or both.

Geocentric. (1) Having the Earth for a center. The geocentric positions of the planets indicating their position. These are now generally calculated from the heliocentric places as given in the Nautical Almanac. The difference between the two is incorrectly termed the parallax. All astrological considerations are based on the geocentric positions of the planets, on the theory that Astrology is concerned with planetary motions only as they affect the Earth. (2) The distance along the Ecliptic from 0° Aries, as viewed from the Earth.
Heliocentric Longitude is expressed in degrees of Right Ascension, from 0° to 360°, while Geocentric Longitude is expressed in terms of the Signs of the Zodiac.

Geomancy, Astrological. A system of divination, employing a map containing twelve divisions, in which arc placed symbols of geomancy, in conjunction with the ruling planets and signs.

Gibbous. v. Phase.

Giver of Life. The Hyleg, or Significator that holds the vital prerogative. *(v. Hyleg.)*

Gnomes. An esoteric name for the invisible Nature-spirits that belong to the Earth Triplicity.

Golden Number. The number of any year in the Metonic Cycle of 235 Lunation *(q.v.)*, which equals 6939d. 16h. 31m., or approximately 19 years. It is used in fixing the date of Easter. The cycle begins with the year in which the lunation falls on January 1st in the tenth degree of Capricorn, which it did in the year beginning the Christian era (1 B.C.). To find the Golden Number of any year: Add 1, divide by 19; the remainder indicates the number of the cycle. If there is no remainder the Golden Number is 19. Because the sum of solar and lunar inequalities vary in different years the matter of determining the date and longitude of the lunations may be in error as much as 2 days - either earlier or later. At the Gregorian Reformation of 1582 it was superseded by the Epacts. *(q.v.)*

Gradial Transit, Arc of. A term employed by Sepharial to indicate the arc a planet traverses from its birth position to its progressed position, when in any given year it is activated by a major transit through the arc. As this arc increases in size from year to year, it affords a possible explanation of the observation that with advancing years transitory aspects become operative for longer periods and in cumulatively increased potencies.

Grand Cross. v. Cosmic Cross.

Grand Trine. Two planets trine to each other, both of which are trined by a third planet.

Gregorian Calendar. v. Calendar.

Guarded. Applied to one or more elevated planets guarded on the East by the Sun and on the West by the Moon.

Hayz. In Horary Questions a masculine diurnal planet above the Earth in a Day Figure, and a feminine nocturnal planet under the Earth in a Night Figure is a Dignity of 1°, and is reckoned fortunate. The Arabians did not conceive it a perfect Hayz except when the masculine planet was in a male Sign, or the feminine planet in a female Sign. A masculine planet in a male Sign under the Earth by day was considered to be only in his light, and the person denoted by it to be in a state of contentment.

Hearing. Deemed to be under the Dominion of Saturn. v. SENSES.

Heart of the Sun. v. CAZIMI.

Heliacal Rising. Lit., rising with the Sun. When a planet or a star, after it has been hidden by the Sun's rays, becomes again visible.

Heliacal Setting. When a star is overtaken by the Sun and is lost in its rays. The Heliacal rising or setting of the Moon occurs when it is within 17° of the Sun; other stars and planets, when within 30° distance.

Heliarc. v. GEOARC.

Heliarc Figure. A Solar Figure based on the Earth's annual revolution around the Sun, employing the Sun's position as an ascendant degree. In a Heliarc Figure each heliarc consists of 30°. v. GEOARC FIGURE.

Heliocentric. The Sun as a center. The science of Astrology is largely based on geocentric observations, since it treats of cosmic forces as perceived or received by an inhabitant of the Earth. Some authorities believe that heliocentric considerations may contribute added testimony of importance, for which reason the heliocentric longitudes 2nd latitudes of the planets are to be found in some ephemerides. In reducing heliocentric positions to geocentric terms, a mean orbit is employed wherein the planets are presumed to move in a circle at a uniform rate. This is corrected by an equation to centre, based upon the eccentricity of the orbit - its departure from a true circle. Having determined the true position in the orbit, a further equation, improperly called parallax, is employed to reduce the position to its geocentric longitude.

Heliocentric Astrology. One wherein the astrological interpretations are based upon a Figure in which the solar system bodies are located according to their heliocentric longitudes. It is more or less experimental and used by but few astrologers.

Heliocentric Longitude and Latitude. That based on the Sun as a center. The Nautical Almanac gives the Heliocentric positions of all celestial bodies. The Astrologer's Ephemeris is now made from the Nautical Almanac by reducing these positions to their Geocentric equivalents.

Helios. The Greek Sun God, who went home every evening at sunset in a winged boat made of gold.

Hemisphere. The half-circle: either that East or West of the meridian, or that North or South of the Equator.

Hermaphrodite. Compounded of both sexes. Derived from the names of the god Hermes or Mercury, and the goddess Aphrodite, or Venus. The combination of the two influences, Art and Science, in the mind of man constitutes the true human, in whom the emotional and rational powers are presumed to be in perfect balance. Astrology under this appellation speaks of a higher order of intellect, combining masculine and feminine qualities or propensities, yet with no inference of bisexual functioning. The term is sometimes applied to Mercury, because of its dual and changeable nature.

Hermes. (1) An olympian god, son of Zeus and Maia, identified by the Romans with Mercury: messenger of the gods; giver of increase to herds; guardian of roads and commerce; the god of science, inven- tion, eloquence, cunning, trickery, theft, and luck in discovering treasure. of course, in creating the god they endowed him with the astrological attributes of the planet, of whose influences he became the personification. (2) Hermes Trismegistus, identified with the Egyptian god Thoth, was the fabled author of Neo-Platonic, judaic, cabalistic, alchemical and astrological works, studied as sacred by the Egyptian priests. Many spurious works have been put forward as Hermetic writings. Theories and philosophics peculiar to the Hermetic writings are characterized as hermetical. (3) A minor planet, or asteroid discovered photographically at Heidelberg on Oct. 28, 1940 by the German astronomer Reinmuth. As it was moving rapidly in its apparent course in the sky only a few observations were secured, hence the orbit determinations are only approximate. Since then the asteroid has passed beyond telescopic reach. The noteworthy feature of Hermes is the nearness of part of its orbit to that of the Earth-about 362,000 Miles, only 110,000 miles farther from the Earth than the Moon's greatest distance. This breaks the record of Eros for the close approach of a heavenly body to the Earth. First known as the Reinmuth Object, the asteroid was given the designation 1937 UB. Later the discoverer gave it the name Hermes. Calculations give it a diameter of about ½ mile. When nearest the Earth it was in the constellation Delphinus, corresponding to an astrological position of approx. 12º Aquarius. Esoteric writers have long applied the name to Mercury - with a mystical significance implying wisdom.

Hermetic. An alchemist.

Herschel. The British name for the planet discovered by Sir Wm. Herschel; otherwise, Uranus, or Georgium Sidus.

Hexagon. The sextile aspect. (v. ASPECT.)

Hindu Astrology. This is apparently based upon a fixed zodiac, determined by taking a birth year, subtracting 498, multiplying by 50 1/3" per year, reducing the product to Arc and subtracting it from all positions computed according to a Geocentric Ephemeris. The equivalent names of the elements in Sanskrit are:

Aries - Mesham

Taurus - Vrishabham
Germimi - Mithuna
Cancer - Katakam
Leo - Simha
Virgo - Kanya
Libra - Tulam
Scorpio - Vrischika
Sagittarius - Dhanus
Capricorn - Makaram
Aquarius - Kumbra
Pisces - Mînam

Sun - Surya
Moon - Chandra
Mercury - Budham
Venus - Shukra
Mars - Kuja
Jupiter - Cura
Saturn - Shani
North Node - Rahu
South Node - Ketu

Angular: Kendra
Succedent: Panapara
Cadent: Apokalima

Ascendant: Lagnam
Trine: Trikonam
Square: Kandra

The Houses are numbered as counted from any significator. Houses 3, 5, 9, 11 are uniformly favorable as regards that significator; 6, 8, 12 uniformly unfavorable; while 1. 2, 4, 7 and 10 are judged according to the planets occupied. It can be seen that this is largely their method of considering aspects. All planets in 10, 11, 12, 2, 3, 4 houses from a significator are benefic, including harmonious planets in the 1st. All others are evil.

Progressed positions are computed by a complex series of periods, which follow the basic series of South Node 7, Venus 20, Sun 6, Moon 10, Mars 7, North Node 18, Jupiter 16, Saturn 19, Mercury 17. The figures give the duration of the period in years. These are divided into 9 subperiods ruled in the same order, but beginning in each case with the planet's own subperiod. The sub-periods are again divided into interperiods, ruled according to the same method and by the same series. These are applied to the Mansions of the Moon (QV.).

Home, Day or Night. V. HOUSE, DIURNAL.

Homodromi (fellow-runners). Applied to the internal, or variously called minor or inferior, planets Mercury and Venus, which have a maximum elongation from the Sun of approximately 28° and 46° respectively.

Honors. These refer to the Sun and Midheaven and their radical aspects, as indicating the degrees of fame and of honor to which a person is predestined. The Luminaries in an Angle and well-aspected is a sign of high honors. Jupiter rising, or in the Mid-heaven, shows a high degree of prestige. Saturn similarly placed denies credit and renown, however much deserved. Rising planets show aspirations to honors and high ambition, but the outcome of such aspirations depends on which planet first culminates. If the majority of the planets are oriental to the Sun and occidental to the Moon the native will arrive at authority and accumulate wealth. The term is seldom employed by modern authorities.

Horary Astrology. The art of interpreting the relationship between cosmic phenomena resulting from the ordered motions of the celestial bodies, and a thought, situation or event. It deals successfully only with concrete, well-defined queries, and its validity is subject to question when the particular problem to be analyzed is hazy in the mind of the querent, or ill-defined in its presentation to the astrologer.

Since the Horary Figure centers around the person of the querent and his consciousness at the time of the query, a clear concept of the problem for which a solution is sought is essential if the heavens are faithfully to reflect the question and portray the outcome. If the query is correctly conceived the resultant Figure is presumed to provide the correct answer, showing the manner in which the subsequent motions of the planets will mold events to their eventual culmination. This does not infer that cosmic influences will suspend the operation of the law of cause and effect, or deny the exercise of free-will; but the heavenly bodies through their House and Sign positions and the qualities they assume in the Figure will indicate the precise factors that are involved.

Horary Astrology has its own canons, apart from those governing other branches of Astrology, but the rules peculiar to it are reasonably simple and easily comprehended. However, the more worldly knowledge the practitioner possesses the more deftly will he interpret the Scheme, and the greater number of details he will be able to extract from it.

According to Zadkiel (Commander R. J. Morrison, R.N.), editor of William Lilly's "Introduction to Astrology," a revised version of Lilly's "Christian Astrology Modestly Treated in Three Books" first published in 1647: "If a proposition of **ANY NATURE** be made to any individual, about the result of which he is dubious, and therefore uncertain whether or not to accede to it, let him but note the hour and minute when it was **FIRST MADE** and erect a Figure of the Heavens, as herein taught, and his doubts will be instantly resolved. He may thus learn infallibly whether the affair will succeed or not; and, consequently, whether it is prudent to accept the offer made. If he examine the Sign on the First House of the Figure, the planet therein, or the planet ruling the Sign, **WILL EXACTLY DESCRIBE THE PARTY MAKING THE OFFER**, both in person and character. Moreover, the descending Sign will describe his own person and character."

Approaching it from a modern viewpoint it would appear that since the solidity of the solar system is reasonably established in the Western mind, there can hardly remain any valid objections to the ancient Doctrine of Signatures, which Albertus Magnus, Trithemius, Agrippa, Paracelsus, Boehme and their followers proclaimed and extensively developed.

The twelfth part of the whole circle of 360° which the Ascendant precedes, is deemed to portray the querent, his physique, disposition and circumstances. If the analogy is extended to embrace the birth of a thought, a project or an event, the precise time thereof establishes the angle of incidence in Nature, and makes it possible to chart its activity, the anticipated results, and its ultimate disposition and object with relation to the person or thing that occasioned it.

Pursuing the analogy further, just as any heavenly body which has ascended to the horizon will keep on rising until it attains to the meridian, so, too, will any person, thought or event that has attained to maturity be similar in nature to the portion of the celestial sphere then culminating.

Therefore Horary Astrology assumes that the Ascendant symbolizes the forces that are emerging into being at a given time, and which will operate through the various divisions of the entire sphere to impart form to whatever is taking place at that point on the Earth. Since the disposition of events are the outward manifestation of thoughts generated in the mind, thoughts are an entity, and are conceived, gestated and delivered, no matter how difficult it may be to trace events from their inception through their subsequent evolution.

Since a man's thoughts are fashioned after himself, they must of necessity reflect that universe of which he is a part; and the concepts he creates, working with whatever materials are available within his environment, will be faithfully reflected in his being and disposition - a perfect mirror of celestial and human correspondence.

A few of the more notable characteristics of a valid Horary Figure are:

The SIGNATURE RERUM, or celestial pattern of the factors involved in any situation under scrutiny, its form, essence and totality, must be viewed in the abstract, free from obfuscating prejudices, emotional involvements and the confusion of surface events that would tend to prejudice the interpretation. One must be willing to read the answer without wishful thinking. These factors will be portrayed in the Scheme, yet they must be observed as things apart, except where they interfere with or complicate the issue.

The time for which the Figure is cast is a subjective factor pertaining to the consciousness and character of the practitioner, in that it represents his own particular connection with the matter at issue. The element of time, his consciousness and the circumstances of his life are thus inseparable.

Whether the watch from which is taken the time for casting the Figure be slow or fast, if the practitioner is unaware of it the Figure will be as correct for him as it would have been had the actual time been known and used. In other words the correct perception of time reposes in his own consciousness.

A Figure cast for a trivial or confused issue or query will be unrevealing, since the significance one is able to extract from an Horary Figure is limited to the precise quality of consciousness brought to bear upon it.

The more vital the issue the greater the extent to which the Figure will conform to it; and this conformity is frequently evidenced by the correspondence of one or more of its salient configurations with equally important features visible in the querent's Nativity. These conformities are often so striking as conclusively to portray the marvellous mosaic of the universe.

It frequently happens that a Figure is cast too soon, for an event that is dependent upon one or more indeterminate factors that have not sufficiently matured; or too late, for an issue which the querent can no longer swerve the course of events to avert. In either case the fact will be shown in the Figure, and the rules applicable to either situation constrain the practitioner to defer or withhold judgment.

A valid Horary Figure indicates the querent's birthmarks, and bodily deformities. This phase of Astrology is useful to prove whether the propounded question is radical, whether or not it con- forms with the querent's Nativity in one or more important features, and perhaps to prove to skeptics the validity. of astrological analysis and prognosis.

Even though divination by Horary Astrology is largely practiced with surprising results by many who are too ignorant or too superficially-inclined to probe the arcana of the science of Nativities, incessant recourse to Horary Art is not recommended, for undue reliance upon it weakens one's true judgment and impairs his power of will and independence of character.

On the other hand, occasions will arise when it can be of great assistance, when formulating judgment with regard to a policy to be pursued when the Nativity is not available. It is used in ascertaining the whereabouts of a missing person; the probability of recovering stolen goods; by what manner of thief they were stolen, the direction in which he went, and his disposal thereof; whether a certain rumor be true or false; whether a case will be prosecuted in court, and its ultimate disposition; whether one ought to accept a proposition made to him and the outcome thereof; whether a contemplated marriage is advisable, and how it may be expected to result; whether one should accept proffered employment, sell or mortgage a piece of property, and so on. Apart from these considerations the study of Horary Astrology, when pursued for the mental training it affords, will prove of value to the student by way of maturing his judgment and sharpening his intuition, and may at some time stand him in excellent service.

-FREDERIC VAN NORSTRAND-

Horary Astrology is thus an application of Astrology predicated on a sympathy that exists between cosmic influences and the human mind, by reason of which people think of and propound questions of serious import at a time when the aspects bear a definite relation to the nature, origin and termination of the matter involved. It has been said to anticipate the emergence of objective thoughts into the physical world. Certain planetary Significators are taken as representative of the querent, the person making the inquiry. Other planets, acting as Promittors, promise assistance or detriment to the concern about which the inquiry is made. The specific natures of the planets ARE LITTLE UTILIZED, the bodies which aspect the Significator regarded as either friendly or the reverse. A Promittor may be angular, succedant or cadent, combust, disposed of, frustrated, applying to, separating from, or in mutual disposition with other planets, and all these considerations are taken into account. There is no purely mathematical measure of time as in Genethlialogy, but days, weeks, months, and years are determined from a consideration of the Signs and Houses involved, whether they be fixed, common or cardinal, and whether angular, succedant, or cadent. The Houses generally retain the same significance as in Nativities. There arc many works dealings with this recognized department of Astrology, among the best of which is that by William Lilly. It is presumed that if the mind is clear regarding the question, the Ascendant will not be in the first or last degrees of a Sign.

Horary Circles. The arcs, or circles, in which the planets appear to move around the Earth by virtue of the Earth's diurnal revolution. They are either diurnal or nocturnal.

Horary Time. The time from the rising of a planet to its setting, divided by 12, gives its horary time, which is 1/12th of the time between the rising and setting of a planet - or the reverse, according as the planet is placed in the diurnal or nocturnal circle. The factors employed in this calculation are the declination of the planet and the latitude of the place. (v. ASCENSIONAL DIFFERENCE.)

Horimea. The rays of the Hyleg after it has passed the Mid-heaven.

Horizon. The circle round the Earth that separates the visible and the invisible hemispheres. The terms sensible, visible or physical horizon are often employed, indicating the line which terminates our vision, where the celestial bodies appear and disappear. The astronomical horizon, termed the rational horizon, is obtained by supposing a line drawn from the Earth's center parallel with the horizon. Astrologically, the eastern horizon is the degree rising in the east, and the Sign then appearing is the Rising Sign.

Horizontal Aspects. Mundane Aspects.

Horizontal Parallel. A parallel in mundo, or a mundane parallel, formed about the horizon instead of the meridian. It is considered by some authorities to be equally powerful.

Horoscope. Strictly speaking the Ascendant, since it is based upon the "hour." As generally employed it refers to the Figure, or Map of the Heavens, for a given date and hour, utilized by astrologers for the judgment of a Nativity and for predictions in Mundane and Horary Astrology; also delineations based thereon.

Hour Angle. The angle between the great circle that passes through the poles, and that which bisects a specific point in the heavens; expressed in hours, as indicating the interval of time before or after its transit of the meridian, at the rate of 15° p.h.

Hours. v. PLANETARY HOURS.

Houses. An astrological Figure is divided into 12 arcs, equal either in terms of space or time. If in terms of space the arcs are of 30° each, one twelfth of the circle of 360°.

If these begin at 0° Aries they are known as the Signs of the Zodiac, from Aries to Pisces, and represent subdivisions of the orbit of the Earth round the Sun. As such they are Signs, not Houses. They bear no relation to the constellations after which they were anciently named, but are measured from the Spring equinoctial point.

If the subdivision begins at a given moment, and each represents the celestial arc that passes over the horizon in 2 hours - one twelfth of the time required for one complete rotation - the divisions are known as Houses.

In considering the divisions of the Figure as consisting of Signs, the Figure is deemed to stand still while one contemplates the actual motions of the planets in their orbits round the Sun, in a counter-clockwise direction. In considering the divisions as Houses, the observer deems the planets to stand still while the Figure (representing the Earth) rotates in a counter-clockwise direction, thus causing the planets to appear to move in a clockwise direction at a uniform rate, one after another passing from below the horizon to above it, and on through the Midheaven to the Descendant, just as the Sun rises and sets.

There are also **Solar Houses** - subdivisions of a Figure which, because the moment of inception, otherwise "birth-moment," is unknown - cast with the Sun's degree at Greenwich noon as the Rising Degree, or Ascendant. In the House-divisions so determined are placed the planets in the positions they tenanted at Greenwich noon on that particular date. Such a Figure is termed by some: a Heliarc Figure (Q.V.).

In any event one should at all times bear in mind that the Signs are divisions of an annual cycle, beginning with the Spring Equinox; while the Houses arc divisions of a daily cycle of apparent motions resulting from the Earth's own daily rotation on its axis. Some modern authorities employ the term Heliarc in lieu of Sign as a subdivision of the Earth's annual orbit, and Geoarc in lieu of House as the subdivision of the orbit of a given point on the Earth's periphery round the axis - hence a subdivision of the Earth's daily rotation. Thus the influence of the Sign-positions, and the pattern of con- figurations resulting from the places the planets occupy therein, are a common experience of everyone born anywhere on the Earth's surface upon that day; but the point at which a personality enters into this cycle is an individual factor which determines the "angle of incidence" at which these cosmic impulses impinge upon his own consciousness.

Due to the inclination of the polar axis in its relationship to the Sun, the number of degrees which pass over the horizon in 2 hours varies with the time of year and the latitude of the place where the birth occurs. While the Midheaven-point moves reasonably steady from day to day throughout the year, the rising and setting-points vary, lengthening into the "long winter evenings" and shortening into the so-called "Daylight Saving" period of long days and short summer nights.

Before considering all the factors entering into the problem of House definition and terminology, remember that a House is a two- hour segment of a twenty-four-hour cycle, repeated each day with minor variants. The beginning of the First House is the degree that from a given point on the Earth's surface was rising above the eastern horizon at a given moment of time. This point is the Ascendant, just as the opposite point is the Descendant. Between them is the Mid- heaven, and the opposite point below the Earth, the so-called **IMMUM COELI**, viz.: the Lowest Heaven. These are the Angles of the Figure. The

Houses which fall away from these Angles are termed the Angular Houses. Note that as your horizon falls down, the planets - which are thus uncovered - rise up. The next Houses are termed the Succedent Houses, and these are midway between the Angles. The remaining four Houses, which precede the Angles, are termed the Cadent Houses. Numerically these are summed up as follows:

ANGULAR: 1, 4, 7, 10 - the strongest positions in any Figure.
SUCCEDENT: 2, 5, 8, 11 - possibly of no less strength than the Angles, though they attract less public notice.
CADENT: 3, 6, 9, 12 - the weakest positions.

In a Birth Figure many planets in Cadent Houses may confer versatility. In Horary Astrology planets in these Houses are considered to produce delays. James Wilson says that a cadent planet seldom brings to pass any event of which it is the Significator, or if at all then it will be when all hope has vanished; also that when obtained it is either useless or detrimental to the querent's interests.

Other groupings are -

Individual or Life Houses: 1, 5, 9 - representing respectively the body, soul, and spirit or mind: the Trinity of Life.

TEMPORAL OR POSSESSIVE HOUSES: representing the temporal status of the native: 2. Possessions and property; 6. Comforts, such as food, clothing, health and servants; 10. Honor and credit, business or professional standing, position in society: the Trinity of Wealth.

RELATIVE OR ASSOCIATION HOUSES: having to do with human relationtionships. 3. Ties of Consanguinity - brothers, sisters, close relatives; 7. Ties of conjugality and legality, such as marriage and partnership; 11. Ties of friendship; close associates and advisers: the Trinity of Association.

TERMINAL OR PSYCHIC HOUSES: referring to eventualities, particularly to the termination of conditions in the native's life, and the psychological reaction to their contemplation. 4. The environment in each epoch of life, with particular reference to old age; 8. The influence of others upon his environment, particularly with respect to the effect upon him of their death, by way of inheritance and inherited responsibilities; 12. Confinement and other hindering influences which retard the fruition of the soul's yearnings: the Trinity of Psychism.

These esoteric realms have been compared to three degrees of death: 4th, of the mind; 8th, of the body; 12th, of the soul. Or, as taken from the Kabala, according to this table:

PERSONAL: 1 The body. 5. The soul. 9. The spirit.
POSSESSIVE: 2. Wealth. 6. The Household. 10. Honor.
RELATIVE: 3. Consanguine. 7. Conjugal. 11. Congenial.
TERMINAL: 4. The grave. 8. Paradise. 12. Heaven.

Another grouping, of modern origin and based largely on statistical research, is:

SELF: 12th, 1st, 2nd, 3rd.
COMPANIONS: 4th, 5th, 6th, 7th.
PUBLIC: 8th, 9th, 10th, 11th.

EASTERN HOUSES: Those in the Eastern half of the Figure, containing planets rising toward the Midheaven; viz.: the 3rd, 2nd, 1st, 12th, 11th, 10th. Of these, the three above the horizon - containing planets which, moving clockwise against the order of the Signs, are passing away from the horizon toward their culmination at the Midheaven - are considered to confer upon these planets added strength "by position."

WESTERN HOUSES: Those in the Western half of the Figure - 4th, 5th, 6th, 7th, 8th, and 9th. Posited in these Houses, malefic planets are said to be strengthened and benefic planets weakened - particularly as regards their influence upon the native's health. An advisable distinction would be to classify the Twelve Houses as Eastern and Western and confine the Oriental Houses to the 12th, 11th and 10th, and the Occidental to the 4th, 5th, and 6th - those which culminate at either the oriental or occidental side of the meridian for which the Figure is cast.

ORIENTAL HOUSES: Those which extend clockwise from the horizon to the meridian: The 12th, 11th, 10th, 6th, 5th and 4th.
OCCIDENTAL HOUSES: Those which extend clockwise from the meridian to the horizon: The 9th, 8th, 7th, 3rd, 2nd and 1st.

Zodiacal House is a misnomer, for that would mean a Sign, a subdivision of an orbital revolution rather than of an axial rotation. The term Mundane House, once used to distinguish between two types of so-called Houses, is thus unnecessary, since properly termed all Houses arc mundane Houses.

Houses, Meaning of. The significance of each House, basically and as related to the other Houses, without considering the modifications that result from the positions and aspects of radical, progressed or transiting planets, is as follows: v. HOUSE, FIRST; HOUSE, SECOND, ETC. - OR CLICK 'NEXT' TO NAVIGATE FROM HERE.

House, First.

IN A NATIVITY: The cusp of the Ascendant, the first and most important of the four Angles of any Figure, marks the Eastern end of the Line of Particular Being; the Irrational Axis, or culminating point of the eastern hemisphere - a Line of Awareness of Self and of Others. Hence, it becomes the Point of Dualism of Consciousness, and the Angle of Fulfillment.

Representing Selfhood, its primary significance is Action: Destiny in the making. It defines and particularizes the native, his personal appearance, disposition and manner, moral and subjective viewpoint and motivating impulses- Personality as distinguished from Individuality; and is an index to his birth, environment in early childhood, outlook upon life, and will to manifest; personal power over himself and others; carriage, mein, walk, and manner of approach; complexion, skin, head, face, brain, and the shape and size of his body; opinion of himself and of others, their opinion of him, and the impression he makes upon them; habits, desires and personal interests; capacity for self-development; vitality, health in consequence of personal habits, the inherent strength of his physical constitution; mental and emotional qualities and attitudes; worldly outlook, and the quality, bent and direction of his cravings and their gratification; attitude toward his possessions, and other things that affect the ego; circumstances and situations that result from his acts; consciousness of the future.

The First House has to do with a man's grandmother, or a woman's grandfather. (v. FOURTH HOUSE.) The Ruler of the Rising Sign indicates the influences that were at work previous to birth.

When the Lord of the First also rules the sign on the cusp of the Twelfth, it becomes an index to his Destiny or Fate.

As the Ascendant provides a key to the native's mentality and the quality of his will power, the Sixth House, its Ruler and occupants, portrays what use he makes of them.

In a Mundane Figure: The body politic. The country and its inhabitants as a whole: the people, the masses; their prosperity and health, or the reverse; their national traits and habits; the country's interior affairs; the public consciousness and collective expression; the psychology of the masses, their reactions and conditions.

In a Political Campaign: the majority.

In a Contest: the public favorite; the holder of the title; the one who is challenged; the decision or decisions of the referee.

In a Lawsuit: the defendant; also the decision or sentence of the Court.

In an Organization: its personnel - including the stockholders and all who work for the company in any capacity; the company's morale and its attitude toward its competitors.

House, Second.

IN A NATIVITY: Repository of the native's strongest desires, it determines the quality of the life-substance used by the Ego - that which the Life is dedicated to redeem; the heredity and social background with which the native is equipped for the pursuit of his destiny, and the bodily chemistry of metabolism; secret thoughts and desires; financial standing, money, moveable property and possessions, the gain or loss and the income derived therefrom; earning and spending capacities, personal debts; the manner in which he meets his obligations.

IN A MUNDANE FIGURE: The nation's wealth; taxation revenue, stocks, bonds, shares, and all places and activities connected in any way with money, such as banks, stock exchanges, trade and commerce; the national exports; taxing power, as distinct from the manner in which the taxes affect the people; the purchasing power of the nation, its national expenditures and receipts, currency and its circulation and liquid assets; hence the wealth and prosperity of the people as measured by their collective earning and buying power; investors and their investments, and those who buy stocks and bonds for investment rather than for speculation.

In a National Figure: the Treasury.

In an Organization: its liquid assets and voluntary expenditures; the ability of the Company to earn profits; its disposition toward investments.

House, Third.

IN A NATIVITY: The synthesizing powers of the mind and its ability to form sense impressions and mold destiny within one's social environment; dexterity, cleverness, duality, restlessness; the rational mind and its adaptability to education; short journeys; brothers, sisters and near blood relationships, and their attitude toward the native; acquaintances and neighbors, their character and reputation; writings and communications, news and rumors; changes and removals; daily comings and goings; accidents; memory, perception, speech; personal advertising and publicity.

IN A MUNDANE FIGURE: Inland transit, traffic and communications by land, air or water; the nature of the public demands upon and the degree of public patronage accorded to the nation's transportation and communication facilities; the postal, telegraph and telephone systems, radio, cinema, newspapers, magazines and ephemeral publications; the people's inclination to travel, move about, make changes and communicate with one another within the nation; the nation's intellectual activities and its relations with neighboring nations; the reading public, and its tendency to patronize the newspapers and other periodicals; indications relative to rumors, public opinion, the mental and psychological attitude of the masses; emigration as distinct from immigration; and the effects of storms, temperature changes and atmospheric conditions within the country.

In a Court of Law: the Court reporter.

In an Organization: first-hand contacts of the Organization with the general public, the traffic, transit, transportation and communication departments; interoffice communications; specific information disseminated within the organization, and departments having to do with the dissemination of such information; public statements of a relatively private nature.

House, Fourth.

IN A NATIVITY: Its cusp, the Northern end of the meridian that passes through the birthplace, is the degree of Integration. Although it is the weakest of the four Angles, it nevertheless exercises a decisive influence throughout the entire Figure. It is the drain through which everything that is to be sloughed off, merges and passes away. Through it the Ego becomes concrete, as the operational base of the physical entity, the seat of the desire-nature - the emotions and the passions. It is an index to the home and all domestic affairs; the imaginative faculty; receptivity of mood; treasured recollections. It counsels him whether to remain in or to leave his birthplace, and the advantages consequent thereon. Thus it defines the nature of one's residence, while the Ascendant indicates in what direction it should lie. It has been called the "grave" because it is so often concerned with hidden things: private affairs, old age, the ultimate end and aim of terrestrial existence.

Considered in connection with the Ascendant, it affords an insight into the nature of the native's early life, his childhood upbringing, the character of his home environment; his domestic concerns throughout life, and their conspicuousness or obscurity; the nature of the termination of every earthly concern: the last illness and demise, the ultimate disposition of the body, the nature of the burial, and the general location of the grave.

It summarizes matters relating to lands, houses, estates, cities, mines, concealed treasures, intimate concerns, curious personal secrets, things accumulated and stored up, leases, rentals, real estate transactions, and similar matters.

In the Figure of a woman it generally characterizes the first child, and a heavily tenanted Fourth House is often an indication that he will pursue a scientific career.

The Fourth House produces changes of environment within the disposition of the native, wherein he can alter or upset his home conditions and those of such as are intimately related to him. Only through this House can he build his reputation and lay the foundation of a successful career, to find expression later through the Tenth House. While one cannot directly control his fortunes insofar as they depend upon the good will of others, by laying a proper Fourth House foundation in obscure beginnings, he can build toward a secure end.

To it is commonly assigned the native's father, his life, disposition and fortunes; and from it are derived inferences relative to cousins on the mother's side. Which parent to assign to the Tenth, its Ruler, and the planets therein, is, however, a moot question: and divergent opinions variously assign (1) the mother to the Tenth in a day-birth, the Fourth in a night-birth - the father represented by the opposite ends of the meridian; (2) to the Tenth the parent of the same sex as the native, and to the Fourth the parent of the opposite sex; (3) to the Tenth the father in a female, and the mother in a male Nativity; (4) on the basis that Cancer represents the womb the Hindus assign to the Fourth the mother, and to the Tenth the father since Capricorn indicates conservatism, repression and firmness; while yet other authorities contend (5) that the determination of the House selected as the parent's significator is dependent upon which parent has most authority over the native. Thus there is need for extended documentation on the subject.

IN A MUNDANE FIGURE: Circumstances and events affecting real estate values, mines and their products, buildings, crops, produce and all agricultural interests, including those of the owners of and workers on the land; miners, builders, the housing and living conditions of the people, and their patriotic inclinations; the land as a locality wherein people are subject to natural forces - terrestrial as distinguished from atmospheric - hence property damages resulting from floods, earthquakes, and mining disasters; the interests of the people as distinguished from those of the government and of the governing class; and democratic as against autocratic tendencies in government, and between governments.

In a National Figure: the Opposition Party, and those individuals who cooperate with or oppose the Chief Executive; the characteristics of any governmental opposition, and the time such opposition may be expected to culminate.

In Ingress, Lunation and Full Moon Figures a planet close to the cusp of this House will affect the weather according to its nature and aspects; and if it be a malefic and powerfully aspected, it will profoundly affect the government.

In a Court of Law: the Jury.

In a Contest: the arena of action; the judges as distinguished from the referee; the end of the contest.

In an Organization: its real estate investments and holdings; its base of operations or field of activity; the location and condition of factory or office buildings it owns or occupies.

House, Fifth.

IN A NATIVITY. The conception of offspring; hence the exteriorization of Self through all manner of creative and procreative urges and activities; recreational, and other pleasurable impulses of mind and heart; mental offspring, such as creative, artistic or literary output; gambling and financial speculations; the operations of the laws of chance - in so far as its effects are under the native's control. As the abode of the heart, it has to do with all impulses arising therefrom, hence all emotional and romantic tendencies. Those who have a strong Fifth House, containing one or more planets giving or receiving strong vibrations, have overpowering impulses with which to contend throughout life, which find emotional expression through dramatic attitudes, pride, the affections, and which contribute to popularity, notoriety or fame, according as the aspects thereto are favorable or adverse. It has been postulated that in a male Nativity this House prefigures the first child. Planets in the Fifth and Eleventh Houses are an index to emotional desires, not infrequently expressed in the more sublimated form of platonic friendships and affiliations.

IN A MUNDANE FIGURE. Children, their attitudes and conditions; circumstances affecting minors; the public school system and children in attendance at primary schools; amusements and amusement places, theatres, concerts, sporting events; public speculations and investments; the inclination of the people to play or express emotion; public happiness and sorrow; circumstances attending those seeking pleasure and amusement; high society and the upper classes; ambassadors, senators and government representatives; formal social functions and all ceremonies of a more or less official character. Public happiness or sorrow; circumstances and dangers affecting those on pleasure bent; and similar activities not engaged in for the specific purpose of making money.

Since it is the realm of the country's creative and procreative activities, it indicates probable changes in the birth rate during the period immediately following that for which the Figure is cast.

In a National Figure: the upper legislative house - in contrast to the Eleventh House which rules the lower house; although the Eleventh represents the legislative branches as a unit, as distinct from the administrative branch of the government.

In an Organization: the executive personnel, its officers and Board of Directors as distinguished from the President or Chairman of the Board; the governing body in a collective sense; any attitude or action of the stockholders or Board of Directors in opposition to the President.

House, Sixth

IN A NATIVITY: Food, clothing, comforts and domestic pets; mental or physical conflicts resulting from the externalization of the Ego. As such it depicts any enmity between the Ego and the physical body, out of which mental, nervous or organic disease may develop. It is an obscure arc, since the nature of service rendered or received is more or less personal, unobtrusive and routine. It has been termed the House of Service in that it portrays one's capacity to serve, as also the character and qualities of those who serve him - his employees and dependents, and his relations with them. As the Sixth House is the Third from the Fourth, it pertains to uncles and aunts on the father's side (Fourth House).

Sixth House action is generally under the Native's control; while Twelfth House derivatives by way of inhibitions, repressions and frustrations, spring from causes over which the Native has no control.

IN A MUNDANE FIGURE: The public health; the armed forces, civil service workers and police, as the servants of the country; and in general, the laboring class and the workers in all trades; and all involuntary services rendered by the people.

In a National Figure: the Labor Party.

In a Court of Law: the deliberations of the jury, and the Court records as the field of activity of the Court reporter.

In an Organization: the workers or employees; their attitude, efficiency and general condition; the health condition of the personnel as affecting the organization. Strikes and labor troubles which have their inception here, will take form in the Twelfth House.

House, Seventh.

IN A NATIVITY: The Seventh cusp, the Angle of Relationship, at the western end of the line of Particular Being, depicts the subjective side of the Nature, the Individuality, as opposed to the Personality that is revealed objectively in the. First House; the correlation of exterior agencies and forces. of the four Angles, it ranks third in importance. Here human relations are on a give-and-take basis, by the interchange of ideas. It has to do with the outcome of all contentions, oppositions, strife, enmities, pleas, and fines. Since it defines the native's reaction to law, it becomes the House of the Public, showing the relation of the native to others; particularly his open adversaries; lawsuits and contracts; one's personal agents and representatives; men's grandfathers or women's grandmothers; nephews and nieces; and every manner of cooperative arrangement or partnership, legal or otherwise - including marriage and the effects thereof upon the native. In an astrological sense marriage is any state of cohabitation prompted by love and attended by a condition of sympathetic understanding, whether or not recognized by civil or ecclesiastical law. Furthermore, when any state of cohabitation, however legalized it may be, ceases to produce a blending of two horoscopes through a condition of mutual regard and understanding harmoniousness, marriage ceases to exist and becomes merely a legalized form of prostitution; as evidenced by laws governing "common law" marriage, divorce, and the support of offspring after divorce. The more profoundly the constructive influence of cohabita- tion affects the lives of the participants, the more it can properly be termed a marriage.

IN A MUNDANE FIGURE. The public as an organized social unit, the social consciousness of the people, the relative status of the nation among the nations of the world, and conditions, circumstances and events affecting its social evolution; those who cooperate with or oppose the people in a national sense, such as anti-social organizations or activities, crime, organized crime and criminals, particularly those who assume the status of a public enemy; anything that contributes to or interferes with public harmony, or tends to build or disintegrate social identities; public support of the nation's foreign policy, friendly or hostile, political or commercial, and the reactions of foreign nations thereto. It is therefore the domain of international disputes, of war and peace; public relations, public gatherings, and meetings between and dealings with strangers. It also indicates the status of women in the nation, particularly the public attitude toward marriage and divorce, and the fluctuations of the marriage and divorce rate as determined by the planet posited there, and its relation to the Fifth House.

In a Contest: the challenger; the decision of the judges.

In a Court of Law: the plaintiff and the lawyers; the point of arbitration where evidence and the rights of opposing factions are weighed; also the verdict of the jury.

In an Organization: its relation to other organizations through contracts, trade agreements, mergers, cartels, or reciprocal arrangements; its lawsuits and legal affairs. Here originate all forces that oppose the growth and free action of the organization as an individual entity, such as competitors and their activities.

House, Eighth.

IN A NATIVITY. Release from personal limitations through human interchange; the Realm of Birth and Rebirth; of evolution through the suffering incident to all human experience; regeneration through enlargement of viewpoint, both spiritual and mental; and the subjugation of the personal Self -- a difficult process since so few realize the horror of its impact upon the mind and consciousness. It has to do with effects of an involuntary nature, such as the healing crisis preceding either recovery or dissolution in death; the manner of death; fateful losses which lead to regeneration through certain enforced changes; the transmutation of emotional stress into spiritual power; wills, legacies, trust funds, insurance; the estate of the marital or business partner; money belonging to other people, especially the deceased, in so far as it applies to the native; hence in general the financial relationship of the world to him, and his responsibilities in connection therewith. However, its consideration of these things is largely as liabilities rather than as assets.

It has been called the Occult House, the house of hidden things, because in most Eighth House operations the Law of Cause and Effect is difficult to identify, and there is the common human temptation to blame everything upon an inscrutable Providence. It is also known as the House of Death, because it represents the refiner's fire wherein through suffering the selfish desires of the Ego are burned away, setting free the pure gold of spiritually-enlightened Selflessness. That death so often comes instead, is a vivid indication of the tenacity with which we mortals cling to our foibles, utterly deaf to the accumulated exhortations of the philosophers throughout the centuries. In the wake of an Eighth House storm there is always a rainbow - if we but lift our eyes to perceive it. The Creative Ruler so devised this planetary system as to administer an automatic and recurrent spur to spiritual growth and emotional self-control. Successive jabs become increasingly severe, and finally to those who refuse to listen and heed, a premature death is inevitable; while to the others, the spiritually adult, every Eighth House operation is a celestial messenger in disguise, and a challenge to penetrate this disguise and become the recipient of the blessing he bears.

As the Second from the Seventh, it represents accumulated non-material riches - that which neither moth nor rust doth corrupt - not the result of the labor of your hand and brain, but of the manner in which you play the game with those to whom you are closely allied.

IN A MUNDANE FIGURE: The public income; the income from exports; earning power of the nation, chiefly from the standpoint of the man who pays; frozen assets in properties, stocks and bonds as distinct from currency; the monetary standard, the National debt, and interest rates; public sales; financial organizations, such as trust and insurance companies. The birth and mortality rate in different class groups, as determined by the planet involved, and its relation to the Fifth House; medical discovery, insofar as it tends to promote longevity.

In a National Figure: The national treasurer as a government official, distinct from the treasury itself; financial relations with and the financial condition and obligations of other countries with respect to the nation for the capital of which the Figure is cast.

In an Organization: Losses and gains through or on account of death, or in connection with the estates of deceased persons; financial conditions involved in partnerships, mergers or lawsuits; financial relations with competitors, and their financial condition; revenue from investments, or through liquidation of frozen assets; loans and income from sources not under immediate control of the Organization; the company treasurer, as distinguished from the Treasury.

House, Ninth.

IN A NATIVITY. The realm of the abstract mind, of intuition and inspiration, of dreams and visions, hence an index to one's reactions to philosophy, success and religion; and to his sense of responsibility toward relatives, by blood or in law. From this arc inferences are drawn concerning grandchildren, especially those of his brother and his sister-in-law; the probability of distant travel, timing, nature and results; the fate and nature of imports and exports; the ultimate result of long-range advertising; world wide contacts and mental adjustment to racial ideas, ideals and collective needs. With an author, his works from the standpoint of publication.

IN A MUNDANE FIGURE. Long-distance passenger and freight transportation and communications, by or over sea, air and land; religion and the clergy; judges and courts of law; the educated classes: universities and institutions of higher learning, and their administrative and teaching personnel; philosophic and scientific societies and institutions and their publications; all facilities designed to meet the public demand in education, religion, transportation and communications; the Ministry of Foreign Affairs; immigration as distinguished from emigration; weather conditions along the coast, particularly incoming storms in process of formation as distinguished from their effects; and the origins of all disturbances, either of an intellectual or atmospheric nature. Observe a distinction drawn between the public's attitude toward the press, as indicated by the Third House, and the attitude of the press toward the public as indicated by the Ninth House.

In a National Figure: The Secretary of State as a government official, as distinguished from the State Department; the educated classes - those who control or govern the reading, writing or travelling habits of the public.

In an Organization: the advertising department; long distance communications; results of mail-order campaigns; relations with educational institutions and publications; professional consultants, publicity and public relations; officials, as distinguished from their departments.

House, Tenth.

IN A NATIVITY. From this arc one traces the native's business or professional life and affairs, his honor, preferment, fame, credit, reputation, career, and position in society; hence his standing before the world. As the operational base for social intercourse, it offers a summation of the native's human relationships. From this arc inferences may be drawn concerning his relations with those who are more or less in authority over him - his employers and clients; his cousins on his father's side, and ordinarily his mother (V. FOURTH HOUSE) in that here racial consciousness, and what may be termed the "national soul," becomes an entity. Of the four angles it is second in importance, the southern end of the meridian running through the birthplace: the Midheaven, the Rational Axis, the Line of Universal Being, the Point of Solar Sustainment, the Line of Concrete Experience and its sublimation. As the apex of the Nativity, it assembles, vitalizes, universalizes and largely summarizes the individual's relationship to society as expressed through his occupational activities.

IN A MUNDANE FIGURE: The Chief Executive, as occupying the control-tower of the nation; the political party in power; eminent and famous persons, and those upon whom rest the nation's honor, reputation and standing among the nations of the world; the national power, trade, culture, ideals and achievements. The most favoring planets in this House in a Mundane Figure, are the Sun and Jupiter.

In a Court of Law: the judge.

In a Contest: the referee.

In an Organization: The supreme or governing authority; the President, or Chairman of the Board.

House, Eleventh.

IN A NATIVITY: One finds here the externalization of the native's social position; the nature and characteristics of his circle of acquaintances and friends; his ideals with respect to human and therefore social relationships; his hopes, wishes, projects and ambitions; the reformer's dreams and his efforts to realize them; flatterers and their machinations; to a certain extent the imagination; his sons and his daughters-in-law. Its Lord and the planets tenanting it are an index to his idea of happiness and the probabilities of his ultimate attainment thereof. When considered in relation to the First, Fifth and Eighth Houses, it becomes an important arc, for with an afflicted Eleventh House little real satisfaction can be extracted from life - riches, a beautiful home, a fond and dutiful wife and children, and all the tangible things for which a heart could wish, yet never the serene contentment wherewith to enjoy them.

The Fifth and Eleventh Houses are an index to the personal-emotional desires and their sublimated form as found in platonic friendship.

The Ninth and Eleventh Houses indicate higher levels of consciousness as to both mind and emotion.

If the Lord of the Eleventh is stronger than the Lord of the Seventh the native's friends and assistants are more numerous and powerful than his adversaries.

IN A MUNDANE FIGURE: The legislative branches of the government, particularly the lower house, with the Fifth more directly concerned with the upper house; town and county councils, and state legislatures; the friends of the nation; the Stock Exchange, as an organization apart from its activities; ceremonies and celebrations; the exchange of amenities with foreign governments; hence the nation's aims, desires, purposes, projects, and alliances.

In a National Figure: The treasury, as distinguished from the Secretary of the Treasury.

In an Organization: Other friendly organizations, in panies closely allied to or associated with its activities; also organizations or facilities which provide social activities, as fraternal groups and clubs; the treasury as distinguished from the treasurer.

House, Twelfth.

IN A NATIVITY. This is the arena wherein transpires the combat against the inertia inherent in all forms of society - the limiting power of the level of race consciousness. Here are expressed the innermost and secret emotions; the source and nature of hidden and underhanded opposition; imprisonment, hospitalization; the uncles and aunts on the mother's side (V. FOURTH HOUSE); the secret effects of sins of omission and commission - defects of character that make necessary a spiritual rebirth. Since we can rid ourselves of the presence of these ghosts of the past only by liquidating our indebtedness to them, the Twelfth may be termed the House of the Hangover; of crime, punishment and grief; the pawnshop of the Ego; the Gethsemane of the soul; the Hell wherein one atones for his errors through compassionate self-sacrifice, whereby ultimately to achieve freedom from conditions that limit and restrict. Thus it is also the House of Charity given and received.

Termed the House of Bondage, and of Self-Undoing, it is also the House of Initiation and ultimate understanding. While it is frequently tenanted by the significators of scandal, self-approbation and hardness of heart, its qualities can be advantageously employed for work done in seclusion, for confidential behind-the-scene activities, and for meditation and inner development.

The Terminal Houses, the Fourth, Eighth and Twelfth, corresponding to the Emotional Triplicity of Signs, are concerned with the three most mysterious phases of life; the Fourth, the end of physical man; the Eighth, the liberation of his soul; the Twelfth, his secret aspirations and his disposition in the after-world.

From this, proponents of the doctrine of Reincarnation deduce that the Nativity we have on this plane of expression we earned in a past incarnation, while the one we will acquire in our next incarnation will depend upon the life we lived in this - and are living now. Thus again is involved the Law of Cause and Effect from which is no escape.

IN A MUNDANE FIGURE: Labor disturbances, plagues and epidemics, conditions that militate against the public welfare; correctional institutions, jails, prisons, workhouses, houses of detention, hospitals and charitable institutions; organizations devoted to forcible control or condemnation of people; involuntary services ordered by law; the nation's secret enemies in war and peace; spies and confidential agents of foreign countries; crimes and criminals; the personal journeyings and writings of those in power in the government; the nation's secret societies, both political and religious.

In an Organization: forces inclining to dissolution of the organization as an entity, hence enemy and secret organizations; the secret intelligence department; investigative agencies in connection with hospitals and prisons; labor unions, insofar as they represent Sixth House personnel; organized and social units, as distinguished from the parent organization; strikes and labor troubles-which have their inception in the Sixth House, but come to fruition in the Twelfth.

Houses, Reciprocal Action of Opposite:

It should be observed that the six Houses below the horizon are departments of demand or of inclination to act; while the six above the horizon afford the facilities for action; the lower six, personal, the upper six, social; the lower six, unorganized, the upper six, organized. Yet each separate House acts in a reciprocal or complimentary manner to its opposing House, as is shown in the following comparisons or polarizations:

FIRST AND SEVENTH. Whereas the First House is productive of effects caused by the native's ego, the Seventh is productive of effects and situations produced by the ego of the marriage partner or any cooperating personality or event. The commonly observed psycho- logical phenomenon wherein one desires or attempts to reproduce his ego in another, is the direct result of this reciprocal action.

SECOND AND EIGHTH. Whereas the Second House is productive of effects upon the native's individual earning capacity as a direct result of his own acts or inertia, Eighth House effects, as concerning his material position, take cognizance of the fact that his ultimate return depends in large measure upon the extent to which others trade or cooperate with him, or are friendly disposed toward him. Thus, although his earning capacity may be exercised through the Second House by means of work and related activities under his own control which leave him free to choose whether he will work or not and to what extent, the ultimate net amount of his income and the extent of his fortunes do not rest wholly within his own control but are distinctly due to outside forces. In the sense in which the Second House registers assets, the Eighth House is more directly concerned with liabilities.

THIRD AND NINTH. The Third House is productive of effects which rest on changes under the direct control of the native and which result from his own acts. These may be various, such as changes of location (travel), or changes of domicile (removal). In contrast, Ninth House operations are not under his control, but involve the wider changes wrought by an evolution that is largely the result of outside forces. Similar facilities are indicated by both Houses, but in the Third their application is confined to the dissemination of information, while in the Ninth they are utilized to educate and mold public opinion.

FOURTH AND TENTH. The Fourth House produces effects involving the environment, which are subject to the control of the native, in that he can alter his environment or upset his home conditions and that of all those who are intimately related to him, to his heart's content. Only through this House can he build his reputation and the foundations of his professional career. In contrast, forces operative through his Tenth House to affect his fortunes in his profession or career, he cannot directly control; since his ultimate fate is largely dependent upon the attitude of others toward him.

FIFTH AND ELEVENTH. The Fifth House involves the ability of the native to take advantage of the Laws of Chance at such times as they become operative in his favor. Its effects are under his control in that he alone decides the nature of the investments, whether or not he will make them, and when. Romance and emotional matters in general partake of the essence of Chance, for the native's acts produce emotional disturbances or yield emotional satisfactions according as the Laws of Chance favor him. This strongly contrasts with the effects resulting from the Eleventh House influences, for these deter- mine whether his hopes, wishes and desires are to be gratified or denied. That for which he wishes and the treasure or resources upon which he can draw wherewith to obtain them, is shown by the Fifth House; but whether his wish will or will not be granted through the influence or intervention of other persons, is in the domain of the Eleventh House.

SIXTH AND TWELFTH. Sixth House affairs, comprising the native's occupational activities, his service and devotion to others, are under the native's control. His bodily health is largely dependent upon his own acts. But Twelfth House matters are beyond his control, in that they comprise inhibitive influences, repressions, frustrations, even the complete loss of personal liberty dependent upon the way others react toward him - and are the class of things which since they cannot be cured must be endured.

In a National Figure, while the Sixth House pertains to the servants of the people, apart from organizations which represent them, the Twelfth represents them in organized form - in unions, brotherhoods, lodges and unions that have to do with strikes and the use of strike-breakers.

Houses, solar. These are Houses, in that they are subdivisions of the twenty-four hour axial rotation of the Earth; but based upon the Sun-position as the Ascendant they divide the terrestrial circle into equal arcs of 30° each. v. SOLAR ASTROLOGY.

House Ruler. Properly speaking, only a Sign has a Ruler. A planet in a House is generally its Ruler; or lacking a planet, the House is said to be ruled by the Ruler of the Sign appearing on its cusp. Some earlier authority attempted to clarify this by introducing the term Lord, whereby one could make the distinction: Lord of a House, and Ruler of a Sign. The intention was excellent, but the result has been an indiscriminate use of Lord and Ruler as inter-changeable terms. For a concise terminology it would appear desirable to determine the planet of strongest influence in a House, either because posited there or because it is the Ruler of the Sign on its cusp, and then refer to the selected planet as the Lord of that House. Any term would serve - except Ruler, which term has to do with a planet's strength in a Sign. In fact, the degrees of lordship are largely dependent upon the strength of the planet in, or by virtue, of its Sign-position: whether in its own Sign, exalted or debilitated.

House, intercepted. One in which a Sign is contained wholly within the House, which sign does not appear upon either cusp of the House. It is more logical to consider the House as intercepted by the Sign - than the reverse although it is frequently referred to as an intercepted sign, instead of an intercepting sign. An intercepted House is generally either preceded or followed by one that has the same sign on both the cusps. The affairs of an intercepted House are generally complicated, and the planets therein are of more than average importance.

House: Diurnal, or day; Nocturnal, or Night. This is another misnomer which should be supplanted by "Day Home," or by any term other than House. It applies to the ruler ship of Signs, viz.: when a planet rules two Signs, one is considered its Day Home, the other its Night Home. The use of the term House in such a connection is misleading, since it has nothing to do with a House as astrologically defined. Each planet's Day Home is located in a Positive or Masculine Sign; its Night Home, in a Negative or Feminine Sign.

Houses, Tables of. By means of tables of houses for different latitudes, one is able to ascertain what degrees of the zodiac appeared upon the Ascendant and the various House cusps on any hour of any day, as calculated from the sidereal time at noon of that day as indicated in the ephemeris. Actually the tables may be said to divide distance by time, showing how many degrees of the ecliptic will pass a given point in two hours, which varies in different latitudes on account of the inclination of the earth's axis.

USES OF, IN DIRECTING. By means of the Tables of Houses for the latitude of birth, planets may be directed to the horizon, as follows: In the Asc. column find the longitude of the planet, then take the related location of the cusp of the X' house, and subtract from it the MC. at birth; the result will be the age at which this direction will be effective. To direct to the opposition of the Asc. add 180º to the longitude of the planet. To direct to the MC locate the planet's longitude in the Tenth House column and count the years backwards to the MC at birth. To direct to the opposition of the MC, count backwards to the degree appearing on the IC or cusp of Fourth House at birth. To direct the Asc. or MC to aspects with planets, note the degree in which it will fall, and bring the degree to the Asc. or MC, as if the planet were there.

Human Signs. Gemini, Virgo, Aquarius, and the first half of Sagittarius. v. SIGNS.

Hyleg. The Giver of Life. Said of a planet so located as to have influence upon the longevity of the native. It is one of the most complex and controversial subjects in the field of astrology, but which has fallen more or less in disfavor as the result of the concept that any attempt to predict the time of death is now generally considered unethical. The strongest planet that occupied one of the Aphetic places became Hyleg, and was deemed to be the Apheta, the giver of life. When it had progressed to an aspect to the place of the Anareta, the taker a way of life, the native was presumed to have run his span and death ensued.

The Aphetic places were from the 25th degree of the Eighth House to the 25th degree of the Eleventh House; from the 25th degree of the Twelfth House to the 25th degree of the First House; and from the 25th degree of the Sixth House to the 25th degree of the Seventh House. If the Sun occupied any of these arcs, it became Hyleg. If not, the Moon was the next choice. Lacking either, the planet which had the most dignities at the moment of the Lunation next preceding birth. Otherwise in a Day birth the Ascendant, or in a Night birth Fortuna, became Hyleg. The Anaretic places were those occupied by Mars or Saturn, or by Sun, Moon, or Mercury if aspected by Mars or Saturn. Otherwise the Descending degree. Wilson's Dictionary gives several pages of rules and exceptions, and then characterizes the whole subject as so much rubbish. It merely amounts to a consideration of aspects formed by progressed or transitory planets to birth positions and aspects, with special attention to a prognosis of death - an application of astrological analysis that is generally frowned upon by modern astrologers.

A planet conjoined to Caput Algol, if joined to the Hyleg, was in earlier days deemed to threaten beheading; the modern equivalent is perhaps defeat at the polls.

Hylegiacal Places. v. PRINCIPAL PLACES.

Hypogeon. Under the Earth. An all-embracing Greek term generalizing the lower heaven: including the Nadir, the IMMUM COELI, and the Fourth House.

Ides. A day in the Roman calendar and seven days before it. It appears that the term applied to the day on which the Sun passed the points of the Equinoxes and the Tropics, and that the seven days constituted the orbs preceding the Sun's crossing of the cusps of the four cardinal signs or angular houses. Shakespeare refers to the baleful influence of "The Ides of March" - evidently the last seven degrees of Pisces, or of the Twelfth House.

Illumination, Period of. That portion of the Moon's orbit, of the duration of approximately 26d 18h, during which it is visible, supplying light after sunset and before sunrise. Obviously it supplies light only to the hemisphere which is turned in its direction; but since the Earth's rotation constantly shifts this hemisphere, the whole of the Earth's surface is illuminated for some portion of every night during this period.

Immersion. Applied to the Sun or Moon as it enters into an eclipse, or to the beginning of an occultation (Q.V.).

Impeded; Impedited. Said of a Luminary or planet when badly aspected, especially by the malefics. Also said of the Moon when passing to a conjunction, square or opposition to the Sun, Mars, or Saturn. The Moon when impeded by the Sun at birth was anciently said to produce a blemish in or near the eye.

Imperfect Signs, Broken Signs. Leo, Scorpio and Pisces. v. SIGNS.

Imum Coeli. The lowest heaven, the North Angle or cusp of the fourth house. v. MIDHEAVEN; CELESTIAL SPHERE.

Inclination. (1) Astrologically, the motion of a body toward a position in the horoscope other than the one it held at birth. (2) Astronomically, the angle at which the orbit of a planet crosses another orbit, particularly the ecliptic. A point in an orbit is reduced to the ecliptic by subtracting from the vector, the cosine of the declination.
The inclination of the Moon's orbit to the ecliptic varies from 4°59' to 5°18'.

The Earth's orbit is, of course, the Ecliptic, hence the Sun can have no latitude. That it has declination is due to the fact that the ecliptic makes an angle with the celestial equator of approx. 23°5' - which is described, not as inclination but as the obliquity of the ecliptic. For the inclination of the planets v. NODES OF THE PLANETS.

Inconjunct. Dissociate. A planet is inconjunct when it forms no aspect and is not in parallel of declination or mutual disposition to another planet. Dissociate was formerly applied by some authorities to the 150° or Quincunx aspect, which they deemed inconsequential; but is now applied to any two Signs or Houses which have no familiarity with each other - meaning those which bear a twelfth, second, sixth and eighth House relationship, as Taurus, with Aries, Gemini, Libra and Sagittarius.

Increasing in Light. Usually said of the Moon, but equally applicable to any planet which, on leaving a conjunction with the Sun, increases in light, as viewed from the Earth; and as it recedes from the opposition, decreases in light.

Increasing in Motion. A planet increases its motion by acceleration from day to day as it approaches perihelion. When it is approaching its apogee, the Moon may advance 12° one day and as much as 13° the next. As its mean motion is 13°10' per day, any excess above this indicates that the Moon is "swift in motion." The condition is regarded as fortunate. Older authorities term it increasing in number.

Individual Houses. v. HOUSES.

Inferior Planets. The minor planets, those whose orbits are within that of the Earth: viz.: Mercury and Venus. v. PLANETS.

Infortunes. Mars and Saturn. v. PLANETS, MALEFIC.

Ingress. Said of the entry of any orbital body into a Sign, or a quadrant. The Sun makes an ingress into the Cardinal Signs at the equinoxes and solstices. The planets also have their ingresses into the various Signs, which result in certain alterations of their influence.

Initiating Signs. The first Sign of each season of the year; the Cardinal Signs - Aries, Cancer, Libra, and Capricorn, characterized by a constant state of mobilization for action.

Initiative Type. Referring to a quality liberally possessed by those born when the Sun was in a leading Sign: Aries, Cancer, Libra, or Capricorn. v. SIGN.

Injunct. An abbreviated form of inconjunct (Q.V.).

Inspirational Natures. Referring to the quality of sensory receptivity and reaction that characterizes those born with the Sun in Aries, Leo and Sagittarius - respectively, the initiative, executive and deductive types of the Inspirational group. It would appear that their chief motivation derives from a super-consciousness of the Ego.

Intellectual Natures. Referring to a quality of sensory receptivity through the mind that characterizes those born with the Sun in Libra, Aquarius and Gemini - respectively, the initiative, executive and deductive types of the Intellectual group. To classify this group as Intellectuals, does not imply that other groups are possessed of inferior intellects.

Interlunar. Of or pertaining to the brief period of time that separates the old and the new Moon. The period of the Moon's invisibility during a lunation, the solar period less 26 d., 18 h., or approximately two days.

Intercepted. Said of a Sign wholly contained within a House; or more precisely, of a House which is intercepted by a Sign which does not appear upon either of its cusps. v. HOUSE.

Interpolation. The process of computing intermediate values in a series of numbers. In astrology it is applied (1) to computing a planet's position for a given moment between two known posi- tions, such as the noon or midnight position prior to and subsequent to the desired moment, as taken from an Ephemeris for that year; and (2) to compute the house cusps for an intermediate latitude between two sets of tables computed for latitudes on either side of that for which the interpolation is required. In making the calculations necessary for an interpolation, use is frequently made of Tables of Diurnal Proportional Logarithms. v. LOGARITHMS.

Interpretation. Applied astrologically to an individual judgment as to the significance of a configuration of birth planets, or of transiting or progressed aspects to a birth configuration.

Invariable Plane. The Solar System possesses two fixed planes: that of the Solar Equator; and the Invariable plane - a central plane of the Solar System discovered by Laplace, which, passing through its center of gravity at a mean inclination of about 1°35' to the Ecliptic, is independent of the mutual perturbations of the planets. The inclination of the orbits of Venus and Mercury to the Solar Equator, slightly more than 3 degrees, is less than that of the other planets. Since these are the two closest planets to the Sun, the Solar Equator can be considered as their reference plane. The Earth's inclination to this plane, of slightly more than 7", is exceeded only by that of Pluto. The Ecliptic, the Earth's plane of revolution around the Sun, intersects the Solar Equator in the middle of Gemini and Sagittarius, at which points the Earth has no heliographic Latitude North or South. However, the values of these inclinations and the longitudes of the planetary Nodes along this plane are all variable due to motions of the orbits themselves with respect to the other great reference plane of the Solar System: the Invariable Plane - so-called because its position remains unaltered by any forces within the system. In this plane the combined angular momenta of all the planets is a maximum. There are two classes of disturbances in the normal undisturbed elliptical motion of the planets in their orbits in space: periodic perturbations and secular perturbations. Periodic perturbations are deviations due to the gravitational pulls of the planets on each other. However, after the planets have revolved a considerable number of times, and thus have been in all possible relations to each other, these periodic perturbations cancel each other. A famous example is the long period inequality in the motions of Jupiter and Saturn, which shifts their positions by a degree or so - one forward and the other backward - in a period of about 918 years. Actually their recurrence cycle in the fixed Zodiac - 46 conjunctions distributed nearly evenly in all 12 Signs of that Zodiac - is about 913½ years, but the inequality lengthens this to 918 years. Therefore the periodic perturbations are determined by the second order recurrence cycles of the planets in the fixed Zodiac. However, at the end of such a cycle of fluctuation the distorting effects have not been completely cancelled out, and small remaining residues show up in what are termed the elements of the planets' orbits. As a result of this residue, the nodical line at which the orbit plane of each planet intersects the invariable plane, is displaced backward, in a processional motion of the whole orbit plane. In addition, the inclination of the orbit plane to the invariable plane is slightly decreased or increased. A third effect is a shift in the position of the major axis - longest axis of the orbital ellipse. This shift may be either forward or backward, but it is more likely to be forward for all of the planets except Venus. Finally the shortest axis of the orbital ellipse - the minor axis which crosses the major axis at the center of the ellipse - increases or decreases its length; i.e, the eccentricity of the ellipse becomes greater or less.

Two great masters of celestial mechanics, Lagrange and Laplace, demonstrated that while there are periodic fluctuations in the lengths of the major axes there are no secular perturbations - long-term oscillations. Since the duration of a planet's revolution around the Sun depends on the major axis alone, this means that except for minor short-term fluctuations the periods of the planets are constant. They further demonstrated that the inclinations and eccentricities oscillate within narrow limits which are never exceeded, thus preserving the stability of the Solar System. Finally they showed that the orbit planes precess backward along the invariable plane, while most of the major axes revolve forward - spending briefer periods in actual retrograde motion. Only the major axis of Venus spends more time revolving backward than forward. Thus the Solar System, through an intricate process of mutual adjustment, maintains its basic configurations of orbits, and its stability. As one planet decreases its eccentricity and inclination, one or more orbits must at the same time be increasing their eccentricities and inclinations: whereby the total amount of eccentricity and of inclination to the invariable plane remains constant! This has been termed the Magna Charta of the Solar System. The late Ernest W. Brown showed that the effects of resonance could not have been great enough within the past hundred million years to have destroyed this stability; nor would it be in the next hundred million years.

Jupiter, the most massive of all the planets, has an orbital inclination to the Invariable Plane which never exceeds 0°28', nor ever less than 0°14'. Its current value is about 0°21'. Furthermore, the Nodes of the Jupiter and Saturn orbits on this plane are never separated from each other by much less than 180°; hence these two planets largely determine the position of the Invariable plane - especially Jupiter. According to Stockwell, the mean period of their common precession is 49,972 years. Similarly the perihelion ends of the major axes of the orbits of Jupiter and Uranus never get much less than 180º from each other. The common mean period for a revolution of their major axes (line of apsides) is 348,700 years. Thus Jupiter is the "flywheel" which balance the Solar System, a perfect symbol of justice and law.

The Earth's orbit - the ecliptic - can never have an inclination to the Invariable plane in excess of 3°6'. The value on January 1, 1850 was 1°35'19.376" - the figures are taken from Stockwell's "Secular Variations of the Eight Principal Planets," in the "Smithsonian Annual Contributions to Knowledge," Volume 18, 1872. According to him the maximum eccentricity of the Earth's orbit is .0693888; the current value .0159. The period of the orbital precession of the Ecliptic on the Invariable Plane is indeterminate, since the minimum inclination of the Ecliptic to that plane is 0°0'0". Similarly, the minimum Eccentricity is also 0, hence the mean period of motion of the line of Apsides is also indeterminate.

LeVerrier, the discoverer of Neptune, and Stockwell, calculated the position of Earth's perihelion, one end of the line of apsides, over a period in excess of 4,000,000 Years. By counting the number of times the line of Apsides revolved within that period, one gains a good estimate of its period in the present Mahayuga. This Mahayuga of the Hindus is a period of approximately 4,320,000 years, in which they say all of the planets recur at nearly the same position. The astronomer Stuart showed that this is correct and that the period is 4,319,936.8663 years: at the end of which Mercury, Venus, Earth, Mars, Jupiter and Saturn return to a position in the Fixed Zodiac about 20° behind where they started. He found this also applied to the "new" planets, Uranus and Neptune; and that an increase in the period of Pluto of only one part in 100,000, or 0.001 per cent, will also bring it into recurrence. It would appear that in the present Mahayuga the mean period of revolution of the Earth's apsides is about 115,000 years from LeVerrier's figures, and about 110,000 from Stockwell's somewhat more accurate figures; and the average period of revolution of the major axis of the Earth's orbit must have a mean value of approximately the same order of magnitude: i.e., 110,000 to 115,000 years.

In the present cycle both of these periods are near minimums, since the eccentricity and inclination of the Earth's orbit are decreasing to minimum values. In the current cosmic Era the length of the Planetary Precession and rotation of the Line of Apsides will be from 72,000 to 75,000 years. The minimum inclination will be reached in about 20,000 years and the minimum eccentricity about 26,000 A.D., one cycle of general Precession after Christ. The last Stationary position of the Perihelion-Stationary-Direct after several thousands of years of retrogressive motion - was about 26,000 years before Christ: again one cycle of the general Precession.

The relationships of these cosmic cycles to the time of the Christ is indeed remarkable, and tends to confirm the belief that a new cycle of general Precession then commenced. Furthermore at that epoch the Nodical line of Ecliptic and Invariable Plane was at right angles to the Nodical line of Ecliptic and Equator - the Equinox - thus making a Cross! The position of the Nodical line of the Planetary precession in the Moving Zodiac was 16°14'6.00" Cancer-Capricorn on January 1, 1850. The present position of the Perihelion end of the Line of Apsides - where the Earth is nearest the Sun - is about 11° Capricorn, i.e., the position of the Sun on or shortly after January 1 of every year (deviation due to Calendar variation or Leap Year effect). Thus it appears that we commence our year at what after all is astronomically the most logical time.

The minimum eccentricity of the Earth's orbit, at about 29,900 A.D., will be the smallest minimum since the greatest maximum, about 850,000 B.C., showing a great cycle, governing all planetary eccentricities in the Solar System, of a duration of approximately 1,750,000 years. According to Madame Blavatsky's "Secret Doctrine" it was around 850,000 B.C. that the first and most serious cataclysm destroyed most of the continent of Atlantis, at the start of what she terms the Fifth Root Race. As a cataclysm by Water, this suggests that the next cataclysm may be by Fire, and will occur about 25,900 A.D., at the start of the Sixth Root Race. Since she maintains that each Root Race has 7 Sub-races and each of these in turn 7 Family Races, there should be 49 Family Races in a Root Race or Lifewave. She also states that the period of a Family Race was that of the general Precession, a little under 26,000 years - although the Root Races overlap, in that a new one commences before an older one has run its course. It is easy to show that the Precession which ended with Christ was the end of the Fifth Family Race of the Fifth Subrace of the Fifth Root Race: making 33 Family Races or Precessions since 850,000 B.C. Therefore the present Sixth Family Race, of the present cycle of Precession, may be considered as a bridging cycle out of which both the Sixth Sub-Race and the Sixth Root Race will in the next cataclysm approach their start around 25,900 A.D.

The foregoing is not put forward dogmatically, but as an interesting explanation of the significance of these long cosmic cycles. The implication is that the present cycle of Precession is a bridging cycle between two great Lifewaves (Root Races), and thus has extraordinary importance; that it commenced with Christ and the cosmic Cross formed by the Equinoxes and the Line of the Planetary Nodes; and that the significance of the Crucifixion is essentially cosmic, and the Mission of the Christ one of initiating the great Precessional cycle of Transition from the Fifth to the Sixth Lifewave. It is a notable fact that on April 1, 25 A.D. (Julian Calendar), when Jesus was 30 years of age and at the start of his mission, according to a consensus of historical researches, there was a Great Cardinal Cross, wherein Uranus in Cancer at its Node on the Invariable Plane opposing Neptune in Capricorn at its Node on the Ecliptic, was in cross relationship to Saturn in Aries at its Node on the Equator opposing Jupiter in Libra - all the Nodes on the three basic planes which at that time were forming the cosmic cross. In addition there was a Full Moon in Libra with the Sun in Aries, Mars in Aries also in the Cross, and at its Node on the Ecliptic. Pluto was in early Sagittarius; and Mercury and Venus were retrograde in the last decan of Pisces - the Sign of Christianity and of the traditionally first of the 12 Ages into which the Precessional cycle is customarily divided. Thus through the crossing of orbit planes, the Nodes, this Planetary Cross shows a remarkable relationship to the Cosmic Cross made at that time by the Equator, Ecliptic and Invariable planes.

This full discussion is warranted on the basis that this date marks the blending of all the chief cycles which affect the Earth, and the significance of the cosmically-indicated Crucifixion of Christ, which could never before have occurred in the two-billion-year history of the Earth. A third Cross is found to be involved, if one considers the four CONSECUTIVE Solar eclipse paths which passed over Jerusalem and Bethlehem, both before and after the life of Jesus. The total Eclipse of July 4, 336 B.C. at 6.3° Cancer; the total Eclipse of April 2, 303 B.C. at 7.5° Aries; the annular Eclipse of January 5, 29 B.C. at 12.6° Capricorn; and the annular Eclipse of October 4, 590 A.D. at 13.2° Libra - all Julian dates. These form a Cross in their positions on the Ecliptic (Zodiac), the positions in near-agreement with the Zodiacal places of the four chief major planets on April 1, 25 A.D.: Uranus, at 10.1° Cancer; Neptune, at 13.8° Capricorn; Saturn, at 4.8° Aries; and Jupiter, at 15.4° Libra - all calculated from Schoch's Tables by Ralph Kraum. Thus the Planetary Cross activated the Eclipse Cross (zodiacal), and the drama of the ensuing Crucifixion was enacted in Jerusalem where the four eclipse-paths had crossed and were to cross (Geographical), while both in turn were the projection of the basic evolutionary Cosmic Cross of the three fundamental planes which signified the commencement of the most vital cycle of Precession (both planetary Precession and general Precession), within the period of two Lifeways (transition from one to the other) - which is about 100 general Precessions or 2,570,000 years: the period of a double Polar Inversion. - CHARLES A. JAYNE, Jr.

Inversion. When any Angle which represents an aspect is subtracted from 180°, that which remains is also an aspect, and either is an inversion of the other. Thus: the inversion of a sextile is a trine; of a semi-square, a sesquiquadrate; and so on.

Ishtar. v. VENUS.

Isis and Osiris. Two hypothetical trans-Plutonic planets which have been the subject of much conjecture.

Issat. (Izzah, glory; from Arabic.) Applied ironically to one who has delusions of grandeur, or who suffers from an exaggerated appraisal of his prestige.

Joined to. Applied to any body that is embraced within the orbs of any aspect to any other body; more specifically applicable to a conjunction.

Joy. A term employed by some of the older authorities to indicate an affinity between certain planets and certain Signs, not necessarily of the character of Dignities. The original application of the term as anciently employed has been lost in the course of the centuries, and other meanings have been attached to the term. According to one theory a planet is in joy when, itself in debility, another planet with which it enjoys some similarity is posited in one of its Dignities. Thus Saturn was presumed to experience a sympathetic joy when Mars is in Capricorn, the Sign ruled by Saturn, and in which Mars is exalted; also that it there opposes and afflicts Cancer, ruled by the Moon. It feels a "joy" when Mercury is posited in either of its triplicities, since the Signs they rule belong to the same Triplicities: Capricorn-Virgo and Aquarius-Gemini. Also when Venus is in either of its Signs, because both trine Saturn's Signs: Taurus-Capricorn, Libra-Aquarius. A malefic experiences "joy" when another malefic afflicts either Sun, Moon, or any benefic which is in one of its Dignities. Thus Jupiter is in its joy when the Sun inhabits a Jupiter-ruled Sign - either Sagittarius or Pisces, or Cancer where Jupiter is in its Exaltation; or any Sign of its Triplicity - which includes all the Fire and Water Signs. Also when the Moon or Mars are in their respective Signs or Triplicities. Mars "joys" when the Sun is exalted; when the Moon is in her Sign, or when Saturn is in Capricorn. While not exalted in Leo, Mars was said to "joy" in the Sign, because both are of a fiery nature. The term belongs to an epoch when astrological writers were more poetic than scientific.

In short, any planet "joys" when another planet is placed in one of its Essential Dignities. Some authorities have confused this with what is termed the Thrones of the planets, viz.: the Signs they rule.

Latterly planets have been said to "joy" in certain Houses: Saturn, in the Twelfth; Jupiter, in the Eleventh; Mars, in the Sixth; Venus, in the Fifth; Mercury, in the First; the Sun, in the Tenth; the Moon, in the Third.

It is also said that the Sun and Jupiter "joy" in each other's Houses, as do Saturn and Mercury, and Venus and the Moon. All of which added together leaves the term in ill-repute, and generally in disuse among modern astrologers. The term has a certain merit and might well be restored, if confined to the congeniality of a planet in a House. In that way it can be said that Dignity and Debility result from Sign placement, and Joy from House placement.

Julian Calendar. v. CALENDAR.

Julian Day. For calculating long intervals of time it was found desirable to eliminate the months and years, and number the days consecutively. Hence one such numbered day is identified by the prefix J.D., meaning Julian Day. (v. DAY.)

This table of Julian Days is a convenience in computing the num- ber of elapsed days between any two dates. Merely set down the J.D. for the two days and subtract: the difference will be the number of elapsed days. For dates that are separated by only 2 or 3 years, it will be necessary to use only the last three or four digits. These tables can be applied to any years, if care is exercised to see that a table for a bissextile year is used for a bissextile year, and one for a common year is used for a common year.

Kabala. v. CABALA.

Kakatyche. Ill-fortune. A greek term for the Sixth House.

Karma. Applied to the end-result of the operation of the Law of Cause and Effect. Perhaps its closest English equivalent is Destiny. Many Western astrologers are inclined to reject the concept of Karma, and its associated doctrines of Predestination and Reincarnation, as escapist theories of help only to those who have been unable to master Destiny through the exercise of Free Will and Self Determination. They feel that if Astrology is to serve any worthy end, by way of aiding in the formulation and pursuit of a Design for Living built to individual specifications, it must avoid any such blind and fatalistic acceptance of limitations as is implied in the doctrine of Karma.

Katababazon. The Dragon's Tail. v. NODES.

Kether. The first Sephira of the Tree of Life; the Crown, situated in the world of Atziluth; known also as the Primum Mobile, the highest point in a Figure of the Heavens. The term pertains chiefly to Hindu astrology.

Key-Cycle. A system of progressions published by Sidney K. Bennett, under the pseudonym of "Wynn." Based upon the fractional quarter-day excess which is corrected by a leap-year every fourth year, it is an adaptation of Solar Return calculations, adjusted to any desired date or geographical location.

Kosmos. The Universe, as distinguished from our earth.

Krishna. A Hindu deity, the incarnation of Vishnu.

Kronos. v. SATURN.

Labha bhava. The Eleventh House in the Hindu system of Astrology.

Lagna. In Hindu Astrology the Ascendant.

Lagna Sphutas. In Hindu Astrology, the calculating of the Ascendant.

Latitude. There are three kinds of Terrestrial latitude: astronomical, geographic and geocentric. **(1) Astronomical:** the angle between the direction of the plumb-line and the plane of the Earth's equator. If the Earth were a homogeneous sphere without rotation, the plumb-line would point toward its center -- but the Earth is not an exact sphere. Deviation due to inequalities of the Earth's surface is termed Station Error. **(2) Geographic:** the latitude used in drawing terrestrial maps. It is astronomical latitude corrected for station error. **(3) Geocentric:** from a given point on the Earth's surface subtend a line to the Earth's center, and there compute the angle between this line and the plane of the equator.

It is important to distinguish between Geographical Latitude measured N. or S. of the Equator, and Celestial Latitude measured N. or S. of the Ecliptic. Geographical Latitude is thus comparable to Declination rather than Celestial Latitude.

There are also GALACTIC LATITUDE, angular distance on the celestial sphere measured from the medium plane of the Milky Way; and HELIOGRAPHIC LATITUDE, angular distance on the Sun's sphere, N. or S. of its Equator.

There are also three varieties of its Celestial equivalent: (a) that which parallels the Horizon, which is called altitude; (b) that which parallels the Equator, which is called declination; and (c) that which parallels the Ecliptic, which is called Latitude. **(v. CELESTIAL SPHERE.)** Since the apparent motion of the Sun, resulting from the Earth's motion in orbit, is itself the Ecliptic, the Sun can have no Latitude. Since the orbits of the planets are inclined to the Ecliptic at an angle of more or less obliquity, each planet, without Latitude when it intersects the Ecliptic, increases in latitude as it approaches the square to its Nodes: for one half its orbit in North Latitude, the other half in South Latitude. The maximum possible Latitude of each planet, and the location of its Node, are as follows:

...Planet........Node as of 1946.....Maximum Latitude
...Moon..................................5°17'

...Mercury.........47°32'................7°
...Venus............76°05'................0°24'
...Mars.............49°02'................1°51'
...Jupiter..........99°46'................1°18'
...Saturn..........113°04'................2°29'
...Uranus..........73°39'................0°46'
...Neptune........131°02'................1°47'
...Pluto............109°25'................17°09'

To Change Geographical to Geocentric Latitude, or the Reverse. These are equal at the equator and the poles. At 45° the Geocentric Latitude is the greater by about 4½ minutes. The following table shows the corrections for each degree of separation from either the horizon or the pole, whichever is the nearer, the correction to be added to Geographic or subtracted from Geocentric Latitude, to change one to the other.

.. 1º .... 24".2
.. 2º .... 24".36
.. 3º ......1'12".47
.. 4º ......1'24".16

Laya Centers. Neutral states between solid, liquid and gaseous; said to be governed by Saturn.

Leap Year. To preserve the coincidence of the vernal equinox in approximately correct relation to the Civil year, Caesar, with the assistance of Sosigines, introduced the Julian calendar about 46 B.C. It called for the intercalation of a day on certain years. The "last year of confusion," which preceded the introduction of this calendar, was prolonged to 445 days. The arrangement was somewhat upset by Augustus Caesar, who insisted that his month of August have as many days in it as that of Julius. Pope Gregory XIII finally corrected the Julian calendar by what is known as the Gregorian rule of intercalation, which was adopted by all Christian countries, except Russia which did not adopt it until 1918. It is: every year divisible by 4 without a remainder is a leap year; excepting Centurial years, which are leap years only when divisible by 4 after the omission of the two ciphers. This still leaves a gain of a day in 3,323 years, which suggests this further addition to the rule: Excepting that a year that is divisible by four after the omission of three ciphers is not a leap year. More exact, and almost as simple would be the rule of a leap year every fourth year for 31 leap years - suppressing the 32nd, which means merely the addition of 31 days every 128 years. This approximates the system which Omar Khayyam, astronomer to Sultan Jelal Ud-Din of Persia, devised about 1079 A.D.

Leo. The fifth Sign of the Zodiac. (v. Signs.)

Life. v. Hyleg; Apheta.

Light. (1) The imponderable agent by which objects are rendered visible to the eye; (2) an illumination that confers mental or spiritual enlightenment.

Light, Collector of. A ponderous planet which receives the aspects of any two significators in some of their Essential Dignities. Both must be lighter planets than the Collector itself. It denotes a mediator who will interest himself in the affairs of both parties to bring to a favorable issue a desired result which could not otherwise be achieved. It is a favorable position for the reconciling of differences, quarrels, lawsuits; the bringing about of marriages and of various agreements.

Light of time. The Sun by day; the Moon by night.

Light Planets. The Moon, Venus and Mercury, referring to their gravities and to their consequent swiftness of motion. The nearer a body is to its gravitational centre, the more its motion is accelerated and its gravity proportionately diminished.

Light, Velocity of. 186,270 miles per second.

Light-year. Unit of measurement of Ultra-solar system distances. A Light-year is the distance light travels in one year - at the rate of 186,000 miles per second, or about six trillion miles: 6 with 12 ciphers. Intra-solar system distances are measured in astronomical units. An astronomical Unit is the mean distance of the Earth from the Sun, about 92,930,000 miles, where it is found in April and October, at which time the Sun's light reaches the Earth in 499 seconds, or about 8 minutes. The inadequacy of this unit for ultra-solar system spaces can be seen by comparing the Pluto distance from the Earth, of 39½ A.U., light from which reaches the Earth in a little over five hours, with the distance of the next closest major body beyond Pluto, the star Alpha Centauri, light from which requires 4.3 years to traverse the intervening 25 trillion miles. Yet, if anyone on Alpha Centauri, despite its relative closeness, were to attempt to observe Pluto he would find it separated from the Sun by an arc of only 1", which means that Pluto and all the planets would be merged into the glare of the Sun, and give the appearance of an average star of the third or fourth magnitude.

Lights. A term frequently applied to the Luminaries (Q.V.), the Sun and Moon as distinguished from the planets.

Lilith. A name sometimes given to asteroid No. 1181, a minor planet, of magnitude 14.1. It is too faint to be seen other than with the aid of a telescope. It is not a "dark moon," but a planet that shines by reflected light from the Sun - as does the Earth. Lilith is mentioned in the apocryphal writings, as the "other woman" in the original triangle that rendered the Garden of Eden no longer a paradise.

Local Mean Time. Based upon the moment when the mean Sun crosses the Midheaven of the place. Local Mean Time was almost universally used prior to the adoption of Standard Time on Nov. 18, 1883, and in some communities it continued to be used for a long time thereafter. V. TIME.

Logarithms. Proportional parts of a quadrant, expressed in numbers, whereby calculations of the planets' places at a given hour, or the Arc of Direction for a given date, can be made by simple addition and subtraction rather than by multiplication or division. They were invented in 1614 by Baron Napier of Murchiston for use in his astrological calculations. Tables of Logarithms are in common use in all schools by students of trigonometry. Tables of natural, proportional and logistic logarithms are also available, each designed for different uses. An improvement in logarithms was introduced by Henry Briggs in 1624.

The astrologer uses Diurnal Proportionate Logarithms in making numerous calculations, but their average use is in calculating the planets' places for a given birth hour. If it is desired to reduce daily motion to hourly motion by the use of Logarithms, proceed as follows:

Subtract the positions of the desired planet on two successive days to determine its daily motion. Also compute the elapsed time between your birth moment adjusted to local mean time, and the previous noon or midnight - dependent on whether your ephemeris for that year gives noon or midnight positions.

Suppose you are seeking the Moon's position for an elapsed time of 7h 35m on a day in which its daily motion is 14° 27': In the tables, select the column with 14 at the top; run down the column to 27; and set it down; also for 35 in the 7 column; thus:
<DIVFONT>
D.M............ 14º27'   prop. log. .22034
Elap.T. .... 7h35m   prop. log. .50035
                          Add   .72069

Looking for this in the tables you would (APOLO NOTE: THERE IS A HUGE LOGARITHM TABLE IN THE ORIGINAL BOOK WHICH WOULD TAKE IMPOSSIBLY LONG TO REPRODUCE - SORRY!) find .72061 at 34 in the 4 column: 4°34'. Add this to the Moon's longitude on the previous noon or midnight, and you have the position for the desired moment. In the case of a planet, note whether it is retrograde, in which event the distance of travel during the elapsed time is subtracted from the previous noon or midnight position.

Verify all Data. When adjusting the planets' places for a given birth moment, cultivate the habit of forming a mental approximation of the intermediate position for a given interval of elapsed time, before you verify it by a calculation. Comprehension of what you are doing is superior to the mere following of a formula. Also bear in mind that exact calculations to an approximate birth moment, or one that is not authentic and precise, is like holding a stop watch on a race when you do not know where the starting line is located. Whoever said "time is of the essence" should have been an astrologer. Is this date before standard time was used in that community? If so, what zone? Is that a Julian or a Gregorian date? Did they observe Daylight Saving Time at that season of the year? These are only a few of many questions that involve discrepancies amounting to hours - so what matter items which at most involve minutes, perhaps only seconds? Exact work is to be admired, but not in trying to make a silk purse out of a sow's car. Verify the authenticity of your data first. If you cannot do that, insert only even degrees, and interpret on the basis of Solar Houses.

Longitude. (1) Terrestrial or Geographical. The distance of any point on the Earth's surface, E. or W. of Greenwich; measured by geographers in degrees; by astronomers, in hours. **(2) Celestial**. Longitude in the heavens; the distance between the first point in the zodiac (Aries 0°) and any celestial body, measured along the ecliptic, in degrees. For example, Antares, to an astrologer is in Sagittarius 8°; to an astronomer, L. 248°. Celestial longitude is of two kinds: (a) Geocentric, figured from the earth as the center; now chiefly used by astrologers to indicate the zodiacal positions of the planets, but rarely used by astronomers, and in the Nautical Almanac is given only for the Sun and Moon. (b) Heliocentric, figured from the Sun as the center. LONGITUDE as used in astronomical terminology is given in degrees from 1 to 360. Thus Long. 125° becomes 5° Leo; 4 signs of 3° degrees each = 120° - hence 5° in the next or 5th Sign. v. CELESTIAL CIRCLE.

Geographical Longitude is measured E. and W. from the Meridian of Greenwich observatory; Celestial Longitude from the Meridian of the Vernal Equinox: 0° Aries.

Lord. Often used synonymously with Ruler. More precise terminology would indicate the Ruler of a Sign and the Lord of a House. Thus a certain planet may be deemed Lord of a House, either because it is posited in the House, or, lacking any planet in the House, because it is the Ruler of the Sign appearing on the cusp thereof. The Lord of the Geniture would be more precisely termed the Ruler of the Figure, meaning that planet having the most Dignities, either Essential or Accidental. The Lord of the Hour is that planet which is presumed to govern the hour during which the Figure was cast. The Lord of the Year is that planet which has the most Dignities in a Solar Revolution Figure, or in an Ingress figure to be interpreted according to the rules of Mundane Astrology.

LORD OF THE YEAR.

In an Ingress Figure judgment is formed on the basis of its position and aspects, especially such aspects as it forms with the Moon. Well placed, it is interpreted as follows; but afflicted, the reverse is prognosticated.

Sun: Propitious for governments and high governmental officers; food plentiful; money in rapid circulation.

Moon: Favors the advancement of women; contributes to the contentment of the common people; good health to the honest and upright.

Mercury: Advances in science and education; favors the development of inventions; prosperity to merchants and traders. Afflicted: changes, reversals of policy.

Venus: Increased leisure for self-advancement and recreation of the laboring classes; arts and artists will flourish; increased birth rate. Afflicted: epidemics.

Mars: Advancement in accident prevention and safety of workers; protection to those in hazardous occupations. Afflicted: wars, fires, storms, strikes.

Jupiter: Prosperity to the upper classes; constructive legislation; abundance and a contented populace with respect for law.

Saturn: Increased construction; propitious to agriculture; class amity. Afflicted: cold; scarcity; mortality among the old; national calamities.

Lucifer. The 'light-bearer'. Applied to Venus when a 'morning star', rising before the Sun; poetically called, 'Son of the Morning'.

Luminaries. The Lights. Said of the Sun and Moon as distinguished from the planets. It is an ancient classification hardly in keeping with the fact that the Sun is the only direct source of energy, and that the light from the Moon, like that from the planets, is reflected from the Sun. Their function with reference to solar energy is that of a filtering reflector whereby certain frequencies are absorbed by chemical properties inherent in the mass, resulting in the transmission to the Earth of an altered ray. However, the astrological significance warrants the classification of the Sun and Moon separately from the planets, in that the Sun and Moon have to do with Man's spiritual consciousness, while the planetary influences operate through the physical mechanism. The Moon is a luminary in the biblical sense that it affords to Man "light by night."

Lunar. Relating to the Moon.

Lunar Declination. The moon's declination varies from year to year. A maximum (18°+) occurred in March 1932 and in 1941. The reason for the variation is the regression of the Moon's nodes. The ecliptic is inclined to the celestial equator by 23°27'. The moon's apparent path on the celestial sphere is inclined to the ecliptic on an average of 5°8', but the intersection points, the nodes, move relatively fast, covering 360° in about 19 years. When the Moon's ascending node lies at the Vernal equinox, the angle between the Moon's apparent path and the equator is at the greatest, for 23°27' must be added to 5°8' making 28°35'. Half a revolution later, or about 9½ years, the descending node is at the Vernal equinox, and the angle between the moon's path and the equator is at the least, and 5°8' is subtracted from 23°27', giving 18°19'. The more the moon's path is inclined to the equator, the greater is the declination.

Lunar Mansions. v. MANSIONS OF THE MOON.

Lunar Month, or more correctly a Synodic Month. The total of the Moon's annual travel in excess of that of the Sun, when reduced to time, gives the duration of the mean synodic revolution of the moon, or the lunar month, as 29.531 days, or 29d. 12h. 44m. 2.8s., in which period the Moon returns to its former position in relation to the Sun. The Sidereal Month is 27.322 days.

Lunar semicircle. From Aquarius to Cancer inclusive.

Lunar Year. Twelve lunar months, a total of 354 days - 11¼ d. shorter than the Solar year. Its point of beginning passes through the circle of seasons in about 34 lunar years. It is used by modern Jews and Mohammedans. In the early days of Greece the year was regulated entirely by the Moon, and Solon was among the first who attempted to reconcile the Solar and Lunar years by a system of intercalations.

Lunation. (1) As usually employed, it is approximately synonymous with New Moon; specifically, the precise moment of the Moon's conjunction with the Sun; a Syzygy. The New Moon falling upon sensitive points in the Figure has much signification as to events of the ensuing month. It is deemed to actuate, within 14 days, any Secondary Directions that are of the same nature, and to nullify those of an opposite nature. Falling upon the places of the Benefics, it produces good; upon the Malefics, evil. Aspects to the position of the lunation are interpreted according to the positions of the aspecting planets. (2) The period of 29d 12h 44m 2.8s between one New Moon and the next - more correctly termed a synodic month. (3) A SIDEREAL lunation, also more correctly termed a sidereal month, is the period of 27d 7h 43m 11.5s intervening between two successive passages of the Moon over the same degree; sometimes termed a PERIODICAL lunation. (4) An EMBOLISMIC lunation, correctly termed an embolismic month, is an intercalary month, inserted in some calendars, such as the Jewish, when the 11-days' annual excess over twelve lunar months adds up to 30. An arbitrary application of this was used by Placidus, who applied the term EMBOLISMIC LUNATION, to a Figure cast for the moment of the Moon's return to the same relation to the Sun that it occupied at birth. It was made the basis for judgment concerning the affairs and conditions of the ensuing year of life. Another type of Lunation Figure quite incorrectly termed an EMBOLISM, employed each successive return of the Moon to its birth relationship to the Sun, as a basis for prognostication concerning a comparable year of life - the Embolism for the fourth lunar month after birth pertaining to the fourth year of life, and so on. (5) Another Lunation Figure, termed a *Synodical Lunation*, was cast for the return of the progressed Moon, after birth, to the same distance from the progressed Sun, as that which the radical Moon was from the radical Sun at birth. A map of the heavens for the moment of the exact return of the Moon to this position is compared with the horoscope of birth, and treated as symbolical of the influences then prevailing.

Lunation, Embolismic. A period of 29d., 12h., 44m., 28s., during which the Moon's phases pass from conjunction to square and to opposition to the Sun. Also applied to the period between one New Moon and the next. (V. LUNAR MONTH.) The New Moon falling upon sensitive points in the Figure has much signification as to events of the ensuing month. It is deemed to actuate, within 14 days, any Secondary Directions that arc of the same nature, and to nullify those of an opposite nature. Falling upon the places of the Benefics, it produces good; upon the Malefics, evil. Aspects to the position of the lunation are interpreted according to the positions of the aspecting planets. The term is synonymous with New Moon, as indicating the moment when the conjunction with the Sun takes place. Sometimes incorrectly called a Synodical Lunation (QV.).

Lunation, Periodical. The period of 27d, 7h, 41m. from the passage of the Moon over a given degree to its return to that degree; a sidereal month.

Lunation, Synodical. The return of the progressed Moon, after birth, to the same distance from the progressed Sun, as that which the radical Moon was from the radical Sun at birth. This takes place once every 29½ days approximately. Each such lunation or month is considered to represent one year of life. A map of the heavens for the moment of the exact return of the Moon to this position is compared with the horoscope of birth, and treated as symbolical of the influences then prevailing. (V. SYZYGY.)

Magic. In occult terminology, a mastery of occult forces and the hidden mysteries of nature. White Magic is that exercised for a beneficent, helpful purpose; Black Magic, the abuse of super-normal powers when applied to a selfish end. Cornell associates magical powers with Uranus and Scorpio and the 8th and 12th Houses.

Magnetism. In occult terminology, a form of elemental electricity which confers the power of attraction and creates polarity. Almost every person and object has magnetic attraction. Physical magnetism is deemed to be allied to electricity, hence associated with Uranus and Scorpio.

Magnitude. An adopted arbitrary geometric scale whereby to indicate the brightness of a celestial object; according to which an increase of 5 magnitudes corresponds to 100-fold decrease in brightness. *Apparent Magnitude* As it actually appears - ranging from -26.7 for our Sun to + 20 for the faintest stars which can be photographed by the largest telescope. ABSOLUTE MAGNITUDE. As it would be perceived if removed to a point from which its parallax would be 0.1" of arc - ranging from -5 for the brightest of stars to +15 for the faintest, with our Sun about +5. The faintest star visible to the unaided eye is of the sixth magnitude. Since greenish yellow registers best on the eye and blue-violet registers best on the photo-plate, magnitudes vary somewhat according to the method of observation employed.

Major Planets. V. PLANETS.

Malefic. (N.) Applied to certain planets deemed to exert a harmful influence; chiefly Mars and Saturn. V. PLANETS. **2. (A)** As usually employed, it is loosely applied to an inharmonious aspect with any planet, and to a conjunction with any malefic planet. (V. PLANETS.)

AFFLICTED BY; IN AFFLICTION WITH. Applied to certain aspects deemed to be inharmonious.

Mansions of the Moon. A series of 28 divisions of the Moon's travel through one complete circuit of 360 degrees, each Mansion representing one day's average travel of the Moon (12° 51' 25.2", or roughly 13 degrees), beginning apparently at the point of the Spring Equinox, or 0° Aries. In the Hindu system they are called Asterisms, and are measured from the beginning of the Hindu Zodiac. The result is this series of cusps:

Cardinal Signs: 0° 0' 0" The nearest even degree:
...............12 51 25 13
...............25 42 50 26
Fixed Signs:... 8 34 15 9
...............21 25 40 21
Mutable Signs:. 4 17 5 4
...............17 8 30 17

Fragmentary interpretations of the Lunar Mansions have come down to us from Arabia, India and China. The precise manner in which they were employed has been lost, but it is known that great importance was attached to them. Sepharial considers that the entrance of the progressed Moon into a Mansion presaged important changes involving affairs pertaining to that Mansion; but it is probable that they had more to do with the transits of the planets, and with the Mansion in which fell the current Lunation and Full Moon. Particular attention was paid to the Mansion in which fell the Lunar Day - the day of the Full Moon

In a later period the cusps were known as Crucial or Critical Degrees, with particular reference to the prognosis of a crisis in the progress of an acute disease; also the days on which the Moon forms inharmonious aspects - the 7th, 14th, 21st and 28th days - are said to be Critical Days. These coincide with the cusps of the First, Eighth, Fifteenth and Twenty-second Mansions.

Except in Horary questions the Hindu system uses only 27 of these asterisms - omitting the 22nd. Each of these groups of 9 representing the following period in years, are ruled in this sequence:

..South Node...Venus...Sun...Moon...Mars...North Node...Jupiter...Saturn...Mercury
.......7.........20.....6.....10......7........18..........16.......19........17

The periods total 120y, the Hindu idea of normal life span. 120/9 gives 13 1/3 years, or the same number of degrees, showing the 1° per year unit of progression, and the probability that the Mansions were largely a device for use in computing progressed influences. Nevertheless the Hindu would state your birth date in terms of the asterism much as we give it in terms of your Sun Sign.

Another Series of Mansions from an Ancient Chinese source indicates that it was chiefly to determine the requests which one propitiates the gods to grant.

Map. v. Figure.

Marduk, or Asaru. The Chaldean equivalent to Jupiter: said to "restore man to happiness." In the Babylonian religion, the god of magicians.

Mark, Noon or Midnight. A term used by Llewellyn George for the equivalent of noon or midnight at Greenwich in the local mean time of the place for which a Figure is cast. By this means the ephemeral places of the planets are corrected by the amount of time the birth moment precedes or follows the noon or midnight Mark - depending on whether the Ephemeris is for noon or midnight.

Martian. One under the influence of, or ruled by, a strongly placed Mars.

Masculine Degrees. According to H. L. Cornell, M.D., these are:

Aries: 8-15-30
Leo: 5-15-30
Sagittarius: 2-12-30
Taurus: 11-21-30
Virgo: 12-30
Capricorn: 11-30
Gemini: 16-26
Libra: 5-20-30
Aquarius: 5-21-27
Cancer: 2-10-23-30
Scorpio: 4-17-30

Pisces: 10-23-30

Should the Ascendant be in one of these degrees the native, even if a woman, will be of masculine appearance in some respects.

Masculine planets. v. PLANETS.

Masculine Signs. v. SIGNS, MASCULINE AND FEMININE.

Maternal Signs. v. SIGNS.

Matutine, Matutinal. Said of Moon, Mercury and Venus when they appear in the morning. When a star or planet rises before the Sun in the morning, it is called matutine until it reaches its first station (Q.V.), where it becomes Retrograde (Q.V.). The Moon is matutine until it passes its first Dichotome. v. ORIENTALITY.

Maya. Illusion. An oriental concept that nothing is what it appears to be: that a man, for example, who exhibits an unruly disposition is only suffering the penalty for deeds committed in a previous incarnation, because of which his spirit is destined in this incarnation to life in a body which fights against itself: hence is entitled to sympathy rather than censure. It is the oriental approach to what to the Occidental is philosophy. The astrological concept is not so much a matter of Karma as of the Omar picture of the vase marred because the potter's hand slipped: the accident of an unfavorable birth moment that subjects the native to a conflict of forces, and entitles him to forbearance in case he is unable to summon to his aid spiritual strength sufficient to resolve the conflict.

Mean Motion. The average motion of any body within a given period. The mean motion of a planet is based on the presumption that it moves in a circle at a uniform rate about the Sun. Actually the planets move in elliptical orbits, in portions of which this motion is accelerated and retarded in ratio to their distance from the gravitational center. The mean daily motions of the planets are:

...Pluto........0° 0' 14".......Jupiter........0° 4'59"
...Neptune......0° 0' 24".......Mars..........0° 31' 0"
...Uranus.......0° 0' 42".......Venus.........1° 36' 0"
...Saturn.......0° 2' 1".......Mercury........4° 6' 0"
...The Moon..(around the Earth).............13° 10'35"
...The Earth.(around the Sun)................0° 59' 8"

The Heliocentric mean motions of the planets differ from their geocentric motions.

Mean Time. A consequence of the ellipticity of the Earth's track is that its orbital motion is faster near perihelion than near aphelion. This has the effect of making the day longer in Winter than in Summer: not the day from sunrise to sunset, but from one noon to the next. We keep our clocks from going haywire by the employment of the device known as mean time, thereby measuring time not by the true Sun, as does the sundial, but by a fictitious mean Sun which moves uniformly along the celestial equator, not along the ecliptic.

Measure of Time. Said of the method of calculating the time of an event from an Arc of Direction. The Ptolemy unit is 1° of R.A. for each year of life. Later authorities divided the arc by the diurnal increment of R.A. made by the Sun on the day of birth. Others employ a mean arc of 1° of RA., as the equivalent of the mean motion of the Sun, thus adjusting the circle of 360 degrees to a year of 365¼ days. A method employed by Worsdale, Simmonite, Morrison and others, consists of adding the Arc of Direction to the Sun's R.A. at birth, taking as years the number of days after birth at which the Sun reaches this Advanced R.A. The method employed by Naibod (Q.V.) is to determine the arc in R.A., and consider each degree equal to 1 year, 5 days, 8 hours - a minute equal to 6 days, 4 hours. V. DIRECTIONS.

Medical Astrology. That branch of Astrology which has to do with the planetary causes of disease.

Medium Coeli. V. MID-HEAVEN.

Mediumship. The psychic, intuitive or telepathic faculty. Presumably attributed to the positions and aspects of Neptune at birth.

Medusa's Head. Medusa, the mental and beautiful one of the three Gorgon sisters, who in one of Minerva's temples became the mother by Neptune of Chrysador and Pegasus; therefore Minerva changed her hair into hissing serpents, whereby everyone who looked at her was changed into stone. She was later decapitated by Perseus. It is represented by Algol, in the constellation Persus. Its diameter is 1,060,000 miles, of the density of cork. To the Hebrews it was Lilith, a nocturnal vampire - the serpent or "other woman" in the Garden of Eden.

Meridian. A circle of longitude passing from the South point of the horizon, through the zenith to the North point of the horizon. It coincides with geographical longitude - a great circle crossing the equator and passing through the poles. Every point on the Earth's surface has its own meridian or circle of longitude, which passes through its zenith. The point on the heavens where the projection of this circle intersects the ecliptic, marks the midheaven (MC) or the cusp of the Tenth House. The Sun's place at noon is on this meridian, and the distance from this point to the horizon in either direction constitutes the Sun's semi-diurnal arc. The same is true of any celestial body. (V. SEMI-ARC.) The term is loosely and incorrectly applied to the midheaven, to the degree of the zodiac thereon, and even to the whole of the X' house. On an astrological map, it is approximated in the vertical line passing from the cusp of the Tenth House, at the top of the map, to the cusp of the Fourth House, at the bottom.

Meridian Distance. The distance between a given point along the celestial equator and the Midheaven or Imum Coeli; usually expressed in hours and minutes.

Meridional. Southerly.

Mesmerism. A word derived from Mesmer, the eighteenth-century physician who applied animal magnetism or psychic influences in the treatment of disease. It has largely been superseded by Hypnotism, with which it is approximately identical.

Metonic Cycle. The discovery about 432 B.C. by Meton, an Athenian astronomer, of the Moon's period of 19 years, at the end of which the New Moon occurs on the same day of the year. Upon this he based certain corrections of the lunar calendar. He figured the 19-year cyclic of 235 lunations to consist of 6,939d, 16.5h. This he divided into 125 full months of 30 days each, and 110 deficient months of 29 days each. (V. LUNAR MONTH.) the 235 full months, of 30 days each, totalled 7,050 days; hence it became necessary to suppress 110 days or 1 in 64. Therefore the month which contained the 64th day became a deficient month. As the true Lunation period is 6,939d, 14.5h, his calculations showed a deviation of only two hours. The average date on which a Lunation will occur can be determined from the following table correlating Sun positions with the calendar:

METONIC CYCLE

Golden Number	Capric 11°-30°	Aqua	Pisc	Aries	Taur	Gemin	Canc	Leo	Virgo	Libra	Scor	Sagit	Capric 1°-11°
1	11	11	11	10	9	7	5	3	1-29	29	29	29	29
2	29	30	29	28	17	25	23	22	19	18	1	18	18
3	18	18	18	18	16	15	14	12	10	8	7	7	7
4	7	7	7	7	6	5	3	1-29	28	26	26	25	26
5	26	25	26	24	24	22	20	19	17	16	15	15	15
6	15	15	15	14	13	12	9	8	6	5	5	5	4
7	4	4	4	3	3	1-29	27	26	24	24	23	23	24
8	24	23	23	22	20	19	17	15	14	12	12	12	12
9	12	12	12	12	10	9	7	4	3	1	1	0	1
10	1	1	1	1	0-28	26	25	22	21	20	20	19	20
11	20	20	20	19	18	17	15	13	10	9	9	8	9
12	8	9	9	8	8	6	4	3	0-29	27	27	27	28
13	28	27	27	26	25	23	22	20	19	17	17	16	16
14	16	17	16	16	15	14	11	10	8	7	6	6	6
15	6	5	5	5	4	3	1-29	27	25	25	24	24	24
16	24	24	24	23	21	20	19	17	16	15	14	13	14
17	14	13	13	12	11	10	8	6	5	3	3	3	3
18	3	3	2	2	1-28	7	25	24	22	22	22	22	21
19	21	22	21	21	19	18	15	13	12	11	10	11	11

To ascertain the Golden number (Q.V.) of any year, add 1 and divide by 19: the remainder is the Golden number. If there is no remainder, the number is 19.

Metonic Return. Said of the recurrence of an eclipse on a given degree on the same date some 19 years later. This should not be confused with the Saros Cycle (Q.V.).

Micron. A millionth part of a metre. Employed in measuring the wave length of light. MILLIMICRON. A thousandth part of a micron.

Midheaven. Variously called Medium Coeli (M.C.), Southern angle, South point, and cusp of the Tenth House. Also improperly called the Zenith. (v. CELESTIAL SPHERE.) More precisely, it is applicable to the South point of the Map, and what it indicates is dependent on the manner of interpretation employed. Sometimes loosely applied to the whole of the Tenth House.

Midpoint. An unoccupied aspected degree between and equidistant from two other planets, resulting in a symmetrical grouping, sometimes called a planetary picture. Such configurations are deemed important by some authorities, although there is some difference of opinion as to the width of orbs across which there can result a "transference of light" through the planet which aspects the Midpoint.

Milky Way. The galaxy of stars of which the Sun is a member, and which pursue an orbit around a Galactic Center located in the direction of 0° Capricorn. The stars of this Galaxy occupy a band that extends in width from 21° Germini to 5° Leo, and that stretches across the sky to from 7° Sagittarius to 16° Capricorn. According to recent astronomical opinion the Milky Way Galaxy resembles a huge wheel with a large hub, 99 per cent of its stars contained within a diameter of 100,000 light-years and a thickness of 10,000 light-years - with the Earth about 30,000 light-years distant from the center.

Minute. The sixtieth part of an hour in time, marked **1m**; or the sixtieth part of a degree in arc, marked **1'**.

Moderators. A term applied by Placidus and Ptolemy to the Significators: Sun, Moon, Ascendant, Midheaven and Fortuna. It implied that aspects from the Significators moderate or condition the influences of the planets, producing a different "mode of motion" in the rays reflected. The term has largely passed into disuse.

Modus Rationalis. A term applied by Regiomontanus to his method of locating the cusps of the intermediate Houses - those which lie between the angular Houses of a Figure - by dividing the Ecliptic by the Equator instead of the semi-arc. Its division into twelve equal parts was accomplished by circles, the cusps located where the circles cut the plane of the Ecliptic. The method has been superceded by one employing Oblique Ascension under the Poles of the Houses for all but the 4th and 10th cusps. v. HOUSE DIVISION.

Moisture. Said to increase when planets are matutine, when the Moon is in her First Quarter, during the winter, and by night.

Monad. In occult terminology, it signifies Nature's pattern for each species, with special reference to differences between contrasting characteristics. In Greek philosophy, a unit; individual; atom. According to Giordano Bruno, a miscroscopic embodiment of the Divine essence which pervades and constitutes the universe.

Month. One of the twelve major subdivisions of the year. The names of the months are of great antiquity, and although they have in more than one sense lost their original significance, they continue to survive as a part of our common language. Originally they were intended to represent the twelve arcs of the Earth's annual revolution in orbit about the Sun, and thus were comparable to the arcs we now know as the Astrological or Astronomical Signs of the Zodiac. The original significance of the months is as follows:

JANUARY. A month of 31 days, the first in the Julian and Gregorian calendars. It was named after Janus, the ancient Roman deity who presided over gates and doors, hence all beginnings. He was represented with two faces, turned in opposite directions, to indicate how every ending is also a beginning. He was propitiated at the beginning of every important undertaking. Both A. B. Cook and J. G. Frazer identify Janus as Jupiter, and indicate that he looked both ways to give better protection to the house over which he stood guard. January 1st was made the beginning of the year in England with the statutory adoption of the Gregorian calendar in 1752, before which date the year began on March 25. Nevertheless, it was in the Temple of Janus that Saturn sought refuge in times of peace.

February. A month of 28 days, except when increased by one intercalary day on bissextile or leap years; the second month of the Julian and Gregorian calendars. It was not contained in the Romulian calendar, and was said to have been introduced in to the Roman calendar by Numa in 713 B.C., as the eleventh month. January and February were transposed by the decemvirs in 452 B.C., making it the twelfth month. The name was derived from Februare, to purify, from which came Februa, the festival of expiation, celebrated at the end of the month, during which the women were "purified" by the priests. By the Anglo-Saxons it was caged Sprout - Kale, as the cabbage-sprouting season. The two martyred Saints Valentine who died on the same day in the reign of Claudius, determined February 14th as St. Valentine's day, but the modern celebration of it as a lover's festival appears to be purely accidental.

MARCH. A month of 31 days, the third in the Julian and Gregorian calendars, the first in the Roman calendar. It was named in honor of Mars, god of war, the reputed father of Romulus, who was traditionally believed to have compiled the first calendar. However, Ovid says the month existed before the time of Romulus. It was the beginning of the legal year in France until 1564, when by decree Charles IX made the year begin in January. Scotland followed this example in 1599, but in England it continued to begin in March until the 18th century. At that time the first three days, the "blind" or "borrowed" days, were deemed so unlucky that no English or Scottish farmer would sow seed on these days.

APRIL. A month of 30 days, the fourth month of the Julian and Gregorian calendars; the second in the Roman calendar. Its etymology is commonly traced to the Latin aperire, "to open," as the season when the blossoms open their petals. The Roman months, however, were named after divinities, and as April was sacred to Venus and the Festum Veneris et Fortunae Virilis was celebrated on the first day, it is possible the month was originally Aphrilis, from Aphrodite - the Greek name for Venus. To the Anglo-Saxon it was the month of Easter, the pagan Saxon goddess of Spring, from which name is derived the modern Easter. April Fools' day as we know it seems to have originated at the time of the adoption of the Gregorian calendar. Prior thereto the celebration of the New Year began on March 25th, and ended April 1st with the general distribution of gifts. With the change of the New Year to January 1st, those who objected thereto made ostentatious presentations of mock gifts to those who under the influence of the church had advocated the adoption of the Gregorian reform.

MAY. A month of 31 days, the fifth of the Julian and Gregorian calendars, the third of the Roman calendar. It is said to have been named in honor of the goddess Maia, daughter of Atlas and mother of Mercury and Jupiter, to whom sacrifices were offered on the first day of this month. Probably, however, it was named in honor of the majors of the government - the senators; June honoring the juniors, or members of the lower house. The month was regarded a unlucky for marriages, owing to the celebration of the Lemuria, the festival of the unhappy dead, held on the 9th, 11th, and 13th. This is reflected in a proverb of unidentified origin - "Marry in May, you'll rue the day." May day, a people's holiday on which to go "a-Maying" in the woods, goes back to medieval and Tudor England. A huge maypole of cedar erected under the supervision of James II was taken down in 1717, and used by Sir Isaac Newton, as part of the support of a large telescope presented to the Royal Society by a French astronomer.

JUNE. A month of 30 days, the sixth in the Julian and Gregorian calendars, the fourth in the Roman calendar. Ovid makes Juno state that the month was named in her honor, but elsewhere he contradicts this origin. Probably June was named after the junior assemblage of the government, and May after the senior assemblage of the Senate. Prior to the Julian reform of the calendar it had 29 days. To the Anglo-Saxons it was the "dry" month.

JULY. A month of 31 days, the seventh in the Julian and Gregorian calendars, the fifth in the Roman calendar. Originally called Quintilius, it was renamed by Mark Antony in honor of Julius Caesar, who was born in that month. Among the Anglo-Saxons it was known as "hay month," as the meadows were then in bloom. Dog days begin on July 30th, and St. Swithin's Day falls on July 15th.

AUGUST. A month of 31 days, the eighth in the Julian and Gregorian calendars, the sixth in the Roman calendar. Originally known as Sextilis, it was renamed by direction of Augustus Caesar, who refusing to be honored by a month of smaller size than that which in honor of Julius Caesar had been named July, ordered it increased to 31 days, taking the extra day from February. In Gallia and remote parts of the Empire it was known as Aust, meaning harvest.

SEPTEMBER. A month of 30 days, the ninth in the Julian and Gregorian calendars, the seventh in the Roman calendar. The Ludi Magni, in honor of Jupiter, Juno and Minerva, was celebrated by the Romans on September 4th. In Charlemagne's calendar it was called the "harvest month," corresponding partly to the Fructidor and partly to the Vendemiaire of the First French Republic. The Anglo-Saxons called it the gerstmonath, or barley month, as the crop was usually harvested in this month. In Switzerland it is still known as the Herbstmonat.

OCTOBER. A month of 31 days, the tenth in the Julian and Gregorian calendars, the eighth in the Roman calendar. The Equiria, when the Equus October was sacrificed to Mars in the Campus Martius, was celebrated on October 15th. Successive attempts were made to rename it Germanicus, Antoninus, Tacitus and Herculeus, but all failed, as did the effort of the Roman Senate to christen it Faustinus in honor of Faustina, wife of Antoninus. The Slavs called it "yellow month" from the fading leaves. To the Anglo-Saxons it was known as the Winter-fylleth (moon), since Winter was supposed to begin with the October Full Moon.

NOVEMBER. A month of 30 days, the eleventh in the Julian and Gregorian calendars, the ninth in the Roman calendar. The Roman winter began on November 11th, and was celebrated on the 13th by a sacred banquet in honor of Jupiter, the Epulum Jovis. The proposal of the Senate to name it Tiberius, was vetoed by the Emperor, with a question as to what they would propose when it came to the thirteenth Caesar. All Saints Day is the 1st, AH Souls Day, the 2nd, and St. Andrew's Day, the 30th.

DECEMBER. (L. DECEM, ten). A month of 31 days, the twelfth in the Julian and Gregorian calendars, the tenth in the Roman calendar. The Saturnalia, or feast of Saturn, was celebrated in this month. During the reign of Commodus it was temporarily styled Amazonius, in honor of his mistress whose portrait he had had painted as an Amazon. The Saxons called it the Winter month; also the Holy month, from the fact that Christmas fell within it.

MONTH. SIDEREAL, 27.3217 d.; SYNODICAL, 29.5306 d.

Motion. According to Newton's law of motion, all bodies traveling in elliptical orbits move faster at certain portions of their orbits, and slower in others. It is therefore important to observe whether the travel between two successive days is greater or less than their mean motion. In erecting a Figure for a specified hour it is necessary to reduce this to hourly motion, to determine the exact position occupied by the faster-moving bodies.

TO REDUCE DAILY MOTION TO HOURLY MOTION Since 1° or 60 m., divided by 24 h. equals 2½; therefore: degrees per day X 2½ = minutes per hour; and minutes per day X 2½ = seconds per hour. Thus: Moon's travel of 14° p. d. X 2½ = 35' p. h.; and 24' less p. d. = 1' less p. h., or 34' p. h.; Mercury's travel of 2° 7' p. d. (computed as 2° X 2.5 = 5'; and 7' X 2.5 = 17.5") gives a rate of 5' 17.5" p. h.

Movable Signs. Leading or Cardinal Signs. V. SIGNS.

Mundane Aspects. Those formed by planets occupying cusps, whereby it can be said that from the 10th to the 12th cusps is a Mundane sextile, though it may be as little as 50° or as much as 80°. V. ASPECTS.

Mundane Astrology. Mundane Interpretations. An interpretation of Astrology in terms of world trends, the destinies of nations and of large groups of individuals, based on an analysis of the effects of Equinoxes, Solstices, New Moons, Eclipses, planetary conjunctions, and similar celestial phenomena; as distinguished from Natal Astrology, specifically applicable to an individual birth horoscope.

Mundane Directions, or Directions in Mundo. These are based solely upon the axial rotation of the Earth in relation to the circle of observation whereby planets arc carried clockwise through the Houses of the Figure, from east to west, forming aspects to the Ascendant, Midheaven, Sun and Moon. Aspects formed by the opposite or Converse Motion are also employed. The use of spherical trigonometry and of logarithms is necessary to reliable use of this so-called Primary System of Directing. Knowledge of the exact place, hour and minute is also essential.

Mundane Parallel, or Parallel in Mundo. A progressed position in which a Significator and a Promittor occupy points on opposite sides and equidistant to any of the four Angles of the geocentric Figure: Ascendant, Midheaven, Descendant, or Imum Coeli. v. PARALLEL.

Music of the Spheres. A phrase utilized by Pythagoras, an early Greek mathematician and astronomer who was the first to discover a mathematical relationship in the frequencies of the various tones of the musical scale. In postulating the planets' orbits as bearing a similar relationship based upon the distance from the center, he characterized their interrelated orbits as "the harmony of the spheres."

Mutable Signs. The Common Signs: Gemini, Virgo, Sagittarius, and Pisces. v. SIGNS.

Mute Signs. Cancer, Scorpio and Pisces; so named by the Arabians because symbolized by dumb creatures that emit no sounds. Arabian astrologers deemed that Mercury afflicted in these signs was liable to indicate dumbness, especially when afflicted by Saturn. v. SIGNS.

Mutilated Degrees. Certain degrees are said by some authorities to indicate lameness if rising at birth, or if the Moon or the Ruler of the Ascendant is posited therein. These are:

6°-10° .... Taurus
9°-15° .... Cancer
18°-25° .... Leo
18°-19° .... Scorpio
1°,7°, 8°,18°,19° .... Sagittarius
26°-29° .... Capricorn
18°-19° .... Aquarius

Other authorities deem that if their influences exist it must be due to the presence of fixed stars in these arcs, in which event the position must be advanced by 1° every 70 years.

Mutual Application. This results when the applying body is in direct motion, and the body to which it applies is in retrograde motion. In other words, each is in motion towards the other.

Mutual Reception. Said of two planets mutually posited in each other's essential dignities. For example, with Jupiter in Aries, the Sun's place of exaltation; and the Sun in Cancer, Jupiter's place of exaltation: Sun and Jupiter are said to be in mutual reception. This is accounted a configuration of singular amity and agreement. By some authorities, the term is confined to the placement of the two planets, each in a house or sign ruled by the other.

Nadir. The lowest point below the Earth, or opposite point to the Zenith. It should not be confused with the Imum Coeli. v. CELESTIAL SPHERE.

Naibod's Table of Times. (For calculating an arc of direction.) Determine the Right Ascension of the bodies and subtract, to yield the length of the arc in degrees and minutes. Then reduce to time, counting each degree equal to 1y 5d 8h, and each minute of arc equal to 6d 4h. v. DIRECTIONS.

Natal Astrology. Genethliacal Astrology. The department of Astrology which deals with nativities - the influence of planets and signs upon the life and character of the individual.

Native. The subject of a Celestial Figure.

Nativity. The Birth moment. (1) The instant wherein the native first inhales, thereby commencing a process of blood conditioning that up to that moment had been accomplished through the receptivities of another. During the first days of life, in accordance with the law of adaptability, there ensues a growth of channels of receptivity to cosmic energy which results in a life-pattern of cosmic stimulation. (2) A Figure, or Horoscope, cast for a date, moment and place of birth, as distinguished from an Electional or Horary Figure.

Natural Day. v. DAY.

Nebo. "The Proclaimer," the Chaldean god which compares to Mercury. He was known as the god of wisdom and learning. There is evidence that the priestly school of Nebo had acquired a commanding position and widespread fame as astrologers, before Babylon rose to political importance.

Nebuchadnezzar, Temple of. A famous temple at Barsippa, unearthed in modern times. A veritable color chart of astrological symbols. Like many others it was built in seven stages, each marked by a different hue. The lowest stage was black and symbolized Saturn; the second, orange (the hue of sandalwood), symbolized Jupiter; the third, red, Mars; the fourth, yellow, the Sun; the fifth, green, Venus; the sixth, blue, Mercury; and the seventh, white or silver, symbolized the Moon.

Nebulae. Star clusters in which the light of the individual stars, because of their distance, merge to give the impression of a cloud with a more or less well-defined center. Great numbers of them are found in the heavens, and when one of them is rising at birth, or is in conjunction with the Moon, it is said to produce blindness or other ocular defect.

The principal nebulae noted in Astrology are: Praesepe, The Hyades, The Pleiades in 29° Taurus-Scorpio; the Aselli in 61, Leo-Aquarius; and Aldebaran-Antares in 8° Gemini-Sagittarius. Ptolemy refers to the "cloudy spot of Cancer, the Pleiades of Taurus, the Arrow-head of Sagittarius, the sting of Scorpio, the parts about the mane of Leo, and the urn of Aquarius" in reference to blindness. The Ascendant or Moon in any of these positions and afflicted by Mars indicates blindness from an accident or by violence; afflicted by Saturn, by a natural defect, such as the inhibiting or decay of the optic nerve, cataract, glaucoma, or obstructing growths.

Negative Sign. An even-numbered sign. v. SIGN.

Neomenium. The new Moon. *Neomenia.* The festival of the new Moon.

Neptune. v. PLANETS.

New Year's Day. v. CALENDAR.

Night Houses. v. HOUSES.

Ninib. Chaldean equivalent of Saturn.

Nodes, Moon's. Variously called the Ascending and Descending Nodes, the North and South Nodes, Caput Draconis or the Dragon's Head, Cauda Draconis, the Katababazon, or the Dragon's Tail. The Nodes regress about 3° of arc per diem. There is much argument as to whether any intrinsic influences repose in the Nodes comparable to the radiation emitted by reflection of a planet. In all probability the ancients read more from a Celestial Figure by virtue of a greater comprehension of the astronomical mechanics it represents, than do most moderns. The position of the Node can show whether there was an eclipse condition shortly before or after birth, whether a planet near the Node would shortly be accented by the Moon's transit, or that of the Sun, and similar and sundry factors which the modern astrologer can trace from the ephemeris but often does not. The Nodes of themselves merely point to places where something may happen at such and such a time - which of itself is no small matter. Things happen because of the time, the place and the planet, and the Node is often the middle factor in that formula (v. MOON.)

In 18 years and 10 or 11 days the Node regresses 349 degrees, hence in that period at a point 11 degrees in advance, an eclipse or a series of eclipses recurs under similar conditions. Astronomers calculate eclipses by means of the Saros Cycle rather than by the use of the ephemeris.

Placement of the Ascending Node oriental of the Line of Advantage is deemed preferable, as stimulating, among other things, increased stature. The Line of advantage joins the third decans of the Third and Ninth Houses.

The position of the Sun on the North Node in the Nativity of H. P. Blavatsky is supposed to have profoundly influenced her life. It might well be for it indicates a prenatal solar eclipse at that point only a matter of days before her birth. The ancients held that the Moon's North Node partook of the nature of Venus and Jupiter, while the South Node partook of the nature of Mars and Saturn. Probably more helpful would be the observation that a planet in close conjunction to the North Node at birth would bring honors or riches; at the South Node, poverty and afflictions and a cruel or usurious nature - according to the character of the planet so placed, as modified by the Houses thus tenanted. It is doubtless also of significance in connection with transit and progressions, particularly those of the Moon, only this would appear to involve the regressed position of the Node at the date for which the transit or progression is computed.

Nodes of the Planets. The points at which the orbits of the planets intersect the ecliptic, because of the inclination of their planes to the plane of the Earth's orbit.

One authority states that a lunation or eclipse on the South Node of a planet tends to release a destructive force of the nature of the planet involved. For example, conditions centering around Saturn's South Node may indicate a drought following an unusually hard winter.

Nomes. Each Nome, or province, of ancient Egypt had its own god or totem, its own capital, frontiers and coat-of-arms. Hence the Nomes were either an ancient equivalent of our later systems of geographical Ruler ships, or an older and better term for what are now termed Houses, as indicating two-hour arcs of ascension.

North Point. The Immum Coeli, or cusp of the Fourth House; placed at the bottom of the map.

Northern Signs. The Commanding Signs, Aries to Virgo, pursuing the order of the Sign. V. SIGNS.

Nova. Literally, a new star. Actually a nova is an old star which from an unknown cause appears to have exploded with cataclysmic violence. The first nova of record appeared suddenly on November 11, 1572, in the Constellation Cassiopeia, in the third decanate of Pisces - known as the decanate of Vicissitudes. It was an ancient belief that from the constellation in which any unusual phenomenon appeared could be judged the department of life that would be most affected. This nova was discovered by Tycho Brahe. On the previous August 24th, the massacre of Bartholomew in Paris with the King's sanction incited the Huguenots to a resort to arms, in the belief that it was a messenger of hope sent from heaven. They made a successful defense of La Rochelle, and in consequence were granted a measure of tolerance. Two years later Henry of Navarre escaped from Paris to become their leader, and thus began a new life for them.

Nova Hercules 1934 was the 79th nova since the one discovered by Tycho Brahe, few of which have been spectacular. The three notable novae during the present century were:

February 1901, in Perseus, in the third or Propaganda decanate of Aries. It was the year of the Pan-American Exposition, in Buffalo, in which Northern Pacific stock touched 1000.

June 1918, in Aquila, in the second or Exploration decanate of Sagittarius. It was the year in which an American Expeditionary Force on foreign soil turned the tide of World War I.

December 1934, in Hercules, in Experience decanate of Virgo, the sign ruling labor, and connotated with the Twelve Labors of Hercules. It increased in brilliance from fourteenth magnitude on November 14th, to first magnitude on December 22nd.

Obeying Signs. V. SIGNS.

Oblique Ascendant. V. ASCENSIONAL DIFFERENCE.

Oblique Ascension. (O.A.) As it rises, a star or planet, not on the equator, forms an angle with that part of the equator which is rising at the same time. This is called its Ascensional difference. (A.D.) This A.D.

ADDED to the R.A. if it have S. declination, and SUBTRACTED therefrom if it have N. declination, gives its Oblique Ascension. In the Southern hemisphere, reverse; add, if N.; subtract, if S.

The equator is always at right angles to a line between the North and South Poles. Any meridian circle can be considered as the horizon of a place on the equator 90 degrees distant from that meridian - hence, from that point such meridian can be called the horizon of the pole.

At either pole a planet on any parallel of declination moves along an arc parallel to the equator, to the horizon of the pole. It has neither ascension nor descension, but remains, day and night, above or below the horizon, according as it is in North or South declination. Viewed from a place on the equator, a star will by the axial rotation of the Earth, be carried along an arc parallel to the equator: hence it rises and sets at right angles to the horizon of that place. All places in latitudes north and south of the equator, have a prime vertical that cuts the equator at an angle equal to the latitude of the place; and the horizon cuts the equator at an angle equal to the complement of the latitude. Stars and planets rise and set obliquely, since they follow arcs parallel to the equator - to which the horizon is oblique. The semi-arc of a body on the equator is always 90 degrees, or 6 hours; the whole arc is always 180 degrees or 12 hours. On the equator days and nights are equal, and the semi-arcs of all bodies are equal; but in latitudes north or south of the equator the arcs above and below the horizon are unequal, although together these make 180 degrees or 12 hours. The difference between 90 degrees and the diurnal or nocturnal semi-arc of a body is thus its Ascensional Difference; and its Right Ascension, plus or minus this Ascensional Difference, is its Oblique Ascension.

Oblique Descension. The complement of Oblique Ascension: 180 degrees, minus the Oblique Ascension, equals the Oblique Descension.

Oblique Sphere. Any sphere that is not in the same vertical as the poles of the Earth. All circles parallel to the equator are oblique to the horizon - caused by the depression of the pole of the place from the Pole of the Earth. All places located between the poles and the equator are in an oblique sphere.

Occidental or Oriental. These terms have various meanings, when differently applied, as: (1) The Moon is oriental of the Sun when it is increasing in light, from the lunation to the full; occidental of the Sun, when decreasing in light. (2) A planet is said to be oriental of the Sun when it rises and sets before the Sun; occidental of the Sun, when it rises and sets after the Sun. Planets are said to be stronger when oriental of the Sun and occidental of the Moon. (3) Applied to the Sun, a special significance is involved in that when the Sun is setting in one hemisphere it is rising in the other. Therefore the Sun is said to be oriental in Houses 12, 11, 10, 6, 5, or 4; and occidental in the opposite Houses. Thus the oriental Houses are those which have passed the horizon and are culminating toward the meridian; the occidental Houses, those which have passed the meridian and are moving toward the horizon. Some authorities speak of the Eastern Houses, the entire eastern half of the Figure, as the oriental Houses; the entire Western half, as the occidental Houses. This practice only introduces confusion and should be discouraged. If one must use the term, it should always be qualified; either as "in an oriental House" or "oriental of the Sun." The same applies to Occidental. v. ORIENTALITY.

Occultation. When a planet or star is hidden or eclipsed by another body, particularly by the Moon, there results what is termed an occultation.

Occursions. Celestial occurrences; such as, ingresses, formation of aspects, and conjunctions.

Occursor. A term applied by Ptolemy to the planet which moves to produce an occursion. Now generally superseded by Promittor.

Old Style. v. CALENDAR.

Opposition. v. ASPECTS.

Omniverse. A technical article applied the word to all creation in all space, as distinguished from "universe," designating all creation in our solar system. As the solar system is entirely under the domination of the Milky Way galaxy of which it is a unit, the term universe should embrace the whole of the galaxy, and omniverse the galaxy of galaxies that embraces all known and unknown stars and star-clusters.

Orbit. The path described by a heavenly body in its revolution around a center of attraction. Since the attracting mass is also in motion, the orbit must necessarily be an ellipse. The position of the center of the attracting mass is the FOCUS of the ellipse. The line from the focus to any point of the orbit is the radius vector. If the plane of the orbit intersects any other plane, the two points of intersection are the nodes. The nearest point to the center is the peri-center, or lower apsis (the smallest-distance); the most distant point, the apocenter, or higher apsis. As indicating the particular attracting center involved, the pericenter becomes perihelion (HELIO, the Sun) to a body revolving around the Sun; and perigee (GEO, the Earth), around the Earth. Thus, according to Kepler's law that "the radius vector sweeps over equal areas (arcs) in equal times," as the body approaches the pericenter, its motion is accelerated; as it recedes, the motion is retarded. These points are collectively termed APSIDES: the diameter running through the Line of Apses. APHELION. The point at which any planet, including the Earth, is at its greatest distance from the Sun, the apo-center of its orbit. PERIHELION. At the closest point to the Sun. APOGEE. Said of the Moon, when at its greatest distance from the Earth. PERIGEE. At the closest point to the Earth.

The so-called six Elements of an orbit are: eccentricity; mean radius vector; inclination of its orbit plane to that of the Ecliptic; longitude of its ascending node; period of revolution; and time of passage across a given point, such as perihelion.

Orbital revolution. The annual motion of the Earth in an elliptical orbit round the Sun. Applicable also to the motion of any celestial body which pursues an orbit around any other body.

Oriental. v. OCCIDENTAL.

Orbs. The space within which an aspect is judged to be effective. The term is employed to describe the arc between the point at which a platic, or wide aspect, is deemed strong enough to be operative, and the point of culmination of a partile or exact aspect. Most authorities agree that orbs should vary with each planet and aspect, and that a larger orb should be allowed for an aspect that is forming than for one that is separating. As to exact orbs, there are few points on which authorities differ so radically. For conjunction or opposition some allow as much as 12° when the Sun aspects the Moon, about 10° when either luminary aspects a planet, and 8° for aspects between planets. Observe whether either body is in retrograde motion. The faster moving applies to the slower.

According to Ptolemy, the following orbs apply to the different bodies: Sun 17°, Moon 12°, Mercury 7,, Venus 8°, Mars 7°, Jupiter 12°, Saturn 9°, Uranus 5°, Neptune 5°. When two planets are approaching conjunction or opposition, add their respective orbs and divide by two to ascertain the arc of separation within which the aspect is supposed to be effective. For the trine and square aspects reduce the arc by one-fourth, and for the minor aspects by one-half. In all cases the closer the aspect the more powerful it becomes; also the heavier and slower moving planets are more powerful than the smaller and faster. v. CELESTIAL SPHERE.

Orphic Mysteries. Secret rites of Dionysiac worship, supposedly founded by Orpheus. Therefore, mystic, esoteric, oracular.

Ortive Difference. A term sometimes applied to the difference between the primary and secondary distances, when directing the Sun at its rising or setting. It appears to indicate an effort to accommodate the fact of horizontal parallax. The term is seldom employed by modern authorities.

Pantheism. Deity in nature. A belief that the forces and laws that are manifest in the universe, are God. The Greeks worshipped the faultlessly contoured human body. Modern pantheism more or less deifies electricity as the universal agent that accelerates humanity's progress. Astrology sees God as He who placed the Sun, Moon and planets in the firmament "as signs, and seasons." GEN. 1:14

Pantheon. The five great gods of the Pantheon, and the planets with which they were identified, were: Marduk, Jupiter; Ishtar, Venus; Ninib, Saturn; Nebo, Mercury; and Nergal, Mars.

Parallel. v. ASPECT.

Pars fortunae; Part of Fortune. v. FORTUNA.

Partile. An exact aspect (Q.V.).

Passive. The Sun and Moon are termed passive, in that they take their coloring from the signs in which they are posited, or the planets with which they are in strongest aspect. PASSIVE QUALITIES: Moisture and dryness.

Pavanna. God of the mental plane represented by the Air Signs.

Penumbral Eclipse. Said of eclipses of the Moon, when the Moon approaches closely enough to the Earth's shadow to cause an appreciable diminution of light though it does not directly touch it. These are often termed appulses. They are not generally classed as eclipses, though from their close resemblance to eclipse conditions they often produce effects similar to those attending an actual eclipse. In fact to an observer on the Moon, the Sun would be partially eclipsed by the Earth.

Peregrine. Foreign, alien. Said of a planet posited in a sign where it possesses no essential dignity: where it is neither dignified nor debilitated. It is employed in Horary Astrology, where it is usually reckoned as a debility. In a question of a theft, a peregrine planet in an angle or in the second house, is the thief. However, no planet is reckoned peregrine if it be in mutual reception with another.

Perigee. v. ORBIT.

Perihelion. v. ORBIT.

Periodical Lunation. A Figure cast for the Moon's synodic period, when it returns to the exact degree held at birth. It is often employed for monthly forecasts in a manner similar to the Solar Revolution (Q.V.) for annual forecasts. A true Figure for the Moon's periodical return is difficult to construct, because of the Moon's acceleration from hour to hour.

Phase. (Obs.) A term formerly used by some authorities for Decanate (Q.V.). Originally one-fourth of a Decanate, or 2½ degrees.

Phases. Said of the Moon, but also applicable to Mercury and Venus. The phases are crescent, shortly before and after lunation; half-moon, at the quarter when one side is a straight line and the other is convex; gibbous, shortly after the quarters, when both sides are convex; and Full Moon, when the Earth and the Moon are in opposition. The Lunation is hardly a phase, since the Moon is invisible except for a slight glow: the Earth-shine resulting from light reflected back from the Earth. According to Kepler, as the Moon waxes all things swell with moisture, which is decreased at the Lunation, increased at the Full, and powerfully stressed at the quadratures. Direct light is heating; reflected light, moistening.

Phenomenon. Any item of experience or reality. Kant divides this into: the noumenon, the thing in itself, which is utterly unknowable; and the phenomenon, which is the object of experience. In c,ccult terminology applied to a cosmical chemical, or psychical impulse, experienced by one who is attuned to Nature's more sensitive forces. PHENOMENA, PL., is applied to supplementary data in the ephemeris indicating the exact times of eclipses, of the passing of the Nodes and other points in the orbit, of conjunctions, of the lunar ingresses, and similar details.

Philosophy. Literally, the love for and the pursuit of knowledge, and its application to daily affairs; in actual usage the knowledge of phenomena as explained by and resolved into reasons and causes, sources and forces and the laws applicable thereto. The philosophical attitude is generally associated with a Jupiter accent.

Philosopher's Stone. An imaginary substance through the means of which the ancient alchemists sought to transmit baser metals into gold. Probably an early concept of a catalytic agent. Used in occult terminology to indicate the power by which all life evolves and through which all minds and souls realize a mutual kinship. It signified the highest aspirations and the purest ideologies of altruism.

Phoenon. Greek name for Saturn. (Q.V.)

Pisces. The twelfth sign of the zodiac. V. SIGNS.

Planets, Classifications of.

Androgynous planet. Mercury, because both dry and moist.

BARREN AND FRUITFUL. Barren: Mars, Saturn, Uranus. Fruitful: Sun, Moon, Venus, Jupiter, Neptune. Moderately fruitful: Mercury.

BENEFIC AND MALEFIC. Benefic: Venus and Jupiter, particularly when not afflicted. Some authorities include the Sun, Moon and Mercury, if favorably aspected. Malefic: The infortunes, Mars and Saturn, and by some modern authorities, Uranus and Neptune, whether afflicted or otherwise. Mercury unfavorably aspected is deemed a malefic with respect to money, law and marriage. Modern authorities consider no planet can be truly termed a malefic, except insofar as its vibrations are improperly applied, and is dependent largely upon its aspects for the nature of its operation.

COLD AND HOT. Cold: The Moon and Saturn; also, according to Sepharial, Mercury and Uranus. Hot: Sun, Mars. Warm: Venus, Jupiter, Neptune.

DIURNAL AND NOCTURNAL. The NOCTURNAL planets are the Moon and Venus, because of their feminine qualities, their cool, moist temperaments, and their passive natures as compared to the Sun and Mars. Also applied to those which at birth were below the horizon, and thereby deemed to represent passive qualities. In this case the DIURNAL planets are those which at birth were above the horizon, and are thereby considered to represent the more active influences.

DRY AND MOIST. Dry: Sun, Mars, Saturn. Moist: Moon, Mercury, Jupiter, Uranus; also, according to Sepharial, Neptune. Mercury is both dry and moist.

ELECTRIC AND MAGNETIC. Electric: Sun, Mars, Jupiter. Magnetic: Moon, Mercury, Saturn, Neptune. According to Sepharial both Sun and Moon are magnetic.

MASCULINE AND FEMININE. Masculine: Sun, Mars, Jupiter, Saturn and Uranus. Feminine: Moon, Venus and Neptune. Also, planets are said to take on masculine attributes in masculine signs; when in advance of the Sun; or in the oriental quadrants; and feminine attributes in feminine signs; when following the Sun; when on the opposite side of the horizon from the Sun; or when in the occidental quadrants.

MORNING AND EVENING. Matitutinal and Nocturnal. This refers particularly to Mercury and Venus, as morning and evening "stars," although all the planets become morning and evening stars at some part of the year, though not all of them are visible to the naked eye. (V. RETROGRADE.) It must be observed that a planet which is "behind" the Sun in its orbital motion, rises in diurnal motion "before" the Sun. The counter-clockwise motion of the Earth's surface causes objects as uncovered on the Eastern horizon to appear to move in a clockwise direction. Thus the planet which is behind the Sun in orbit, rises in diurnal motion **BEFORE** the Sun.

SUPERIOR AND INFERIOR. The Major or Superior planets are those that have orbits larger than that of the Earth, and which lie at a greater distance from the Sun. They are: Mars, Jupiter, Saturn, Uranus, Neptune and Pluto. Also called the Ponderous or Ponderable planets. Their motion appears to us to be slower, due to their greater distance from the Sun. Their effects are more enduring than those of the Minor or Inferior planets. The Minor or Inferior planets are those that have orbits smaller than that of the Earth, and which lie closer to the Sun. They are Mercury and Venus.

The order of the planets outward from the Sun is used in a recent work in psychology, in illustration of a memory aid in the form of the sentence: "men very easily make jugs serve usual needy purposes" - the first initial of each word corresponding to that of a planet: Mercury, Venus, Earth, Mars, Jupiter, Saturn, Uranus, Neptune and Pluto. Also the word Vibgyor, for the colors of the Solar spectrum, from the top downwards: Violet, Indigo, Blue, Green, Yellow, Orange, Red.

Planetary Ages of Man. By the ancients the planets were caned chronocrators, or markers of time. It was presumed that different periods of life are ruled by different planets, as:

Planet..................Period.....Ages
Moon - growth...........4 years.....1-4 the mewling babe
Mercury - education....10 years....5-14 the scholar
Venus - emotion.........8 years...15-22 the lover
Sun - virility.........19 years...23-42 the citizen
Mars - ambition........15 years...43-57 the soldier
Jupiter - reflection...12 years...58-69 the judge
Saturn - resignation...30 years...70-99 slippers

These appear to correspond to the Seven Ages of Man, as listed by Shakespeare in "As You Like It," which he apparently took from the Chaldeans. Sepharial suggests a slightly altered set of measures, to include the planets of recent discovery:

...Planet........Duration of Years...Age Period
...Moon.................7...............0-7
...Mercury..............8...............7-15
...Venus................9...............15-24
...Sun..................10..............24-34
...Mars.................11..............35-45
...Jupiter..............12..............46-57
...Saturn...............13..............57-70
...Uranus...............14..............70-84
...Neptune..............15..............84-99

...Pluto................16...............99-115

From the sign position and aspects to the chronocrators, judgment was formed as to the fortunes of the native and his environment during the period ruled by each planet. Thus an afflicted Moon indicates ill health and an adverse environment in infancy; an afflicted Mercury, retarded education; an afflicted Mars, unfortunate in love; and so on.

Planetary Anatomy.

Sun: Operates chiefly through the anterior pituitary gland, to affect the circulation of the blood through the heart and the arteries; the tear ducts; the spinal cord.

MOON: The substance of the body, as distinguished from the vitality flowing through it; the alimentary canal; the child-bearing female organs and functions; the lymphs; the sympathetic nervous system; the cerebellum, the lower ganglia.

MERCURY: The thyroid gland; the brain and the cerebro-spinal nervous system; the sense of sight; the tongue and the organs of speech; the hands as instruments of intelligence.

VENUS: The thymus gland, the sense of touch; the throat, kidneys, and to some extent the generative system. Its influence has been said to operate through the solar plexus, upon the functions of digestion and nutrition. It has an indirect influence upon features, complexion, hair - in so far as those express beauty.

MARS: The cortex, or cortical portion of the adrenal gland; the head, externally; the sense of taste; the breasts and the maternal functions, and in part the generative organs; the motor nerves; the excretory organs; the red corpuscles of the blood.

JUPITER: The posterior pituitary gland; feet, thighs, liver, intestines, blood plasma, muscles, growth; also control of shoulders and arms, in motions that for effectiveness depend upon good timing.

SATURN: The medullary portion of the adrenal gland; the skin and the secretive system; teeth; bones, joints and tendons-particularly the knee and the calf of the leg; the spleen; the organs and sense of hearing.

URANUS: The parathyroid gland; the brain and nervous system; the electric and magnetic emanations.

NEPTUNE: The pineal gland, the organs of extra-sensory perception; intuitive and psychic receptivity.

PLUTO. The Pancreas, and the digestive glands; the enzymes which effect catalytic and hydrolitic transformations essential to proper metabolism.

Planetary Angels. Sun, Michael; Moon, Gabriel; Mercury, Raphael; Venus, Arnad; Mars, Samael; Jupiter, Zadkiel; Saturn, Cassiel; Uranus, Arvath.

Planetary Colors. All authorities, though variously, associate the colors of the spectrum with specific planets. In fact there are almost as many versions as there are authorities. Nevertheless the following planetary associations represent a consensus of opinion:

SUN: Orange, gold, deep yellows.
MOON: White, pearl, opal, light, pale blues; iridescent and silvery hues.
MERCURY: Insofar as Mercury can be said to have any appropriate colors of its own, slate color, spotted mixtures. Most authorities agree that Mercury generally assumes the color of that planet with which it is in nearest aspect.
VENUS: Sky-blue to pale green, lemon yellow; and tints in general as contrasted to colors.
MARS: Red, scarlet, carmine.
JUPITER: Royal purple, violet, some blends of red and indigo, deep blue.
URANUS: Streaked mixtures, checks and plaids like Joseph's coat "of many colors."
NEPTUNE: Lavender, sea-green, mauve, smoke-blue and possibly peculiar shades of gray.
PLUTO. Luminous pigments, in unusual shades containing a large percentage of red.

Planetary Days. Certain planets are by some deemed to have added strength on, or to exercise ruler ship over, certain days of the week, which was considered in the assignment of names to the days. (v. P. HOURS.)

Planetary Flavors. According to Sepharial, these are:

SUN: Sweet, pungent.
MOON: Odorless, insipid.
MERCURY: Cold, mildly astringent.
Venus: Warm, sweet.
MARS: Sharp astringents, acids, pungent odors.
JUPITER: Fragrant, bland.
SATURN: Cold, sour, astringent.
URANUS: Cold, brackish, astringent.
NEPTUNE: Subtile, seductive.
PLUTO. The so-called aromatic flavors, in which solubility releases both taste and aroma.

Planetary Forms. According to Sepharial, these are:

SUN: Circles, full curves, helical scrolls.
MOON: Irregular curves, crooked lines.
MERCURY: Slender curves, short incisive lines.
VENUS: Curved lines, rhythmic scrolls.
MARS: Sharp angles and barbs; fine straight lines.
JUPITER: Full generous curves.
SATURN: Cramped forms, straight short lines, sharp, clear-cut outlines.
URANUS: Mixed forms, broken lines.

NEPTUNE: Curved lines, rhythmic curves, nebulous and chaotic forms.
PLUTO. Heavy straight lines and sharp angles, in complex combinations.

Planetary Hours. Hours. Egyptian astronomy had only seven planets, arranged in this order: Saturn, Jupiter, Mars, Sun, Venus, Mercury, Moon - based seemingly on the apparent velocities of the bodies. In rotation, each hour of the 24-hour day was consecrated to a planet. If Saturn ruled the first hour, it also ruled the 8th, 15th and 22nd. As Jupiter would then rule the 23rd, and Mars the 24th hour, the first hour of the following day would be ruled by the Sun; and so on. The days thus came to be known by the ruler of the first hour, resulting in our present order of the days of the week. Thus the order of the days of the week, which can be harmonized with no observable cosmic plan, are explainable only by a student of astrology. The hatred of the Jews for the Egyptians after their flight from Egypt is said to have caused them to "demote" Saturn from the ruler ship of the first day, by beginning the week on Sunday, making Saturn's day the last day of the week. Probably some symbolical association of the Sun with the Hebrew idea of Jehovah, had something to do with it. The evolution of the English names of the days, from the Latin, through the Saxon, resulted as follows:

```
Norse...Latin............French.......Saxon..........English
........Sol..............Le Dimanche..Sun's day......Sunday
........Luna.............Lundi........Moon's day.....Monday
Tyr.....Martis (Mars)....Mardi........Tiw's day......Tuesday
Wotan...Mercurius........Mercredi.....Woden's day....Wednesday
Thor....Jove (Jupiter)...Jeudi........Thor's day.....Thursday
Freya...Veneris (Venus)..Vendredi.....Frigg's day....Friday
........Saturni..........Samedi.......Seterne's day..Saturday
```

Under this system an hour was not uniformly 60 minutes, except at the equinoxes. It was one-twelfth of the interval between sunrise and sunset, by day; and the reverse, by night. A planet favorably aspected suggests that action be initiated during that planet's hour; or if unfavorably aspected, that one should wait for others to act. Wilson goes to some length in expressing doubt as to the efficacy and logic of this system.

The astonishing thing about this sequence is the placing of the Sun between Venus and Mars, showing that the ancients realized that in speaking of the Sun they were actually making reference to the position of the Earth as determined by the apparent position of the Sun.

Planetary Jewels, or Precious Stones. Here, again, there are almost as many opinions as there are authorities, but the following list expresses a consensus:

SUN: Diamond, Ruby, carbuncle.
MOON: Crystal, pearl, opal, moonstone; all milk-white stones.
MERCURY: Quicksilver, loadstone.
VENUS: Emerald and, possibly, sapphire.
MARS: Bloodstone, flint, malachite, red haematite.
JUPITER: Amethyst, turquoise.

SATURN: Garnet, jet, all black stones.
URANUS: Chalcedony, lapis lazuli, jacinth, amber.
NEPTUNE: Coral, aquamarine, ivory.
PLUTO: Beryl and, presumably, sardonyx; jade, cloissone enamels, ceramics.

It should be realized that all stones, precious and semi-precious, as stones, come more or less directly under Saturn, the overall ruler of all hard minerals. As for many, authorities differ so widely that to settle the question each stone would have to be examined with respect to its mineral components before deciding the planet to which it should rightfully be assigned.

Planetary Metals.

SUN: Gold
MOON: Silver, aluminum
MERCURY: Quicksilver
VENUS: Copper, brass
MARS: Iron, steel.
JUPITER: Tin.
SATURN: Lead.
URANUS: Radium, uranium.
NEPTUNE: Lithium, platinum.
PLUTO: Tungsten, plutonium.

Planetary Motions.

CONVERSE. Said of a progressed or directed motion to a point of aspect, in a clockwise direction or opposite to the order of the Signs. The term is frequently employed in a contradictory manner, in the sense of the reverse of the accustomed motion. In the case of a Secondary Progression that would mean a clockwise motion, since the accustomed motion of a planet in orbit is counter-clockwise. In Primary Directions the apparent motion of the planets and the House-cusps is clockwise, resulting from the counter-clockwise motion of the Earth's periphery. The entire doctrine of converse motion is debatable.

DIRECT The true motion of the planets in the order of the Signs, or counter-clockwise, within the Zodiac: a narrow band that parallels the Earth's path around the Sun. As applied to progressed or directed motion it is the opposite of converse motion. As to transits, it is the opposite of retrograde. (Q.V.)

DIURNAL (by day) A diurnal planet is one that was above the horizon at the time for which the Figure was cast. Such planets are said to be less passive. The DIURNAL ARC of a planet is the time it remains above the Earth, measured either in degrees of Right Ascension, or in Sidereal Time. The opposition arc is the NOCTURNAL ARC. The declination of the body, or its distance from the Equator, is the controlling factor: the greater the declination the higher the body will ascend in the heavens and the longer it will remain above the horizon.

HOURLY. Subtracting a planet's position on one day, as shown in the ephemeris, from its position on the preceding or following day yields its daily motion.

RAPT. RAPTUS, carried away. The apparent diurnal motion of the heavens, in consequence of the Earth's axial rotation; the manner in which the fixed stars and the planetary bodies are caused to make one complete revolution in 24 hours, is termed their Rapt Motion, in accordance with the ancient theory of the Primum Mobile (Q.V.).

RE-DIRECT. Said of the reversal to direct motion following the second station of the retrograde.

RETROGRADE. The apparent motion in the Zodiac of certain planets, as viewed from the Earth during certain portions of the year. (Q.V.)

SLOW OF COURSE: slow in motion. Said of any planet whose travel in 24 hours is less than its mean motion. It is reckoned a debility, especially in horary astrology.

STATIONARY. When a planet appears to have no motion, as when changing from retrograde to direct or the reverse, it is said to be stationary.

STATIONS, IN RETROGRADE. Each planet has two stations, or stationary points: **(1)** the place in its orbit where it becomes stationary before it turns retrograde, abbreviated S.R.; **(2)** when it again becomes stationary preparatory to resuming its direct motion, abbreviated S.D.

SWIFT IN MOTION. Planets that at the moment are moving at a speed in excess of their mean motion, are said to be "swift in motion."

Planetary Objects and Substances.

SUN: Precious metals, diamonds-things valuable and scarce; glistening substances.
MOON: Utensils in common use in the laundry; or in the silversmith's trade. Soft, smooth substances.
MERCURY: Papers connected with money; legal documents; books, pictures, writing materials, anything connected with education and communications. Flowing and veined substances.
VENUS: Jewelry and ornaments; women's wearing apparel; bed linens; polished reflecting substances.
MARS: Steel; cutlery, and anything that is sharp; instruments of war; sparkling substances.
JUPITER: Men's wearing apparel, merchandisable sweets; horses, domestic pets; common and useful substances, cloth, paper.
SATURN: Land, minerals, agriculture and garden implements; heavy materials; dull and heavy substances; dross.
URANUS: Machinery, old coins and antiques, baths, public institutions; everything uncommon and unusual; radioactive and magnetic substances.
NEPTUNE: Poison, liquids, habit-forming drugs; mysterious and unidentifiable substances.
PLUTO. Synthetics, through splitting and recondensing processes; plastics; atomic fission.

Planetary Pathology, or physical ailments. Associated with planetary influences are the ailments affecting the portion of the body represented by the Sign position of the planet - at birth, in transit, or by direction; and by the Signs and Houses ruled by the planet.

SUN: Ailments of heart and upper spinal region; fevers and breaking down of tissues; organic ailments; fainting spells; diseases of the spleen.

MOON: Endocrine imbalance resulting in inflamed glands and defective eyesight; functional ailments and irregularities; allergies; mental instabilities; female disorders; emotional depression that impairs normal functioning; dropsy and excess fluidity; catarrhal infection of the mucous membranes.

In matters of health it is generally the significator of the bodily afflictions of its Sign position, as follows:

Aries, head
Taurus, neck
Gemini, arms
Cancer, chest
Leo, back and heart
Virgo, abdomen
Libra, loins, kidneys
Scorpio, organs of generation
Sagittarius, thighs
Capricorn, knees
Aquarius, legs
Pisces, feet

MERCURY: Nervous disorders or debility from excitement, stress, overwork or worry; headaches; losses of memory; salivation; goitre; impaired respiration and sluggish elimination.

VENUS: Blood impurities that poison the system, resulting in tonsilitis; pustural diseases, as measles or smallpox; sloughing sores and susceptibility to contagion; kidney disease; venereal diseases; poisoning; impaired functioning, resulting from uncontrolled eroticism.

MARS: Infectious, contagious and cruptive diseases; fevers, high blood pressure, internal hemorrhages, inflammations producing sharp pains; burns, scalds; inflammatory conditions requiring surgical treatment; hysterical outbursts producing violent reactions due to high temperatures.

JUPITER: Maladies arising from surfeit; congestion; chronic acidity and hyperfluidity of functional activity; subnormal blood pressure; apoplexy.

SATURN: Inhibited functioning due to fears and morbid conditions; debilities due to accidental falls or subnormal temperatures; depressed vital activity or impaired circulation due to inhibited emotions; rheumatism; melancholia; decayed and abscessed teeth; malnutrition, often from sheer miserliness; skin diseases; atrophy; spinal ailments.

URANUS: Inflammations resulting from deposit of precipitated min- erals; fractures, ruptures, lesions, spasmodic disorders.

NEPTUNE: Oxygen deficiency; glandular imbalance from unexplainable causes; energy depletion and wasting diseases; anaemia; neuroses; catalepsy, often the result of undirected or undisciplined psychic activity; hypochrondriasis; drug addiction.

PLUTO. Ailments resulting from deposits of precipitated mineral products in consequence of chronic acidosis; arthritic and arteriosclerotic afflictions.

Planetary Pattern. A symmetrical arrangement of two or more planets or sensitive points around a common axis. A Planetary Picture as employed in Uranian Astrology, represents the interactivity of two planets, connected through a third planet or sensitive point at or in hard aspect to their midpoint. In figuring a midpoint between, for example, planets at 2" and 28" of the same sign, one does not subtract, and add half the difference to the longitude of the first planet; but adds and halves, thus: (2 + 28) / 2 = 15° - the midpoint. A third planet or sensitive point which forms a hard angle aspect to this midpoint within a 2° orb completes the planetary pattern, and renders interactive the three planets or points. Two planets equidistant from and on opposite sides of the 0° Cancer-Capricorn axis become Antiscions and form a planetary pattern that is interactivated without the addition of a third.planet. Where a third point falls short of an aspect to the midpoint by a certain number of degrees, a fourth planet that is the same number of degrees on the opposite side of the midpoint will complete the sym- metrical arrangement and activate the pattern. A planetary pattern may also be formed between any two planets and a cardinal degree on this formula: A planet at 10° Leo is 130° (4 X 30 + 10) distant from 0° Aries, and one at 5° Taurus is 35° (30 + 5) distant. The sum of these distances (165°) indicates 15° Virgo as the point of activation by a fourth element. To be effective there must participate in the pattern one of the native's "personal" points: Sun, Moon, Ascendant, Midheaven, and the four cardinal points - 0° of Aries, Cancer, Libra and Capricorn.

JONES PATTERNS Another set of pattern classifications for flash appraisal, as advanced by Marc Edmund Jones, consists of the following: **(1)** SPLASH type, in which actual bodies excluding Fortuna and the Moon's Nodes, are scattered around the circle, with no noticeable gaps in the daily rising sequence. **(2)** BUNDLE type, all planets contained within a 120° arc. **(3)** LOCOMOTIVE type, all planets within a 240° arc leaving an unoccupied 120° arc. **(4)** BOWL type, all planets within a 180° arc, leaving one half of the Figure untenanted. **(5)** BUCKET type, approximating the Bowl type, but with one planet in the opposite arc as a bail, thereby transforming the bowl into a bucket. **(6)** SEE SAW type, in which the planets are generally polarized around opposite ends of a diameter, leaving two vacant arcs of from 60° to 90° at opposite sides of the continuity. **(7)** SPLAY type. Strong and sharp aggregations of planets irregularly spaced.

Characteristic qualities of each group, are described as: **(1)** A well-balanced nature with a capacity for universal interest, whose only genius is that of versatility and the seeming ability to find order in apparent confusion. **(2)** Apparent self-gathering of interests and unresponsiveness to universal stimuli. **(3)** A dynamic and practical capacity, which while in a sense, eccentric, lacks extremes of universality or obsession. **(4)** An extreme degree of self-containment. **(5)** An effective capacity for some special activity. **(6)** A consciousness of opposing views in a world of conflict, with success dependent on correct alignment. **(7)** A purposeful individuality, which chooses its outlet of self-expression and refuses to be pigeon-holed.

Planetary Periods, or Cycles.

The mean symbolical periods of the various bodies are the length of time between two successive conjunctions of that body with the Sun at the same geocentric longitude, i.e, falling on the same day of a year. In other words the Sun in its apparent annual revolution forms conjunctions with each of the other bodies as viewed from the Earth, each successive annual conjunction with the same body taking place at an advanced point in the Zodiac. After a time these conjunctions themselves form a cycle of conjunctions, beginning on approximately the same degree of the Zodiac, or days of the year. The length of this cycle with reference to a particular planet constitutes the planetary periods. These are:

MOON: 19 years, the Cycle of Meton (q.v.).
MERCURY: 79 years, with an inconstant mean advance of 1°37' each cycle.
VENUS: 8 years, with an inconstant mean advance of 1°32' each cycle.
MARS: 79 years, with an inconstant mean advance of 1°34' each cycle.
JUPITER: 83 years exact.
SATURN: 59 years, with a mean advance of 1°53'
URANUS: 84 years, with a mean advance of 40'
NEPTUNE: 164 years, 280 days; a mean annual motion of 2°10'54"
PLUTO. 247.7 years, with a mean annual motion that, because of the extreme ellipticity of its orbit, varies from 1° in Pisces through Gemini, to 2.5° in Virgo through Sagittarius.

Ptolemy cites these time-measures as follows: Moon 4y, Mercury 10y, Venus 8y, Sun 19y, Mars 15y, Jupiter 12y, Saturn 30y. Those moderns who use his system add Uranus 90y, Neptune 18oy, Pluto 360y. Lilley alters this, as regards the Moon to 25y, and Mercury to 20y; others assign 27y to Mercury.

By means of these periods one is able to arrive at a rough approximation of a planet's position at a given date in a year for which an ephemeris is unavailable; as follows:

Example: To determine the longitude of Uranus on October 15th, 1672 (new style), add multiples of 84y and subtract the mean advance. To do this in one operation: assume any year in this epoch, say 1902. From this subtract 1672. This gives an interval of 230 years. Divide this by 84; the result, 2 periods and 62 years. Subtract 62 from 1902, which gives the year 1840: two Uranus periods subsequent to the desired date. To illustrate: the longitude of Uranus, as perceived in the ephemeris for 1940, on October 15th, is 17°09' Pisces. The 40' advance, times the two periods, is 1°20'. Subtract this from 17°09' and you have 15°19' Pisces as the longitude of Uranus on October 15th, 1672 (N.S.).

These and additional periods, arranged in tabular form for reference use, are as follows:

PLANET.......REVOLUTIONS..YEARS.....REMAINDER.........OTHER PERIODS IN YEARS

Moon.............254.......19....Cycle of Meton.......8-372-1040*#
Mercury..........318.......79....+1°37'(a)............7-13-33-46-204*
Venus.............13........8....+1°32'(a)............235-243
Mars..............42.......79....+1°34'...............16-32147-205*
Jupiter............7.......83....+0°1'*
Saturn.............2.......59....+1°53'...............206*

* Unusually exact. # Not an eclipse cycle. (a) Inconstant mean advance.

The three outer planets are usually computed by other methods: either (a) the first return, in even years, with a plus or minus correction showing excess over 360 degrees; or (b) the net mean annual motion.

..Planet..........Period....Remainder...Advance*
..Uranus............84y.......+1°4'.....4°17'55"
..Neptune..........164y.......+0°34'....2°11"55"
..Pluto............245y.......-0°29'....1°28'03"

*Mean annual advance, based on mean precession.

Planetary Physiology.

Consideration of the ruling planet, the Ruler of the ascending Decanate and its aspects, assists at arriving at a judgment as to sub-active and hyper-active functioning, as follows:

SUN: Generation of vital force, circulation, physical growth, expansion of areas of sensitivity.
MOON: Impregnation, generation, flow of secretions.
MERCURY: Nerve functions, nerve reflexes, volition, coordination of motivity.
VENUS: Exosmosis, filtration, venereal functions.
MARS: Rapid energy combustion under stress, bodily distribution of metallic elements.
JUPITER: Cell nutrition and development, flesh building, formation of hemoglobin and red corpuscles.
SATURN: Calcification, congestion, conditions affecting tendons, cartilages and articulation of bones.
URANUS: Electro-magnetic forces, growth of long bones.
NEPTUNE: Functioning of telepathic, psychic or occult faculties; formation of white corpuscles.
PLUTO. Balance between the anabolistic and katabolistic phases of metabolism.

Planetary Physiques.

SUN: Powerful, well formed body, with large bones; large face and forehead, clear complexion; hair, light but inclined to baldness; commanding eyes.

MOON: of middle stature, inclined to heaviness; round face, pale complexion; large, soft eyes; short but thick hands and feet; and usually small boned.

MERCURY: Slender body and face; full forehead, long nose, thin lips; slender, expressive hands; dark hair, thin beard, poor com- plexion, penetrating eyes.

VENUS: Short but graceful body; inclined to stoutness in advancing years; round face, dark hair, large and wandering eyes; soft voice and vivacious manner.

MARS: Strong, stocky body, but not overly tall, military deportment; black or red hair; often curly or wiry; sharp, quick eyes; often very ruddy complexion; when angry face is livid.

JUPITER: Large, well-formed body, inclined to become portly in advancing years; wide chest; high forehead; kindly and widely spaced eyes; dark, wavy hair; paternal attitude.

SATURN: Slender, angular body, with large bones - back bends with increasing years; stern features; small, beady eyes; dark, curly hair; indifferent complexion.

URANUS: Slender body, pleasing appearance; irregular but prepossessing features; usually large light eyes, brilliant and keen; some types ascetic in appearance, often giving the impression of being effeminate.

NEPTUNE: Finely organized, slender body; long head, sharp features, often cruel expression; always mysterious; hypnotic eyes; hair retreats from temples.

PLUTO. Medium stature, of rugged and sturdy build, yet with a delicate skin; soft fine hair on the scalp, but little hair elsewhere on the body.

Planetary Psychology.

Planetary influences upon the unfolding psyche, are as follows:

SUN: Individual faculties; consciousness of Ego, the Individuality as distinguished from the Personality. The vital energy that flows from the Sun through the solar system, enabling life to exist and its activities to be pursued; inspiring men to the consciousness of a destiny to be achieved: the sense of purpose that is recognized by MacDougal and the psychologists of the Purposivistic School; ambitious, with good organizing and executive ability. The solar influence is reflected in an impression of power in reserve; an outspoken and worldly-wise counselor; a strong individuality with an urge toward acquisition of power. Emanates an impression of dignity, grandeur, wisdom, authority, will and lofty spirituality. Restless under restraint, it operates more through inspiration than intellect. A strong paternal instinct. Generous, masterful, honest, truthful and creative; vital, forceful, sanguine, dignified. Power, honor, fame, pride, influence. When frustrated may become ostentatious, despotic, ceremonious, and fond of pomp and ritual.

MOON: Higher emotional faculties such as faith, hope and charity, veneration, peace-loving. The instinctive mind, the desire-nature with respect to material things; the external reactions to every-day affairs and to those pertaining to the home and domestic life; moods that fluctuate between the extremes of optimism and pessimism; ideas that are not abstract; ingenuity applicable to concrete purposes and practical ends; a mind that fluctuates and that lacks the ability to concentrate, hence easily influenced; sympathy, not compassion; respect for the old and regard for the young; suavity, kindness; love for animals; strong protective sense, and an inclination to defend those incapable of self-defense; acute maternal instinct not based on sex; modesty, timidity, economy, receptivity, imagination, impressionability, changeableness; fond of travel; personal magnetism; psychic qualities; extra-sensory receptivity; lymphatic, changeful, plastic, wandering, romantic, visionary, frivolous, capricious, fanciful, unstable, procrastinating, lazy.

MERCURY: Concrete mental faculties: perception of size, weight, form, color, order, position, motion; memory, speech, intonation, phonetic inflection; thought, understanding, reason, intelligence; vacillation, hesitancy to face issues; mental waywardness; brilliant and facile but not profound; intellect in the abstract but not the concrete; industrious in acquiring knowledge for its own sake, apart from any practical application or any question of right or wrong; amasses evidence and eloquently cites statistics in support of his thesis; loves argument and debate; cunning, crafty, subtle; a skilled technician enjoying a superficial proficiency; literary, though not a ready writer. Mercury's highest application appears to be in the realm of "pure reason," which, however, knows so much on both sides of a subject it experiences difficulty in drawing a conclusion, or in holding to a conclusion once arrived at. From the planet Mercury we have the word for the element Mercury, and its derivative effect, mercurial. Its mental direction is largely determined by aspecting planets. **v. ASPECTS, PLANETARY.**

MERCURY: Active, excitable, impressionable, nervous, gossipy, worrisome, witty, dextrous.

MERCURY EXPRESSIONS: Literature, writings, oratory, study, memory. If frustrated may become conceited, profane, unprincipled, tale-bearing, forgetful, addicted to gambling.

VENUS: Physical faculties: friendship, romantic amativeness; the affections, particularly love and the emotions derived therefrom; aesthetic sense, but not analytical; responsive to beauty whether of person, adornment, art or environment; enjoys elegance, comfort and pleasure; good taste; sex sensitivity, but discriminating; parental instinct; a youthful, almost childlike simplicity of approach and viewpoint; a gracious yet almost patronizing attitude; subject to negative moods and extremes of feeling; given to self-pity in moments of depression; mind highly receptive but largely concerned with social affairs; memory sense frequently unreliable; gentle, amiable, pacific, graceful, cheerful, temperate, passive. When thwarted, inclines to extravagance in self-indulgence; slothful, licentious, sensual, vain, dissolute, and generally abandoned; fond of gaudy apparel. Evolved venusian sensibilities incline to art, music, peace, justice, grace, faithfulness, fruitfulness.

MARS: The vital faculties: combativeness, acquisitiveness, desire, enthusiasm, passionate amativeness, courage, ardor in pursuit, not easily rebuffed and seldom discouraged, indiscriminate sexuality, haste, anger, intolerance, fretfulness; a centre of power and energy, whether for good or ill; acute, penetrative mind, largely concerned with physical accomplishment, through direct-action methods, rather than aims, and fitted for enterprises requiring seer-assurance; dynamic force, whether applied constructively or destructively; domineering, brooks no interference and is often ruthless in disregard of others; fearless and unhesitating as to hazardous undertakings and occupations; love of family - and on a wider plane, patriotism; ever ready to protect its own, whether family, country or organization; strong sense of brotherhood with humanity at large, though appearing to be self-centered. Mars is forceful, active, inflammatory, generally careless and destructive, expert, high-spirited. Normally synonymous with force, activity, ambition, pluck, endurance, desire, strife. When thwarted, Mars becomes cruel, egotistical, sarcastic, quarrelsome, coarse, vulgar.

JUPITER: The abstract and creative faculties: comparison applied in generalizations upon the broader aspects; idealism; powerful sense of the dramatic, and obsessed with the desire to be of service to society; symbolizes a person of sound judgment with an ample store of common sense; optimism, order, harmony; the principle of expansion and growth as expressed in the accumulation of material wealth, but without the miserliness of a marked Saturnian trait. Idealism generosity; a balance of feeling and thought, of heart and mind, that yields optimism, devotion, benevolence, good nature, generosity, temperateness, sociability, hopefulness; peace-loving, law-abiding, philosophical; usually of marked religious tendencies, especially of a ritu- alistic order; convinced of the integrity of his motives and that his judgments are tempered with mercy; love of beauty as applied to grandeur and the sublime, with a leaning toward art, especially sculpture; the ability to overcome opposition with forceful but impersonal arguments; broad vision, open-mindedness; listens to reason.

Jupiter creates conditions through which these qualities can bc expressed: health, as physical harmony; law, as social harmony; religion, as spiritual harmony - not as channels of intellect, or the means of making money. It represents judgment, power in the benevolent sense, profit, good fortune, honesty, dignity - or just plain respectability.

At its best Jupiter is generous, expansive, genial, temperate, vital, benevolent, respectful, self-controlled; but when frustrated it inclines to pride, dissipation, boastfulness, gambling, extravagance, procrastination, complacency, hypocrisy.

SATURN: The concrete creative faculties: asceticism; practical ability to achieve the external expression of thought forms; well ordered mind for the technical and concrete with an emphasis on detail; inclined toward scientific research involving mathematics; the conservative realist who asserts the authority of experience; secretive, noncommittal, noncommunicative; cautious, inhibited and reserved; laconic in expression; apostle of justice meted out with a firm hand, yet fair and impartial, a strong sense of justice - particularly injustice; a slave to customs and conventions, even when railing against them; patient, prudent, constant but jealous, yet not easily offended. Its emphasis on the personal ego and inability to give outward expression to affection, tends to separation and isolation; a serious outlook on life; inclined to learn everything the hard way; avoids strenuous effort or exertion - but generally finds more than his share of it to do. Its strong sense of self-preservation is deliberately purposeful and holds the emotions in check through the exercise of thought and will power, more completely than does any other planet.

Where Uranus makes a show of strength when freedom is threatened, and Mars when the passions are aroused, Saturn is cold, slow and deliberate, but inexorable when fully aroused. Plots his way to positions of authority, wherein he discharges his duties with tyrannical conservatism; generally a reactionary, but faithful.

Normally fearful, secretive, cautious, defensive, binding, cold, hard, persevering, steadfast; when frustrated Saturn develops avarice, materialism, ultra-conservatism, tradition-bound narrow-mindedness, pessimism and fatalism.

URANUS: The iconoclastic tendency: characterized by an aloof, offhand manner and approach; imagination, constructive or otherwise; reacts violently against anything that would deprive him of his free and conscious choice of thought and action. Unbending will, insistent upon independence at any price; not readily amenable to any sort of control, much less to arbitrary authority; strong sense of power and authority; assertiveness, with crushing positiveness; self-reliant; inventive; interest in scientific and religious principles; unconventional, altruistic; perseverance to cope with and conquer material obstacles, yet subject to sudden changes of attitude; organizer, promoter, scientific investigator along materialistic lines; originality, with a tendency to break new ground, start new occupations, advance new ideas, utilize new methods, depart from established customs, and hold in disdain the arbitrary restrictions of conventional morality; strong mechanical sense and executive ability that leans toward construction engineering; unerring ability to sense people's motives, hence often becomes a refractory spirit, more or less alienated from his relatives; moves spontaneously from an inner urge - hence impulsive and generally classed as eccentric.

Uranus is deemed a higher octave of Mercury. often fails to know his own mind, but is moved by providential circumstances; often a fatalist who considers his destiny beyond his control.

Naturally inclined to be variable, spasmodic, impulsive, prophetic, and heroic, under restriction - even that of an inferiority complex - it becomes eccentric, refractory, bohemian, fanatical, anarchistic, and given to hurling sarcastic invectives at anybody or anything on any pretext and without provocation. Uranus is eminently the planet of science and invention, particularly aviation, electricity, and astrology.

NEPTUNE: The Social Unrest; follow-the-trend illusive and intangible emotions, of which we know so little; entertains false hopes and indulges in tricky schemes, yet is highest in human sympathy; loves mystery; acts dictated by powerful but inexplicable motives, directed toward invisible, intangible ends; reacts to harmony, sympathy, symmetry, rhythm, poetry, and the dance, which is the poetry of motion, with a partiality for stringed instruments; also for the morbid and erotic.

Neptune pertains to feeling, desire, emotion, imagination. aesthetics, intuition, the psychic faculties or extra-sensory perceptions. When thwarted it becomes psycho-neurotic, theatric, and susceptible to flattery, the power of suggestion, and appearances. On the merest whim it will break a bargain or go back on its word. It exhibits a high regard for uniformity yet often succeeds in enterprises that require more than the average measure of mental effort. Neptune is deemed a higher octave of Venus.

PLUTO. Sociological Urge. The organized group as the instrument with which to amputate parasitic growths on the body politic, in order to reconstruct society along more altruistic lines. Depending upon the spiritual development they have attained, these individuals become leaders of eleemosynary organizations. Foundations for the advancement of human welfare and relations, professional associations or trade unions through which to achieve better social conditions, or mere racketeers and gang leaders. It affords incentive to great literary or dramatic geniuses who inculcate in their works

Plutonian doctrines calculated to bear fruit through the succeeding generation; total disregard for constituted authority or vested rights, except as administered for the good of all; and even at its worst, more likely to be activated by a sense of righteous indignation on behalf of society than by personal vindictiveness.

Planetary Significators. In external affairs the solar system bodies exercise influence as follows:

SUN: Leaders and persons of authority in government, religious and industrial organizations.

MOON: Public life and the fickleness of the public; fluctuations of popularity, changing fortunes; the common people, and the transportation and distribution systems that serve them; the home and home life; the place of residence; the mother, and women generally; in the State, women of title; the ocean, and voyages by water; water and liquids in general, and persons who follow occupations connected with them; places and houses near water; removals, mystery, romance.

MERCURY: Business matters, letter writing, short travels, the neigh- bors and their gossip; schools, colleges, and all places where teaching and learning are pursued; scientific and literary organizations; printing-works, publishing offices, and all who are occupied at these places; buying, selling, bargaining, trading.

VENUS: Social activities; women, especially those younger; art, music, literature; beautiful objects, and anything that is prized for its beauty; ornaments; things of luxury and pleasure; jewels, toys, fine clothes, articles of adornment; pictures, flowers, dancing, singing, acting in so far as these express beauty or pleasure, apart from skill or intelligence; all places where these things belong, and where such occupations are carried on; sweethearts, wives, the home and household; conjugal love, as embodying affection rather than passion.

MARS: Steel, cutlery, weapons of war, sharp tools, and those who use them, fires, slaughter houses, mortuaries; brick and lime kilns; athletics and sports, in so far as they express courage, enterprise, strength and dexterity.

JUPITER: Expansion and growth, and their expression in terms of material wealth; occupations, persons, and places associated with religion, law, and education; public functions and assemblies of a state or official character; charitable and philanthropic movements and institutions; social gatherings, theatres and clothing.

SATURN: Restrictions, delay, poverty, defects, darkness, decay; the father; stability in friendship; secrets, misfortunes, sorrows, fatalities; the ultimate uncombined atomic condition of matter; also the state of matter called "earth," and those whose occupations are concerned with it; ascetics of every description, whether religious or not; hermits, misers, and those who fast or starve; workers employed by municipalities or the State; older people; old plans, matters already started; del)ts and their payment; karma; practicality; good advice; widows and widowers; mountainous and hilly places, or open country, especially rocky and uncultivated; caves, ruins; corpses, graves, and churchyards.

URANUS: Those who have power and authority over others, either on a large or small scale - from King, Parliament and Prime Minister downwards; the chief, the ruler, the wielder of authority; inventors, discoverers, pioneers and antiquarians.

NEPTUNE: Democratic and popular movements, mobs, the common people; mystics, dreamers, visionaries, psychics, mediums; perhaps hospitals and charities.

PLUTO. Idealistic organizations that attack the social ills; social organizations designed to combat groups of individuals who believe they belong to a privileged class. Ideas that are ahead of their time, that will not bear fruit until readvocated by some disciple thereof in the next generation.

Planetary Significators - Horary.

In Horary Astrology the solar system bodies are subject to the following interpretations:

SUN: The querent - if a man. Rich and powerful relations; the person in authority, from whom an honor or favor is desired; the one capable of saving the querent from embarrassment; goldsmiths, jewelers, reformers, educators.

MOON: The querent - if a woman. The mother, or the woman in the case; servants, sailors, navigators, and those in contact with fluids or liquids.

MERCURY: The bringer of tidings; news of that which is lost; artificers, thieves, ingenious and clever persons, who live by their wits; mathematicians, secretaries, merchants, travelers, teachers, orators, ambassadors.

VENUS: The person in whom the querent may be interested, particularly if a young woman; embroiderers, perfumers, entertainers, artists, dealers in ornamentation, designers of clothing, interior decorators, lovers of pleasure, managers of places of amusement.

MARS: If favorably aspected, a strong and aggressive friend; if unfavorably aspected, a revengeful enemy; surgeons, chemists, soldiers, munition manufacturers; all who use sharp instruments; rough and uncultured persons; thieves, and such as live by violence.

JUPITER: The wise friend of the querent upon whom he depends for protection or assistance; a person of advanced years noted for integrity; rich and generous friends or relations; clothiers and dealers in essential commodities; mountebanks, dissipated relatives or friends; the black sheep of the family; counsellors, ecclesiastical dignitaries, judges, lawyers.

SATURN: Persons who, through narrowness of outlook, endanger the success of querent; aged and conservative or indigent friends or relatives; day laborers, religious recluses, those engaged in agriculture and mining, paupers, beggars, clowns; sometimes prudent counsellors; if unfavorably aspected, a person with ulterior motive.

URANUS: The querent's friend in an emergency; unexpected elements, persons from afar, inventors, electricians, indicators of change; astrologers, humanitarians, psychologists, mental specialists. If favorably aspected, a person bringing new and important propositions. If unfavorably aspected, losses through impostors or unwise speculation.

NEPTUNE: Those concerned with the investigation of scientific or metaphysical secrets; profoundly wise and eccentric individuals geniuses, prophets, spiritual counsellors; persons of mysterious origin; those engaged in water pursuits.

PLUTO. The leader of an organization waging a strike, boycott or lockout, to establish a precedent for some principle; the writer who instigates a reform movement or mass reaction.

Planetary Significator s - Mundane. In Mundane Astrology, the significance of the solar system bodies is as follows:

In a consideration of world affairs, the planets supply the initiating factor, whether personalities or environment; the aspects, its favorable or unfavorable action; the signs, the geographical divisions of the earth's surface to be affected; and the houses, the economic or political conditions of the people to be affected or activated.

SUN: Executive heads; governmental and legislative.

MOON: The proletariat, particularly the women; crowds; subjects or objects of popular interest; water transport conditions and occupations; land and crops.

MERCURY: The intelligentsia, the literary world; the transportation and communications industry; the press, educators, speakers, news commentators; change.

VENUS: Ambassadors of good will and preservers of the peace; artists, musicians; theatres and festivals; births, children; courtship and marriage. Unfavoring aspects bring plagues and pestilences.

MARS: Military leaders; surgeons; persons liable to die; engineers; agitators, incendiaries, criminals and crimes of violence; epidemics of infectious and contagious diseases; wars. Commotions are stirred up by Mars aspects to the Sun.

JUPITER: judiciary; ecclesiastical heads; industrialists and capitalists; philanthropists and philanthropic movements; influences in support of order; peace, prosperity and plenty. If afflicted, over-production.

SATURN: The minor state executives and law enforcement authorities; Civil Service employees; land owners and mine operators; elderly persons; public buildings, national calamities, scarcities.

URANUS: Air and rail transport; labor organizations, strikes and riots; civic organizations; anarchy, explosions, inventions; the electrical and radio industry.

NEPTUNE: The little people; social movements; socialized medicine and hospitalization; charities; seditions; socialistic political movements; widespread unrest.

PLUTO. Organized labor; chain store syndicates; group activities; mob psychology - whether the mob be capitalists drunk with power or unemployed crazed by hunger.

Planetary Spirits. In Occultism, the seven highest hierarchies, corresponding to the Christian archangels, which have passed through states of evolution in past cycles.

Planetary Vegetation and Herbs. According to Alan Leo, herbs are classified according to planetary influences as follows:

SUN: Almond, angelica, ash tree, bay tree, celandine, centaury, chamomile, corn hornwort, eyebright, frankincense and other aromatic herbs, heart trefoil, juniper, male peony, poppy, marigold, mistletoe, olive, pimpernel, rice, rosemary, rue, saffron, St. John's wort, sun dew, tormentil, turnsole, vine, wiper's bugloss; also bay, citrus, and walnut trees.

MOON: Adder's tongue, cabbage, chickweed, clary, coral-wort, cuckoo flowers, cucumber, dog-tooth, duck's meat, gourd, hyssop, iris, lettuce, melon, mercury, moonwort, mouse-car, mushrooms, pearlwort, privet, pumpkin, purslain, rattle grass, rosemary, seaweed, spunk, turnips, wallflowers, water arrowhead, watercress, water lily, water violet, white lily, white poppy, white rose, white saxifrage, whitlow grass, wild wallflower, willow, winter green, and all night blooming plants; also maple, olive, palm, and other trees rich in sap.

MERCURY: Azaleas, bitter sweet, calamint, caraway, carrots, cascara, coraline, dill, elecampane, endive, fennel, hare's foot, hazel, horehound, hound's tongue, lavender, lily of the valley, liquorice, male fern, mandrake, majoram, mulberry, myrtle, olive spurger parsley, pellitory, southernwood, star-wort, trefoil, valerian, wild carrots, winter savory; also hazel, and filbert trees.

VENUS. Apples, archangel, artichoke, beans, bearberry, bishop's weed, black alder, bubbleholly, burdock, cloves, cock's head, couch grass, cowslip, cranebill, cudweed, daffodils, elder, featherfew, ferns, foxgloves, goldenrod, gooseberry, grapes and other vines, groundsel, kidneywort, lily, little daisy, marshmallows, mint, pennyroyal, pennywort, peppermint, red cherries, roses, sanicle, sea holly, sorrel, spearmint, tansy, throatwort, vervain, violets, wheat; also almond, apple, apricot, ash, cypress, pecan and pomegranate trees.

MARS: All-heal, aloes, anemone, arsmart, barberry, basil, box tree, broom, butcher's broom, cactus, capers, catmint, coriander, crowfoot, flax-weed, furze-bush, garden cress, garlic, gentian, ginger, hawthorn, honeysuckle, hops, horse radish, horsetongue, hyssop, leadwort, leeks, madder, masterwort, mousetail, mustard, nettles, onions, peppers, plantain, radish, savin, tobacco, wake-robin, wormwood, and all briars and thistles; also trees with thorns.

JUPITER: Agrimony, aniseed, apricots, asparagus, balm, balsam, betony, bloodwort, borage, chestnut, cinquefoil, cloves, currants, daisy, dandelion, hart's tongue, house leek, jessamine, liver wort, mint, myrrh, nailwort, nutmeg, polypody, rhubarb, sage, scurvy grass, small samphire swallow wort, strawberry, sugar cane, thorn apple, wild pinks, wild succory; also ash, almond, birch, fig, lime, linden, mulberry and oak trees.

SATURN: Aconite, barley, barren wort, beech, black hellebore, blue bottle, comfrey, crosswort, flaxweed, fleawort, fumitory, gladwin, ground moss, hemlock, hemp, henbane, holly, horsetail, ivy, jew's ear, knapweed, knotgrass, mandrake, mangel, medlar, moss, navelwort, nightshade, pansies, parsnips, quince, rue, rupture wort, rushes, rye, sciatica wort, senna, shepherd's purse, sloes, Solomon's seal, spinach, tamarisk, vervain, wintergreen. Also cypress, elm, pine, willow and yew trees.

PLUTO. Modern astrology seldom concerns itself with adding to or even using these classifications. Furthermore, the second-octave planets externalize more on the mental and spiritual plane than the physical, hence no additions to these ancient lists have been made as applicable to Uranus, Neptune and Pluto.

Planetary Vocations and Avocations. The ruling planet, and the signs in which posited, considered with reference to occupational aptitude, gives the following testimony.

SUN: Positions of power, dignity, authority and responsibility, judges, magistrates, law observance authorities; superintendents and directors of public utilities, banks and businesses where huge sums of money are handled; goldsmiths, money lenders, writers, makers of ornaments, as luxuries and for display.

MOON: All common employments; persons dealing with public commodities, or holding inferior positions chiefly in the transit industry; women officials and female occupations, as maids, children's nurses, midwives; those having to do with water, as seamen, fishermen, beavers, longshoremen; dealers in liquids; bath attendants; traveling salesmen, tradesmen, purveyors of food.

MERCURY: Authors, actors, orators, teachers, inventors, men of science, journalists and those engaged in gathering and disseminating information and in basing of judgment thereon; merchants, book sellers, postal workers, telegraph operators and messengers, or clerks engaged in the communications industry; artisans who exercise skill and intelligence; accountants, civil engineers, lawyers.

VENUS: All professions connected with music and the fine arts; jewellers, embroiderers, perfumers, botanists; all businesses connected with women and their adornment: domestic servants, dancers and actors who impersonate beauty or grace, apart from skill or intelligence; painters, clothing designers, makers and dealers in toilet accessories.

MARS: All military professions; surgeons, chemists, blacksmiths, engineers, merchants, butchers, barbers, carpenters, and those who use cutlery or sharp instruments; workers in iron and steel, and those who make implements of war; bakers, dyers, and au common employments.

JUPITER: All professions connected with religion and the law; legislators, physicians, bankers, philanthropists, clothiers and businesses connected with woollen clothing; restaurant workers.

SATURN: All conservative businesses and all who deal in land, or in commodities produced by or taken out of the earth; those having to do with places of confinement, or of the dead; common laborers, and those who undertake laborious tasks, or who work underground, or by night. Employments where much labor is necessary to acquire gain. Builders, bridge makers, potters, plumbers, bricklayers, dyers, cattlemen, policemen, scavengers.

URANUS: Public figures, not holding office; travelers, inventors, pioneers, discoverers, original thinkers, lecturers; aviators, and those in the development of air transport; electricians, radio technicians, astrologists, scientists, psychologists, psychoanalysts, physical researchers and all new and uncommon occupations.

NEPTUNE: Artistic and literary geniuses, philosophers, occultists, occupations connected with water, or liquids.

PLUTO. Leaders in large organizations and movements, whether socialistic or capitalistic. Writers along sociological lines, or of works in which sociological doctrines are disguised; activities conducted anonymously or under a pseudonym.

Planetary Years. The ancients presumed the planets to have definite periods of ruler ship, at the end of which changes of constitution or environment might be expected to occur to persons or in the places ruled by them. What they called "the shortest years" can be traced to the orbital motions in most cases; but it is difficult to trace a justification for the other groups. They are:

...Planet.....Short..Mean..Greater..Greatest
...Saturn......30....43.5.....57......465
...Jupiter.....12....45.......79......428
...Mars.........15....40.......66......264
...Sun..........19....69......120.....1460
...Venus........8....45.......82......151
...Mercury.....20....48.......76......450
. Moon........25....66......108......320

By the use of the short years one deduces that, for example, if Saturn conjoins the Moon at birth, its opposition will occur at 15 years of age; if Jupiter conjoins any planet it will form its sextile in 2 years from birth. In other words, it was a method whereby, without the aid of an ephemeris, to determine when the planets wig form aspects or directions to the radical places of the Sun and Moon, and they to the radical places of the planets - called "periodical directions." It is principally of value in mundane astrology, when considering world-trends over long epochs.

Platic. v. ASPECTS.

Pluto v. SOLAR SYSTEM.

Point of Life. A progressed point, obtained by advancing 0° Aries at the rate of 7y per Sign. A planet at this point is presumed to affect the native according to its nature and strength. The theory appears to recognize the importance of the equinoctial degree as an individual point, and to associate it somehow with the Uranus motion, and the progressed motion of the Moon.

Point of Love. As this represents the position of Venus in a Solar figure, and as Venus never has a greater elongation from the Sun than 48°, this Arabian Point can never be in other than the 11th, 12th, 1st or 2nd Houses.

Polar Elevation. The Elevation of the Pole, or the Pole of the Descendant, is relative to the north or south latitude of the place for which a map is erected. Proceeding northward from the Equator the North Pole appears to rise up toward the zenith. The elevation of the Pole at London is 51° 30' - the latitude of the city. The Poles of the Houses increase as they recede from the Imum Coeli and the Mid-heaven, which have no polar elevation, toward the Ascendant and Descendant. The cusps of the intermediate Houses, have polar elevation proportional to the positions at which they cut the Prime Vertical or Circle of Observation - the circle in which a person stands when facing South.

The formula whereby to ascertain the Pole of a planet, is one-third of the planet's semi-arc: the difference of elevation of the two cusps:: the planet's cuspal distance: its proportional polar distance. To ascertain the cuspal distance of a planet from the Oblique Ascension of the cusp, subtract the planet's Oblique Ascension or Descension under the pole of that cusp.

To find the Oblique Ascension of a cusp - add 30° to the Right Ascension of the Mid-heaven for each successive House eastward.

To find the Oblique Descension, subtract 30° for every House westward from the Mid-heaven.

Polarity. Literally, that quality or condition in virtue of which a body exhibits opposite, or contrasted, properties or powers, in opposite or contrasted, parts or directions.

(1) The opposite point in the zodiac to the Sun position in any nativity may be spoken of as its Sun's polarity; usually employed in the harmonization of two maps.

(2) Since opposing signs are said to complement each other, any diameter can be termed a polarity. It is through this principle that Air and Fire signs are deemed more harmonious, since belonging to the same polarity. Similarly with the Water and Earth signs. This polarization of two groups through the polarization of one member of each group is illustrated in Solomon's Seal (q.v.) a six pointed star produced by the juxtaposition of two triangles.

(3) In any one nativity, polarity as used by Leo refers to a relationship between the Sun and Moon positions; viz., Sun in Leo, as polarized by the Moon in Libra. The basic thought is probably that a life revolves around an axis which has as one pole its Sun destiny, and the other pole its Moon desires, the character of the polarization dependent upon the degree of harmony or disharmony that exists between the signs positing the two luminaries.

Maurice Weymss classifies the polarities as follows:

POLARITY:....SIGNS..................ROOT INSTINCT....SIMPLE INSTINCT
Electric:....Aries and Libra.........Food obtaining...Acquisitiveness
Crystalline:.Taurus and Scorpio......Reproductive.....Constructiveness
Energy:......Gemini and Sagittarius..Imitative........Mimicry
Solid:.......Cancer and Capricorn....Precautionary....Acquisitive
Gaseous:.....Leo and Aquarius........Communicative....Sympathy
Liquid:......Virgo and Pisces........Herd.............Service

Pole - of the Ascendant; of the Horoscope. The geographical latitude of the place for which the figure is cast. v. POLAR ELEVATION.

Ponderous, or Ponderable planets. v. PLANETS.

Posited. The position actually occupied by a body, in the heavens or in the signs and houses of a geocentric map.

Positive sign. An odd-numbered sign. v. SIGNS, POSITIVE.

Practical Natures. Referring to a balance between idealism and the ability to enjoy realities and actualities, and to do whatever has to be done, that is shared in common by those born with the Sun in Capricorn, Taurus and Virgo - respectively the Initiative, Executive and Deductive types of the Practical group.

Precession of Equinox and Pole. The shape of the Earth is that of an ellipsoid: flattened at the poles and bulging at the Equator. The gravitational pull of the Moon, and to a lesser extent of the Sun, on this equatorial bulge is said to create a precessional "couple," which causes the Earth's poles of rotation to gyrate or slightly nod in a conical manner. The periods of these Nutations are diurnal, monthly and annual, in addition to the chief one, of the same period as the precessional motion of the Moon's orbit, as noted by its receding Nodes. These slight periodic perturbations of the Earth's polar axis leave residues which accumulate slowly to cause the Soli-Lunar Precession - a more extensive motion and longer in period, hence a Secular perturbation. Stockwell, taking into account all the changes in the orbits of the Earth and Moon due to the action of the planets, has shown that the mean period of this Soli-Lunar Precession is 25,694.8 years. This is the period of that steady precession of the Poles which causes it to point at different stars. Thus in 2102 A.D. the North Pole will point nearly direct at Polaris. As exactly as we can tell, the North Pole pointed as nearly to Vega as it ever does - 6° away - just one-half of the cycle of Precession before the Mission of Christ. Thus the bulk of evidence of an astronomical character, mentioned under Invariable Plane (q.v.), indicates that a new cycle of Polar Precession started around 25 to 28 A.D.

If we measure the backward motion of the line of intersection of the Equator and the Ecliptic on a hypothetical Fixed Ecliptic plane, its motion would be a steady one of the same period as the Pole. This line of intersection is the Equinox, 0° Aries-Libra, which forms the start and midpoint of our Moving Zodiac. It moves backward because the Equator is shifting its position in space, due to the slow gyration or nodding motion of the precessing Polar Axis.

However, the Ecliptic plane is not fixed. The precessing of the Ecliptic with respect to the Invariable Plane, is analogous to the motion of the Earth's Equator with respect to the Ecliptic. In addition it librates, or tilts slowly back and forth, with respect to the Invariable Plane. This has the effect of slightly changing the backward rate of motion of 0° Aries - the Equinox: now speeding it, and again retarding it. The variation is such that the general Precession - the actual as opposed to the Mean motion of the Equinox - can be plus or minus, by 281.2y, that of the Soli-Lunar Precession of 25,694.8y. Thus it can occur at rates of from 25,413.6y to 25,976 1/2 years. Observe that this range of variation includes: the present rate, 25,868y; the period mentioned by Plato, 25,920 years; and that memorialized in the Great Pyramid of the Egyptians, 25,827½y.

Another effect of this variation is the lag and lead, plus or minus 3°56', of the variable Equinox with respect to the steady poles. As the line of intersection of Ecliptic and Invariable Plane was at right angles to that of the Equinox at the time of Christ, this discrepancy had its maximum value and the Equinox led the pole. If we count back about 281 years before the three year Mission of Christ ended in the Crucifixion and Resurrection, 28 A.D., we reach early 254 B.C. as the approximate time when the Moving and Fixed Zodiacs coincided. This is in close agreement with the date 255 B.C., given by Gerald Massey, based on his extensive knowledge of Hebraic and Egyptian Culture. This may be regarded as a period of transition, whose midpoint came about 115 B.C., not greatly at variance with the date, 97 B.C., advanced by Rudhyar, and 125 B.C., by Thierens, for the start of the Piscean Age. It indicates that on the basis of actual motion the Aquarian Age commenced about 1906, although the Pole will not reach this point until about 2170 A.D. It is notable in this connection that a Great Cardinal Cross of the major planets, similar to that at the time of Christ, 25 A.D., took place on January 11, 1910, with Mars and Saturn again in Aries, and again opposing Jupiter in Libra; but with the positions of Uranus and Neptune interchanged - ranus in Capricorn, where Neptune had been, and vice versa. Instead of a Full Moon on the Jupiter-Saturn arm of the Cross, there was a new Moon on the Uranus-Neptune arm, conjoining Uranus, the planet of the Aquarian Age, and Mercury and Venus were both in Aquarius and both direct - significant of the New Era now commencing. In 25 A.D. Neptune, the planet of the Piscean Age, had the Capricorn position, with both Mercury and Venus in Pisces, and both Retrograde.

The overall pattern seems to piece together a number of factors, and the Precession emerges as a cycle of great vitality (v. Cycles). The entrance of the Equinox into Aquarius and the Great Cross of 1910 thus account for the tremendous changes and readjustments now taking place in this predominantly Uranian cycle of transition in which we live - which gains added importance perhaps, through the fact that only in the past two Centuries have the extra Saturnian planets been discovered. An additional significator of the crucial importance of the present Era is the fact that the Meta-Galactic Plane, the Milky Way, is crossing the plane of the Equator at 0° Cancer- Capricorn, thus making another Cross with the Equinox. The Cross is the symbol not only of crisis and readjustment, but also of "crossing over" from one phase of evolution into another. Therefore the start (Polar) of the Piscean Age and (Equinoctial) of the Aquarian Age are heralded by rare cosmic crosses that mark the Epoch as of unique significance in the evolution of humanity, wherein Man is stimulated by new energies. - CHARLES A. JAYNE, JR.

Precession of the Equinoxes. In a recent astronomical work it is defined as "that westward march of the intersection of the planes of the equator and the ecliptic, caused by the attraction of the sun, moon and planets on the protuberant mass at the earth's equator." In doubting the correctness of this explanation, offered blandly by astronomers as an accepted fact, I maintain that this precession is due to causes similar to those which produce the precession of Moon's node - where there is no equatorial protuberating to which to attribute the phenomenon. More likely it is the result of an oscillatory or undulating motion of the entire plane of the orbit, the rate of oscillation determinable by ratios between such factors as the rate of motion of the body and of the center around which it revolves, and the relative diameters of the intersecting orbits. Although our Sun is presumed to be a member of the Milky Way Galaxy, the theory has been advanced that the Sun is a member of a sub-galaxy that is itself a part of the Milky Way Galaxy. This would mean a revolution of the Sun around the center of the sub-galaxy in a much shorter period than that of the entire Milky Way galaxy.

Predictions, in Mundane Astrology. Although predictions, as drawn from a birth Figure, often show a high percentage of correctness, the practice teaches a fatalistic philosophy that denies the gift of Free Will and Self Determination. The high percentage of correctness proves only that a high percentage of people permit themselves to be ruled by the emotions instead of the dominance of the reasoning faculties. It is only in the realm of Mundane Astrology, which deals with the mass reaction of large political or geographical groups, that predicting can be indulged in without inculcating a harmful philosophy.

Predictions in Mundane Astrology are certainly no more damaging than those based upon Gallup polls, or the experience and judgment of practical politicians. Even the weatherman is often wrong, yet he stacks up a pretty good average, but in doing so he uses an efficient communications system to get advance warning of movements that must have had their inception in some cosmic condition. Weather predicting is therefore no more and no less legitimate than predictions in Mundane Astrology. Whether based upon an eclipse path, a chart of an ingress or lunation, or a national chart erected for some presumed moment of inception or initiation, and whether or not the predictions are substantiated by ensuing events, the important factor is that, right or wrong, there is no harm done. Mass reactions generally follow cosmic trends, for the same reason that only the minority is ever consistently right. However, when it comes to the individual, astrology cannot be helpful other than by teaching that man has the inherent ability, if he will use it, to negate unfavorable urges and work in harmony with favorable ones. For that reason, the future value of astrology rests upon the willingness of astrologers to discourage anything that smacks of fortune-telling and confine its use to the diagnosis of conditions, and the giving of a formula of prescribed thinking calculated to free the individual from subserviency to mere emotional stimulations.

Predictive Astrology. The branch of Astrology that deals with "Directions," the methods by which future influences are ascertained. The consideration of this branch opens up the whole question of Fate versus Free Will, and at once determines the difference between the "exoteric" and the "esoteric" astrologer. The one is a confirmed fatalist who believes himself forever under the bane of Destiny, with an entire life mapped out for him over which he has no control: no re-embodiment of the soul, no continuity of existence and with no sense of purpose - because a cruel or a kind Fate has brought him into existence against his will and imposed upon him an environment he did not choose. The other is sustained by a belief that as a man sows so must he reap. His motto is "Man know thyself," that he may choose to sow in such manner as to reap a harvest of his own enlightened desires. It is from this standpoint that all "Directions" should be made, and all rules based upon the dictum that while the stars may impel they do not compel. This presents Astrology as cosmic conditioning, but over which Man is capable of conscious control.

One supposedly historic prediction that is of interest in the epoch of world history in which this is written, dates from about 1660 and has been ascribed to Friar Jehan; in which he is reputed, according to CORONET, to have said that in the Twentieth Century "the land of the Black Eagle (Germany) would invade the country of the Cock (France), and that the Leopard (England) would rush to the Cock's aid. The Black Eagle would claw its antagonists almost to defeat but would turn, before finishing them off, to attack the White Eagle (Russia). There would then take place a struggle more terrible than words can tell, where the dead would be piled in mounds as high as cities. The nation of the Black Eagle (also referred to in the prophecy as the country of Luther) would at last succumb and, deprived of all its weapons, would be divided into twenty-two separate states. Then, at long last, would follow the true golden age of mankind."

Prenatal Epoch. The theoretical moment of conception. v. EPOCH.

PRENATAL BIRTH CHART: A BIRTH CHART BASED ON THE MOMENT OF CONCEPTION 9 MONTHS OR 40 WEEKS BEFORE BIRTH.

Prescience. Foreknowledge. An excellent word, used by Ptolemy in the affirmation ... "only prescience by astronomy will afford premonition of such events as happen to men by the influence of the Ambient." It suggests preparedness for the exercise of discretion, rather than the fatalistic terror inspired by a prediction.

Primary Directions. Any method, for determining the changing influences of the altered relationship between the cuspal and the planets' places on successive days or years after birth, that is based upon the diurnal rotation of the Earth upon its axis, arc known as Primary Directions. The measure employed is the elapsed time during which one complete degree of Right Ascension (Q.V.) passes across the meridian, or approximately 4 minutes of Sidereal Time. The calculations are too complicated and too laborious for the average astrological student. All Primary Arcs which can be formed between the sensitive points in a Nativity during an entire lifetime are formed during some 6 hours after birth, and are produced solely by the rotation of the Earth on its axis: the planets retaining their radical places and thus carried round the heavens to form aspects to the places of the significator. For its reliability the method is dependent upon the correctness of the birth time to within a fraction of a minute, since an error of 4 minutes in the birth time results in an error of a year in the timing of an event.

As actually described by the ancients, the planets, by motion of the Primum Mobile (Q.V.) are gradually carried round the Earth past the cusps of the Houses, and are brought into sundry successive mundane aspects one with another. The calculation of these aspects and their times of formation is termed "directing"; the result is described as "the directions in force" for the calculated time. The number of degrees and minutes of Right Ascension passing over the meridian between the moment of birth and that when the aspect is complete, constitutes the Arc of Direction, each degree equivalent to one year of life.

There are various systems of Primary Directions, their one object to determine the times of events. Ptolemy's system of measurement employed arcs of direction based upon the apparent motion of the heavens about the Earth by virtue of the rotation of the Earth on its axis, in which the body of one planet is brought to the place of another in a proportion of its ascensional or descensional time as measured by its semi-arc. Thus a planet will progress to the Midheaven by degrees of Right Ascension, while one below the horizon will progress to the Ascendant by degrees of Oblique Ascension, which takes cognizance of the latitude of the place of birth. Since a planet must be directed under the Pole (elevation), due to its proportional distance from the meridian, one on the Midheaven has no Pole, while one on the Ascendant has the same Pole as the Ascendant, which is the latitude of the birthplace. All others between the Midheaven and Ascendant, whether above or below the horizon, have a Pole proportionate to their distance therefrom. Ptolemy confined his directions to aspects between the bodies and the places of the planets.

Placidus de Titus added mundane aspects. In his system one third of the semi-arc of a planet was equal to the space of one House. In both systems the motions of the planets are due to the motion of the Earth on its axis after birth. The radical positions of the planets, taken in connection with the planet to which direction is made, are held to determine the nature of the event. The Significators - Sun, Moon, Midheaven and Ascendant - were directed to the points where conjunctions or aspects would form to mundane and zodiacal positions.

Most Primary Directions can be worked to within 15' of arc, or 3 months' time, by means of Tables of Houses, provided one knows the Poles of the various planets: the degree of elevation in the Nativity in proportion to the latitude of the birthplace.

To direct the Ascendant to an aspect with a promittor first bring the longitude of the point of aspect to the horizon. This can bc done roughly from the Table of Houses for the latitude of birth. Observe that the passage of the Midheaven is uniform while that of the Ascendant is irregular.

Take the Ascendant degree, find the related Midheaven, then find the degree of the point of aspect and its related Midheaven; whence deduct the difference in time at the rate of 1° per year. That these calculations involve the use of so uncertain a factor as the exact moment of birth is a perpetual hindrance.

For that reason resort has been made to easier methods. The method most generally employed is that on which is based a system of so-called Secondary Progressions (Q.V.) (V. DIRECTIONS).

Prime Vertical. The vertical circle that lies at right angles to the meridian, and passes through the East point, Zenith, West point and Nadir of any place.

Primum Mobile. The first mover, the outermost, or tenth sphere of the ancients, which in its daily motion carried all of the fixed stars. It is purely a Ptolemaic concept, exploded in theory by the Copernican concept of a solar system revolving about the Sun instead of the Earth. From the standpoint of Astrology, which deals with the effect of those apparent motions around the Earth by virtue of the Earth's own motion, the concept is as valid today as it was in Ptolemy's time.

Principal Places. The five places in which the luminaries are said to have the most beneficial effects in a Nativity; the hylegiacal places: the 1st, 11th, 10th, 9th and 7th Houses. V. HYLEG.

Process. v. PROGRESSION.

Profections. A term used by Ptolemy to indicate the successional rising of the Signs, hence of the Sun and other Significators, at the rate of one Sign per year, or 2°30' per month. First study the rules for determining the Hyleg, or hylegiacal degree. With that located advance it 30° for each year. Bearing in mind that the year from your third to your fourth birthday is your fourth year, proceed as follows: Assume a Profectional Figure for the year beginning on your 27th birthday with the Hyleg at Pisces 15°. 28 Signs minus 24 - two circles - equals 4 Signs, hence the annual Profection extends from Cancer 15° to Leo 15°. The Moon and the Sun thus become the chronocrators for the 28th year. v. DIRECTIONS.

Prognosis. Originally synonymous with Prediction, usage has attached to it a more conservative meaning, that of "a probability of outcome." Astrologers who adhere to the doctrine of Free-Will, and who seek only to render helpful assistance and wise guidance through a crisis, rather than to mystify and astound, generally prefer this terminology. They do not hesitate to draw forth a complete case-history of everything that might have bearing on the matter under consideration, before passing judgment, in preference to the exhibitionist feat of telling the client what he reads from the chart concerning the past. A recent treatise on a phase of scientific astrology says the "astrological prognosis must be guided by every personal fact or situation of the person in question. The researcher should take into consideration these attendant circumstances and from them deduce the logical results of the indicated astrological conditioning. By this procedure, astrology supplies the factor for psychological analysis that psychology alone could never authoritatively deduce." With utter frankness, the author adds: "There is no infallible certainty in astrological prediction any more than there is in medical or meteorological prognosis. A doctor can only prog- nosticate within limits of probability the course an illness will run, and can err even as the meteorologist in a weather forecast." Medicine achieved respectability through the impersonal approach, and Astrology might with profit emulate the example.

Progressed Horoscope. One erected for a date that is as many days after a given birth date as the native's age in years. v. DIRECTIONS.

Progressions. Alterations in the birth chart aiming to show the changing influences that result from motions of the celestial bodies after birth. v. DIRECTIONS.

Progressions vs. Directions. To clarify astrological terminology it is perhaps well to emphasize a distinction between these two terms so often loosely applied to the same process: DIRECTIONS, to indicate the theoretical advance of some one body or point in a chart, by applying to it an arc of direction for a given period of time, or by measuring the arc between it and some other sensitive point, cuspal point or place formerly tenanted by a planet, and by reducing it to time by some such measure as that employed in the Primary System of Directions. PROGRESSIONS, indicating the advanced positions of the Ascendant, Midheaven and planets as shown in a Progressed Figure cast for a given date, as employed in the system of Secondary Progressions (q.v.). Alan Leo employs both terms rather indiscriminately, defining Directions as "calculations made from the Nativity for the purpose of ascertaining the time when events will happen. Properly speaking this is predictive Astrology, since it is concerned with the future of the person for whom the calculations are made. Directions are classed under two heads: Primary and

Secondary. The former is similar to the small hand of a clock which marks off the hours, while the latter are like the long hand which marks off the exact time."

Although Alan Leo wrote an imposing volume on the "Progressed Horoscope" he says in his Dictionary that "the question of the progressed birthday at the rate of a day for a year needs investigation."

Progressive Solar Revolution. A map similar to the Solar Revolution (q.v.) erected for the moment of the Sun's return to the exact location it occupied on the equivalent birth hour of a date determined by adding one day to the birth date for each year of life up to the year for which the p.s.r. figure is to be erected. From the computed longitude of the Sun, refer to the ephemeris of the current year for the calculation of the planets' places, and aspects, Transits, eclipses and lunations in important places of the p.s.r. map are deemed by some authorities to have great significance.

Prohibition. v. Frustration.

Promittor. A planet, to which a significator may be "directed" in order to form an aspect between the "progressed position" of the Significator and the "birth position" of the promittor, whereby certain events or conditions are promised as concerns the significator so directed. The distance the significator must travel to form this aspect is termed the "arc of direction," to be reduced to time, usually at the rate of 1° for a year and 5' for a month.

Proper Motion. (1) Said of the motion of planet in space, as compared to any apparent motion which results from any movement of the Earth: either axial rotation, annual revolution, or the motion through space of our entire solar system. (2) Loosely applied to the direct motion of a planet through the signs, in distinction to the diurnal rising and setting caused by the Earth's rotation.

Prophecy. The ability to foretell the future. According to occult teachings anyone who is able to prophecy accurately must be psychically equipped to read the Akashic, or astral, records. When there is faulty interpretation it is not the astral light which falters but the adept who is not in tune with the vibratory beam.

Proportional Arcs. Additional sensitive degrees proposed by Sepharial on the theory that each planet has a point of influence at the same distance on the opposite side of the radical Sun, Moon, Ascendant and M.C. Thus the p.a. of Venus in 19°, Aries to the Sun in 5° Aries falls upon 21° Pisces where its influence would be felt when a New Moon falls thereon, or the directional Moon or transit of any planet. Each planet has a p.a. to the Ascendant and M.C., making 9 points; also 8 points each for the Sun and Moon, a total of 34. When the influence of the planet is thus brought out it supposedly brings into activity the affairs of the House in which the arc falls. It is an extension of the theory of Converse Directions.

Prorogator. A term used by Ptolemy in connection with a method of direction, effected by proportion of horary times - semi-arcs. One must distinguish between the Prorogator, the body directed and the Prorogation or method by which it is directed. The Prorogator is the Apheta or Life Giver, in contrast to the Anareta. By day and in aphetical places, the Sun holds the position of Prorogator; by night the Moon. (v. "Hyleg.")

Psychography. In occult terminology it signifies automatic writing in which the hand supposedly transcribes supernal concepts without mental direction.

Psychometry. (1) The art of measuring the duration of mental processes; of establishing the time relations between mental phenomena. (2) As employed by occultists it applies to an adept's supposed ability to weigh or determine psychically the qualities of inanimate objects - such as metals, textiles, antiques or potentially active chemicals. It is explained as the reading of the "memory" of innate powers of material things.

Psychophobia. Fear of the unseen. Literally a horror of destiny. A psychosomatic manifestation, often of astrological genesis.

Ptolemaic Astrology. A correct appraisal of Ptolemy's work might well begin, not with what he knew but with what he did not know. From a careful study of the TETRABIBLOS, one must classify his work under three headings: (1) A valid philosophy that treats in theoretical terms of the plausible value of astrology and the benefits it would confer if properly assayed and applied. (2) A compilation of knowledge from "ancient" sources, for which he erected a consistent framework of practice: an excellent piece of editorial work in any day. (3) An attempted scientific explanation of how and why it works in terms of what was then known of astronomy and physics.

In the first classification his work is superb. He shows the importance of giving consideration to education and environment as modifying factors in delineation; of continued study to establish the actual factors upon which judgment should be based; and the damage done to all sciences by unprincipled charlatans who use their little knowledge for personal gain. His contributions under this heading are as vital today as when he wrote them.

In the second classification he shows that while astrology must have advanced a long way, interpretation had suffered from a lack of knowledge of the mechanics through which it operates, and this knowledge he attempted to supply.

It is in this third classification that instead of clarifying issues, he succeeded mainly in introducing a maze of superfluities, complexities and contradictions.

Of all the theories which he advanced none has been restated more often in contradictory terms than his Doctrine of Orientality. Even Placidus remarked that "everyone knows how largely and to what little purpose authors have treated of the orientality of the planets." To this James Wilson, in his most personal of dictionaries since the days of the ubiquitous Samuel Johnson, adds that "this may well be the case, when the whole was unintelligible even to these authors themselves." Ironically he says: "Orientality I do not comprehend any better than Ptolemy himself, and therefore can say little on the subject." When Ptolemy speaks of the nearness of Mercury's sphere to that of the Moon, Wilson's comment is to the effect that it doesn't make sense. No wonder.

To make sense out of Ptolemy's doctrines one must first reconstruct the firmament as he saw it. Around the Earth were ten spheres; one each for the Moon, Mercury, Venus, the Sun, Mars, Jupiter and Saturn, in which the planets "struggle against the primum mobile"; in an eighth sphere, two small circles wherein the beginning of Aries and Libra "trembles and vibrates" - referring no doubt to the then unexplainable phenomenon of precession; in a ninth sphere, "a crystalline or watery heaven in which no star has been discovered"; and around them all, like a steel tire on a wagon wheel, a tenth sphere, the PRIMUM MOBILE, which by its superior force carries all within it in a diurnal rotation from the east through the meridian to the west.

Forgetting that which we have since learned, one must realize that all Ptolemy knew about the proper or orbital motions of the bodies was that they struggled ineffectually against the compelling force of the "ambient" - which incidentally is a good word. Every concept in his system is based upon apparent motion - and he did not know that it was merely apparent. Since the Sun's motion is faster than that of any of the major planets, they did indeed separate from the Sun in a clockwise direction, rising and eventually culminating at the Midheaven. The minor planets, of course, never got far enough away from the Sun to culminate, so they were differentiated by whether they rose in the morning before the Sun, or set in the evening after the Sun.

It is apparent that astrologers, even in his day, realized the increased strength of planets by virtue of elevation into the Twelfth, Eleventh and Tenth Houses; but it is also apparent that in trying to explain it, he attributed this potency to their visible light rather than to gravitation; hence he deemed it essential that the Sun be below the Horizon, so that the planets might "rise and shine" ahead of the Sun. In ascribing extreme potency to the visibility of the planets' rays, he could not know that light itself is only a symptom of energy radiation from the Sun, and that the octave of visible light eventually would be extended to some 30 octaves of invisible infra-red and ultra-violet frequencies, charging an ambient magnetic field that envelops the Earth, and affects the lower Earth as well as the arc of visibility.

The Moon was the problem, for with its faster motion it did not separate from the Sun, but eventually the Sun caught up with it. Planets mounted to the Sun in one direction, and to the Moon in the other. Only he stated it more vaguely in saying that oriental and matitudinal planets ascend to the Sun, occidental and vespertine, to the Moon. That is the reason he gave the preferential position for a planet, as oriental of the Sun and occidental of the Moon. In these positions it should find the maximum opportunity to shine before Sunrise, and after Moonset.

This picture of a satellitium of planets above the horizon guarded on the East by the Sun and on the West by the Moon, represented an array of power - even though his reasons were somewhat awry. At that, one might be willing to concede something in order to have a waxing Moon; but Ptolemy lacked knowledge of the Moon's proper motion, hence was unable to differentiate between the good qualities of a waxing moon as compared to those conferred upon a weak Fourth Quarter Moon by virtue of the accidental dignity of elevation.

When it came to the Sun itself, there must be a reason why it too was more powerful in the quadrant between the Ascendant and the Midheaven, so to it was given another variety of orientality - that to the Horizon, IM MUNDO. It was more powerful in the three houses through which it culminated to the

Midheaven, but since it must do the same thing in the other half of the Earth as it descended into the west and proceeded to rise on the other side, the Fourth, Fifth and Sixth were also oriental Houses. Therefore as regards the Sun, it was oriental "of the horizon," or IM MUNDO, in the north-west quadrants as it was in the south-east, and occidental in the other two quadrants.

It is strange how truth persists in defiance of all efforts to explain it - or explain it away. Sepharial says a planet is oriental when it rises after the Sun - that one needs only to look at the Sun in the Midheaven and he can see which is the oriental side. He neglects to note that one has but to picture the Sun at the IC to see that it then becomes oriental on the other side. What Sepharial particularly overlooked was the fact that Ptolemy knew nothing about proper motion, and that BEFORE the Sun did not mean before it in orbital motion in the order of the signs, but before it in rising as it comes above the horizon and mounts to the Midheaven. All that Ptolemy meant by oriental he said again when he described a planet as matutine. Wilson tried to remedy this by suggesting that it was matutine for three signs and oriental for the next three signs, but obviously it cannot be farther removed from the Sun than 90º, or it would rise BEFORE the Sun, not in the morning but before midnight of the night before; or it would not set until after midnight, which would be the next day after today's sunset. Naturally this problem does not arise in connection with Mercury and Venus, which never get that far away from the Sun.

Evidently oriental was intended to apply to the major planets and the Moon; while matutine and vespertine, which meant the same thing, were intended to apply to the inferior planets; but Ptolemy lost himself in his own words, and by using both terms in abandoned redundancy managed to leave posterity in a hopeless muddle in its efforts to find some difficult explanation for a very simple thing. Both Wm. Lilly and Alan Leo list all of the houses from the IC to the MC as oriental, yet Leo goes on to add that the Fourth, Fifth, Sixth, and Tenth, Eleventh and Twelfth are the oriental Houses - which calls forth from Wilson the scornful observation that a planet can thus be oriental and occidental at one and the same time.

The fact is that none of these terms are of value today, simply because we have better ways of stating the same thing. Truth born of experience, despite anyone's efforts to explain it, and aided by Copernicus, has led us to an inescapable correlation between the Geocentric and the Solar Houses, until today we recognize that a planet in the Tenth, Eleventh and Twelfth Geocentric Houses enjoys the same added strength by elevation that Ptolemy tried to describe in his use of the terms Matutine, and oriental IM MUNDO; also that in the Tenth, Eleventh and Twelfth Solar Houses they enjoy the strength that he expressed by his terms "oriental of the Sun." Venus matutine is now Venus in the Eleventh or Twelfth Solar House; Vespertine, in the First or Second Solar House. Sun or planets oriental of the horizon, or IM MUNDO, are now expressed as in either the Tenth, Eleventh or Twelfth Geocentric House, as the case may be. A planet "oriental of the Sun" is better located by its Solar House position, either the Tenth, Eleventh or Twelfth.

Another peculiar symptom of the power Ptolemy attached to visi- bility is seen in his classifications of Beholding Signs or signs of Equal Power, and those of Commanding and Obeying. The Beholding Signs, those of equal power, were those whose cusps were equidistant from the Meridian. Both are either visible or invisible, hence equally strong or equally weak. On the other hand, the Commanding and Obeying Signs were equidistant from the Equator, hence one was in the light and the other in darkness, because of which the one above the horizon was Commanding and the other Obeying. Furthermore it has often been overlooked that this distinction applied only when the respective Signs were occupied by planets that were thereby configurated, and that the distinction was only a means of determining which end of the aspect was the more powerful. of course, the elevated planet is the stronger by virtue of House position - which has naught to do with Sign position. That the presence of the Sun in a Commanding Sign made it longer, hence conferred upon the Sign a right to be considered a Commanding Sign, seems particularly naive; and one wonders what would happen if the Sun chanced to be in a Sign of rapid ascension below the horizon. Naturally it would make it smaller, but what privileges would that confer or deny? Since the Signs are of equal size, what he really meant was a House, for only a House could be "longer."

He classifies Sextiles and Trines as harmonious because they join Signs that are either both male or both female. The square is inharmonious because it joins Signs "of different natures and SEXES." The oriental quadrants are masculine; the occidental, feminine. He overlooks the fact that the explanation he gives for his pairs of Commanding and Obeying sextiles and trines would with better logic describe the opposition polarities which in modern practice are found to possess such validity. The 144 so-called polarities between Sun and Moon, the importance of which was given emphasis by Alan Leo, found no place in his system. Truly astrology has made great advances since he gave it the initial impetus that has projected it so powerfully into our modern world.

It seems that Ptolemy, finding a lot of scattered truths and sundry devices for applying them, devoted his ingenuity to an effort to hook them all together into a unified system. In this it appears that in a sense he was a precursor of Freud, in that he seemed bent on reducing everything to terms of sex. of course, this may not be literally true, for his eternal harping on masculine and feminine had to do not so much with sex as with the polarity of positive and negative and the reciprocal action that presumably takes places between adjacent Signs, whereby each even-numbered Sign complements the preceding odd-numbered Sign. That he called them masculine and feminine instead of positive and negative, or active and passive, was a matter of terminology in keeping with the symbolism of his epoch. Even the positive-negative terminology is not ideal, for it still supports his concept that the even-numbered Sign is the underdog who helps the preceding odd-numbered Sign to make good on his positiveness, hence is in an unfortunate position. Nevertheless, since Fortunate and Unfortunate is a classification that exactly parallels what today we prefer to speak of as positive and negative, these and many similarly unnecessary terms that only serve to create confusion might well be discarded.

There is some doubt today as in his day, as to whether this basic distinction is a valid one, for Ptolemy himself reports that many of the astrological savants of his time rejected the distinction. Nevertheless, it was essential to his thesis, so he persisted, for only by this could he justify and explain his system of essential dignities, whereby to arrive at a delineation of untenanted Signs and Houses. These Signs are not wholly untenanted, for from time to time they are actuated by transits, and these concern themselves not at all with the presumed ruler of the territory they transit - but Ptolemy knew naught about Transits.

Since the Sun and Moon rose to the greatest third-dimensional elevation in North declination in Cancer and Leo, he assigned to them the Sun and Moon as Rulers. The Moon, because she was moist, was a female, so he gave her the feminine even-numbered Sign; and since the Sun was dry, hence masculine, he got the odd-numbered masculine Sign. The planets then had to have two Houses each, so they could configure with both Sun and Moon; hence Mercury, which never gets farther away from the Sun than one Sign, he allocated to Gemini and Virgo, a feminine one for his night house, since the moist night must of course be feminine, and a dry masculine one for his day House. Venus, which never gets farther away from the Sun than two Signs, necessarily came next; followed by Mars and then Jupiter - all on the same theory. To Saturn, which was far away and hence out in the cold, was assigned the remaining two Signs - but again a moist female one for his night home and a dry masculine one for his day throne. From this arrangement came the Solar semicircle, and the Lunar - planets in Aquarius to Cancer "mounting" to the Moon in the order of the Signs, and those in Capricorn clockwise to Leo, mounting to the Sun AGAINST the order of the Signs.

After that came masculine and feminine quadrants, Signs and Houses, and masculine and feminine planets, whereby any House, whether or not tenanted, could be delineated by joining them up in sundry ways through this consideration of sex.

The idea that a female is moist is repugnant, and has nothing to do with planets moving in cycles. He started by classifying adjacent Signs into pairs according to sex "as the male is coupled with the female" - yet throughout his entire application of the sex principle he reversed his logic to emphasize the unfavorable influence to which a male planet is subjected when tenanting a female area - and the reverse.

It is small wonder that Wilson, a man of strong opinions but penetrating vision, said of the Ptolemy classification of planets as masculine and feminine that "it is an idle distinction, and no more founded on reason than his essential dignities." Pointing out that Placidus also differed with Ptolemy in the matter, he remarks that "this is not to be wondered at, when he differed so much in opinion with himself." Then he adds, as a sage piece of advice: "I would advise the student to give himself no trouble about the sex of the planets, but to study their influence."

Ptolemy's emphasis on heat and cold, moisture and dryness, may be valid, but can only be accepted when verified by scientific demonstration. Arrived at by a loose symbolic analogy tied in with sex, they are unworthy of perpetuation in our modern terminology. Actually they mean nothing to today's astrology, for through the accumulated testimony of research, experiment, and observation, we have learned how each planet's influence externalizes; and whether it does so because its moist nature makes it female, or the reverse, is of no consequence. Certainly we must reject any such contradictory reasoning as that which makes Jupiter beneficent because of its heat, and Mars malefic because of its excess of dryness, yet on that reasoning Mars should become beneficent when below the horizon, for there it becomes nocturnal, hence feminine.

He said also that in the parts of the Earth "where the Sun's heat is most strongly felt, the inhabitants are more, disposed after his image." Perhaps that, rather than the hookworm, explains the lazy South. A fair sample of the wangling by which ruler ship of the Trigons were awarded, is that the west should be ruled by Mars, "who delights in West winds because they scorch the Egyptians," and that the North should be ruled by Jupiter, "who brings the fruitful showers from that quarter" - to which Wilson suggests that "it would be no bad policy were the Europeans to assign him the government of the South, which would enable him to accommodate them in a similar way." His further complaint against this jockeying for position, as described by Ptolemy, is that "Instead of considering the heavenly bodies as ponderous masses of matter operating by their sympathetic attraction on each other, they are represented as school boys always quarreling and fighting about their playthings."

One need not go so far as to eliminate the entire matter of ruler ships, but the Ptolemy explanations cannot well be the explanation. If the ruler ship system of Essential Dignities is valid, it is merely because of a discovered similarity of influence that renders one planet more congenial in a certain Sign than in any other, whence in congenial surroundings one can expect it to function more advantageously. To expand Wilson's advice: knowledge of the Signs and planets, of the aspects between them, and of the dominions of the Houses, is of supreme importance. Superior to Ptolemy's sex method of arriving at the strength of aspects in different portions of the Figure, is our present method of considering first the Signs which condition the planets, then the Houses which are joined by means of the aspect. In fact, this is what Ptolemy attempted to do, with the limited knowledge at his command. His emphasis on the importance of knowledge concerning the motions of the planetary orbs, of correct place-time identification of the event for which a Figure is to be cast, and of the then concurrent configurations, "improved by an acquaintance with the nature of the bodies and their effective influences" as contributory to a proper prescience of Destiny and Disposition - is something every practicing astrologer might well take to heart. To apply his advice in the light of today's knowledge would leave us with a greatly simplified terminology, for into the discard would go a host of words for things we are now able to describe in terms that at one and the same time are simpler and more comprehensive.

It is not intended to make light of the contributions of Ptolemy, for his philosophy has been a beacon through the ages, while his work as a compiler has saved to us much knowledge that might otherwise have been lost. As to the third category, as initially set forth, it is not reasonable to expect that correct explanations of and justifications for observed operations should come from a man, however brilliant, who did not know that the planets had a proper motion as they revolved about the Sun, as well as an apparent motion by virtue of the Earth's rotation; who did not know that his Primum Mobile was a mirage; and who had never been initiated into any of the mysteries that have been unveiled to us by the telescope, the microscope, the spectroscope, the X-ray and the cyclotron. The contributions he made to learning, in view of the meagre tools at his command, inspires only veneration for those scientists who lived in an age when men still had time to think. The fact that a man of his intellectual attainments found nothing fallacious in the premise that human life and destiny may be influenced by the motions and cycles of the planets, and their reflected solar radiations as transmitted to the Earth, indicates a measure of scientific open-mindedness that is somewhat conspicuous by its absence among many of today's unimaginative and materialistic-minded scientific pedants.

Astrology has persisted in spite of all attempts to explain it; but in accordance with Ptolemy's sound philosophy it is every astrologer's duty to avail himself, with the utmost of understanding, of all knowledge that is applicable to the science, whereby to arrive at the true and correct explanations which alone can bring the improved technic that will enhance Astrology's value to society.

Pyrois. Greek name for Mars, referring to its fiery nature.

Quadrantine Lunation. An ill-advised term sometimes applied to the conjunctions, squares and oppositions of the Sun and Moon.

Quadrants. The four quarters of the Celestial Figure, representative of the four quarters of the heavens, measured from the cusps of the four angular Houses. The oriental quadrants consist of Houses X to XII inclusive, and IV to VI inclusive. The occidental quadrants, of Houses I to Iii inclusive, and VII to IX inclusive. If applied to the Zodiac the oriental quadrants arc from Aries to Gemini and from Libra to Sagittarius inclusive, the occidental quadrants consisting of the opposite Signs. Confusion will be avoided if the term be applied only to the Houses of the geocentric Figure. v. ORIENTAL.

Quadrate, or Quartile. A 90º or Square Aspect (Q.V.).

Quadratures. The Moon's dichotomes (Q.V.)

Quadrupedal. The four-footed Signs: Aries, Taurus, Leo, Sagittarius and Capricorn, all of which represent quadrupeds. Those born when these ascend were said by the ancient astrologers to have the qualities of such animals: as bold as the lion, or as lustful as the goat.

Quadruplicity. The four signs which have the same quality; either cardinal, fixed or mutable. v. SIGNS.

Quartile. A 90º, or Square aspect. (v. ASPECTS.)

Querent. Employed in Horary astrology to indicate the one who asks the question.

Quesited. Employed in horary astrology to indicate the person or thing that is the subject of an inquiry.

Quincunx. An aspect of 150°, or five Signs of separation. v. ASPECTS.

Quintile. An aspect proposed by Kepler, consisting of 72 degrees, or one-fifth of the circle. The Biquintile is 144°, or two-fifths of the circle. A Decile is 36°, or half a Quintile. It has not been universally adopted. v. ASPECT.

Radical. 1. Pertaining to the radix, or horoscope of birth. **2.** In Horary astrology, a term employed to indicate a figure which can appropriately be judged in a given matter; one that is likely to give the correct answer.

Radical Position. Said of a planet's position in a birth horoscope; as distinguished from the transitory or progressed position it occupies at a later date. v. RADIX.

Radix. 1. The radical map: the horoscope of birth, the root from which everything is judged. **2.** The radical or birth positions of the planets, as distinguished from their progressed or directed positions. Progressed aspects can never entirely contradict or negate a radical aspect; but must be interpreted only as modifying or mitigating the influences shown in the Radix.

Radix System. v. DIRECTIONS.

Rahu. The Sanskrit name for the Dragon's Head - the Moon's North node. In Hindu mythology Rahu is a Daitya (demon) who possessed an appendage like a dragon's tail, and made himself immortal by stealing from the gods some Amrita - elixir of divine life - which they obtained by churning an ocean of milk. Unable to deprive him of his immortality, Vishnu exiled him from Earth and made of him the constellation Draco: his head called Rahu, and tail Ketu - astronomically speaking, the Moon's ascending and descending nodes. Using his appendage as a weapon, he has ever since waged a destructive war on the denouncers of his robbery, the Sun and the Moon, which he swallows during the eclipse. The fable is presumed to have a mystic or occult meaning. (v. NODES, MOON'S.)

Rapt Motion. v. MOTION.

Rapt Parallel. Two bodies, which by Rapt motion are carried to a point where they are equidistant from and on opposite sides of the meridian or the horizon, are said to be in Rapt Parallel. (v. ASPECTS.)

Rays, Under the. In astrology a planet is "under the rays" of another when it is within orbs of an aspect. Rarely used by modern authorities.

Reception. (1) A planet posited in a sign not its own, is said to be received by the Ruler of that sign, as if one were visitor and the other host. (2) The condition in which a planet is receiving an aspect from some faster-moving planet.

Reception, Mutual. When two planets are in each other's sign or exaltation.

Recessional Directions. v. DIRECTIONS.

Rectification. The process of verification or correction of the birth moment or ascendant degree of the map, by reference to known events or characteristics pertaining to the native. This may be necessitated by the inaccuracy of time-pieces; the carelessness of those whose business it should be to make a careful record of the correct moment of birth; or it may consist of a hypothetical determination of a birth-hour wholly unknown to the native. The entire subject is a matter of controversy. Some contend that it is unscientific to prove a thesis by altering the premise to fit the conclusion. Among numerous methods are: (1) the Prenatal Epoch, the Arc of the Moon's travel from its birth position to the point where it forms its first aspect, converted into time and compared with the circumstances which attended, is presumed to afford an indication of the Native's exact age, whereby to rectify the degree of the Ascendant; (2) comparisons between the house positions of the planets, and the Native's circumstances and disposition; and (3) the computing of the directions attending the first accident or illness, the death of a parent, the conferring of an honor, marriage, the birth of a child.

Argol and Morinus used a method of rectification by directions timed to an important event. Hermes observed a certain relationship between the place of the Moon at birth and the Ascendant at conception, and vice versa, out of which developed the Prenatal Epoch, as advanced by E. H. Bailey in the 'Prenatal

Epoch" and Sepharial in "The Solar Epoch." Various other methods have been advanced but none has received universal acceptance.

Recurrence Cycles. Periods of time in which a conjunction of any two given planets will recur in approximately the same degree of the zodiac. These are of value, not only in the study of Cycles (q.v.) but as a means of erecting a chart for remote periods for which Ephemerides are unavailable. A fairly accurate list of recurrence cycles, follows:

Planets	Order	Number of Conjunctions	Tropical Years
Moon-Mercury	1	74	8
Moon-Venus	1	94	8
Moon-Mars	1	411	32
	2	5242	410
Moon-Jupiter	2	3467	261
Moon-Saturn	2	4715	353
Moon-Uranus	1	1074	84
Moon-Neptune	1	2149	168
Moon-Pluto	1	6562	494
Mercury-Venus	2	545	243
Mercury-Mars	1	276	79
Mercury-Jupiter	2	827	474
Mercury-Saturn	1	102	59
Mercury-Uranus	1	146	85
Mercury-Neptune	1	682	165
Mercury-Pluto	2	2553	1486
Venus-Mars	1	37	32
	2	1279	1215
Venus-Jupiter	1	37	24
	2	749	486
Venus-Saturn	2	208	235
Venus-Uranus	2	221	251
Venus-Neptune	2	443	494
Venus-Pluto	1	310	494
Mars-Jupiter	2	106	237
Mars-Saturn	2	228	442
Mars-Uranus	1	131	252
Mars-Neptune	1	174	331
Mars-Pluto	2	888	1734
Jupiter-Saturn$	1	3	59.6
	2	40	794.4
Jupiter-Uranus	1	6	83
	2	97	1340
Jupiter-Neptune	1	13	166

	2	64	818
Jupiter-Pluto	1	20	249
	2	59	735
Saturn-Uranus$	1	2	90.7
	2	24	1088.7
Saturn-Neptune	1	23	824
	2	41	1471
Saturn-Pluto	1#	25	736
	1*	37	1237s.y.
Uranus-Neptune$	1	1	171.4
	2	21	3599.4
Uranus-Pluto$	1	2	254.3
	2	27	3432.8
Neptune-Pluto$	1	1	492.3
	2	147	72,372.3

In the zodiac of precession. * In the fixed zodiac. $ More detailed data concerning these cycles are appended to the discussion under Cycles.

Refranation. A term used in Horary Astrology when one of two planets applying to an aspect turns retrograde before the aspect is complete. It is taken as an indication that the matter under negotiation will not be brought to a successful conclusion.

Relative Houses. v. HOUSES.

Retrograde. The term applied to an apparent backward motion in the Zodiac of certain planets when decreasing in longitude as viewed from the Earth. It can be compared to the effect of a slow-moving train as viewed from another train traveling parallel to it but at a more rapid rate, wherein the slower train appears to be moving backwards. However, in the case of the celestial bodies it is not a matter of their actual speed or travel, but of the rate at which they change their angular relationship.

Retrograde planets in a birth map were anciently said to be weak or debilitated, but a more logical interpretation would seem to indicate that the influence is rendered stronger, which in the case of a malefic planet is definitely unfortunate. That it continues to retrograde for a period after birth might detract from its capacity to incite progress, but if so the extent of retardation must be judged from its relative nearness to its second station.

It is averred by some astrologers that a planet in retrograde motion partakes of the nature of the Mars end of the spectrum. This hardly appears a safe generalization, for according to the laws of spectroscopy a planet moving away from us - the distance between it and the Earth increasing - produces a slight shift of frequencies toward the red end of the spectrum, and with diminishing distance a relative shift towards the red end begins immediately after the opposition of a major planet to the Sun, and continues until just before the conjunction; and that it can hardly be said to apply at all to a minor planet.

It would appear that consideration of this factor involves the direction of the planet's motion, whether toward or away from the Earth, rather than the character of the motion as either direct or retrograde. In fact it appears to have bearing on the doctrine of orientality. This Doppler displacement has been noted in observations of Venus, which indicated that a differentiation of influence should be studied as between Venus when in motion away from the Earth, and when moving toward it.

To be able to visualize and thus thoroughly understand the phenomenon of retrograde motion it is advisable to study the cycles of two groups of planets: the minor planets, those between the Earth and the Sun; and the major planets, those whose orbits lie outside that of the Earth.

Analyzing the cycle of Mercury, as typical of the orbits of the minor planets, shows this succession of phenomena:

SUPERIOR CONJUNCTION, when it passes on the far side of the Sun in direct motion, at which time it is invisible. Since thereafter it rises after the Sun and remains invisible during the daylight hours, it becomes visible only after the Sun has set in the west: the Evening Star. About fifteen days after the Superior conjunction it is at its smallest, a small circular orb.

GREATEST ELONGATION EAST: Some six months later it reaches the point of the greatest distance ahead of the Sun in its counterclockwise direct motion in orbit, hence East. At this time it passes out of its gibbous phase, showing only half of its surface illuminated, yet seemingly larger and brighter because it comes closer to the Earth.

ENTERS RETROGRADE ARC: Some two weeks later it enters the arc over which it will shortly retrograde.

MAXIMUM BRILLIANCE AS EVENING STAR: Even though reduced to a crescent of illumination it appears still larger, and with its elevation it remains longer above the horizon and is at its greatest brilliance.

FIRST STATION: Another two weeks and it becomes stationary, in preparation for retrograde (S.R.) motion. In another two weeks, about six days before the Inferior conjunction, it becomes a slender crescent.

INFERIOR CONJUNCTION, when it passes in retrograde between the Earth and the Sun and is lost from sight in the Sun's rays. This conjunction is shorter in duration. They separate faster because Mercury's motion is opposite to the apparent motion of the Sun. In another five days it again becomes visible on the other side of the Sun, the West, when as the Morning Star it appears before sunrise as a slender crescent, but turned in the opposite direction.

SECOND STATION: Another six days and it again becomes stationary, in preparation to resume its direct, or re-direct motion.

MAXIMUM BRILLIANCE AS MORNING STAR: Some fifteen days later it is reduced to a broad crescent and is again at its brightest, now as a morning star.

EMERGES FROM RETROGRADE ARC: As it advances beyond the degree of its First Station it leaves the retrograde arc and enters territory over which it will not retrograde during this cycle.

GREATEST ELONGATION WEST: Although no longer in retrograde it has not yet accelerated to the extent that it equals the Sun's motion, hence it continues to increase behind the Sun in elongation and elevation for some ten or twelve days to the point of greatest elevation West just before it commences its gibbous phase.

SMALLEST PHASE: Some seven months later, about fifteen days before the superior conjunction, it has decreased in visible size until it appears as a small but fully illuminated disc of less than one-third the diameter it had at its brightest phase. Then comes the next superior conjunction and invisibility, completing one cycle from one superior conjunction to the next.

Venus's motion is entirely similar, although the intervals are longer. Where the Mercury sidereal period is approx. 88 d. and its synodic period is 116 d. the Venus orbit of 225 days has a synodic period of 584 days.

The cycle of the major planets is not greatly different, except that at the opposition, the Sun and the planet arc on opposite sides of the Earth. Figure 2, a comparative illustration of the motion of Venus as an inside planet and Mars as an outside planet, in reference to the motion of the Earth, facilitates a ready understanding of the relationship of the orbits which produces the phenomenon known as retrograde motion.

While the Inferior Conjunctions with a minor planet, and the oppositions to a major planet ALWAYS OCCUR DURING THE RETROGRADE; the similarity ceases when gravitation is considered, since at the opposition of the major planet the Earth is in between, hence the planet and the Sun are exercising a gravitational pull upon the Earth from opposite sides; while at both conjunctions of a minor planet the gravitational pull from the Sun and the planet are always in the same direction.

It is generally considered that a transiting planet is more likely to develop its negative qualities when it is in retrograde. That it is turning back for a recheck of ground already covered need not necessarily be bad, except for the fact that the future is held in abeyance. Some people look upon any delay as a tragedy, but the real difference has to do with whose neck is in the noose when the postponement of execution is decreed. In some cases it may mean only a temporary delay that is compensated for when the planet resumes its direct motion.

This proximity of Mars to the Earth may be one of the most important of considerations, since it considerably augments the strength of its reception - what the radio engineer calls signal strength. Wilson speaks of Mars Retrograde as Mars perigee, and attributes to it a wave of robberies, vicious murders and calamities. At the Sun-Mars opposition of August 1924 Mars was closer to the Earth than it had been for 800 years.

It should be found, however, that the period of slower motion and of increasing intensity when the transiting planet is approaching its First Station, and of slower but accelerating motion after it passes its Second Station, are important arcs, because any birth planet which falls within the arc over which the transiting planet will retrograde will receive three separate and successive accents, of the combined nature of the radical and the transiting planet.

When Mars in transit retrogrades over a birth Saturn position, it means that this is already the second transit of Mars over the birth Saturn position, and that when it resumes Redirect motion there will occur a third contact. If a contact can be expected to crystalize into an event, then three contacts can mean three events. Even if one resists the temptations, three are certainly worse than one - particularly three slow ones that linger and thus burn more deeply. There is the further and important consideration of declination to be taken into account, and a parallel of Latitude reinforcing the first or third contact may render one of them more effective even than the retrograde contact. Thus it would appear that the important differentiation of a transiting planet's influence requires the dividing of its apparent orbit into two arcs: that over which the planet will traverse but once, and that which it will traverse three times in one cycle. These two arcs might be termed the Arc of Advance, and the Arc of Retrograde. This distinction emphasizes the fact that it is not merely the slow motion of the Retrograde which is involved, or the matter of replacing steps over territory previously traversed, but that there will be three separate contacts with each degree within the Arc of Retrograde, as compared to one brief contact with each degree within the Arc of Advance.

The Arc of Retrograde is thus marked by four points: (a) the Pre-First-Station point at which the arc begins, when it first passes the degree which later marks the Second Station; (b) the First Station, where the motion turns Retrograde; (c) the Second Station, where the motion turns direct; and (d) the Post-Second-Station point, where the arc ends, marked by the passing of the degree of the First Station.

A further consideration is in the fact that with the major planets the opposition to the Sun occurs always in the middle of the Arc of Retrograde, while the conjunction occurs in the middle of the Arc of Advance. Also, that at the opposition the Earth is nearer to the planet, by the length of the diameter of its own orbit. This is for the reason that at any planet's opposition to the Sun, the Earth is between that planet and the Sun: while at the conjunction the Earth is on the far side of the Sun opposite the planet.

In the case of the minor planets, the Earth never passes between them and the Sun, hence they never oppose the Sun. However, the Superior conjunction which occurs when the earth and the planet are on opposite sides of the Sun, falls in the middle of the Arc of Advance, and the Inferior Conjunction, when the planet passes between the Earth and the Sun, is midway in the Arc of Retrograde.

Modern students take these various factors into consideration in analyzing the influence of a transiting planet in different portions of its orbit, and in different relationships to the position of the Earth in its orbit.

By way of illustrating the Retrograde Arc, the data on two cycles of Mars is given:

..**Enters Arc**.........1945....10-3...14° 6' Cancer..|..1947....11-3.......18° 6' Leo

..**First Station SR**...1947....12-5....3°14' Leo.....|..1948.....1-9.......7°36' Virgo
..**Second Station SD**..1946.....2-22..14°06' Cancer..|...........3-30.....18°06' Leo
..**Leaves Arc**.................4-30...3°14' Leo.....|...........6-5.......7°36' Virgo

Retrograde Application. Said of a planet which during and by virtue of its retrograde motion is applying to an aspect with another planet; or of two planets, both in retrograde motion, which nevertheless are applying to an aspect to each other.

Revolution. Orbital Revolution. (1) Loosely applied to any- thing that describes a circle, or pursues an orbit, in contradistinction to one which rotates upon an axis. (2) In connection with Directions (Q.V.), the return of Sun, Moon, or any planet to its radical place. Revolution, Solar. v. SOLAR REVOLUTION.

Revolutionary Additives. v. SOLAR REVOLUTION.

Right Ascension. Distance measured along the celestial equator, Eastward from the point of the Spring Equinox; or, as sometimes described, distance along the circle of declination. v. CELESTIAL SPHERE.

Right Distance. That from one point to any other, in terms of Right Ascension.

Right Sphere. One in which all equatorial parallels are at right angles to the horizon: a sphere that has the equator for prime vertical, and the poles for horizon. Days and nights would always be of equal duration. Any point on the equator has a zenith in a right Sphere.

Rising Sign. The Sign or the subdivision of the Sign which was rising on the eastern horizon at the moment of birth, is deemed to exercise a strong influence upon the personality and physical appearance of the native. This is subject to modification by virtue of concurrent aspects. The placement of the Lord of the Ascendant, of the Moon, or of the planet aspecting the ascending degree, are also deemed to accent the particular subdivision of the Rising Sun in which the ascending degree falls. Interpretations by numerous authorities are available by Signs, by Decans and by demi-Decans - both incorrectly termed Faces by some authorities. In applying any of the interpretations attached to a Rising Sign it should be remembered that the presence of a planet in the Ascendant will always modify the influence of the Sign itself. v. SIDEREAL TIME.

Rising Time of a Planet, How to Approximate the. In the Ephemeris note the sidereal time for the day. If it is for 0h or midnight instead of 12h or noon, add 12 hours. Also note the degree position of the planet. In a Table of Houses for your latitude, find the sidereal time that corresponds to the degree position. The time difference between the S.T. of the planet's position and the S.T. noon position for the day, will be the elapsed time before or after noon that the planet will rise. For example, on Jan. 1, 1940, the Sun was in 9° Capricorn. The S. T. of 6h 38m at 24h Standard Time, becames S.T. at noon, 18h 38m. In Lat. 40°, a 9° Capricorn Ascendant corresponds with S.T. 14h 6m. The difference is 4h 32m before noon, or 7h 28m local civil or mean time - which varies by only a few minutes from the sunrise time given in the almanac. This local mean time should be further corrected to Standard Time by 4m per degree to the nearest Standard meridian. The rising time of any planet can be determined by the same method. v. TABLE OF HOUSES.

The following formula can also be employed:

From Ephemeris take:

...(1) Sidereal Time on MC at Midnight of desired day.
...(2) Add or subtract 12 = ST at Noon.
...(3) Degree occupied by Sun on the same day.

From Table of Houses for desired Latitude, locate in Ascendant column the degree occupied by the Sun, and take from the first column (4) the equivalent ST.

Then: (4) - (1) = the arc from Noon to Sunrise, stated in hours;
.................hence the approximate time of Sunrise;
......(2) - (4) = approximate hour of Sunset.

Example: For Dec. 17, 1946 at Lat. 40° N

...(1) ST at Midnight, 5h 40m + 12 = (2) ST at Noon, 17h 40m
...(3) Long. 24°26'
...(4) Equivalent S.T. 13h 2m

.........Sunrise.............Sunset
.......(4) 13h 2m..........(2) 17h 40m
.... - (1) 5h 40m....... - (4) 13h 2m
...........7h 22m AM............4h 38m PM

Rice gives 7h 16m AM and 4h 13m PM.

To find the approximate time of rising and setting of Venus on that day:

From Ephemeris take Venus Long., 20°10'
From Table of Houses take (5) the equivalent S.T....14h 46m
.....Subtract (4) Sun's equivalent S.T..............13h 2m
....1h 44m

Since Capricorn rises AFTER Sagittarius:

Venus rises 1h 44m after Sunrise, or 9h 6m AM; and sets 1h 44m after Sunset; or 6h 22m PM.

The same process will yield the rising and setting time of any planet.

Rotation. Preferably confined to the motion of a spherical body upon an axis, in contradistinction to its orbital revolution about another body. A more precise terminology would employ the compound forms: axial rotation, and orbital revolution.

Royal Stars. v. WATCHERS.

Ruler. This rather over-worked and at times loosely-applied term is principally concerned with a schematic arrangement of the Signs, whereby certain planets are deemed to have special potency or congeniality in a certain sign or signs. The entire subject of ruler ship is involved in much controversy, particularly since the modern discovery of additional planets for which there is no place in the ancient scheme of ruler ships.

This ancient scheme was based on the reasoning that since Leo is deemed the most regal of the signs, the Sun must naturally be its ruler. Similarly Cancer, as the most maternal of signs, should be ruled by the Moon. The planets, beginning with Mercury and moving outward from the Sun, were then ascribed to the next adjacent pairs: Mercury, to Gemini and Virgo; Venus, to Taurus and Libra; Mars, to Aries and Scorpio; Jupiter, to Sagittarius and Pisces; and Saturn, to Capricorn and Aquarius. A planet in a sign of which it is the Ruler is said to be in its own sign. In the case of the dual ruler ships, the Positive sign is its "day home" and the Negative sign its "night home." The use of "day house" is unfortunate in that "house" is a subdivision of a 24-hour orbit, while the sign over which the planet is presumed to rule is a subdivision of a 365-day orbit.

Many modern authorities have broken down this scheme by ascribing Uranus to the ruler ship or co-ruler ship of Aquarius, Neptune to Pisces, and Pluto variously to Aries or Scorpio. Others deem these distant planets to represent a second octave, indicating higher concepts, and conferring greater possibilities upon those sufficiently developed to be able to handle a high-tension current, but threatening catastrophe to elemental and undisciplined types. On this theory, Uranus would be the super-ruler of Gemini and Virgo; Neptune of Taurus and Libra; and Pluto of Aries and Scorpio - leaving the second octave planets of Jupiter and Saturn yet to be discovered.

The use of "ruler" in connection with the Houses, is confusing, and the rule generally recommended is: "Lord of a House; Ruler of a Sign." As indicating anatomical and geographical areas it is more precise to say "has dominion over" than to say "ruled by."

The Lord of a House is deemed to be the Ruler of the Sign that occupies the cusp. The Lord of the Nativity, or as often termed the Ruler of the Horoscope, is variously the most strongly placed planet in the map, especially that planet which is in the First House and close to the ascending degree. Lacking a planet so placed, the Ruler of the ascending sign is the Lord of the Nativity.

It is presumed by some that the Arabians employed a system of House ruler ships which consists of the planets arranged in converse order: the Sun as Lord of the First House; Moon, of the Twelfth; Mercury, the Eleventh; Venus, the Tenth; Mars, the Ninth; Jupiter, the Eighth; Saturn, the Seventh; Uranus, the Sixth; Neptune, the Fifth; Pluto, the Fourth; with three as yet undiscovered planets for the remaining Houses.

The commonly observed rules for determining the Lord of the Nativity are: (1) If the Lord of the Ascendant is poorly aspected and in an uncongenial sign, a more elevated planet should be considered, if there be such. (2) If the Lord of the Ascendant is strongly placed and well aspected, but there is another planet which by position and aspects is deemed of equal power, both planets may be considered as co-rulers in a dual Lordship. Some deem that with an Aquarian Ascendant, Saturn and Uranus are co-rulers of the map; and that a Piscean Ascendant makes Jupiter and Neptune co-rulers - because these are major planets and exceedingly strong. (3) If the choice is between two planets of which one is more afflicted than the other, the afflicted planet is to be selected - in that unfavorable aspects are positive and favorable aspects negative. (4) If the Lord of the Ascendant is weak, the Ruler of the Sun sign may be the Lord of the Nativity, if it is in powerful aspect to the Sun and Moon. (5) Either Sun or Moon may be the Lord of the Nativity if strongly placed and in the sign of its Ruler ship or Exaltation. (6) An Exalted planet is generally deemed to be a co-ruler. (7) The Ruler of an intercepted sign in the First House is generally accepted as a co-ruler - after such time as by progression the cusp will have advanced into the intercepted sign. (8) Accidental Dignities are deemed to outweigh Essential Dignities, especially where a planet occupies the Tenth House.

Conditions affecting the Ruler of the Sign on the cusp of a House, or of the Sign intercepting a House, are of secondary importance to the influence of a planet actually posited in the House. However, the considerations affecting the Ruler are consulted for testimony concerning a House in which no planet is posited, on the principle that the planet's dignity with reference to a house on the cusp of which its sign appears, persists even though its owner may be absent. **v. Dignities.**

Ruler ship, Geographical. For the interpreting of Horary figures, certain countries and cities are said to be under the ruler ship of different signs. The following list is from Alan Leo, a British authority:

SIGN RULER SHIP OF COUNTRIES

ARIES: Britain, Denmark, Galitia, Germany, Lithuania, Lower Poland, Palestine, Syria.
TAURUS: Azerbaijan, Asia Minor, Caucasus, Georgia, Holland, Ire- land, Mozendaran, Persia, Poland, White Russia.
GEMINI: Armenia, Belgium, Brabant, Egypt (Lower), England (West), Flanders, Lombardy, Sardinia, Tripoli, United States.
CANCER: Africa (North and West), Holland, Scotland, Zealand.
LEO: Alps, Bohemia, Cappadocia, Chaldea, France, Italy, Sicily, Coast of Sidon, and Tyre.
VIRGO: Assyria, Babylon, Candia, Corinth, Crete, Croatia, Mesopotamia, Morea, Silesia (Lower), Switzerland, Thessaly, Turkey.
LIBRA: Argentina, Austria, China, Egypt, Japan, Livonia, Savoy, Thibet, Burma.
SCORPIO: Algeria, Barbary, Bavaria, Catatonia, Fez, Judea, Jutland, Morocco, Norway.
SAGITTARIUS: Arabia, Cape Finisterre, Dalmatia, France, Hungary, Italy, Moravia, Provence, Spain, Slavonia, Tuscany.
CAPRICORN: Bosnia, Bulgaria, Hesse, India, Illyria, Khorassan, Lithuania, Macedonia, Mexico, Morea, Mecklenburg, Punjab, Thrace, Styria, Saxony.

AQUARIUS: Arabia, Abyssinia, Circassia, Lithuania, Lower Sweden, Prussia, Poland, Piedmont, Russia, Tartary, Westphalia.

PISCES: Asia (Southern), Africa (North), Sahara Desert, Calabria, Egypt, Galicia (Spain), Nubia, Normandy, Portugal.

SIGN RULERSHIP OF CITIES

ARIES: Brunswick, Capua, Cracow, Florence, Leicester, Marseilles, Naples, Padua, Saragossa, Utrecht.
TAURUS: Dublin, Franconia, Leipsic, Mantua, Palermo, Parma.
GEMINI: Cordova, London, Louvain, Mentz, Nuremburg, Versailles.
CANCER: Amsterdam, Berne, Cadiz, Constantinople, Genoa, Lubeck, Manchester, Milan, St. Andrews, Stockholm, Tunis, Venice, York.
LEO: Bath, Bolton-le-Moors, Bombay, Bristol, Damascus, Portsmouth, Prague, Ravenna, Rome, Taunton.
VIRGO: Basle, Bagdad, Cheltenham, Heidelburg, Jerusalem, Lyons, Navarre, Padua, Paris, Reading.
LIBRA: Antwerp, Charlestown, Frankfort, Fribourg, Lisbon, Speyer, Plasencia, Vienna.
SCORPIO: Frankfort on the Oder, Ghent, Liverpool, and Messina. **SAGITTARIUS**: Avignon, Buda, Cologne, Narbonne, Naples, Sheffield.
CAPRICORN: Brussels, Constance, Oxford, Port Said.
AQUARIUS: Bremen, Hamburg, Ingoldstadt, Salsburg, Trent.
PISCES: Alexandria, Compostela, Ratisbon, Seville, Tiverton, Worms.

RULERSHIP OF AMERICAN CITIES. Opinion concerning the rulership of cities in the United States is not always unanimous. The following rulerships are taken from various sources. Those marked by an asterisk are deemed slightly conjectural by one American writer, Charles Bates, who has devoted considerable research to the subject.

```
                    Ascendant....Sun
...Baltimore, Md.......Scorpio*
...Boston..............Capricorn*...Virgo
...Chicago.............Libra........Leo
...Cleveland...        Scorpio*.....Pisces*
...Detroit.............Leo..........Leo
...Los Angeles.........Libra........Virgo
...Miami...............Libra........Leo
...New Orleans.........Scorpio*
...New York............Cancer.......Taurus
...Philadelphia........Virgo*.......Cancer
...St. Louis...........Taurus.......Aquarius
...San Francisco.......Scorpio#
...Toledo..............Sagittarius*
...Washington, D.C.....Scorpio......Virgo
```

*Slightly conjectural. #Others say Gemini or Leo.

Ruminant Signs. Aries, Taurus, Capricorn. v. SIGNS.

Sagittarius. The ninth sign of the zodiac. v. SIGNS.

Saros. (1) A Chaldean and Babylonian interpretation of a cycle of 60 days as 60 years. **(2)** 60 sixties, or 3,600. **(3)** A lunar cycle of 6,585.32 days - 223 lunations; or 18 years, 11 1/3 days. In this period the centers of Sun and Moon return so nearly to the same relative places that the eclipses of the next period recur in approximately the same sequence - but with their zone of visibility shifted 120° to the Westward. (v. ECLIPSES.)

Because the Node recedes 19.5 a year, the Sun meets the same Node in 346.62 days - the eclipse year. As this does not coincide with the Lunar periods, the Sun moves past the node a degree a day for as many days as it takes for the Moon to reach a conjunction or opposition. Thus either a Solar or Lunar Eclipse may occur before or after the Sun reaches the Node, or both before and after. If the Lunation occurs within 2 or 3 days before or after the Sun reaches the Node there may be no accompanying Lunar Eclipse, as on Dec. 3, 1918 and May 29, 1919 (Saros Series 11).

If the Lunation or Full Moon occurs from 4 to 9 days before the Sun reaches the Node, there will be a Lunar Eclipse followed by a Solar Eclipse, or the reverse. If the Lunation occurs from 10 to 12 days before the Sun reaches the Node there may be a series of three Eclipses: a Solar before the Node, a Lunar at the Node, and another Solar when the Sun has passed beyond the Node. Associated with this are certain values:

```
.......................................DAYS
...242 returns of the Moon to a particular Node.......6585.36
....19 returns of the Sun to the same Node............6585.78
...233 Synodic months................................6585.32
```

Saturn chasing the Moon. This is one of the most powerful of Saturnian conditions. Since the progressed Moon takes twenty-eight and Saturn thirty years to complete the circle, the two may in rare cases, approximately coincide. An affliction of the Moon by Saturn is of itself one of the most unfortunate of aspects; for when the aspect is close and the progressing Moon moves at about the same rate as Saturn, a transit of Saturn to the Moon can persist indefinitely - often for a lifetime: thus resulting in a double affliction. However, the condition can occur only where the Moon at birth is in conjunction, square or opposition to Saturn.

Saturnine. One of a dour disposition - a meaning borrowed wholly from Astrology, which defines it as one who has a strong Saturn accent.

Saturnalia. The Roman festival of Saturn which annually on Dec. 17 began a week of feasting.

Satellite. A planet or moon that revolves about another. The Moon is a satellite of the Earth; and according to Newton, both are satellites of the Sun. In modern Astrology it is confined to a body which revolves around one of the planets in our solar system.

Stellium: A group of five or more planets in one Sign or House. In an angle it portends great changes of fortune, the good and the bad coming in patches. Heavy falls are succeeded in due course by a spectacular comeback, and vice versa. Such persons usually have many acquaintances, but few real friends. They can hardly fail of considerable recognition at some periods of their lives.

Scorpio. The eighth sign of the zodiac. v. SIGNS.

Secondary Progressions. Zodiacal aspects formed by the orbital motions of the planets on successive days after birth, each day accounted the equivalent of one year of life. Aspects are calculated to the birth positions of the luminaries, planets and angles, and mutual aspects are formed between the progressed planets. The application of this system of forecasting future conditioning that may be expected to crystallize in events, involves the directing of the Midheaven, Ascendant and the Sun by their natural progress in the heavens after birth. The Sun and the Midheaven progress at an average rate of 59'08" per day (the so-called "Naibod Arc"), to form aspects to the radical positions of the planets, while the planets move at varying rates to form aspects to the radical positions of the Significators. The most dependable factor in Secondary Progressions is the advancing of the progressed Moon, forming aspects to the radical and progressed places of the planets and to the places of the Significators, which are interpreted according to the places in which the aspects fall by Sign and House.

With specific reference to the progressions of the Moon it is generally considered: that such aspects produce strong though gradual effects of about one month's duration; that the month when the progressed Moon is approaching a square to her own radical place is generally marked by accidents and infirmities, the next preceding semi-square usually giving an indication of the nature of the crisis or physical ailment that can be expected to develop; that trine and sextile aspects of the transitory and of the progressed Moon to the radical Moon generally outline favorable days and months; and that square and opposition aspects also strongly influence and that adversely, forming critical periods around the 7th, 14th, 21st and 28th day and year.

In general it is held that directions act in terms of the Radix and that when the Nativity is unfortunate no favorable direction can have the same efficacy as an adverse one; and vice versa when the Nativity is fortunate. In other words, the accidental good cannot overcome the radical evil. (v. RADIX SYSTEM.)

The revised Sepharial Dictionary defines Secondary Progressions somewhat misleadingly as those based upon the progress of the Moon in the zodiac. However, the aspects formed by the Moon in the Secondary system are important, and some authorities hold that unless they are of the same nature as the Primary Directions, hence tend to strengthen their operation, the primary directions will have little effect; but when they do coincide, a decided influence will be traceable in the life of the person whose chart is under consideration. According to this a Primary Direction would not function until such time as the progressed Moon forms an aspect of a similar nature. v. DIRECTIONS.

In calculating Progressions by the system of taking the positions of the planets as given in the Ephemeris for the next day following birth, as the equivalent of their progressed positions at the end of the first year of life, use may be made of this table. [*Apolo's Note:* 'd.' MEANS 'DAY'; 'h.' MEANS 'HOUR(S)'; 'm.' MEANS 'MINUTE(S)'; 's.' MEANS 'SECOND(S)'.]

......1 d. = 1 year
......2 h. = 1 month
.....30 m. = 1 week
......4 m. = 1 day
......1 m. = 6 hours
.....10 s. = 1 hour
......1 s. = 6 minutes

Seer. One who sees; a crystal gazer; a person endowed with second sight; one who foresees future events - a prophet; astrologically, one whose extra-sensory perceptions enable him to visualize the ultimate effects that will result from the cosmic causes portrayed in a birth Figure.

Semi-Arc. That portion of a celestial body's apparent daily travel, during which it remains above the horizon, from its rising to its setting, is called its diurnal arc; hence half of the arc, from horizon to Midheaven, is its Diurnal Semi-Arc. The other half, most of which is under the earth, is its nocturnal arc, and half of it becomes the Nocturnal Semi-Arc. The Sun's semi-arc, diurnal or nocturnal, when in 0° Aries or 0° Libra, is six hours or 90° all over the Earth. At other seasons the one is greater or less than the other, according to the time of the year and the latitude of the place. The greatest discrepancy occurs where the N. or S. latitude is high, and when the Sun is in 0° Cancer or 0° Capricorn. The semi-arc is usually measured in degrees of R. A. passing over the Meridian; although it can be expressed in terms of time.

Semi-Quintile. An 36º aspect (V. QUINTILE).

Semicircle. V. LUNAR; SOLAR.

Semi-sextile. A 30º aspect. (Q.V.)

Semi-square. A 45º aspect. (Q.V.)

Senses, Significators of the. Generally accepted as the significators of the five physical senses, are:

Mercury,....sight
Venus,......touch
Mars,.......taste
Jupiter,....smell
Saturn,.....hearing

Separating, separation. V. ASPECTS.

Sesqui-quadrate. A 135º aspect (q.v.)

Sesquiquintile. A 108º aspect (q.v.)

Seven. Anciently the number of the bodies presumed to make up our solar system, to which number was ascribed a magical significance. Identified with them were the days of the week and the seven notes of the Diatonic scale. In 1666 Newton ascribed to them the seven hues of the spectrum.

Man was presumed to be a seven-fold being:

Sun:.......His life-forces; the spiritual being within.
Moon:......His psychic being; the vegetable kingdom.
Mercury:..His intellect; the realm of Mind.
Venus:.....His divine, immortal self; the benevolent nature.
Mars:......His bestial nature; the animal nature.
Jupiter:...His higher physical nature; the quality of optimism.
Saturn:....His physical being; the mineral kingdom.

The seven deadly sins of the ancient theologians were said to have been of astrological origin: Pride, Jupiter; covetousness, Saturn; lust, Venus; wrath, Mars; gluttony, Mercury; envy, Moon; indolence, Sun.

Also the seven virtues: Chastity, Moon; love, Venus; courage, Mars; faith, Jupiter; hope, Sun; wisdom, Mercury; and prudence, Saturn.

There were also seven wise men of Greece; the seven-fold Amen; the Seven Wonders of the World; the Book of the Seven Seals (REV. 5,5), and the seven angels (REV. 5,8).

The Seven against Thebes were the seven heroes who undertook an expedition to aid Polynices against his brother Eteoclus. The oracle promised success to whichever brother Oedipus favored; but he cursed both, and the brothers slew each other.

Seven has been explained as compounded of "The Ternary of God and the Quarternary of the world," as representing "three-fold and four-fold happiness," making 3 + 4 = 7 a sacred number: a reference to the 4 quadruplicities and the 3 triplicities. Any multiple of seven became a "great number": a jubilee year of restitution.

Since every seventh year from time immemorial was believed to form some material alteration, it has been observed in some professions as a sabbatical year of rest, comparable to the seventh day on which the Creator rested from his labors - as recounted in the Book of Genesis. For the Seven Ages of Man, v. PLANETARY, AGES OF MAN.

Sexagenary. (1) A scale of numbers or a method of computation that proceeds by sixties - as in degree, minutes and seconds. (2) Said of tables prepared for the purpose of showing proportional parts of the number 60°: giving the product of two sexagenary numbers multiplied; or the quotient of two such when divided.

Sextile. A 60º aspect (q.v.)

Sextiles. A body sextiles another toward which it is approaching from a distance of from 53º to 60º.

Sidereal Clock. A clock found in every astronomical observatory, which is set to register oh om os when 0° Aries is on the Zenith. Formerly a noon point, but since 1925 a midnight point, it moves forward in the zodiac by 1°, or 4 minutes, each day, hence the Sidereal Time at noon (or midnight if since 1925) on any day shows what sign and degree is on the M.C. at that particular moment. For example, ST at 0h, or midnight, on May 1, 1945 is 14h 34m 14s: approx. 874m / 4 = 218 degrees = approx. 8° Scorpio on M.C. The Sidereal Clock indicates 24h, while the solar chronometer registers 23h 56m 4.0906s of Mean Solar Time. It does not register A.M. or P.M., but divides the dial into 24 hourly periods. The so-called Army and Navy time of World War 11 indicates the eventual universal use of the same system applied to solar time, whereby for example, 2 P.M. will be known as 1400.

After the Sidereal clock has been set at 0h to coincide with the moment of the Earth's crossing the intersecting point of the Ecliptic and Equator, the next noon it will read something like 12:04 - the distance the Earth has travelled in orbit in one solar day, shown in units of time. Thus each successive day at noon it shows the cumulative amount of the Earth's orbital travel since noon on the day of the equinox. Thereby sidereal time becomes the hour angle of the Vernal Equinox, and the Earth's position at Greenwich Noon on any day can be expressed in terms of hours, minutes and seconds. Its position along the ecliptic is expressed in degrees and minutes of longitude, and along the equator in degrees and minutes of Right Ascension.

Sidereal Day. The interval between two successive transits of the first point of Aries over the upper meridian of any place. The Sidereal Day is equal to 23h 56m 4.09s of mean solar time, and it has sidereal hours, each of 60 sidereal minutes, each minute of 60 sidereal seconds.

Sidereal Time. A method of time-reckoning based upon the period elapsing between two successive passages of some particular star, taken as a fixed celestial point, over a given point on the circumference of the Earth. During one such rotation the Sun's apparent orbital travel has amounted to approximately 1°, hence the return of a given point on the Earth to the same relationship with the Sun requires added travel to the extent of 1° of arc or 4 minutes of time. Thus each calendar anniversary shows an annual net gain of 1°, which is the basis of all systems of progressed influences. The S.T. at any moment is the angular distance along the Ecliptic from 0° Aries, the point of the Spring Equinox, to the meridian of a given place at noon on a given day, expressed in h. m. s. The Right Ascension of the Meridian (RAMC) is a similar angular distance along the Equator expressed in degrees and minutes of arc.

When the Spring equinoctial point is on the observer's meridian it is S.T. 0h. When that degree has moved 15° it is 1h S.T. Thus the time required for the equinoctial degree to move to a certain advanced position becomes the unit through which that position is expressed. To determine the sidereal time for a given moment at a certain place, take from the ephemeris the ST for that date and apply certain corrections, viz.: If the ephemeris is for any other meridian than Greenwich make sure to take that into account, adding or subtracting your distance from this meridian, not from Greenwich; also add or subtract 12 hours if you are calculating your time-interval from midnight.

Additions to this S.T. for stations west of the zone meridian are made in degrees expressed in solar mean time, four minutes for each degree, which must be further converted by adding 0s.657 for each degree to reduce the additions to sidereal time. The hours added for the elapsed time since oh must also be adjusted in the same proportion. v. TIME.

Sidereal Year. v. YEAR.

Sign. One of the Twelve Signs of the Zodiac. The annual revolution of the Earth round the Sun is divided into the 360° of a circle, a division that mathematically and astronomically is universally accepted. The subdivisions of the circle into 12 equal arcs, distinguished by names, are known as the Signs of the Zodiac. They no longer bear any relationship to the constellations of the same name.

These arcs are measured from the point where the Sun crosses the celestial equator at the beginning of Spring on or about March 21st each year. As this is coincidental with the position of the Earth's axis at right angles to the radius of its orbit, the days and nights are of equal duration all over the Earth. The point is termed the Vernal Equinox. That the Zodiacal year seems at one period of history to have begun with Taurus indicates that these records date from between 2,000 and 4,000 B.C., during which period the equinoctial point fell in Taurus.

The further fact that the Equinox still continues to fall in 0° Aries indicates that at some time since the beginning of the Christian era the fixed Zodiac of constellations was abandoned and the names reapplied to a moving Zodiac based upon the equinoctial point, then recognized as the beginning of the astrological year. The year's arc of precession was thus ignored - an annual loss of a moment of time that shows up in no calculation at present in use, other than in a consideration of the Precession of the equinoctial point and the one degree revision of star positions every seventy years.

Can it be that our only record of one of these early readjustments of the calendar is that of Joshua having commanded the Sun to stand still?

Thus for at least 40 centuries astrologers have recognized the receding point of the Node of intersection of the Ecliptic and the Celestial Equator as the commencement of a scheme of magnetic conditioning. (v. SOLAR SYSTEM.)

Of the twelve signs there are four basic groups:

The Inspirational Group - the Fire signs.
The Emotional Group - the Water signs.
The Mental Group - the Air signs.
The Practical Group - the Earth signs.

These are termed the Elements, or Triplicities - since three signs are embraced in each group, as follows:

```
...............Cardinal......Fixed.......Mutable
......Fire:.......Aries.........Leo.........Sagittarius
......Water:.....Cancer........Scorpio.....Pisces
......Air:........Libra.........Aquarius....Gemini
......Earth:.....Capricorn.....Taurus......Virgo
```

As the English language abounds in words which had their origin in the symbology of the ancients, the use of terms such as fire, earth, air and water, do not indicate any present-day adherence to the ancient concept that matter is composed of these four primary elements. They are merely terms, but as such they appear aptly to symbolize, now as then, an outstanding characteristic of each of the four basic groups into which mankind is classified according to astrology. In fact, it becomes doubtful whether this grouping was ever intended to apply to the elements of matter, since fire could hardly have been looked upon even in that day as a physical element. More than likely it is a modern misconception of their symbolic interpretation of the psychological elements discerned in zodiacal influences.

Of each of these elemental groups or triplicities there are three types, or qualities, as shown in the previous arrangement: the Cardinal or Initiative signs, the Fixed or Executive signs, and the Mutable or Deductive signs. As there are four of each, these are known as the Quadruplicities.

Key words often associated with the twelve Signs are:

```
..Aries:.....Aspiration...|..Libra:........Equilibrium
..Taurus:....Integration..|..Scorpio:......Creativity
..Gemini:....Vivification.|..Sagittarius:..Administration
..Cancer:....Expansion....|..Capricorn:....Discrimination
..Leo:.......Assurance....|..Aquarius:.....Loyalty
..Virgo:.....Assimilation.|..Pisces:.......Appreciation
```

Another classification into four groups representing the four seasons, is known as the Trinities:

```
..INTELLECTUAL..MATERNAL....REPRODUCTIVE....SERVING
..(Spring)......(Summer)....(Autumn)........(Winter)
..1. Aries......4. Cancer...7. Libra........10. Capricorn
..2. Taurus.....5. Leo......8. Scorpio......11. Aquarius
..3. Gemini.....6. Virgo....9. Sagittarius..12. Pisces
```

CARDINAL SIGNS. So called because they are placed at the East, West, North and South points of the astrological figure, hence compare to the four Cardinal points of the compass-the points usually marked by a red arrow. They are variously termed, the Leading, Movable, Acute, Changeable or Initiating signs or types, and as they represent the active temperament are said to partake of the nature of the Ascendant.

FIXED SIGNS, because they represent a balance of conflicting forces, are more uniformly referred to as the Fixed or Grave signs or Executive types; although occasionally referred to as the "foundation" signs - those which most distinctly typify each element, because of which they were said to have been dominant in the formulation of the Mosaic laws. They have also been called the Seismic or "earthquake" signs, on the assumption that earthquakes most frequently occur when the Sun or Moon is in a Fixed sign. They are the power-houses of the zodiac - reservoirs of energy; the Formators of the Chaldeans, the Cherubim of the Hebrews - the builders of the world. The fixed sign tenacity is depended upon to support or stabilize the leading signs.

MUTABLE SIGNS, representing the arcs in which there is a perpetual condition of slowing down in readiness to turn a corner; a mobilization for action, and the indecision which results or accompanies it; were symbolized by concepts which would express this duality - the twins, the two deep-water sea-horses, or the half-man, half-horse of the Archer; hence also called the Dual or the Double-bodied Signs; and by some, the Common or Flexed Signs. They are the minds of their Triplicity, with their quickness and versatility acting as mediators between the Leading and Fixed Signs. They have been called the "reconcilers of the universe."

The Signs of the Zodiac should not be confounded with the Zodiac of Constellations with which they have only an historic relationship. Somewhat before the Christian era the Constellations (q.v.) and the Signs coincided. Since then the Precession (q.v.) of the Equinoctial point has produced a separation of approximately 1° in seventy-two years, or a total of about thirty degrees in 2000 years. It is not possible to establish with exactness the date upon which they coincided, for there is no sharp line or boundary between the general areas associated with the group of stars that make up a constellation, as compared to the Signs which are measured in 30° arcs along the Ecliptic beginning at the point of the Spring Equinox. Aries 0° is now in or about to enter the last degrees of the constellation of Aquarius, hence current references to the Aquarian Age; also to the two thousand years of the Piscean Age through which the Equinoctial Point has receded since the dawn of the Christian era - an epoch symbolized in the parable of the Loaves and the Fishes.

The four elements go farther than the mere locating of the Sun position. The qualities contained in the signs positing the Moon and the planets are gradually developed by every stimulation that reaches the native through these points of receptivity. Every planet and every angle, as it passes over each birth sensitivity, results in an accent. This means that each of a dozen points of receptivity are daily stimulated by an accent from each of a dozen points of electro-magnetic radiation, resulting in something like 144 daily accents - not counting the changes resulting from the orbital motion of each energy-radiating body. That is why planets well distributed among signs of the different elements, produce the well-rounded individual. The Greek philosophers built on this basis their thesis that the whole man consisted of the interweaving of the four categories, into one of which can be placed every human activity. These are:

...CATEGORY..........FROM CONTEMPLATION OF....................BECAUSE OF ACCENTS IN
1. Physical......Body: functions and needs....................Earth
2. Intellectual..Mind: concepts and thought processes.........Air
3. Aesthetic.....Soul: yearnings; emotional processes.........Water
4. Moral.........Spirit: aspirations, conduct, and character..Fire

The terminology of the trigons, or triplicities of Elements, is universal: fire, water, air and earth; although some moderns prefer to call them the Inspirational, Emotional, Mental and Practical Natures.

These four Elements, as represented by the fixed type of each group, are symbolized in the figures of the Cherubim, and in the Assyrian "winged lion." Also in the Egyptian Sphynx, in which the Bull's body (Taurus), the Lion's paws and tail (Leo), the Eagle's wings (Scorpio), and the Human head (Aquarius), repre- sent the four types which combine to form the body politic.

They are also embodied in the deck of cards: clubs for fire, diamonds for earth, hearts for water, and spades for air; the black suits representing the positive signs and the red suits the negative signs.

They are depicted symbolically in the Four Horsemen of the Apocalypse, and are builded into the Paris Notre Dame Cathedral, which is as completely an astrological edifice as is the great Pyramid. In **REVELATION V:7** one reads that "the first beast was ne a lion, and the second beast like a calf, and the third beast had a face as a man, and the fourth beast was like a flying eagle." Later on are described horses with the faces of men, the teeth of lions, wings, and a sting in the tall like unto a scorpion. In Chaucer, Shakespeare and all the writers of the Elizabethan age, astrological allusions are frequent; in fact, the symbolism of the fixed signs as representing the four elementary types of the GENUS HOMO, are the subject of innumerable allusions in art and literature.

The "earthiness" of the materialistic or practical Earth sign group is quite generally represented by the thick-necked bull - the Taurus. In Hindu lore the chariot of Vishnu is symbolized by a Bull. The Legend of St. George and the Dragon depicts the opposition of Taurus to Scorpio.

In Chinese astrology, Taurus was the White Tiger: Leo, the Red Bird; Scorpio, the Black Dragon; and Aquarius, the Black Warrior - again a "human" sign.

The inspirational Fire sign group are almost universally symbolized by the Lion.

The sympathetic, sensitive and often vindictive, emotional Water sign group are frequently represented by the Scorpion, not only because of its "sting" but also for the frequency with which it was anciently supposed to sting itself to death rather than face a ring of fire. It is also symbolized by the serpent - perhaps connotating the "wisdom of the serpent" of the Garden of Eden. In the Roman Sphynx it is represented by the asp on the man's forehead. Its "lone wolf" proclivities, and the frequency with which strength in Scorpio is reflected in a Roman nose - the eagle's beak - have been symbolized at some periods of antiquity by the Eagle, as evidenced by the eagle's wings on the Egyptian Sphynx.

The intellectual or mental Air sign group is almost universally represented by a man, usually pouring out water from a jug - symbolizing the giving of the water of knowledge to a thirsting world. The three air signs have been spoken of as the "triangle of harmony, peace and equilibrium."

Signs, and the Disciples. It is commonly considered from the many New Testament pronouncements of astrological doctrine, that the Twelve Disciples were chosen, each to represent a different one of the twelve fundamental types and qualities with a ruling Trinity of the central Sun (the Father) whose spiritual and intellectual light (the Holy Spirit) reflected by the Moon (the Son) flowed out through these twelve apostles into all the world-representing humanity divided into its twelve basic types. The disciples considered this order so important that after Judas's betrayal Mathias took his place as one of the twelve.

ARIES: Peter, the fiery, impulsive, changeable, pioneering leader, who eventually became the rock upon which was founded the New Church "of the Lamb." (Initiating: inspirational)
TAURUS: Simon Zelotes, the dogmatic, determined zealot; who was concerned with property and finances, rebelled against the payment of taxes, and received from Jesus the admonition - "Render unto Caesar the things that are Caesar's." (Fixed: materialistic)
GEMINI: James, "the lesser." Slow to accept the authenticity of the Messiah, but became the eloquent preacher of the church in Jerusalem, and an active evangelist and exhorter. (Mutable: intellectual)
CANCER: Andrew, the sympathetic homebody, a follower of John the Baptist, whose first thought when he discovered the Messiah was to run quickly and fetch his brother Simon. (Initiating: sympathetic)
LEO: John, the most beloved apostle. (Fixed: inspirational)
VIRGO: Philip, always precise, calculating, enquiring, and practical. (Mutable: materialistic)
LIBRA: Bartholomew-Nathaniel, the innocently pure one "in whom there is no guile." The tactful, persuasive evangelist. (Initiating: intellectual)
SCORPIO: Thomas, the doubting skeptic, yet bold and courageous. (Fixed: sympathetic)
SAGITTARIUS: James, the great teacher, who with Peter and John became the spiritual leaders of the early church: the three fire sign types cooperating. (Mutable: inspirational)
CAPRICORN: Matthew, the tax gatherer, the politician, the one in authority in the governing seat in Rome. (Initiating: materialistic)
AQUARIUS: Thaddeus-Jude, who considered the lot of the peasant, and sought to better the living and working conditions of the masses; and who interrogated Jesus at the Last Supper as to how he would manifest himself. (Fixed: intellectual)
PISCES: Judas Iscariot, who when he succumbed to temptation suf- fered severe pangs of remorse. (Mutable: sympathetic)

Signs, The Symbology of Twelve. Dr. Curtiss characterized the evangelistic authors of the four gospels, in terms of the fixed types of the four elemental groups, in this fashion:

.......Matthew-Aquarius........To Know.
.......Mark-Leo................To Dare.
.......Luke-Taurus.............To Do.
.......John-Scorpio............To Keep Silent.

In the Book of Revelations we read that by the River of Life grew a Tree of Life and of its twelve manner of fruits whereby it yielded a different fruit for each month of the year.

Elsewhere in the Bible, which is a great repository of astrological truths, we find God referred to as the Logos, out of which went four rivers. In Abraham's effort to restore the Logos, we find the symbol of an earlier Trinity: Abraham, the spiritual father; Isaac, the thought concept; and Jacob, the physical externalization.

Jacob's twelve sons were the chiefs of the Twelve Tribes of Israel. These are listed at birth in Genesis XXIX, and again shortly before his death (Gen. XLIX). Ezekiel lists the tribes in the distribution of land, substituting Manasseh and Ephraim, as perhaps the sons of deceased fathers, Joseph and Levi; yet in the last chapter in listing the Temple dates he employs the names of the twelve sons, as recounted in Genesis. The symbolic descriptions accompanying the names leave little doubt that they were representative of the twelve astrological types.

In the order of their birth the twelve sons were named Reuben, Simeon, Levi, Judah, Dan, Naphtali, Gad, Asher, Issacher, Zebulon, Joseph and Benjamin. There is disagreement among authorities as to which Sign represents each one, but none as to the fact that they were astrological. In fact Dan is definitely established as representing Scorpio in Jacob's last blessing, when he said: "Dan is a snake, a serpent in the path, that biteth at the horse's heels so that the rider falleth backward," referring to Scorpio at the heels of the Centaur or Sagittarius.

It is generally considered that the modern prototype of the tribe of judah is the British nation; of Dan, Italy; of Naphtali, the United States; and of Reuben, the Jews.

The twelve layers of the foundation walls of the New Jerusalem **(REV. XXI: 19-20)** were builded of:

1. Jasper, an opalescent or greenish stone.
2. Sapphire, a blue, transparent gem.
3. Chalcedony, pale gray, translucent quartz.
4. Emerald, green, transparent beryl.
5. Sardonyx, onyx with layers of sard, a brownish, red chalcedony.
6. Sardius, probably a Ruby.
7. Chrysolite, blue-green magnesium iron silicate.
8. Beryl, probably bluish-green or aquamarine.
9. Topaz, a yellow sapphire.
10. Chrysoprase, a light green chalcedony.
11. Jacinth, a stone the color of hyacinth.
12. Amethyst, purple or blue-violet quartz.

From another period we find the Twelve Labors of Hercules, as emblematic of the tasks which Destiny metes out to each of the twelve basic types, whereby to attain to an heroic stature. Hercules, or Heracles, is a mythological hero celebrated for his strength in the performance of super-human tasks, imposed by Eurysthcus because of the hatred of Hera (Juno) for Alcmena, the mother of Hercules by Zeus (Jupiter). After the death of Hercules he was deified as the husband of Hebe.

The Twelve tasks are not listed in the same order by all his-torians, and there are differences of opinion as to the signs to which they pertain, but presumably the hero took the worst traits of each sign and transmuted them into the nobility of which each sign is capable. The "labors" are:

1. Wrestling with and killing by strangulation the invulnerable Nemean lion.

2. Destruction of the Lernean hydra.
3. Capture of the Arcadian or Cerynean hind - or stag.
4. Capture of the boar of Erymanthus, when he fought the Centaurs, killing two friends, Chiron and Pholus. V. DEMETER'S MYSTERIES (NOT IN THIS DICTIONARY!)
5. Cleansing the stables of Augeas.
6. Killing of the man-eating Stymphalean birds.
7. Capture of the Cretan bull - afterwards killed by Theseus.
8. Capture of the man-eating mares of the Thracian Diomedes.
9. Seizure of the girdle of Hippolyte, queen of the Amazons.
10. Bringing the oxen of Geryones from Erythria in the Far West. On this adventure he set up the Pillars of Hercules at the Straits of Gibraltar.
11. Bringing the golden apples from the garden of the Hesperides.
12. Carrying Cerberus from Hades to the upper world.

Sign, Aries.

The Ram. The first sign of the zodiac. Its symbol represents the head and horns of the ram. It is a symbol of offensive power - a weapon of the gods, hence an implement of the will. The Babylonians sacrificed rams during the period when the Sun occupied this sign, which occurs annually from March 21 to April 20. Astrologically and astronomically it is the first thirty-degree arc beginning at the point of the Spring Equinox. It is the Leading quality of the Fire element: positive, diurnal, movable, dry, hot, fiery, choleric and violent.

RULER: Mars. EXALTATION: Sun. DETRIMENT: Venus. FALL: Saturn.

TEMPERAMENTAL ARIES

...Who works from morn to set of Sun,
...And never likes to be outdone?
...Whose walk is almost like a run?
......Who? Aries.

SYMBOLIC INTERPRETATION: Sprouting seed; fire in eruption; a fountain of water; a ram's horns.

Aries is the embodiment of Self, the will to manifest, the adventurous spirit; desire, initiative and courage.

...First from the east, the Ram conducts the year;
...Whom Ptolemy with twice nine stars adorns. - ARATUS.

FIRST DECAN: activity, adventure, zeal, notoriety, dishonor, misfortune. SECOND DECAN: noble affections as the source of power to sway others - the head joined to the impulses of the heart. It is the decan of Exaltation, in that the Sun is exalted in the nineteenth degree of the Sign.
THIRD DECAN: Propaganda, the spiritual possibilities of the valiant heart at grips with sordid conditions.

Sign, Taurus. The Bull. The second sign of the zodiac. Its symbol represents the head and horns of a bull. The sacred Apis was presumed to be the incarnation of the god Osiris - hence a symbol of a sepulchre or tomb. The Sun's entry into Taurus was celebrated as a Feast of Maya (Maia) - our May Day - the Sun represented by a white bull with a golden disc between his horns, followed by a procession of virgins, exemplifying the fecundity of Nature in Spring. The Sun is in Taurus annually from April 21 to May 20. Astrologically and astronomically it is in the second thirty-degree arc from the Spring Equinox, from 30° to 60° along the Ecliptic. It is the Fixed quality of the Earth element, conferring external will power that, ordinarily passive, and negative, becomes obstinate and unbending when aroused. Negative, nocturnal, cold, dry and melancholy. RULER: Venus. EXALTATION: Moon. DETRIMENT: Mars. FALL: Uranus.

........HEADSTRONG TAURUS
...Who smiles through life - except when crossed?
...Who knows, or thinks he knows, the most?
...Who loves good things: baked, boiled or roast?
.......Oh, Taurus.

SYMBOLIC INTERPRETATION: The head and horns of a bull; the sacred Apis in whom the god Osiris was incarnate; a sepulchre or tomb.

Taurus represents the manifestations of the Self, hence his basic possessions, and inherited tendencies.

...........The mighty Bull trudges the stellar lanes. - **ARATUS**

FIRST DECAN: Determination, the soul's exaltation; materialistic and mediumistic tendencies.
SECOND DECAN: Struggle, the conflict for supremacy.
THIRD DECAN: Mastership, triumph over physical limitations and environment; utilizing physical things for spiritual progress.

Sign, Gemini. The Twins. The third sign of the zodiac. Its symbol represents two pieces of wood bound together, symbolical of the unremitting conflict of contradictory mental processes. The Sun is in Gemini annually from May 21 to June 20. Astrologically it is the thirty degree arc immediately preceding the Summer Solstice, marked by the passing of the Sun over the Tropic of Cancer, and occupying a position along the ecliptic from 60° to 90°. It is the Mutable quality of the element: positive, dual.

RULER: Mercury. DETRIMENT: Jupiter.

................WORRISOME GEMINI.
...Who's fond of life and jest and pleasure;
...Who vacillates and changes ever?
...Who loves attention without measure?
........Why? Gemini.

Symbolic interpretation: Castor and Pollux; Bohas and Jakin, of Solomon's Temple; the Pillars of Hercules.

Gemini establishes a relationship between the Self and substance, the linkage of rhythm and form.

.....Fair Leda's twins, in time to stars decreed,
.....One fought on foot, one curbed the fiery steed. - VIRGIL

FIRST DECAN: Mastership, activities on the mental plane, deduction after assimilation.
SECOND DECAN: Fidelity, the espousal of progressive causes.
THIRD DECAN: Reason, the power of the objective mind.

Sign: Cancer. The Crab. The fourth sign of the zodiac. Its symbol presumably the folded claws of a crab, probably is intended to symbolize the joining together of a male and female spermatozoa -- as indicative of the most maternal of all the signs. The Sun is in Cancer annually from June 21 to July 22. Astrologically and astronomically it is the first thirty-degree arc following the Summer Solstice, marked by the Sun's passing of the Tropic of Cancer, and occupying a position along the Ecliptic from 90° to 120°). It is the Leading quality of the Water element: negative, cold, moist, phlegmatic, nocturnal, commanding, moveable, fruitful, weak, unfortunate, crooked, mute. RULER, Moon. EXALTATION: Jupiter. DETRIMENT: Saturn. FALL: Mars.

...............HARD-SHELLED SYMPATHETIC CANCER.
.......Who changes like a changeful season:
.......Holds fast and lets go without reason?
.......Who is there can give adhesion
............To Cancer?

Symbolic interpretation: The claws of the celestial crab; two spermatozoa intertwined, signifying the male and female seed, implying retirement and nurturing; the crab or scarab.

Cancer expresses the living organism, its capacity to grow.

............Soon as the evening shades prevail
............The Moon takes up the wondrous tale,
............And nightly to the listening Earth
............Proclaims the story of her birth.
..................................- ADDISON.

FIRST DECAN: Moods, strong emotions, poetic and dramatic expression.
SECOND DECAN: Revelation, resourcefulness, energy; powerful emotions; the struggle with sex.
THIRD DECAN: Research, curiosity, discontent, restlessness; love of Nature; a stormy life.

Sign: Leo. The Lion. The fifth sign of the zodiac. Its symbol is possibly an emblem representing the phallus, as used in ancient Dionysian mysteries. It is also an emblem of the Sun's fire, heat or creative energy. The Sun is in Leo annually from July 23 to August 22. Astrologically and astronomically it is the second thirty-degree arc after the Summer Solstice, marked by the Sun's passing of the Tropic of Cancer and occupying a position along the ecliptic from 120° to 150°. It is the Fixed quality of the Fire element, conferring an internal will motivated by an impulse of the heart. It is positive, hot, dry, choleric, eastern, diurnal, commanding, brutish, sterile, broken, changeable, fortunate, strong, hoarse, bitter, and violent. RULER: Sun. DETRIMENT: Saturn. FALL: Mercury.

>..........................*Loving Leo*
>...............Who praises all his kindred do;
>..............Expects his friends to praise them too
>..............And cannot see their senseless view?
>...................Ah, Leo.

Leo exemplifies the principle of cosmic splendor; wherein character defects due to planets in Leo persist through long periods, and good qualities from planets favorably aspecting the Sign are never lost.

>..........The Lion flames: There the Sun's course runs hottest.
>..........Empty of grain the and fields appear
>..........When first the Sun into Leo enters.
>..- ARATUS

FIRST DECAN: Ruler ship, fiery love, and the desire to rule others; extremes of pleasure whether in love or asceticism.
SECOND DECAN: Reformation, a convincing leader, given to ruthless onslaughts against his enemies; clear vision as to weaknesses in politics and religion.
THIRD DECAN: Ambition, a determination to rise in life, at the sacrifice of anything and anybody.

Sign: Virgo.

The Virgin. The sixth sign of the zodiac. Its symbol is probably a representation of the Girdle of Hymen, and has reference to the Immaculate Conception of a Messiah. It is usually pictured by a virgin holding in her hand a green branch, an car of corn, or a spike of grain. Spica is a star in the constellation of Virgo. Here was commemorated the Festival of Ishtar, goddess of fertility. The Sun is in Virgo annually from August 23 to September 22. Astrologically and astronomically it is the thirty-degree arc immediately preceding the Sun's passing over the Fall Equinoctial point, occupying a position along the Ecliptic from 150° to 180°. It is the Mutable quality of the Earth element: negative, cold, dry, sterile, human; also critical, practical, helpful. RULER: Mercury. DETRIMENT: Jupiter. FALL: Venus.

>...............CRITICAL VIRGO
>.........Who criticizes all she sees:
>........Yes, e'en would analyze a sneeze?
>........Who hugs and loves her own disease?
>.................Humpf, Virgo.

SYMBOLIC INTERPRETATION: A green branch; an car of wheat or corn; the Immaculate Virgin who gives birth to a world-saviour.

Form and the differentiation of sex. Discrimination through a critical analysis of the fruits of action.

> But modest Virgo's rays give polished parts,
> And fill men's breasts with honesty and arts;
> No tricks for gain, nor love of wealth dispense,
> But piercing thoughts and winning eloquence.
> - MANILIUS

FIRST DECAN: Achievement, a good mentality, gigantic tasks.
SECOND DECAN: Experience, an assimilative mind, skilled in diplomacy; great temptations; powers of discernment and compassion; love of worldly honor; susceptible to allurements of the flesh.
THIRD DECAN: Renunciation, the Crown of Thorns: work on behalf of others or of science, without thought of reward; forsakes everything for duty.

Sign: Libra. The Balances, or Scales. The seventh sign of the zodiac. Its symbol, representing the balancing scales, is emblematic of equilibrium and justice. The Sun is in Libra annually from September 23 to October 23. Astrologically and astronomically it is the first thirty-degree arc following the passing of the Sun over the Fall Equinoctial point, occupying a position along the ecliptic from 180° to 210°. It is the Leading quality of the Air element: positive, hot, moist, sweet, obeying: also restless, judicial. RULER: Venus. EXALTATION: Saturn. DETRIMENT: Mars. FALL: Sun.

> *Introspective Libra*
> Who puts you off with promise gay,
> And keeps you waiting half the day?
> Who compromises all the way?
> Sweet Libra.

Symbolic interpretation: The setting Sun; the central part of a balance, signifying equilibrium and justice.

The sign of cosmic reciprocity, of cooperation rather than competition, of consciousness objectified through associations and partnerships.

> Now dreadful deeds
> Might have ensued, nor only Paradise
> In this commotion, but the starry cope
> Of heaven perhaps, or all the elements
> At least, had gone to wrack, disturbed and torn
> With violence of this conflict, had not soon
> The Eternal, to prevent such horrid fray,
> Hung forth in heaven his golden scales, yet seen
> Betwixt Astraea and the Scorpion sign.
> - John Milton, in PARADISE LOST

FIRST DECAN: Policy, the quality of wisdom; subtlety in public relations; adventurous in human relations.
SECOND DECAN: Independence, strong individuality; exponent of liberty in thought and action; in rebellion against restrictions and centralized conservatism; espouses progressive movements.
THIRD DECAN: Expiation, a superiority in art and letters; mind often used to enslave others, ending in a fatality.

Sign: Scorpio.

The Scorpion. The eighth sign of the zodiac. Its symbol resembles that of Virgo, but with an arrow on the tail - doubtless to represent the sting. It is symbolized by the asp or serpent, harking back to the serpent of the Garden of Eden, and indicating that the will governs or is governed by the reproductive urge. It is sometimes symbolized by the Dragon, and is frequently linked with the constellation Aquilla - the Eagle. The Sun is in Scorpio annually from October 23 to November 22. Astrologically and astronomically it is the second thirty-degree arc after the Sun's passing of the Fall Equinox, occupying a position along the Ecliptic from 210° to 240°. It is the Fixed quality of the Water element: negative, nocturnal, cold, moist, watery, mute, phlegmatic. RULER: Mars. EXALTATION: Uranus. DETRIMENT: Venus. FALL: Moon.

..................ULTIMATE SCORPIO
.............Who keeps an arrow in his bow,
............And if you prod, he lets it go?
............A fervent friend, a subtle foe -
................Scorpio.

Symbolic interpretation: The legs and tail of: a scorpion: the tail with the sting, the serpent.

The alembic of the Zodiac, the sign of cosmic purpose, Scorpio is a success Sign. Self-contained, self-centered, and concentrated, it usually succeeds in what it sets out to accomplish; great personal magnetism and healing power.

..........Bright Scorpio, armed with poisonous tail, prepares
..........Men's martial minds for violence and for wars.
..........His venom heats and boils their blood to rage,
..........And rapine spreads o'er the unlucky age.
....- MANILIUS.

First Decan: Resourcefulness, an excess of creative energy that ever goads to action; creatice imagination; fertility of ideas; absence of repressions.
Second Decan: Responsibility, restrictions in expression; strong character, for good or bad; vivid passions.
Third Decan: Attainment, the Laurel Crown of Victory. Intense intuitions, vivid ideals, the potency of sex to stimulate ideals and ambitions.

Sign: Sagittarius.

The Archer. The ninth sign of the zodiac. In Hindu astrology: Dhanus. Its symbol represents an arrow and a section of a bow, typifying aspiration. It is usually pictured as the Centaur: half horse, half man - representing the conflict between the philosophical mind and the carnal instinct of conquest; also aspiration supported by effort that aims at the stars. Said to have been named for the Babylonian god of war. A typical Sagittarian sentiment is:

................Go plant a ladder: climb it!
...................Even if it doubles up
................'Tis better than to lounge below
...................And sip Life's idle cup.

The Sun is in Sagittarius annually from November 23 to December 21. Astrologically and astronomically it is the thirty-degree arc immediately preceding the Sun's passing over the Tropic of Capricorn, occupying a position along the Ecliptic from 240° to 270°. It is the Mutable quality of the Fire element: positive, hot, dry, changeable, bicorporeal, obeying. **Ruler:** Jupiter. DETRIMENT: Mercury.

.....................***Pursuing Sagittarius***
................Who loves the dim religious light:
................Who always keeps a star in sight?
................An optimist, both gay and bright -
...................Sagittarius.

SYMBOLIC INTERPRETATION: The centaur; an arrow with a short section of the bow, the symbol of enthusiasm and effort, aiming at the stars.

Significator of cosmic progress and abundance, that perverted becomes prodigality.

..............Midst golden stars he stands resplendent now
..............And thrusts the Scorpion with his bended bow.
....- OVID.

FIRST DECAN: Devotion, cosmic consciousness, operating from instinct rather than upon advice.
SECOND DECAN: Expiation, a restless search for new fields to conquer; demands work of a definite importance.
THIRD DECAN: Illumination, piercing the illusion of matter.

Sign: Capricorn.

The mountain-climbing goat. The tenth sign of the zodiac. In Hindu astrology, Makarar - and considered by the ancients to be the most important of all the signs. Is it possible the ancients recognized in the Winter Solstice the point of gravitation that controls the Sun's orbit? Its symbol represents the figure by which the sign is often pictured - that of the forepart of a goat, with the tail of a fish - vaguely suggesting the mermaid. Sometimes also by the sea-goat, or dolphin.

It is said to have a reference to the legend of the goat and the Sun gods.

Dryden makes reference to it:

.....And, what was ominous, that very morn
.....The Sun was entered into Capricorn.

The Sun is in Capricorn annually from December 22 to January 20. Astrologically and astronomically It is the first thirty degrees following the Winter Solstice, marked by the passing of the Sun over the Tropic of Capricorn and occupying a position along the ecliptic from 270° to 300°. It is the Leading quality of the Earth element: nega- tive, nocturnal, cold, dry, obeying. RULER: Saturn. EXALTATION: Mars. DETRIMENT: Moon. FALL: Jupiter.

.....................*Relentless Capricorn*
........Who climbs and schemes for wealth and place,
........And mourns his brother's fall from grace -
........But takes what's due in any case?
.............Safe Capricorn.

SYMBOLIC INTERPRETATION: A goat with a fish's tail, signifying extremes of height and depth; changes wrought by time; union of the Christian and Jewish religious dispensations.

The sign of Initiation, of Cosmic Order and justice, wherein the Individuality is developed, and humanity fulfills its obligations to others.

.....................Pitiless
...............Siroccos lash the main, when Capricorn
...............Lodges the Sun and Zeus sends bitter cold
...............To numb the frozen sailors. -ARATUS.

FIRST DECAN: Organization, coordination, a forerunner of better things; conciliates factions.
SECOND DECAN: Martyrdom; dauntless, again and again it comes back for more; by indefatigable effort, scaling heights of success.
THIRD DECAN: Idealism, natural ability to grasp high ideals, and to express them in concrete form; powerful imagination joined to intensive labor; draws knowledge from the infinite.

Sign: Aquarius.

The Water Bearer. The eleventh sign of the zodiac. Its symbol represents a stream of water, symbolizing the servant of humanity who pours out the water of knowledge to quench the thirst of the world. The Sun is in Aquarius annually from January 21 to February 20. Astrologically and astronomically it is the second thirty-degree arc following the Sun's passing of the Winter Solstice, occupying a position along the Ecliptic from 300° to 330°. It is the Fixed quality of the Air element, in which the will is largely motivated by reasoning processes - whether sound or unsound. It is positive, hot, moist, sanguine, rational and obeying. RULER: Saturn; or by some moderns: Uranus. EXALTATION: Mercury. **Detriment:** Sun.

..................DELIBERATE AQUARIUS
......Who gives to all a helping hand,
......But bows his head to no command -
......And higher laws doth understand?
......Inventor, Genius, Superman - Aquarius.

SYMBOLIC INTERPRETATION: Waves, of water, or the vibrationary waves of electricity; parallel lines of force.

The humanitarian principle coordinating spirit and matter, that prompts all acts of unselfish love; that sees, feels, and acts for others as though all were one Self.

............Men at some time are masters of their fates;
............The fault, dear Brutus, is not in our stars,
............But in ourselves, that we are underlings.
........................Shakespeare, JULIUS CAESAR.

FIRST DECAN: Originality, remarkable knowledge of human nature; progressive tendencies; ever in pursuit of this own ideas; ability to handle people; to impart to others his enthusiasm for advanced ideas and methods.

SECOND DECAN: Inspiration, ability to gain ideas from the invisible; imaginative power; dramatic, convincing.

THIRD DECAN: Repression, reaches highest expression through association with opposite sex; must work with and for others.

Sign: Pisces.

The Fishes. The twelfth sign of the zodiac. Its symbol represents a pair of great sea-horses or sea-lions, yoked together, who dwell in the innermost regions of the sea; symbolical of life after death; of bondage - the inhibiting of self-expression except through others; and of the struggle of the soul within the body. The Sun is in Pisces annually from February 21 to March 20. Astrologically and astronomically it is the thirty degree arc immediately preceding the passing of the Sun over the point of the Spring Equinox occupying a position along the Ecliptic from 330° to 360°. It is the Mutable quality of the Water element; negative, cold, moist, obeying, fruitful; also effeminate, idle, sickly and unfortunate.

RULER: Jupiter; or by some moderns: NEPTUNE. Exaltation: Venus. DETRIMENT: Mercury. FALL: Mercury.

..............................SOULFUL PISCES

..........Who prays, and serves, and prays some more;
..........And feeds the beggar at the door -
..........And weeps o'er loves lost long before?
...............Poor Pisces.

SYMBOLIC INTERPRETATION: Bondage, captivity; the inhibition of natural expression.

Silent, passionless, all-comprehending, granting to every creature the power to act according to its development and capacity. Its imaginative faculties are a great contradiction. The ability to abstract one's self from his immediate surroundings and throw himself into an imaginary life, often termed the Sign of Self-denial and of withdrawal; of the Messiah or Outcast.

........Westward, and further in the South wind's path,
........The Fishes float; one ever uppermost
........First hears the boisterous coming of the North.
........Both are united by a band.
........Their tails point to an angle
........Filled by a single goodly star,
........Called the Conjoiner of the Fishes' Tails.
...................................- ARATUS

FIRST DECAN: Verity, mystic, psychic; seekers of truth through psychic faculties rather than through the exact sciences; detectives of a high order, either materially or spiritually.

SECOND DECAN: Self-sacrifice, lives hemmed around by restrictions, often voluntarily assumed, as the price exacted by the world for the sake of assisting in its progress; gets most from life through alleviating the distress of others.

THIRD DECAN: Vicissitudes; sex decanate of the Sign of Imprisonment; eventful lives; wide variety of careers, recapitulating in their lives the events and conditions expected from other decanates; reach highest expression through psychic research, and in adopting and advocating a regime that best prepares Man for a life after death.

Signs, Classifications of: There are many groupings and classifications of Signs according to a variety of characteristics and effects. It must be emphasized that these are not based solely on the presence of the Sun in the Sign, but may be evidenced in greater or lesser degree by virtue of any accent in the Sign; such as the presence therein of the Ascendant, Moon, several planets, or a strongly aspected planet. Some of the following classifications are ignored by modern authorities:

ASCENDING :: DESCENDING. The ASCENDING signs are those from Capricorn to Gemini, inclusive, proceeding counter-clockwise in the order of the signs. These are the signs through which the solar system bodies approach the North celestial pole, and wherein the declination of the Sun is increasing.

The DESCENDING signs are those from Cancer to Sagittarius.

ASCENSION - LONG :: SHORT. The SIGNS OF LONG ASCENSION are those which, due to the obliquity of the Ecliptic, require more than two hours to rise over the Eastern horizon. The SIGNS OF SHORT ASCENSION are those which rise in Less than two hours. For example, in Latitude 40°N, approximately that of New York, Leo may require as much as 2h 45m to rise, while Aries and Pisces may rise in 1h 10m. In the Northern hemisphere, the Ascending signs are the signs of Short Ascension; the Descending signs, those of Long Ascension. In the Southern hemisphere, these are reversed. Thus by the law of averages the majority of birth maps in the Northern hemisphere have an Ascendant in an Ascending sign; while in the Southern hemisphere the majority of Ascendants are in a Descending sign.

BARREN :: FRUITFUL. The so-called BARREN or Sterile signs, are Gemini, Leo and Virgo; and by some authorities, Aries - with a mild tendency attributed to Sagittarius and Aquarius. Generally classed as the *Fruitful* signs are those the Water triplicity, Cancer, Scorpio and Pisces, in that the Lord of the Ascendant or of the Fifth house in a fruitful sign, or such sign on the Asc. or the cusp of the Fifth, are taken as an indication of the probability of offspring. Taurus and Capricorn, and by some Libra and Aquarius, are classed as MODERATELY FRUITFUL.

BESTIAL :: HUMAN. The BESTIAL Signs are those named after animals: Aries, Taurus, Leo, Scorpio, Capricorn and the last half of Sagittarius; also spoken of as feral, or four-footed. The HUMAN Signs are Gemini, Virgo and Aquarius, and the first half of Sagittarius, so-called to distinguish them from Signs named after animals. Sepharial insists that the first half of Sagittarius is the animal portion and that the human portion is the last half, and cites in proof Jacob's words concerning Dan. **(GENESIS 49:17)** In a different sense Ptolemy rated Libra a humane Sign, since he discovered that the Lord of the Ascendant posited in Libra conferred a humane disposition.

BICORPOREAL. The Double bodied, or dual Signs: Gemini, Virgo, Sagittarius and Pisces.

BITTER :: SWEET. Older authorities classed Aries, Leo and Sagittarius as hot, fiery and bitter, and often referred to them as the BITTER Signs. The SWEET Signs, Gemini, Libra and Aquarius, were presumably sweet-tempered.

BOREAL. From Boreas, the north wind. The six northern Signs: Aries to Virgo inclusive.

BROKEN AND WHOLE. Perfect :: Imperfect. Signs deemed more likely to produce distortions of the body or limbs, when in the Ascendant and unfavorably aspected, are variously known as Broken, Mutilated, or Imperfect Signs. These are Leo, Scorpio and Pisces, to which many authorities add Capricorn and Cancer. Any rising Sign may have its defects if severely afflicted planets are posited therein. The WHOLE or Perfect Signs are Gemini, Libra and Aquarius because those born thereunder are said to be strong, robust and less liable to accidents.

BRUTISH. Leo and the last half of Sagittarius were so classified, because unfavorable as cots accenting these arcs appear to produce savage, coarse mannered, intractable and inhuman traits.

CHANGEABLE. Certain Signs were so classed because they are said to change their natures according to their positions. These are:

```
                  IN THE EAST.......IN THE WEST
...Taurus................Hot...............Cold
...Gemini................Hot and dry.......Cold and moist
...Leo...................Hot and dry.......Hot and Moist
...Virgo.................Hottish Cold......Moist
...Sagittarius...........Cold and moist....Hot and dry
...Capricorn.............Cold and dry......Cold and moist
```

Wilson in his dictionary calls these foolish distinctions.

CHOLERIC: said of the Fire Signs, Aries, Leo and Sagittarius.

COLD::HOT. THE COLD SIGNS: The ancients classed all the even-numbered Signs as *Cold Signs*, but most modern authorities list only Cancer and Capricorn in this classification. The odd-numbered Signs were termed HOT SIGNS. The modern terms Positive and Negative have largely displaced the designations Hot and Cold.

COMMANDING. v. NORTHERN.

COMMON. v. MUTABLE.

CONCEPTIVE. The four Fixed Signs: Taurus, Leo, Scorpio and Aquarius.

CROOKED. Taurus, Capricorn, Pisces are listed by Wilson as liable to produce crooked legs or arms when an afflicted Moon is posited in one of them; yet he scoffs at the classification.

DESCENDING. v. ASCENDING.

DIURNAL. v. POSITIVE.

DRY AND MOIST. The DRY Signs are Aries, Taurus, Leo, Virgo, Sagittarius and Capricorn; the MOIST, Cancer, Scorpio and Pisces, and by some, Gemini, Libra and Aquarius.

DUAL, or DOUBLE-BODIED. v. BICORPOREAL.

DUMB. v. MUTE.

EFFEMINATE. The Sign Pisces is so characterized by Wilson.

EQUINOCTIAL :: TROPICAL. The *Equinoctial* Signs are Aries and Libra: those marked by the Sun's passing of the Equinox at the beginning of Spring and Autumn. The TROPICAL signs are Cancer and

Capricorn: so called because they limit the course of the Sun, which reverses its direction after entrance therein, and thereafter diminishes in elevation. The Sun's passing over the Tropic of Cancer announces the beginning of summer; and of Capricorn, winter.

ESTIVAL (aestival) :: **HIEMAL** (Hyemal). The ESTIVAL Signs are those belonging to the Summer; the HIEMAL, the Winter.

FEMININE. v. Negative.

FERAL. v. Bestial.

FLEXED. Applied by Sepharial to the Mutable Signs (Q.V.).

FORTUNATE. v. Positive.

FOUR-FOOTED: Aries, Taurus, Leo, Sagittarius, Capricorn.

FRUITFUL. v. Barren.

HIEMAL, or Hyemal. v. Estival.

HOARSE or **MUTE.** According to Manly Hall these are Cancer, Scorpio and Pisces.

HOT. v. Cold.

HUMAN. v. Bestial.

IDLE. Pisces is so classed by Wilson.

LONG ASCENSION. v. Ascension.

LUXURIOUS. Aries is so classed, because of a propensity to luxury and intemperance.

MASCULINE. V. POSITIVE.

MELANCHOLY. The Earth Signs Taurus, Virgo and Capricorn are so classified by Wilson.

MOIST. V. DRY.

MOVEABLE. The Cardinal Signs.

MUTE. The Signs of the Water element, Cancer, Scorpio and Pisces. Also termed Dumb Signs, in that afflictions to planets therein often produce speech defects.

NEGATIVE. v. POSITIVE.

NOCTURNAL. v. POSITIVE.

NORTHERN :: SOUTHERN. NORTHERN, or Commanding Signs constitute the first six, Aries to Virgo inclusive since planets posited therein are said to command, while those in the opposite Signs obey. They are considered to be more powerful because nearer to our Earth, hence by some are presumed to confer the ability to command. The scientist who first applied the term possibly and perhaps properly assumed that this portion of the Earth's orbit lay above the plane of the Sun's orbit. The *Southern,* or Obeying Signs are those from Libra to Pisces inclusive.

Strictly speaking, the Northern Signs are those in which the Sun has North declination from March 21 to September 23; the Southern Signs, those in which the Sun has South declination, from September 23 to March 21. The commanding and obeying appears to apply more properly to Houses than Signs. v. PTOLEMAIC ASTROLOGY.

OBEYING. The Southern Signs. v. **NORTHERN.**

PERFECT. v. BROKEN.

POSITIVE :: NEGATIVE, or **MASCULINE :: FEMININE.** The odd-numbered Fire and Air Signs are considered to be more fortunate when rising, and are spoken of as the Positive, Masculine, Diurnal or Fortunate Signs; while the even-numbered Earth and Water Signs are termed the Negative, Feminine, Nocturnal or Unfortunate Signs. For some untenable reason the ancients deemed the Negative Signs to be unfortunate in the general tenor of their lives; Capricorn, particularly, possibly due to its Saturn ruler ship. The extent to which good aspects from well-placed planets, and the reverse, can overbalance the intrinsic nature of the Sun Sign has largely thrown these classifications into the discard. Nevertheless it can readily be seen that for objective results, public acclaim and personal glamor the Fire and Air Signs hold a certain advantage over the more self-contained and introspective Earth and Water Sign groups. An ancient aphorism held that the first half of each Positive Sign and the last half of each Negative Sign is dominated by the Sun and thereby has a tendency to lightness of complection; while the reverse half is dominated by the Moon and tends to the brunette types.

RUMINANT. Those named after animals that chew the cud: Aries, Taurus and Capricorn. Some authorities advise against the administering of drugs during the Moon's transit through these Signs.

SHORT ASCENSION. v. ASCENSION.

SOUTHERN. v. NORTHERN.

SPEAKING. v. VOICE.

STERILE: v. BARREN.

STRONG :: WEAK.

Cancer, Capricorn and Pisces are termed WEAK SIGNS; and Scorpio and Aquarius, said to give strong, athletic bodies, are termed STRONG SIGNS. One can see why Cancer and Pisces, which compare to the Fourth and Twelfth Houses, might be reckoned weak and unfortunate, but why Capricorn should be so classed is less apparent unless because of its ruler ship by Saturn. These terms are little used by modern authorities. Some class all of the Fixed or Foundation signs, as Strong Signs, in that they confer strength of character, fixity of purpose, and general ruggedness of constitution.

SWEET. Gemini, Libra and Aquarius. v. BITTER.

SYMPATHETIC. Those of the same polarity, consisting of each opposition Sign: Air and Fire, or Earth and Water. Some confine the term to those Signs which together form either a trine or a sextile. Planets in trine are always in the same element; those in sextile, are in elements that are sympathetic.

TROPICAL. Cancer and Capricorn. v. Equinoctial.

VIOLENT. Those ruled by the malefics, or wherein the malefics are exalted, viz: Aries, Libra, Scorpio, Capricorn and Aquarius; also applied to parts of Signs in which are any remarkably violent stars, such as Caput Algol in 25° Taurus. v. STARS.

VITAL. The Fire Signs, Aries, Leo and Sagittarius; so termed not because they have more vitality, but because they spend it to excess - hence are often prone to anemia and nervous debility. Since the measure of lung capacity in actual use is the index to vital energy, one must limit this classification to a certain psychological quality of vitality or "punch."

VOICE. Gemini, Libra, the latter part of Virgo, and the first part of Sagittarius; so-called because when posited upon the Ascendant, with Mercury or the Moon well placed and unafflicted, it is deemed to indicate one with the capacity to become a good speaker or orator. Some authorities include Aquarius.

WATERY. The Signs of the Watery Triplicity. Cancer, Scorpio and Pisces.

WHOLE. Taurus, Gemini, Leo, Scorpio, Sagittarius and Aquarius; also termed Strong Signs, by Alvidas, since the Sun in these Signs, unafflicted or rising, gives a strong body and greater powers of endurance.

Significator. A planet may be taken as a significator of a person or of an event, or of affairs ruled by a House. Its strength by virtue of its Sign and House position and its relationship by aspects are then consulted in arriving at a judgment concerning a desired condition. In general the strongest planet in the Figure, usually the ruler of the Ascendant, is taken as the Significator of the native. Similarly the Ruler of the Sign on the cusp of the Second House is taken as the Significator of wealth, of the Seventh House of the partner, of the Eighth of the partner's wealth, and so on. Sepharial speaks of the Sun, Moon, Ascendant and Midheaven as Significators, but Alan Leo prefers to speak of them as Moderators, and includes Fortuna. The Sun and Midheaven are by some authorities deemed to have affinity as Significators of the honor, credit, and standing of the subject of the Figure, or of the surviving male head of the family;

the Moon and Ascendant to have affinity as Significators of the personal fortunes, changes and accidents befalling the native; Mercury, of his learning, intellectual accomplishments or business acumen; Venus, of his love-affairs, social arts and accomplishments; Mars, of strikes, contentions, enterprises and risks; Jupiter, of wealth and increase; and Saturn, of disease, loss, death and decay. In this use there is danger of confusing the distinction between a Significator, as representing persons in Horary Astrology, and Promittors as representative of things promised or desired; but every planet in the Figure can be taken not only as the significator of something, but also as the Promittor of something.

Sinister. A left-handed aspect - not, however, with reference to the proper motion of the aspecting body, but to its apparent motion. v. DEXTER.

Slow of Course. v. PLANETARY MOTIONS.

Sol. The Sun.

Solar Astrology. The presumption that the Solar Horoscope is of value only as a make-shift when an exact hour of birth is unobtainable, is rapidly giving way to a realization of its genuine merits. Strictly speaking, it is not an hour-scope but a day-scope; yet it is the same cycle of hour-to-hour daily experiences through a rising series of sensitive points, whether it begins with an ascendant degree or with the omnipotent Sun degree.

When the Arabians devised their system of Parts, it evidenced a realization of the importance of the relationship between a planet's position and the Sun's position. The Part of Fortune merely locates in a Rising Sign Figure the position the Moon occupies in a Solar chart. Similarly the Part of Commerce or Understanding is the Solar house position of Mercury: the Part of Love, that of Venus; of Passion, that of Mars; of Increase, that of Jupiter; of Fatality, that of Saturn; to which the moderns have added the Part of Catastrophe, that of the Uranus position; of Treachery, that of Neptune; and of Organization, that of Pluto.

The Sign positions of the planets are an important element in any horoscopic analysis and these are the same in a Solar chart as in a chart based upon an ascending degree. Likewise the birth aspects, and even the aspects of transitory planets to birth sensitivities, remain the same. Thus the entire daily cycle of sensitive points is identical, except for those of or based upon the ascendant and Midheaven.

To appraise the relative importance of Ascending degree and the Sun's degree as a point of beginning, consider the first return of the Ascendant degree on the second day of life: With the Sun advanced to a new position, one senses the incompleteness of the sidereal cycle, and the added four minutes necessary to complete a solar day. One must either advance the Ascendant by one degree, or retard the Sun four minutes. The next day and each succeeding day repeats the process. A year later the Ascendant has gained a day, but while one can revise the memory of a Rising degree, one cannot order the Sun to stand still.

In a few years the unvarying regularity of the Sun's return begins to exercise a rapidly augmented potency. Since life is lived by the Sun - the Giver of Life in a keenly actual sense - it is no make-shift that one gradually finds he reacts less and less to the reiterations of the advancing Ascendant cycle, and more and more to the eternally unchanging cycle of Solar returns.

This helps to explain why the Rising Sign influence is so largely physical, pertaining to bodily growth during the first plastic weeks and months of life, and why individuality and character take on the quality of the Sun Sign as we approach adulthood. It also explains why some young people undergo such radical changes of individuality on their approach to the age at which they are said to have attained their majority, for when an Aquarian Sun takes command over a Pisces-rising boy, it is a shock to his family, his friends and himself; while the transition from a Gemini-rising boy to one with the Sun in Libra is so imperceptible as hardly to occasion comment.

The Solar chart is in reality only an assumption that to the native of each Sun Sign the independent absorption of life-giving energy begins with its first sunrise. The cycle of sensitivities which daily passes over the horizon is a vital experience, but the cycle is the same cycle whether one begins with the Sun, or with an annually-advanced ascendant. That you eventually count your laps on the daily and annual course by the Sun instead of the Ascendant, makes less difference than at first appears - otherwise a removal to another time zone would create a far greater condition of pandemonium, and entail a far greater degree of readjustment than seems proven by experience. The Solar House cusps have added significance in the fact that each cusp represents an aspect to the Sun, in a series that is unalterable and unvarying

Secondary progressions can even be applied to the Solar chart, and despite the lack of enthusiasm with which some astrologers contemplate the Solar chart, it is doubtful if a tenth-of-one-percent of them compute primary directions. To what extent the Table of Houses is fallacious, which system of cusp division is the more nearly correct, whether to employ the Latitude of birth or of domicile, and doubt concerning the authenticity of the birth moment, are only a few of the embarrassing questions obviated by its use. The Arabian astrologers discovered the importance of the solar houses, as demonstrated in their system of Arabian Points (q.v.).

As Astrology evolves out of the realm of prestidigitation, wherein it seeks only to impress by the predicting of specific events, into that of a psychological diagnosis of predispositions, wherein it defineates reactions to cosmic stimuli in terms of traits, trends and tendencies, the Solar chart wig become increasingly acceptable as a true cycle of adult experience, and a reliable index to the character development of the matured individuality.

Solar Cycle, or Cycle of the Sun. A 28-year period applicable to the Julian calendar, in which the first day of the year is restored to the same day of the week. Since the days of the week are 7, and the number of years in an intercalary period are 4, their product (4 x 7 = 28) must include all possible combinations. At the end of each cycle, the Dominical letters return again in the same order on the same days of the month. v. CALENDAR.

Solar Day The time clasping between two consecutive passages of the Sun over a fixed point on the Earth. It is in excess of one complete revolution, by 1° of longitude or 4 minutes of time. v. DAY.

Solar Equilibrium. A term used by recent astrologers with reference to the Solar Figure: one cast for sunrise on a given day, but with houses of uniformly thirty degrees each.

Solar Revolution. A horoscopical figure erected for the moment in any year when the Sun has reached the exact Longitude it occupies in the Radix. From this figure and from aspects of Radical planets to significators - Sun, Moon, Ascendant and Midheaven degrees - in the Solar Revolution map predictions are made cov- ering the ensuing year. For example, the Solar Revolution Moon conjunct radical Mars, indicates a year ominous of accidents - especially on the days on which the Sun or Moon conjoins Mars. Also it can be judged within itself, in which case, current Solar transits should be observed.

REVOLUTIONARY ADDITIVES. For computing the time of the return of the Sun to its radical longitude, the following table gives the amounts to be added to the sidereal time of the meridian of the radical map to ascertain the meridian for the solar return for any given year of life:

...................**REVOLUTIONARY ADDITIVES**......................
```
YEARS H.  M.   |YEARS H.  M.   |YEARS H.  M.   |YEARS H.  M.   |YEARS H.  M.  |
..1... 5..49.. |.19...14..36.. |.37...23..23.. |.55....8..10.. |.73...16..56..|
..2...11..38.. |.20...20..25.. |.38....5..12.. |.56...13..59.. |.74...22..45..|
..3...17..28.. |.21....2..14.. |.39...11...2.. |.57...19..48.. |.75....4..35..|
..4...23..17.. |.22....8...3.. |.40...16..51.. |.58....1..37.. |.76...10..24..|
..5....5...6.. |.23...13..53.. |.41...22..40.. |.59....7..27.. |.77...16..13..|
..6...10..55.. |.24...19..43.. |.42....4..29.. |.60...13..16.. |.78...22...2..|
..7...16..45.. |.25....1..32.. |.43...10..19.. |.61...19...5.. |.79....3..52..|
..8...22..34.. |.26....7..21.. |.44...16...8.. |.62....0..54.. |.80....9..41..|
..9....4..23.. |.27...13..11.. |.45...21..57.. |.63....6..44.. |.81...15..30..|
.10...10..12.. |.28...19...0.. |.46....3..46.. |.64...12..33.. |.82...21..19..|
.11...16...2.. |.9....0..49.. |.47....9..36.. |.65...18..22.. |.83....3...9..|
.12...21..51.. |.30....6..38.. |.48...15..23.. |.66....0..11.. |.84....8..59..|
.13....3..40.. |.31...12..28.. |.49...21..14.. |.67....6...1.. |.85...14..48..|
.14....9..29.. |.32...18..17.. |.50....3...3.. |.68...11..50.. |.86...20..37..|
.15...15..19.. |.33....0...6.. |.51....8..53.. |.69...17..39.. |.87....2..27..|
.16...21...8.. |.34....5..55.. |.52...14..42.. |.70...23..28.. |.88....8..16..|
.17....2..57.. |.5....11..45.. |.53...20..31.. |.71....5..18.. |.89...14...5..|
.18....8..46.. |.36...17..34.. |.54....2..20.. |.72...11...7.. |.90...19..54..|
```

Continental astrologers use a table in which the Revolutionary Additives are given in degrees, to be added to the degree of the Midheaven in the Radical Figure to yield the Midheaven degree of the Solar Revolution Figure. The relative cusps are then taken from the Table of Houses.

............REVOLUTIONARY ADDITIVES, IN DEGREES.........
```
....y....º......y....º.......y....º.......y....º.......y....º
....1....87.....16...315.....31...183.....46....51.....61...279
....2...174.....17....42.....32...270.....47...138.....62.....6
....3...262.....18...130.....33...358.....48...226.....63....94
```

....4...349.....19...217.....34....85.....49...313.....64...181
....5....76......20...304.....35...172.....50....40.....65...268
....6...163.....21....31.....36...259.....51...127.....66...355
....7...250.....22...118.....37...346.....52...214.....67....82
....8...338.....23...206.....38....74.....53...302.....68...170
....9....65.....24...293.....39...161.....54....29.....69...257
...10...152.....25....20.....40...248.....55...116.....70...344
...11...239.....26...107.....41...335.....56...203.....71....71
...12...326.....27...194.....42....62.....57...290.....72...158
...13....54.....28...282.....43...150.....58....18.....73...245
...14...141.....29.....9.....44...273.....59...105.....74...333
...15...228.....30....96.....45...324.....60...192.....75....60

By referring this meridian to the sidereal time at noon on the given anniversary of birth, one determines the time before or after noon for which to erect the figure, and to calculate the planets' places.

An adaptation of this principle is to cast the Figure for the day when the Sun is nearest to the longtitude it had at birth, and the hour and minute when R.A. of the M.C. is the same as at birth, whereby the cusps will be the same as those in the Radix. The one method employs the Sun's position as the measure of time, and is equivalent to placing the transitory positions of the planets in a Solar Nativity; the other, to placing the transiting positions of the planets in a Geocentric Nativity. If Primary Directions are to be considered within the year, from either Figure, the time of day on which the revolution will be complete (either the Sun's return or the Ascendant's return), and the places of the planets, must be computed with great exactness for that precise moment. Otherwise it suffices to insert in the Nativity, the current noon positions of the transiting planets.

Modern practice considers that a lingering aspect from a Transitor, a slow-moving major planet in transit, to a radical sensitivity produces displacement of equilibrium; which is activated by an additional aspect from a Culminator, a faster moving body such as the Sun or Moon, to the same or another planet, thereby precipitating the externalization. The interpretation, however, is based not alone upon the aspected planet, but upon the entire radical configuration in which it participates, and which is thereby altered by the addition of the transiting planet's influence.

Solar Semicircle. Leo to Capricorn, inclusive.

Solar System. The cosmic influences by which a dweller on the Earth is conditioned (v. COSMIC CONDITIONING), and motivated, are almost exclusively confined to forces present and manifest within the Solar System, which consists of the Sun, and the planets which revolve in orbits around the Sun chiefly in response to its gravitational pull. The Sun is the sole source of radiating energy that makes possible every form of life found on the Earth. This energy is received, both direct and by reflection from the planets and the Moon. Due, however, to the varying chemical constituency of the Sun's reflectors, each absorbs certain frequencies of the Solar emanations, and delivers to the Earth an altered spectrum. The Sun's energy raditaion is estimated in a continuous flow of 80,000 horsepower from each square year of its surface.

Around it are so far discovered ten planetary cycles, the bodies of which emit no light except that reflected from the sun. These, in order from the Sun outward, i.e: Mercury, Venus, the Earth, Mars, the Asteroids, Jupiter, Saturn, Uranus, Neptune, and Pluto. The astrological significance of the Asteroid has not received sufficient study to warrant any judgments in reference thereto, but it is generally presumed that they consist of the matter for what was intended to be another planet in the vacant orbit between Mars and Jupiter, but which was dispersed by the influence of the ponderous nearby planet Jupiter.

Astronomers and astrologers have speculated on the possible existence of an intramercurial planet, so close to the Sun as to be lost in its rays and indistinguishable by any known method - but this is mere hypothesis. As three of the known planets have been discovered since i781, and Pluto as late as 1930, there is an everpresent possibility that additional outside planets may yet be discovered. In this connection it should not be forgotten that Pythagoras, on both astrological and mathematical evidence, contended some 2500 years ago that there must be 10 planets in the Solar atom. From Pythagorcus came the concept that Copernicus developed into his heliocentric theory, and that gave Einstein, no doubt, a Vision of the Creator as a mathematician rather than an engineer.

In occult teaching there are in our solar system ten schemes of evolution, each presided over by a planetary Logos. As the ancients knew of only the Sun, Moon and five planets, each system consisted of a chain of seven globes, and each chain had passed through seven incarnations. Their idea of ten schemes of evolution was a further prophetic indication of the three additional plants since discovered.

However, with the inclusion of the Earth and the orbit of the asteroids, we now recognize in the solar system twelve planetary cycles: the Sun, moving in an undetermined orbit around some remote galactic center; the 8 planets, the Earth and the asteroids, moving in 10 channels around the Sun; and the Moon moving in an orbit around the Earth.

Astronomically the Moon is too tiny an object for inclusion in such an enumeration. Besides, there are other moons revolving around other planets in our solar atom. Astrologically, however, our Moon, because of its nearness to us, assumes an importance that is disproportionate to its size, while the moons of other planets have no significance for us, other than as they enter into the composite ray reflected in our direction.

In this general picture of our solar system we find three distinct and known forces in evidence: energy radiations, orbital motion, and gravitation.

Considering the Sun, particularly, one must take cognizance of the fact that its influence as a source of energy radiation should bc entirely disassociated from the influence it exerts by way of gravitational pull and orbital motion. Experiment with the little ball on the end of a rubber string, and you will find that a horizontal motion of the hand will change the vertical motion of the ball into a circular motion that can become an orbit. While the Sun is exerting a pull upon the Earth, it is moving at right angles to the direction of its pull. If in response to the pull the Sun exerts upon the Earth at this particular moment we were to plunge precipitately in that direction, by the time we arrived the Sun would be gone. From the continuance of such a pursuit an elliptical orbit must necessarily result. However, both radiation and the gravitation from the Sun, considered alone, are constants. To introduce differences in different portions of the Earth's orbit, other and changing factors must be introduced.

As to the Sun's energy radiations, we have long recognized the differentiating effect of variously combined reflections from the planets, each of which by virtue of its chemical components absorbs certain bands of the spectrum and thus emits an altered ray. Hence aspects are the differentiating factor that alters the constant of the Sun's energy radiation.

To find the differentiating element in the constant of the Sun's gravitational influence, suppose we consider relationship between two known orbits: those of the Moon and the Earth, and the Earth around the Sun.

The constant of the Earth-Moon gravitation is altered by the Sun-Earth gravitation whereby at the lunation, the Sun and the Earth are pulling from OPPOSITE sides of the Moon, while at the Full Moon, both Sun and Earth are pulling in the SAME direction. Furthermore from the dichotome at the end of the First Quarter to that at the end of the Third the Moon's travel is faster than that of the Earth, its own motion added to that of the Earth, while in the other half of its orbit it is traveling slower than the Earth. Thus the dichotomes are the points where the Moon's orbit intersects that of the Earth.

Applying this to the Earth-Sun orbit, one sees that the direction of the Sun's travel, and at right angles thereto the source of the gravitational pull that governs the Sun's motion, are the missing factors necessary to an explanation of the changes of conditioning in the various arcs of the Earth's annual orbit, the so-called signs of the zodiac, the heliarcs into which the Ecliptic path is divided.

If we assume 0° Capricorn to be the direction of the Galactic Center, then the Aries-Libra cusps must represent the line of the Sun's travel. The fact is that the Galactic Center HAS to be 0° Capricorn, or astrology needs revision. Assuming this factor, let us see what we discover: The inclination of the North polar axis in the direction of the Galactic Center suddenly appears to have a plausible justification. Also it explains the coincidence of the Equinox (when the inclination is at right angles to the radius) and the points where the Earth crosses the Sun's path.

Tracing some of the conditions the Earth encounters in the course of one annual cycle, we see that when the Sun is at 0° Capricorn the Earth is actually at the opposite point 0° Cancer, hence at its greatest distance from G.C. From this point it moves toward and in the direction of G.C. accelerating to its maximum speed at the midway point, and slowing down to a dead center when the Sun reaches 0° Cancer, where it reverses its motion and for the next half year travels against the gravitational pull from G.C. This identifies four points at which a motion in a given direction comes to a dead center and reverses itself. From Aries 0° to Libra 0° the Earth would travel slower than the Sun-its orbital motion subtracted from that of the Sun; and faster than the Sun during the other half of the orbit. Also that with the Sun at Capricorn 0° the Earth is farthest from the Galactic center, hence the gravitational pull from the Sun and the G.C. operates in the same direction. After traveling half its orbit in the direction of the Galactic Center the Earth comes to the closest point where the gravitational pull from the two centers comes from opposite sides of the Earth.

In the motion from these points of reversal to the opposite points, there can be recognized a division into two periods: one of acceleration, and one of retardation. The motion from Capricorn 0º, in reference to gravitation, reaches its maximum at the point where the motion against momentum reverses itself; also at a midway point in that quadrant the second motion balances the first-after which the first slows down to a full stop, and reverses its direction.

Thus there results a natural subdivision of the year in accordance with this formula:

```
............PORTION OF ORBIT.........
|Sun in-............|..................|
|....Aries..........| M c 1 a :: G w 3 r |
|....Taurus.........| M c 2 a :: G w 2 r |
|....Gemini.........| M c 3 a :: G w 1 r |
|....Cancer.........| M c 3 r :: G c 1 a |
|....Leo............| M c 2 r :: G c 2 a |
|....Virgo..........| M c 1 r :: G c 3 a |
|....Libra..........| M w 1 a :: G c 3 r |
|....Scorpio........| M w 2 a :: G c 2 r |
|....Sagittarius....| M w 3 a :: G c 1 r |
|....Capricorn......| M w 3 r :: G w 1 a |
|....Aquarius.......| M w 2 r :: G w 2 a |
|....Pisces.........| M w 1 r :: G w 3 a |
|..................|..................|
```

G - Gravitation: w - with, or c - contra to attraction from Galactic Center
M - Momentum:... w - with, or c - contra to the Sun's orbital motion
at: 1, minimum; 2, mean; or 3, maximum rate of speed.
a - acceleration
r - retardation

From this it can be judged that the line of demarcation between any Mutable Sign and the Cardinal Sign which follows it, is a sharp and thinly drawn line; while those between a Cardinal and Fixed Sign, and between a Fixed and Mutable Sign, are a gradual merging or dissolving effect which culminates in a complete balancing of two forces in the middle of each Fixed Sign. Therefore one finds occasion for consideration of cuspal influences only in connection with the intermediate cusps, in which case the orb should be fairly large - as much perhaps as five degrees on either side. This would mean that a person with the Sun in 25° Aries or in 5° Taurus, or any of the degrees between, would be spoken of as an Aries-Taurus cusp; and so on for all but the Cardinal cusps.

In addition, there is undoubtedly a third-dimensional motion above and below the plane of the Sun's travel. Latest astronomical opinion is that the 14° band in which the planets revolve is inclined by approximately 60° to a similar band in which the stars in the Milky Way galaxy revolve around the Galactic Center. This would appear to indicate that the locating of the Earth's nodes of intersection of the Sun's orbital plane are a third factor that is necessary to a true three-dimensional analysis of the conditioning one acquires by virtue of birth when the Earth is in some one of these twelve heliarcs of its annual travel.

There are thus (a) four arcs in which there is a reversal of motion and a new start in the opposite direction; viz: The four Initiating Cardinal or Leading signs: (b) four arcs wherein two motions strike a balance, the Executive or Fixed signs; and (c) four arcs wherein a motion is retarding to a dead center, preparing for a reversal of motion; the Deductive Common or Mutable signs. These three groups of four signs each are generally spoken of as the Quadruplicities or Qualities.

Another and quite different relationship exists between the arc in which a motion starts, that wherein it is balanced by another motion, and that wherein the overcoming motion slows to a dead stop. These four groups of three signs each, are spoken of as the four basic types: the Elements or the Triplicities. These are:

..........Inspirational type: Spirit - aspirational, imaginative.
..........Emotional type:......Soul - intuitive, passionate.
..........Mental type:........Mind - reasoning, intellectual.
..........Practical type:......Body - matter-of-fact, materialistic but sensory.

Thus of each of the four types, there are three qualities - Initiating, Executive and Deductive, as follows:

QUALITIES
..............*Inspirational.....Emotional.....Mental.........Practical*
Initiating....1 Aries...........4 Cancer......7 Libra.......10 Capricorn
Executive.....5 Leo.............8 Scorpio....11 Aquarius.....2 Taurus
Deductive.....9 Sagittarius....12 Pisces......3 Gemini.......6 Virgo

Out of the cosmic conditioning inherent in these formulas, it is possible to deduce delineations of each of the twelve arcs, that to an amazing extent are in accord with the analyses that are the cumulative result of some 50 centuries of observation.

Solar System bodies: Sun.

To the Egyptians it was Ra, Amen, Aten, or Osiris, each with a different religious significance. The winged globe in Egyptian art is a familiar representation of the solar orb. Atenism, the first impersonal concept of the Deity, worshipped only "the power which came from the Sun," and forbade any emblem or idol that would tend to substitute a symbol for the thing itself. To The Persian it was Mithras; to the Hindu, Brahma; to the Chaldean, Bel; and to the Greek, Adonis and Apollo. In Free-masonry Sol-om-on, the name of the Sun in three languages, is an expression of light.

Actually the Sun has no visible motion, although we know it moves because nothing in the universe can hold its place by standing still. However, ancient astrology dealt with things as they appear rather than as they are; just as the wind which blows South was to the ancients the North wind because it came out of the North. Therefore, when astrology speaks of the Sun's motion we must not overlook the fact that what we actually mean is the Earth's motion which we measure by or describe in the terms of the apparent motion of the Sun. That the ancient masters knew this, can be seen in the order of the planetary hours:

Saturn, Jupiter, Mars, Sun, Venus - the placing of the Sun between Mars and Venus clearly showing that it represents the Earth in this sequence.

The Nodes at which the Earth intercepts the plane of the Sun's equator, lie at heliocentric longitudes 75° and 255°, which the Earth crosses in June and December. The Sun's North Pole is inclined toward the Earth by 7° in July, and away from the Earth by 7° in January. The plane of the Sun's orbit is not known, but since the Milky Way galaxy is a flat disc of stars it is probable that the Sun's orbit does not deviate to any great extent from the average of the stars within the galaxy - similar to the orbits of the planets which lie within a narrow band that extends some 7° on either side of the Ecliptic.

We do know that the plane of our ecliptic is inclined to the plane of the Milky Way galaxy at a steep angle of approximately 50° hence the three-dimensional motion of the Earth with reference to the orbit of the Sun must involve a considerable degree of elevation and depression above and below the plane of the Sun's orbit; also that there must be a considerable declination of the Sun's pole with reference to its orbit, not unlike that of the Earth's pole to which we ascribe our seasonal variations. Because of this, the Nodes where the Earth intersects the Sun's equator are not the same as those at which the Earth intersects the plane of the Sun's orbit. It is not improbable that the latter nodes may pursue a precessional cycle not unlike that of the Moon's Nodes.

The Sun is a variable star, unlike any other star yet discovered. It revolves from East to West; i.e., looking down on its North pole, it moves counter-clockwise. Its period of rotation at the Equator is 24.65 d.; at the pole, 34 d. Its mean period as seen by the Earth is 25.38 d.; but its synodical period of rotation is 27.25 d.

The diameter of the Sun is 864,392 miles. Driving in an automobile at the rate of 500 miles a day, it would require 14 y, 10 m, 2 d, to circle the Sun.

Its weight in tons is 2,200 plus 24 ciphers, or 2.2 octillion tons. In bulk it could contain 1,300,000 Earths.

The Sun-Earth distance - 92,897,416 miles - is taken as a unit of measurement of inter-solar system space, and is known as one Astronomical Unit. Its light requires 498.59 seconds, or about 8 1/3 minutes, to reach the Earth. To travel the distance by an airplane at 300 miles per hour, would consume 35 years; to walk at 4 m.p.h., 6300 y.

Hugh Rice, astronomer of the Hayden Planetarium of New York, says, "The Sun is the source of almost all the power, heat and life on the Earth." Heat reaching the Earth amounts to 1.94 calories per minute, per square mile of the Earth's surface. One caloric is the amount of heat required to raise one gram of water by one degree of temperature.

In terms of power the Sun's radiation amounts to 1.51 h.p. per sq. yard of the Earth's surface, or 643,000 h.p. per sq. mile. Were it not for loss by curvature and reflection it would amount to 4,690,000 h.p. per sq. mile, or for the entire surface of the Earth, 127 plus twelve ciphers, or 127 trillions of horsepower - more than we could possibly use. Actually our absorption amounts to from 0.34 to 0.38 h.p. per sq. yard, or the equivalent of a 60-watt lamp in continuous operation. When it is recalled that the Earth as seen from the Sun is a point in the sky apparently less than half as large as Venus when it is our brilliant evening star, and that this is the tiny object which intercepts a total of 230 million-million horsepower of solar radiation, it becomes evident that the Sun radiates an incomprehensible amount of energy. Indeed, we find that it radiates nearly 2,200,000,000 times as much energy as that which lights and warms and gives life to our planet, and hundreds of millions of times as much energy as is intercepted by all the planets, satellites, and planetoids combined.

Most of the Sun has a temperature of a million degrees. Its energy travels at the rate of 186,271 miles per second. The Sun's heat would melt a block of ice the size of the Earth in 16.6 minutes; a block of iron of the same size, in Less than 3 hours. Its heat for a year is equal to the burning of tons of coal amounting to 400 Plus 21 ciphers.

The Sun's Spectrum of visible light extends from 7700 Angstrom units on the red end, to 3600 Angstrom units on the violet end. An Angstrom unit is one ten-millionth of a millimeter. A millimeter is 1/25th of an inch. A wave of red light measures one 32-thousandths of an inch; of violet, one 64-thousandths. Hence the visible Spectrum consists of one octave, although 40 octaves are known to Science. The ultra-violet band extends from 3600 to 1000 Angstrom units. However, the ozone in the Earth's atmosphere cuts out all rays shorter than 2900 A.U. Tanning is nature's way of protecting the body against an excess of ultra-violet radiation.

The light of the Sun is 465,000 times brighter than the Full Moon; 900,000,000 times brighter than Venus at its brightest. In the Zenith this has been computed at 103,000 meter-candles. A meter-candle is the light received from a candle at a distance of a meter.

According to the latest astronomical computations the Sun's proper motion in orbit is approx. 200 miles per second; its apparent motion towards a point in the constellation Hercules is 12 miles per second.

Solar System Bodies: Moon.
A satellite of the Earth, which to different civilizations has also been known as Luna, Soma, Isis; the "mother of the Earth." It has given us the name for the first day of the week-Monday; also lunacy, lunatic, moonstruck.

The Moon, reflecting the light of the Sun, emits a degree of heat which can be registered by concentrating the rays on the bulb of a thermometer. It may have some slight vegetation, but because of the apparent absence of atmosphere or clouds it lacks sufficient water to support vegetation such as is on the Earth.

The period of the Moon's axial rotation is the same as its period of revolution, hence the same side of the Moon is always turned toward the Earth. That its orbit was formerly smaller and its velocity correspondingly greater is proved by comparing records of ancient eclipses to tables based on observation of its present motion. The Moon's mean distance from the Earth is 238,840 miles, or 60 times the Earth's radius. It travels a trifle faster than its diameter per hour. Nor is it entirely the nearest body to the Earth, for in part of its orbit the minor planet Hermes (disc. in 1937) approaches to a distance of only 200,000 Miles. Traveling by airplane at 200 m.p.h. one would traverse the Earth-Moon distance in 5o days; but it would take a rocket ship speed of 7 m.p.s. to get beyond the Earth's gravitational field-at which rate we could arrive in 2 days.

Lifetimes have been devoted to the study of its incredibly complex motions. Among its various perturbations are the Equation of the Center, the retrogression of the Nodes, Evection, the anomalistic period, Lunar Variation, Annual Equation, and Secular Acceleration.

Galilee, in 1610, was the first selenographer to study the Moon through a telescope. In 1647 Hevelius published a chart of the Moon's surface that was not improved upon for a century. Its phases are familiar: The crescent of the new moon, and the reverse crescent of the fourth quarter of its circuit; the gibbous phase of the second and third quarters, when more than half of the moon is light; and the Earth-shine, when the Earth reflects a dim light upon the surface of the Moon during a few days before and after the Lunation.

Because of its faster motion near perigee we are able to see 7°45' around the Eastern and Western edges. This is termed its Libration in Longitude. Because of the inclination of the plane of the Moon's orbit to that of the Earth, we are able at times to see 6°41' beyond each of the poles. This is termed Libration in Latitude. There is also a Diurnal Libration of 1° on the Eastern limb of the Moon when rising, and on the Western when setting. The net combined result is that 41% of the Moon's surface is visible all the time, with another 18% that is visible part of the time, leaving 41% that has never been seen from the Earth.

Meton discovered the recession of the Moon's node in 432 B.C. and reformed the calendar in accordance therewith. He determined that there were 235 synodic periods in 19 years, varying by i day according to the number of leap years contained in the period.

The node recesses 360° in 6793.5 days or 18 2/3 years, or roughly 1½ years to a sign.

The Draconitic period of the Moon's motion, that from node to node, is 27.2122 days.

The moon rises 50 minutes later each night.

Harvest Moon. At this season of the year the Moon's path more nearly parallels that of the Earth, hence it remains near to the horizon for several days, at the same hour. Similarly with the Hunter's Moon, which is the nearest Full Moon to September 23rd. This effect is further intensified when the descending node is at 0° Aries. For example, with the Ascending node at 0° Aries : 23° 27', Plus 5° 9', equals 28° 36'. With the Descending node at 0° Aries : 23° 27', minus 5° 9', equals 18° 18°'. The Full Moon rides low in Summer but high in Winter, thus making Winter the season of least sunlight but of most moonlight.

Moonlight contains streaks of bright rays, apparently from some special mineral that fails to absorb light, or which may have some such property as radio-activity - to conjecture on a point regarding which scientists fail to agree. The rays consist largely of shades of yellow and gray, and from certain areas a shade of green. The Earth's surface has a reflective power six times greater than that of the Moon.

The Lunar spectrum is much the same as that of the Sun, except that the light is yellower, and more diffused because of the roughness of the Moon's surface. At the quarter, the Moon's light has a brilliance of one-millionth that of the Sun; at the Full, 1/465 thousandths. However, the Moon absorbs 93% of the light it could reflect.

The Moon's aspects by Right Ascension differ some minutes from those by Geocentric Longitude.

Tropical period minus Precession from 0° Aries : 6.9 seconds per period.

The color white is often associated with the Moon to symbolize purity. That it is chemically white is due to the absence of all color. Prismatically it is the presence of all colors of the spectrum, or the three primary colors in the proportions of three parts of yellow, five of red, and eight of blue.

Solar System Bodies: Mercury.

A small planet, with pale bluish light; the planet closest to the Sun. Never more than 28 degrees from the Sun, it is rarely visible to the naked eye. The Roman god Mercury and the Greek god Hercules, the winged messenger of the Gods, were endowed with the qualities that are associated with the influence of the planet Mercury. To the Chaldeans it was Nebo, the planet of warning; also associated with Buddha, the wise.

Ancient astrologers considered the existence of a planet nearer to the Sun than Mercury, to which they gave the name Vulcan. It has not as yet been discovered by astronomers.

From a stationary point about 28° in advance of the Sun, it retrogrades to an inferior conjunction with the Sun - after which it becomes a "morning star," visible on the Eastern horizon shortly before Sunrise. From a stationary point about 20° behind the Sun, it advances by direct motion to a superior conjunction with the Sun - after which it becomes an "evening star," visible on the Western horizon shortly after Sunset.

As with the Moon, and all satellites with reference to the planet around which they revolve, Mercury always turns the same face toward the Sun, except for a libration of 23° 7' in both directions: making a 47° zone of temperate conditions, and 132° zones of perpetual heat and cold.

As seen from the Earth, Mercury presents phases, similar to those of the Moon, because of which its visible size varies from 30' to 104' -- its crescent or new moon phase occurs at its inferior conjunction; its full moon phase at its superior conjunction. Its minor elongation, about 18°, occurs 22 days before and after its inferior conjunction; its major elongation, about 28°, 36 days before and after its superior conjunction. At its maximum its visible size is 3¼ times its diameter. Two of Jupiter's moons are larger than the planet Mercury.

To locate Mercury in the evening sky, find in the ephemeris the dates of its major elongation before or after a superior conjunction, and for 10 and 5 days before and after. Transfer into hours its R.A. and declination on these five dates, and plot its course on a star map, making note its nearness to known bright stars. Tilt this map toward the celestial North pole, and assume a horizon about 23° below the Mercury position. If weather conditions permit it can be seen with the aid of a field glass - sometimes even with the naked eye.

Mercury made a transit across the face of the Sun on May 11, 1937.

Solar System bodies: Venus.

A brilliant planet reflecting a silvery-white light, it is the most brilliant object that illuminates the evening sky. The Greeks associated it with Aphrodite. To the Romans, it was known as Lucifer, when the Morning Star: and Vesper, when the Evening Star. To the Chaldeans it was Ishtar, and compared to the Sumerian virgin mother, the "Lady of Heaven," and the goddess of fertility.

Like Mercury, Venus exhibits phases, from a large twin crescent at the Inferior Conjunction, when it is closest to the Earth, and some- times visible in daylight if you know where to look for it, to a small round orb at the Superior Conjunction, when it is on the opposite side of the Sun from the Earth. After the Superior Conjunction it is an Evening Star, and thus is visible in the evening, sky after sun-down, setting later each evening until it reaches its maximum elongation of about 47° - at which time it sets about 3 hours after the Sun.

Shortly thereafter it attains to its greatest brilliancy, then grows rapidly smaller as it again comes closer behind the Sun, until at its Inferior Conjunction it becomes invisible. Thereafter it reappears on the other side of the Sun and becomes again visible as the Morning Star. Its motion as a Morning Star, as measured from the Earth, is slower because of its greater distance from the Earth: 26 million miles at the Inferior Conjunction, as compared to 160 million miles at the Superior Conjunction.

Its rotation period has never been established because of the layer of clouds in which it is perpetually enveloped. Its period has been variously estimated at from 68 hours to 225 days. Its axis is inclined to its orbit plane at an angle of 5 degrees. Its low albedo, or reflecting power (.59), is due to this constant cloud covering. The periods when it is a Morning and Evening Star are of about 10 months' duration each.

Transits over the Sun are rare and occur only when the Sun is within 1°45' of the node, with the Earth also at the node. Though infrequent, they come in pairs. The last such transits occurred in 1874 and 1882. It will not recur until June 8, 2004 and June 6, 2012. The duration of such a transit is about 8 hours.

Solar System Bodies: Earth.
The planet we inhabit. Astrologically, the Earth is the center of its universe, since one is concerned not with the position of the planets in reference to the Sun, but with the angle from which their reflected frequencies enter into the experience of those who dwell upon the Earth. When one speaks of the Sun's position he is but expressing the position of the Earth in its orbit in terms of the apparent position of the Sun. The Earth's orbit is an ellipse, of an eccentricity of about 1:60 - but which is slowly diminishing. Its longest diameter is its major axis. Its half length, or semi-axis, taken as the Mean distance from the Earth to Sun, amounts to about 92,900,000 miles. At perihelion the Earth is more than three million miles closer to the Sun than at aphelion; or about 3% of the maximum distance. The velocity of the Earth in its orbit is approximately 18.5 miles per second.

The Precession of the Equinoctial Point amounts to 360 degrees in about 24,800 years. The Earth's rotation appears to be slowing down at a rate which if continued will amount to 1 second in about 120,000 years.

The common center around which the Earth and the Moon revolve has been computed to be about 3000 miles from the Earth's center - or 1000 miles below the crust of the Earth. That this point is a variable one has been used by some as a basis for a computation based on the assumption that as this point approaches the surface of the Earth there result phenomena known as Earthquakes. The Earth curves from a straight line at the rate of about 1/9th of a degree per second. Its Diameter at the poles is 7900 m.; at the Equator, 7926 m.

The inclination of its axis to the Ecliptic, 66°33'.

Solar System Bodies: Mars. The nearest planet to the Earth, and frequently visible, it may be recognized through the distinct reddish hue of its ray. Mars was known as Ares, the god of war; and as Nimrod, the god of the chase, whose mission it was apparently to dispel terror and fear. To the Greeks, it was Pyrois, the fire. The Romans celebrated the festival of Mars in March, before an altar in the Campus Martius. From it comes our word martial, war like - as martial music. To the Chaldeans it was Nergal, called the "raging king" and the "furious one"; to the Babylonians, the god of war and pestilence, said to preside over the nether-world. For the Alchemists, it represented Iron. Mars has two satelites: Deimos, 6 miles in diameter, distant from Mars by 6.9 radii; and Phoetus, with a revolutionary period of 7h 39M. Deimos has a sidereal period of 30h 18m. Phoetus makes 1330 eclipses a year.

Solar System Bodies: Asteroids. An orbit, approximately midway between those of Mars and Jupiter, occupied by a large number of planetoids or minor planets: variously explained as fragments of a major planet broken up in some prehistoric catastrophe; or particles drawn out of the Sun which failed to coalesce into a single planet. In all there are estimated to be some 50,000 of these Asteroids, of which 1380 had been identified in 1937. As many as 5000 are estimated to have been seen, and again lost. Many of them are more readily visible than Pluto, and may have some astrological significance not as yet identified. Their average diameter is less than 100 miles.

The Astronomischer Rechen-Institut at Dahlem, near Berlin, was world headquarters for Asteroid research, and up to World War 11 published a yearly ephemeris of the larger Asteroids for the periods when they are best observed.

Statistics of the five principal Asteroids are as follows:

```
............Diameter..................Albedo
...Name.......(miles)...Magnitude....(rel. to Sun)...Discovered
...Ceres.......480........7.4...........0.06...........1801
...Pallas......304........8.0...........0.07...........1802
...Juno........120........8.7...........0.12...........1804
...Vesta.......240........6.5...........0.26...........1807
...Astraea................9.9.......................1845
```

The next five, in the order of their discovery, are Hebe (1847), Iris (1847), Flora (1847), Metis (1848), Hygeia (1849).

The orbit of 944 Hidalgo has an eccentricity of 0.65 - more elongated than some comets. At its aphelion distance (9.6 units) it extends into Saturn's orbit.

That of 1177 Gounessia, has an eccentricity of 0.006399, more circular than that of Venus, the most circular among the major planets.

That of 846 Lipperta, is almost parallel with that of the Earth, with an inclination of 0°.244 - more nearly parallel than that of Uranus 0°.77.

That of 2 Pallas has an inclination of 34°.726 - double that of Pluto's 17°.1.

Three Asteroids come closer to the Earth than do any of the major planets. They are Amor, Apollo, and Adonis. 1936 CA or Adonis was discovered in 1936 by Delporte in Belgium. Its orbit has an eccentricity of 0.78, an inclination to the Ecliptic of 1°.48, and a major axis of 1.969 units. On February 7, 1936, it approached to within 1,200,000 miles of the Earth, in the sign Leo. It had reached perihelion in December 1935, at a point slightly outside Mercury's orbit, at a distance of less than half an astrom. unit. Its diameter is less than ½ mile. At aphelion it will go almost to the Jupiter orbit. Its period is about 2 years.

Another asteroid was discovered in 1940 that had approached to within 110,000 miles beyond the Moon's orbit. **V. HERMES.**

Jupiter: The largest planet in the solar family: larger in fact than all other planets combined. Yet it is exceeded in brightness by Venus, because of her greater proximity to the Earth. To the Greeks, known as Zeus; also associated with Marduk, one of the gods of the Pantheon; known to the Hindus as Brahmanaspati. Jupiter has 11 satellites. The first four were among the earliest discoveries of Galileo, and can be seen with the aid of a field glass. Statistics concerning the first five are as follows:

	PERIOD	DISTANCE	DIAMETER
Io	1d.8	262,000	2109
Europa	3d.6		1865
Ganymede	7d.2		3273
Callesta	16d.7	1,000,000	3142
V	11h.57m	112,600	100 est.
VI			100
VII			40

The dates of discovery are V, 1892; VI, 1904; VII, 1905; VIII, 1908; IX, 1914; X, 1938; XI, 1938. The orbits of the outer four are so far distant from the planet that their motion is affected by perturbations due to the Sun's attraction, to such an extent that they can hardly be said to have an orbit.

No. IX has an orbital inclination in excess of 90°, to that of Jupiter's orbit. No. VIII has an orbital eccentricity of 0.38, whereby its distance varies from 9 to 20 million miles.

Saturn: The planet next smaller in magnitude to Jupiter, and next more remote from the Sun, is remarkable for its engirdling system of rings. It was the most remote planet known to the ancients. The surface of Saturn shows markings somewhat similar to those of Jupiter, but fainter. Spectroscopic observations have confirmed the theory that the rings are composed of a dense swarm of small solid bodies. of ten identified satellites of Saturn, the brightest is Titan. The ninth, Phobe, is fainter and more distant than any of the others. The tenth, Themis, lies between Titan and Hyperion. When the Alchemists and early Chemists used the name Saturn they referred to its association with the metal lead. Lead poisoning was once called the Saturnine colic.

Saturn was the ancient god of the seed sowing. His temple in Rome, founded in 497 B.C., was used as a state treasury. In 217 B.C. the worship of Saturn was conformed to that of its Greek counterpart, Cronus, son of Uranus, and god of Boundless Time and the Cycles. There was a myth that Saturn in Italy, as Cronus in Greece, had been king during an ancient golden age - hence was the founder of Italian civilization. Also associated with the Greek god Phoenon, "the cruel one," and the Assyrian god Ninib, patron of Agriculture, and one of the gods of the Pantheon. From it we have the English word Saturnian or Saturnine. The Saturnine colic was lead poisoning. Its atmosphere contains a high percentage of methane and ammonium gases, with no oxygen. For some unexplained reason it changes color from year to year.

There are 25,824 Saturn days in one Saturn year.

The Saturn rings consist of: A, the outermost ring, about 11,000 miles in width; B, the middle ring, about 18,000 miles in width; and C, the inside ring, the gauze or crepe ring, about 11,000 miles in width. Between it and the surface of the planet is a gap of about 5,000 miles. Separating A and B is the Cassini division, a dark strip some 2,300 miles in width.

Because the planet's equator is inclined about 28° to the plane of the ecliptic, the Saturn ring as seen from the Earth passes through phases: from Saturn's equinoctial point, where the rings are visible only as a thin line, to Saturn's solstices, where they lie transverse to us in a wide expanse. The edgewise view occurs in longitudes 172° and 352°; the maximum elongation, in longitudes 82° and 262°. The edgewise view was had in 1921 and 1936; the full-faced view in 1929 and 1944. As this constitutes a 15-year cycle, it is possible that there are related variations and fluctuations in the resultant astrological influences, which further research will be able to reduce to usable distinctions.

...SATURN'S MOONS	DISC.	DISTANCE THOUSANDS	PERIOD DAYS	ECCENT	DIAM. MILES
.1...Mimas	1789	115	0.9	0.0190	370
.2...Enceladus	1789	148	1.4	0.0046	460
.3...Tethys	1684	183	001.9	0.0000	750
.4...Dione	1684	234	002.7	0.0020	900
.5...Rhea	1672	327	004.5	0.0009	1150
.6...Titan	1655	759	015.9	0.0289	3550

.7...Hyperion..........1848.......919.......021.3......0.119..........310
.8...Iapetus............1671.....2,210.......079.3......0.029.........1100
.9...Phoebe.............1898.....8,044.......550.4......0.1659.........160
10...Themis............1905.....c.800

Uranus: Its discovery by Sir William Herschel on March 13, 1781, added a new factor to the problems of Astrology, and incidentally widened the horizon of observation of planetary influence upon human life. Inserting the planet into the existing horoscopes, revealed that Uranus had been the previously inexplicable cause of violent dislocations, fractures, separations, mental disturbances and deaths. With its discovery there came a new interpretation to the old phrase "by visitation of God." Herschel called it Georgium Sidus, but England continues to use the name Herschel - from which derives the symbol although the rest of the world adopted the name Uranus by which Bode referred to it in 1783. Astrologers had long speculated upon its existence, referring to it as Ouranos. It is sometimes called "The cataclysmic planet."

The astronomers' symbol is one of the few cases in which astronomers and astrologers fall to employ the same symbols.

As its Equator is inclined by 82° to the plane of its orbit, the regions of perpetual day and night reach to within 8° of the Equator.

Its satellites are:

..............DISC. ..SIDEREAL PERIOD...MAGNITUDE..DIAM.
...Ariel.......1851.......2d 12.489h.........16......560
...Umbriel.....1851.......4d 3.460h.........16-17...430
...Titania.....1787.......8d 16.941h.........14.....1000
...Oberon......1787......13d 11.118h.........14......900

Solar System bodies:
Neptune: Until the discovery of Pluto in 1930, Neptune was supposed to be the outermost member of the solar system. It was discovered September 23, 1846 by Galle in Berlin, in the region suggested by Leverrier of Paris; but later was identified as the "star" observed in 1795 by Lalande of Paris. Agrippa dedicated a temple to Neptune in honor of the naval victory of Actium. To the Greeks, known as Poseidon. It is a greenish disc of the magnitude of 7.7, and is distant from Earth by 30 astrom. units. Its revolutionary period is 164y.

It has one known satellite, Triton, about the size of our Moon, and 220,000 miles distant from the planet. It has a magnitude of 13. Its period is 5d, 21h, its orbit inclined to the Neptune orbit by an angle of 40°; its motion retrograde, with a recession period of 580y, or 140° direct. Inclination of Triton's orbit to Neptune's equator is 20°.

Neptune was in Virgo from 1435 to 1449; from 1600 to 1614; from 1761 to 1778; and most recently from 1921 to 1942. It was in Libra from 1450 to 1465; from 1615 to 1635; from 1779 to 1793; and 1943 to 1957.

Pluto: The outermost planet of the solar system so far identified, was discovered in 1930. It lies 800 million miles beyond Neptune. The nearest conjunction of Neptune and Pluto occurred in 1892.. A previous exact conjunction occurred in prehistoric times, and will not recur for several thousand years, when they will remain close together for 100 years. As 3 Neptune revolutions take 494y. and 2 of Pluto 496y, an approximate conjunction occurs every 492.328 years.

Pluto was discovered by Percival Lowell, who delayed publication of the news until his birthday, March 13, 1930 - the day on which Uranus had been discovered 140 years before.

The name Pluto, beginning with P.L., the initials of the discoverer was suggested by an eleven-year-old English girl.

The size or volume of Pluto has not been ascertained, but its mass is less than that of the Earth. The extreme eccentricity of its orbit brings it at times nearer to the Sun than Neptune. There is no certainty that the orbits do not cross, in which event a collision is not impossible. Experience seems to increase the probability of the eventual discovery of other Trans-Neptune planets.

Solar Time. v. TIME.

Solar Year. v. YEAR.

SOL-om-on. The name of the Sun in three languages: an expression of light, knowledge, understanding.

Solomon's Seal. Two interlaced triangles, the angles of which form the six-pointed star. often one of the triangles is dark and the other light, symbolizing the union of soul and body. According to occult symbology the apex of the emblem represents the human head or intelligence; the two upper outstretched points, sympathy with everything that lives; the two lower, human responsibility; the angle at the bottom, pointing earthward, procreative power - the cryptograph, in its entirety, denoting complete individuality or human entity.

Solomon's Temple. Solomon, Son of David, by Bathsheba, King of Israel in the 10th century B.C., was noted for his superior wisdom, and his great wealth. To the great temple he built at Jerusalem has been attributed many symbolic interpretations. In occult literature the human body, as developed by divine principle, is referred to as Solomon's Temple.

Solstices. The points in the Ecliptic at which the Sun is at its greatest distance north or south of the Equator, so-called because the Sun then appears to stand still. The Summer Solstice occurs when the Sun is at 0° Cancer, about June 21; the Winter Solstice, at 0° Capricorn, about December 21.

South Latitudes. Those south of the celestial equator. In utilizing the Table of Houses for South Latitudes, change the signs to their opposites: Aries becomes Libra, and so on.

Southern Signs. v. NORTHERN SIGNS.

Spectroscope. A device whereby to disperse and separate a beam of radiation into its component wave lengths. Spectroscopic observation of moving bodies shows that with an approaching body there is a shift to the violet end, while with a receding body the shift is toward the red end: the angular amount of the shift proportional to the velocity of motion of the light source and inversely to the wave length and velocity of the light. This is a confirmation of the altered astrological influence resulting from motion toward or away from a gravitational center, and with or contra to the orbital motion of the controlling body.

Speculum. A table appended to a horoscope, comprising its astronomical elements: the planets' latitude, declination, Right Ascension, Ascensional Difference, Pole and Semi-arc. It is employed in the practice of directing by Primary Directions (Q.V.) as taught by Ptolemy.

Sphere. A globe. Also applied to a planet's orbit.

Sphinx. The most famous sphinx in Greek mythology was that of Thebes in Boetia, mentioned by Hesiod. It was symbolic of the fixed types of the four elements: the body of a bull - Taurus; the feet and tail of a lion - Leo; the wings of the eagle - Scorpio; a human head - Aquarius. Variations are found in all parts of the ancient world, showing its art influence upon those who knew naught of its symbolic significance. of interest is the parallel found in Ezekiel's description of the Markaba. (EZ. 1:10.)

Square. N. A separation of 900 between any bodies or zodiacal points (V. ASPECT). Syn. quartile.

Square, VB. Moving to form an aspect, through an arc of approximately 7 degrees, according to the bodies involved, on either side of the point where their Longitudinal separation becomes exactly 90 degrees.

Standard Time. V. TIME.

Star of Bethlehem. Commonly conjectured to have been the conjunction of Saturn, Jupiter and Mars which occurred about 2 B.C. It is supposed that the astrologers, the "wise men of the East," were endeavoring to locate a child born at the point in terrestrial latitude and longitude from which this triple conjunction would occur in the same celestial latitude and longitude, and in the midheaven of that particular geographical location. As this was one of the grand mutations (Q.V.) it was presumed that a child born at the exact place and hour that would posit this important satellitium (Q.V.) at the cusp of the Tenth House, would be marked by Destiny to become the initiator of a new epoch in world history. It may be that the legend of the manger was devised as a record of a birth, connotated to this grand conjunction in 2 B.C.

Stars. Stars were classified by the ancients as "fixed stars" to distinguish them from the "wandering" stars - which, when their orbits were discovered, became known as planets, in that they revolve in a plane. Stars have a proper motion of their own, but owing to their remoteness this motion could be measured only by observations taken over a protracted period - far in excess of a mere lifetime. There is no reason why the term should not now be abandoned in favor of the simple designation of "star."

By some astrological authorities the stars are credited with an influence of their own, when in conjunction and parallel with a planet, either at birth or in transit. A star of the first magnitude on the Ascendant or

Midheaven at birth is said to indicate that the native will become illustrious within his sphere of life - a "star" in social, political, or commercial life. The two large stars, Aldebaran and Antares, which are in the tenth degree of Gemini and Sagittarius, respectively, when directed to the angles of the horoscope, are said to produce periods of severe stress. They are deemed more powerful when in the angles.

Those who include the stars in their delineations appear to agree that the influence is entirely confined to a close conjunction with a birth planet to within from 2° to 5° in Longitude, and 1° in Latitude, and that it has no influence by aspect. Certain individual degrees of the zodiac appear to possess specific influences, and these may have some connection with stars which tenant these degrees, even when untenanted by planets. Further confirmation of this theory is to be found in a work by Salmon, wherein he divided each sign into six Faces of 5 degrees each, "because in every sign there are various stars of differing natures." v. Degrees, Individual.

Stars visible to the unaided eye number less than five thousand. Those near Polaris can be seen only in the Northern Hemisphere, while the Southern Cross and nearby stars can be seen only from the Southern Hemisphere.

Stationary. A planet appears to be stationary in its orbit at that point, or station, from which it reverses its motion from direct to retrograde, or the reverse. The Sun and Moon are never stationary. v. Stations.

Stations. Those points in the orbit of a planet where it becomes either retrograde or direct; so termed because it remains stationary there for a few days before it changes its course. The first station is where it becomes retrograde; the second station, where it abandons retrograde and resumes direct motion. From these Stations orientality is reckoned. From apogee to the first station it is matutine, because it rises in the morning before the Sun, hence is in the first degree of orientality. From the first station to perigee, the lowest apsis, it is vespertine, because it rises in the evening before Sunset, hence is in the first degree of occidentality.

Stations of the Moon. The Moon is never retrograde, but in a different sense her first and second dichotomies are often loosely termed her first and second stations.

Stellium. v. Satellitium.

Strength of a planet. v. Dignity, accidental or essential.

Succedent Houses. Those which follow the angular houses: 2, 5, 8 and 11. v. Houses.

Sunspot Cycle. The phenomenon of Sunspot cycles is one which has increasingly engaged the attention of astrophysicists for more than two centuries. Useful records of the sunspot cycle are available from 1610 to the present day. For a long time the cycle was said to be of a duration of 11.3 years, but more recently it has been noted that successive eleven-year cycles produce similar but opposite phenomena, and that a complete cycle is of a duration of 22.6 years. It has also been noted that while the Sun's surface is hotter at times of sunspot maxima, the Earth's land surface is cooler, apparently due to the increased cloudiness that attends the phenomena. It is also found that magnetic disturbances in the Sun - are reflected on the Earth with increased display of the **AURORA BOREALIS** and magnetic disturbances that interrupt telegraphic service. Economic cycles are also found to correspond with the Sunspot Cycle. Trees grow more during the years of Sunspot maxima, when ultra-violet radiation increases by as much as 30 Per cent. Some plant life grows better with an excess of ultra-violet light, while other species thrive better on an excess of infra-red rays. Ellsworth Huntingdon, of Yale University, says solar radiation affects the health and behavior of man. Harlan E. Stetson, of Massachusetts Institute of Technology, finds business activity, output of automobiles and new building construction follow the Sunspot cycle. For lack of reliable data on weather conditions, Dr. William Herschel used the price of wheat as an index on which to base his observations of this and similar cosmic cycles. Thus sciences establish the fact that man is influenced by cosmic phenomena, and the step to recognition of the validity of astrological influences has only the hurdle of prejudice to overcome before it is accorded scientific recognition.

Supercycle. A term applied by Richard and Jaggar to a cycle of 132 years, or approximately 6 sun-spot cycles.

Superior Planets. Those which lie outside of the Earth's orbit. v. **PLANETS.**

Synodical Lunation. v. **LUNATION.**

Synthesis. The art of blending together separate influences in a nativity, and deducing a summary thereof. The ability to synthesize a nativity is the mark of an experienced astrologer.

Syzygy. Literally a yoking together. often loosely applied to any conjunction or opposition; particularly of a planet with the Sun, and close to the ecliptic whereby the Earth and the two bodies are in a straight line. In its use in connection with the calculation of Tide Tables it applies to the conjunctions and oppositions of Sun and Moon near the Node.

Tables of Houses. Tables showing the degrees of the Signs which occupy the cusps of the several Houses in different latitudes for every degree of Right Ascension, or for every 4 minutes of Sidereal Time. Generally available are those by Dalton (1913), Raphael (1920) and Hugh Rice (1935).
There is much argument anent the various systems of calculating the cusps of the intermediate Houses, until one wonders sometimes why not use a stop watch to locate the degree on the horizon every two hours. Of course it would have to be done over again in all latitudes, and besides it would not be very scientific. Nevertheless the general opinion is that none of the existing methods are correct for all latitudes, even though they may be near enough for practical purposes. The four best known systems are as follows:
Campanus. The vertical circle from the zenith to the cast and west points of the horizon is trisected. Through these points are drawn great circles, the House circles, from the north and south points of the horizon. Thus the intersections will be at altitudes of 30° and 60° above the horizon, on both cast and west branches of the prime vertical. This divides the sky into six great sectors. Similarly divide the hemisphere below the horizon. The house cusps are the points at which the ecliptic at that moment intersects the horizon.

Regiomontanus. The celestial circle is trisected, instead of the prime vertical, and great circles extend from north and south points of the horizon to the points of trisection. The house cusps are at the points at which the ecliptic intersects the horizon. At the Equator the two systems give the same cusps, the disparity increasing as one approaches the Earth's poles.

Horizontal. Starting with great circles at the meridian and ante-meridian, the horizon and the prime vertical, add other great circles from Zenith to Nadir which trisect each quadrant of the horizon. The cusps will then be the points at which on a given moment the ecliptic intersects the vertical circles.

Placidus Instead of using great circles, the diurnal motion of the Earth causes a celestial object to intersect the cusp of the 12th House, after a sidereal-time interval equal to one-third of its semi-diurnal arc; to intersect the cusp of the 11th House after a sidereal-time interval equal to two-thirds of its semi-diurnal arc; and to culminate at the meridian after an interval of sidereal time that corresponds to the semi-diurnal arc. The semi-arc from the meridian that intersects the Eastern horizon gives the Ascendant; and the 2nd and 3rd house cusps are similarly extended below the horizon. The Placidian cusps are in almost universal use at the present time. Maurice Wemyss takes exception to the Placidus cusps on the grounds that the Ascendant is located according to one system and the intermediate cusps by another. He prefers what he terms the "Rational Method" of Regiomontanus.

A set of Tables of Houses for Lat. 40° N., which is approximately the latitude of New York, in which can be seen a comparison of these four systems, is to be found in the American Astrology Ephemeris for the year 1941. The Tenth House is common to an four systems, and this is theoretically correct. The discrepancies show in the intermediate cusps between the IC and MC. The Ascendant is also the same for three of the four systems, but the Horizontal system has its own Ascendants. Different Latitudes require different sets of tables. Published volumes containing Tables of Houses for all Latitudes are available, most of them, however, confined to the Placidus system, which is the one most generally used. The one by Hugh Rice is the most recent and the most elaborate, with the cusps computed to several decimals.

Unless you have a birth moment that is correct to the minute, and beyond doubt, detailed methods are futile and misleading, and one might well confine himself to whole degrees and ignore the decimals. By means of these tables of houses computed for different latitudes, one is able to ascertain what degrees of the zodiac appeared upon the Ascendant and the various House cusps on any hour of any day, as calculated from the siderial time at noon of that day as indicated in the ephemeris. Actually the tables may be said to divide distance by time, showing how many degrees of the equator will pass the ASC or MC, as if the planet were there. It is to be understood, of course, that this is a rule-of-thumb short-cut for average use when one is not too certain of the reliability of his birth data, and is not to be used when seeking exactness.

T-cross. *v. Cosmic Cross.*

Taurus. The second sign of the zodiac. *v. Signs.*

Telepathy. Transmission of thoughts from one to another of two minds that presumably are in attunement or affinity, without the aid of any orthodox means of communication through ordinary channels of sensation. It is generally supposed that an accent on Neptune confers sensitive receptivity to telepathic communications. This may occur at close range or over a long distance.

Telescope. An optical instrument assisting the eye or camera in viewing or photographing distant objects, magnifying the celestial bodies, and concentrating a larger beam of light to render the image more distinct. Some ancient references suggest that it was known to the Greeks and Romans. In the Pyramid is found evidence that at some period the Egyptians had a form of reflecting telescope. Refracting telescopes were first made in Holland in 1608. Hearing about them, Galileo made one for himself and in 1620 began his experiments. The earliest known reflecting telescope was that perfected by James Gregory of Edinborough in 1663.

Temporal Houses. 2, 6, 10. v. Houses.

Terminal Houses, The. 4th, 8th, 12th Houses *(q.v.)*, corresponding to the Signs of the Watery Triplicity. So called because they govern the terminations of three occult or mysterious phases of life: the 4th, the end of the physical man; the 8th, the liberation of the soul; and the 12th, of the hopes to which the native secretly aspires.

Terms of the planets. The planetary Terms comprises a system of subruler ships of portions of a Sign by different planets, whereby the nature of a planet posited in a Sign is altered to that of the planet in whose term it happens to be posited. These subdivisions - applicable only to the interpretation of a Horary Figure - are largely disregarded by the moderns, most of whom deem them the fanciful invention of the Egyptians to account for effects now ascribed to the influences of formerly unknown planets. Other authorities who use them in the practice of Horary Astrology claim that they yield excellent results. Ptolemy made light of the Egyptian Tables as devoid of either rhyme or reason. He then laid down a set of rules and made his own Tables - to which he himself failed to conform. Sepharial, Alan Leo and Wilson all give Tables of these Terms - no two, however, exactly alike - while all more or less scoff at their value. Ptolemy gave 6° to each of the five planets. Any planet whether or not a malefic, which had two dignities came first; otherwise the malefics came last. He next gave to each planet extra points of valuation, two for Sign-position and one each for Exaltation and Triplicity, subtracting these points from the value of the malefics. The Term occupied by a planet denotes that the person it signifies is of a disposition indicated by the Lord of the Term, but with no reference to his wealth, poverty, or station in life.

.SIGN........	TERMS AS REVISED BY PTOLEMY......................
Aries........	Jupiter..0-5*	Venus....6-13	Mercury..14-20	Mars.....21-25	Saturn..26-29
Taurus.......	Venus....0-7.	Mercury..8-14	Jupiter..15-21	Saturn...22-25	Mars....26-29
Gemini.......	Mercury..0-6.	Jupiter..7-13	Venus....14-20	Saturn...21-24	Mars....25-29
Cancer.......	Mars.....0-5.	Jupiter..6-12	Mercury..13-19	Venus....20-26	Saturn..27-29
Leo..........	Saturn...0-5.	Mercury..6-12	Venus....13-18	Jupiter..19-24	Mars....25-29
Virgo........	Mercury..0-6.	Venus....7-12	Jupiter..13-17	Saturn...18-23	Mars....24-29
Libra........	Saturn...0-5.	Venus....6-10	Jupiter..11-18	Mercury..19-23	Mars....24-29
Scorpio......	Mars.....0-5.	Jupiter..6-13	Venus....14-20	Mercury..21-26	Saturn..27-29
Sagittarius..	Jupiter..0-7.	Venus....8-13	Mercury..14-18	Saturn...19-24	Mars....25-29
Capricorn....	Venus....0-5.	Mercury..6-11	Jupiter..12-18	Mars.....19-24	Saturn..25-29
Aquarius.....	Saturn...0-5.	Mercury..6-11	Venus....12-19	Jupiter..20-24	Mars....25-29
Pisces.......	Venus....0-7.	Jupiter..8-13	Mercury..14-19	Mars.....20-25	Saturn..26-29

*Meaning the first six degrees, from 0°0' to 5°59' - and so on.

The planet sequence for Gemini is Lilly's variant. See "Christian Astrology" by W.Lilly. But the Tetrabiblos says this sequence is (in meaning as above) "Mercury 0-6, Jupiter 7-12, Venus 13-19, Mars 20-25, Saturn 26-29". See: *Ptolemy. Tetrabiblos / Edited and translated by F.E.Robbins. - Cambridge, Massachusetts; London: Harvard University Press, 2001*. [A.Z.]

The series of terms according to the Egyptians, were as follows:
...Aries....... Jupiter 6, Venus 6, Mercury 8, Mars 5, Saturn 5.
...Taurus...... Venus 8, Mercury 6, Jupiter 8, Saturn 5, Mars 3.
...Gemini...... Mercury 6, Jupiter 6, Venus 5, Mars 7, Saturn 6.
...Cancer...... Mars 7, Venus 6, Mercury 6, Jupiter 7, Saturn 4.
...Leo.......... Jupiter 6, Venus 5, Saturn 7, Mercury 6, Mars 6.
...Virgo....... Mercury 7, Venus 10, Jupiter 4, Mars 7, Saturn 2.
...Libra....... Saturn 6, Venus 8, Jupiter 7, Mercury 7, Mars 2.
...Scorpio..... Mars 7, Venus 4, Mercury 8, Jupiter 5, Saturn 6.
...Sagittarius. Jupiter 12, Venus 5, Mercury 4, Saturn 5, Mars 4.
...Capricorn... Mercury 7, Venus 6, Jupiter 7, Mars 5, Saturn 5.
...Aquarius.... Mercury 7, Venus 6, Jupiter 7, Mars 5, Saturn 5.
...Pisces...... Venus 12, Jupiter 4, Mercury 3, Mars 9, Saturn 2.

Testimony. A partial judgment based upon the influence of a certain planet as conditioned by Sign and House, strength of position and aspects, or of a certain configuration of planets in a Figure. The synthesis of several testimonies constitutes a judgment. The term as used by Ptolemy is approximately synonymous with Argument.

Tetrabiblios. Literally four books. The oldest record of the astrological system of the ancients which has survived. It dates from about 132-160 A.D. In it the author, Claudius Ptolemy, the great Egyptian mathematician, says that it was compiled from "ancient" sources. *v. Ptolemaic Astrology.*

Tetractys - ten symbolic dots. A theory advanced by Pythagoras, who affirmed the existence of ten bodies in our Solar System. The ancients knew only seven such bodies, but modern astronomers have discovered the other three: Uranus, Neptune and Pluto.

.
. .
. . .
. . . .

This symbol as used by Pythagoras consisted of ten dots arranged in triangular form, as illustrated. By connecting the dots in different ways many rectangles and triangles were formed, all intimately associated with the Pythagorean mathematical system by means of which he explains his conception of the truths of the universe. This may explain the missing apex of the pyramid, as can be seen in the great seal of the United States, as printed on some of the paper currency.

Tetragon, N. Tetragonous, A. Syn. of quartile, or a square aspect. v. ASPECT.

Thema Coeli. The figure of the heavens. v. *Figure*.

Throne. Some astrologers who lean to hyperbole rather than consistency and lucidity describe a planet as on its throne when in a Sign of which it is the Ruler. In a more ancient and more logical usage it was applied to a planet posited in that part of a Sign wherein it had more than one Dignity.

Time. The measurement of time is inseparable from considerations of place, and of a point of reference. The establishing of the actual moment of an occurrence, and its statement in terms of Universal Time, is one of the most difficult problems with which the astrologer deals, because of the prevalent neglect on the part of those who make the record of the moment of an event, to qualify it by stating in what manner of time it is noted: whether apparent solar time, as shown on a sundial; mean time, as shown by a clock adjusted to the meridian of the place; local Standard Time, as shown by a clock adjusted to a Standard time meridian, and if so, which one; or whether in Daylight Saving Time, War Time, Double Summer Time; and so on.

SIDEREAL TIME. That in which the point of reference is a star - as the most nearly fixed point in the universe as it appears from the Earth. Two successive crossings of a star is the measurement of a sidereal day, which is divided into 24 hours, beginning with 0h and continuing to 23h 59m. It is used by astronomers, chiefly to express in hours and minutes of sidereal time the Midheaven longitude of a given place. Prior to 1925 0h of the astronomical day coincided with noon but in that year astronomical and civil time were made to coincide, since when 0h has coincided with midnight.

SOLAR TIME. That in which the point of reference is the Sun. This may be APPARENT Solar time, as shown by a sundial; or local Mean Time, as shown by a clock adjusted to an average rather than an actual day. This is explained more fully under Equation of Time (Q.V.). With Solar Time, noon was approximately four minutes earlier or later with every increase of distance of 1° East or West of Greenwich Observatory, which at zero longitude is the point for which Universal or World Time is computed. Apparent and Mean Solar Time coincide four times a year: on April 15, June 14, Sept. 1 and Dec. 25. At all other times the Sun is FAST or SLOW by from one to sixteen minutes.

STANDARD TIME. Since the meeting of train schedules is impossible on the basis of local time, Standard time-zone meridians were spaced at intervals of 15° of longitude East and West of Greenwich, and all clocks within each zone were adjusted to the mean Solar time of the midpoint of the zone. Standard Time was generally adopted on Nov. 18, 1883, but it did not come into common use in some localities until after many years had elapsed. Even yet there are communities in which the time of day is given in Sun time; unless you wish to catch a train, in which case you are given Railway Time. Not only that, but longitude is becoming an increasingly unreliable guide, for some communities which are actually in the Central Standard Time zone run by Eastern Standard Time, to make their business day coincide with that of some nearby city across the meridian; and similarly at various points throughout the world. Lacking such exceptions, all places in the United States east of 82°39' W. Long. are theoretically in the Eastern Standard Time zone, and their time is 5h earlier than that of Greenwich; Central Standard Time, 6h earlier than Greenwich, applies to points between 82°30' and 97°30' W. Long.; Mountain Standard Time, 7h earlier than Greenwich, between 97°30' and 112°30' W. Long.; and Pacific Standard Time, 8h earlier than Greenwich, to all points in the United States west of Long. 112°30'. However, one need but observe on any time zone map the irregular lines which indicate the Time Zone meridians across the country, to realize how important it is that any statement of time of an event is incomplete and unreliable unless it carries with it a statement of the kind of time in which the event was recorded, and the standard meridian adopted by that community.

DAYLIGHT SAVING TIME. This was originated in England in 1916, where it was called Summer Time. It consists of an arbitrary setting ahead of the clock by one hour, thereby shifting all the day's activities an hour earlier, ending the work day that much sooner and leaving an hour more of daylight in which to indulge in seasonal recreations. In general, it commences at 2 A.M. of the Sunday following the third Saturday in April, and ends on the Sunday after the first Saturday in October. This is not a reliable guide, for in its earlier years it sometimes began as early as March 24. Furthermore, during World War II England set the clock ahead by two hours, making Double Summer Time. During the same period, beginning Feb. 9, 1942 at 2 P.M., the United States had War Time, a year-round setting ahead of the clock by one hour. Prior to that, some parts of the United States observed Daylight Saving Time during certain periods in certain years, but other localities refused to accept or ratify it; and even in those where it was legally authorized, many refused to abide by it. Even though a record of the vagaries of time observance is attempted in a volume called WORLD DAYLIGHT SAVING TIME, by Curran and Taylor, the only safe way to record an event is not only to state in what kind of time it was recorded, but in addition to give its equivalent in Greenwich Standard or Universal Time. In most other countries the problem is still more complicated. All of Mexico is -6h, except part of Lower California, which is -8h. Some adopt a time meridian that involves a half-hour adjustment, like Hawaii, which is GMT - 10h 30m. All of Russia adjusts to a time unit which is the virtual equivalent of permanent daylight saving. Bolivia is -4:33 and Venezuela -4:30. In addition, there is for some Middle European countries an adjustment of the date itself from the old-style to the new-style calendar, and the impossible determination whether time was given in apparent Sun time or Solar Mean time, or whether some arbitrarily selected meridian became the basis for the standard time of the country.

The important factors for the astrologer to establish are: (1) the exact equivalent of a given moment as expressed in Universal Time, in order therefrom to compute from the Ephemeris the exact position occupied by the planets at that precise moment; and (2) the exact equivalent of the same moment in Local Mean Time for the place where the event occurred, wherefrom with the aid of the sidereal time of noon or midnight on that date, and of Tables of Houses for the Latitude of the place, to calculate the Midheaven position, the Ascendant degree, and the intermediate cusps of the Figure. Universal Time is variously called World Time, Greenwich Civil Time, Greenwich Standard Time, or zero zone time.

An ephemeris calculated for other than zero meridian is a simplification that is of doubtful value, in that it introduces the possibility of confusion on the part of those who work by formulas rather than by a comprehension of the elements involved. In using an ephemeris calculated, let us say, for 75° W. Long., one bases his calculations on that time meridian, instead of the zero meridian, correcting zone time to local time by subtracting 4m for each degree of longitude W., or adding it for each degree of Long. E., OF THE 75TH MERIDIAN.

ARMY AND NAVY TIME. Just as the Navy has long since abandoned the traditional method of "boxing the compass" and instead indicates direction in degrees from 1 to 360, so both Army and Navy have abandoned the twelve-hour clock in favor of the 24-hour clock, which begins at midnight as 0000h, is 1200 at noon, 1330h at half-past-one, and so on until 2359h, which is one minute before oh of the next day. Thus A.M. and P.M. become no longer necessary in connection with the time of day or night. The public will be slow to demand 24-hour clocks and watches, but indications and efficiency point to the probability of their eventual general use.

RECORDING A BIRTH MOMENT. Never make record of or state a birth hour as midnight, for the day both begins and ends with midnight, and in time you yourself will not know which it was - resulting in a tiny difference of twenty-four hours. The day begins with 0h; noon is 12h. A minute before midnight can be 11:59 P.M., or 23:59h - but midnight is oh OF THE NEXT DAY.

Time. CORRECTION OF MEAN TO SIDEREAL TIME. In calculating the Sidereal Time for a given moment of birth, add the solar hours elapsed since the previous noon to the Sun's noon position at Greenwich as given in the ephemeris in Sidereal Time. (*Apolo's Note:* THIS APPLIES ONLY IF YOU ARE USING AN EPHEMERIS WITH READINGS FOR NOON; IF USING ONE FOR MIDNIGHT, WHICH IS EASIER, THEN ADD THE SOLAR HOURS ELAPSED SINCE MIDNIGHT ON THE START OF THE DAY OF BIRTH.) This requires the further addition of a little less than ten seconds (9.86 SECONDS) per hour to compensate for the difference between solar and sidereal time.

[A further correction for longitude is made by way of adjusting the Greenwich position to that of the place for which the correction is made.]

Transit. The ephemeral passage of a planet over the place of any Significator, moderator or planet, or any point where it forms an aspect thereto, whether in a radix, progressed, Solar Revolution or Horary Figure. Transits are taken from the ephemeris for the current year. Generally speaking the passage of the benefic planets over, or in aspect to, the radical and progressed places of the several Significators is favorable; of the malefics unfavorable.

Kuno Foelsch, Ph.D., in his work on Transits, which actually treats of the Solar Revolution, concurs in the suggestion that during the Middle Ages it became necessary to devise some system of approximating future conditions, for the reason that Ephemerides calculated for years in advance were not then obtainable. Speaking of Transits, he expresses the confident belief that "other methods will eventually disappear, especially those which are dependent upon hypothetical elements which have no connection with the actual astronomical positions of the planets as recorded by scientifically operated observations."

Transit of a planet across the Sun. A transit of Venus across the Sun can occur only when the Sun is within 1° 45' of the Node, and the Earth is passing the Node. These occur in pairs - the last two in 1874 and 1882. The next recurrence will be June 8, 2004, and June 6, 2012. Mercury transits are more frequent.

Transitor. A slow-moving major planet whose lingering aspect to a birth planet produces a displacement of equilibrium, which is then activated by an additional aspect from a Culminator, a faster-moving body such as the Sun or Moon, to the same or another planet, thereby precipitating the externalization.

Translation of Light. The conveyance of influence which occurs when a transiting planet, while separating from an aspect to one planet is found to be applying to an aspect to another, in which event some of the influence of the first aspected planet is imparted to the second aspected planet by a translation of light. For example, assume an Horary Figure in which Jupiter or Saturn, the Significators of the parties to the negotiation of an agreement, are in no aspect to each other; but Venus while separating from Jupiter is applying to an aspect of Saturn. There results a translation of light from Jupiter to Saturn, which is a powerful testimony that Venus represents a person or an idea that will bring about a settlement. The nature of the aspect, and of the aspecting and aspected planets through which the translation is accomplished, determines whether the outcome will be fortuitous.

Transmutation. The advantageous utilization, on the part of a controlled and developed character, of an astrological influence which otherwise might exert a destructive and disruptive force. It is a term borrowed from the alchemists who sought to transmute baser metals into gold, whereby to suggest a process of spiritual alchemy through which a baser emotion is dedicated to a noble purpose.

Trigon. A term applied to the three signs of the same triplicity.

Trigonocrators. Rulers of Trigons

	ANCIENT	MODERN
FIRE:	Sun, Jupiter	Sun, Jupiter, Mars
EARTH:	Venus, Moon	Venus, Mercury, Saturn
AIR:	Saturn, Mercury	Venus, Saturn
WATER:	Mars	Moon, Mars, Mercury

Some modern authorities confine the Moon and Mars to a Nocturnal Figure, substituting Venus and Mars if a Day Figure.

Trimorion. An aspect in Mundo which embraces three Houses, hence a Mundane square, but which in some instances may actually extend to as much as 120°; hence in Primary Directions It was sometimes called the killing arc, since 120 years were deemed the natural limit of life.

Trine, N. An aspect of 120°.

Trine, VB. Used in describing the motion of a planet to a trine aspect with the body or place of another planet.

Trinities. V. SIGNS.

Triplicities. V. SIGNS.

Tropical Signs. Cancer and Capricorn. V. SIGNS.

Tropical Year. The Solar Year; the period of 365d, 5h, 48m, 4.5s, during which the Sun's centre passes from one Vernal Equinox to the next. Because of the precession, it is shorter than the Sidereal Year by 20m, 23.5s.

True Solar Day. v. DAY.

Trutine. A term employed by Hermes in the process of rectification (Q.V.).

Twilight. The illumination of the Earth's atmosphere after sunset, visible until the Sun is about 18° below the horizon. Its duration depends upon the time required for the Sun to traverse this distance. At the Equator this requires about an hour at any time of year, but during Summer lasts for a much longer period. As one passes beyond 40° N. latitude, the interval is lengthened in the Summer and shortened in the Winter.

Umbral Eclipse. Said of an eclipse of the Moon, when the Moon definitely enters the Earth's shadow. If the Moon is completely immersed in the Earth's shadow a total eclipse results; otherwise, a partial eclipse. Applied to an eclipse of the Sun it does not include a partial eclipse, but only those in which the Moon's disc is fully contained within that of the Sun, either total, annular, or annular-total. *v. Eclipse.*

Under the Sunbeams. Said of a planet that is less than 17° distant in longitude from the Sun. It was once reckoned unfavorable though not as much so as combust. Modern authorities, however, form more discriminating and less categorical judgments, by taking into consideration the intrinsic character of the planets and other attending conditions. *v. Cazimi.*

Unfortunate Signs. The Negative Signs Taurus, Cancer, Virgo, Scorpio, Capricorn and Aquarius. *v. Signs.*

Urania. One of the Nine Muses, representing Astronomy. Often applied to things astrologic.

Uranian. Said of a person of erratic and independent nature, with original and unorthodox ideas and viewpoints, due to a strong Uranus birth receptivity. Usually tall blond types.

Uranian Astrology. A system based upon the teachings of Alfred Witte of the Hamburg (Ger.) Astrology School. Its chief differences from the orthodox school consist in the use of Planetary Patterns *(q.v.)* based upon Midpoints, the cardinal points, Antiscia, and certain hypothetical planets; also the exclusion of all but the "hard" angles: conjunction, semi-square, quadrate, sesquiquadrate and opposition - which are termed effective connections. The personal points are 0° of Aries, Cancer, Libra and Capricorn, the Ascendant, Midheaven, Sun and Moon.

Uranus. The first of the trans-Saturnian planets of modern discovery. *v. Solar System.*

Vernal Equinox, The Spring Equinox. *v. Equinox; Celestial Sphere.*

Vertical. Virtually synonymous with perpendicular, save that vertical applies more to abstract things and implies the general direction of the zenith, while perpendicular applies more to concrete things and implies a general downward direction toward Earth's center. Astronomically and astrologically it is employed with reference to the celestial circle, the circle in which one stands when facing south. v. *Celestial Sphere*.

Vespertine. Said of a planet which sets in the West after the Sun. The reverse of Matutine *(q.v.)*.

Via Combusta. The combust path. As employed by the ancients this doubtless referred to a cluster of fixed stars in the early degrees of the constellation Scorpio. A birth Moon in that arc was considered to be as afflicted as if it was in an eclipse condition - at or near one of the Nodes. If so, the description would have to be revised by 1° every 70 years, to compensate for the Precessional arc. This would probably place the Via Combusta in the region occupied by Antares and opposed by Aldebaran, an arc now centering around 10° Sagittarius. A birth planet or birth Moon in that arc would thus be described "in Via Combusta." Some of the older authorities gave its location as the last half of Libra and the whole of Capricorn; others, from Libra 15° to Scorpio 15°.

Vibrations. It is common to speak of impressions as vibrations. Bodies doubtless exude some variety of emanations, which we now deem to be energy radiations, and whose vibratory characteristics are termed frequencies. just as the thought embodied in music or audible sounds is conveyed to the ear in sound frequencies, of a range from 60 to 6000 cycles a second, and color in art and all things visible is conveyed to the eye in light frequencies of from 400 to 800 milli-micron wave lengths, so must there be a range of frequencies in which otherwise unexpressed thoughts are projected from one brain to that of another attuned to receive it. Occultists define Vibrations as psychic pulsations or magnetic waves.

Violent Signs. Aries, Libra, Scorpio, Capricorn, and Aquarius. v. *Signs*.

Virgo. The sixth sign of the zodiac. v. *Signs*.

Visibility.
Moon. As the New Moon begins to separate from its conjunction with the Sun, it becomes visible in the West just after Sunset. Each successive evening it is higher in the sky, hence sheds its light for nearly an hour longer before it sets. A first quarter Moon is always seen directly overhead immediately after sunset. At the Full Moon the Sun's setting reveals the Moon just rising in the East, hence the Full Moon shines throughout the entire night. As each night it rises an hour later, by the time it reaches its last quarter it does not rise until midnight, and is overhead when the morning Sun, rising in the East, blots it from view. At the next Lunation the Moon traverses the sky along with the Sun, and is invisible - except as it eclipses the Sun, when it shows as a dark shadow crossing the Sun. A day later it reappears in the West, just after the fading light of the Sun renders it visible. *Mercury*. Its periods of visibility follow a pattern similar to that of the Moon, in a cycle of from 3½ and 4½ months. A few days after its inferior conjunction it fades into view in the West about an hour after sunset. Each night for about three nights it climbs higher in the western sky to its point of greatest elongation; then falls back until it disappears. Five to six weeks later, in the middle of its retrograde period, occurs its superior conjunction, when its rays are completely enveloped by those of the Sun. In another five or six weeks it attains to a sufficient elongation to become

visible in the East just before Sunrise. Each of three mornings finds it a little higher in the sky, after which it as quickly recedes - and another cycle begins. *Venus.* Its cycle is strikingly similar to that of the Moon - including its phases; but while Mercury makes its superior conjunction approximately every four months at an advance of four Signs, the Venus superior conjunction occurs every two years, approximately, at an advance of nine signs. *Mars, Jupiter* and *Saturn.* Similarly the major planets depend for visibility upon their positions relative to the Sun, whereby the planet can be above the horizon at a time when the Sun is below it. A study of the phenomena of visibility of a planet with regards to the relative positions of the Sun and Moon, will contribute to a better understanding of the Doctrine of Orientality, which decrees that a planet is more advantageously placed when oriental of the Sun, and occidental of the Moon.

Mercury was an Evening Star in November of 1943-1944, and will be on every sixth year thereafter; 1949-1950, and so on.

Venus was an Evening Star in November 1941, 1944, 1946 and 1947, and will be on every eighth year after each of these dates.

Mars was a Morning Star in 1947, and was to be every second year thereafter for many years.

Jupiter was visible in the evening

Saturn will have been a Morning Star for several years from 1945.

The major planets are brightest when in opposition to the Sun, when they are visible throughout the entire night.

Uranus is sometimes visible to the unaided eye on a Moonless night, when it is in a near conjunction with Mars.

Neptune and *Pluto* are never visible except with the aid of a telescope.

Vital Signs. *v. Signs.*

Vocal Signs. Gemini, Libra and Aquarius. *v. Signs.*

Voice, Signs of. Said to be Gemini, Virgo, Libra, Aquarius and the first half of Sagittarius, so called because when one of these Signs ascend and Mercury is strong, the person is deemed to have the capacity to become an orator.

Void of Course: Said of a planet which forms no complete aspect before leaving the Sign in which it is posited at birth. When the Moon is so placed it denies fruition to much of the good otherwise promised. In Horary Astrology a planet so placed is said to indicate a person devoid of objective or purpose, hence one who abandons himself to aimless endeavor.

Vulcan. A hypothetical planet, said to be yet undiscovered and possibly the ruler of Virgo. Much conjectured among ancient astrologers, the orbit of which is supposed to lie inside that of Mercury. Astronomers have so far found no justification for any assumption of its existence.

War Time. *v. Time.*

Watchers of the Heavens. Applied by the Persians (c. 3000 B.C.) to the four Royal Stars then at the angles of the Zodiac: the Watcher of the East, then at the Vernal Equinox - Aldebaran; the Watcher of the North, which then marked the Summer Solstice - Regulus; the Watcher of the West, then at the Autumnal Equinox - Antares, the Watcher of the South, which then marked the Winter Solstice - Fomalhaut.

Water-bearer, Waterman. The zodiacal Sign Aquarius. *v. Signs.*

Water Signs. Cancer, Scorpio, Pisces. *v. Signs.*

Wave Length. Radio waves may be measured either in length or in frequency: the higher the frequency, the shorter the length of the waves. For example, your WMCA, at the top of the dial, has a frequency of 570 kilocycles, in a wave that has a length of approximately 527 metres. Multiply one by the other and you have about 300,000. WQXR, near the bottom, has a frequency of 1560 kc., and a wave length of approximately 192 metres. These multiplied yield also approximately 300,000 - thereby showing a definite inverse ratio between frequency and length of wave. The ultra-short wave lengths in the light band are measured in millimicrons, or angstrom units. A micron is a millionth part of a metre; a millimicron, a thousandth part of a micron; an angstrom, one-tenth of a millimicron. Red light has a wave length of about 780 M M or 7800 A (angstrom units); yellow, 590 M M or 5900 A; and violet, 390 M M or 3900 A. The range of visibility is thus one octave: from approximately 400 M M to 800 M M. Above that are the ultra-violet rays, and below it, the infra-red. It is also discovered that refraction increases in inverse ratio to the wave length - hence the dispersion of light as it passes through a glass prism. It is a matter of wave length that Mars yields a red light, stimulates the adrenal glands, and thus produces the sundry emotional reactions that astrologers have learned to associate with a Mars accent: and similarly with all the other planetary rays, as distinguished from those of the luminaries.

Weak Signs. Cancer, Capricorn and Pisces. *v. Signs.*

Whole Signs. Gemini, Libra and Aquarius, and by some authorities Taurus. *v. Signs.*

Year. The Solar or Tropical Year is the period of time in which the earth performs a revolution in its orbit about the Sun, or passes from any point of the ecliptic to the same point again. It consists of 365.2422 days, or 365d 5h 48M 46s. (The Sun's motion in longitude in a Julian year of 365.25 days is 360° 27'7.)

The Sidereal Year is a period of 365d.256 or 365d 6h 9m 9s.5, during which time the Sun's center, departing eastward from the ecliptic meridian of a given star, returns to the same; an astral year. It is about 20 minutes longer than the tropical year. The sidereal month is of a duration of 27d.322. The *Anomalistic Year*, that between two successive perihelion passages of the Earth, is 365d.26, or 4m 43s.5 longer than the sidereal year, although it is increasing in length even faster than the sidereal year. v. DAY.

Zenith. Mathematically, the Pole of the Horizon. The point directly overhead, through which pass the Prime Vertical *(q.v.)* and Meridian circles. Every place has its own zenith, and the nearer a planet is to that zenith, the more powerful is its influence.. The term is sometimes loosely applied to the cusp of the Tenth House, which strictly speaking is only the point of the zodiac or ecliptic through which the meridian circle passes. *v. Celestial Sphere.*

Zero Hour Circles. The Secondary Hour Circles drawn through the celestial poles and perpendicular to the celestial equator are termed Hour Circles, while those drawn parallel to the celestial equator are called parallels of declination. The angle at the pole which this circle makes with the meridian through any other place is called longitude.

The Hour Circle passing through the point of the Spring Equinox is known as the Zero Hour Circle. At the time the Great Pyramid was built, the Zero Hour Circle cut the Earth at that point, just as some centuries later it cut the location fot eh Greenwich Observatory when that was constructed. The world time should follow the precession of the Equinoxes, but this would entail not only the relocation of the Observatory every 70 or 700 years but of all the time zone meridians - obviously a difficulty not easily overcome. To obviate that, world time has been made synonymous with Greenwich Standard Time. However, the measurement in degrees of Right Ascension of points along the Ecliptic, beginning at the point of the Spring Equinox, must of necessity be correct, and while the required adjustment is but a matter of seconds per year, there is little we can do but disregard the interval, much as we arbitrarily correct the calender by an intercalary day every four years. Thus it becomes the one passage of time of which no record is kept other than in the changed relationship between the signs and the constellations. The result, however, is that Sidereal Time as utilized in locating the daily noon-pint is in increasing disagreement with Standard world-time as observed on the Earth. However, since an hour's discrepancy as created by law during Daylight Saving Time has entailed no serious difficulties, the failure to shift our world time zones in keeping with the precession will entail no greater inconvenience for some 2,000 years, at which time we could relocate another observatory and still maintain the same boundaries for our Standard Time Zones. v. *Signs* and *Constellations*

Zodiac. A circle or belt, which anciently was said to extend some 8 degrees on either side of the ecliptic (q.v.). Modern astronomers have widened it to 9 degrees either side, because of the extreme latitudes to which Venus and Mars attain. The position of any planet within, or of any star within or outside of the zodiax, is measured by a perpendicular to the ecliptic. The point where this perpendicular meets the ecliptic is the geocentric longitude of the star or planet. In a sense, the zodiac is identical with the ecliptic, for both are measured from a point of beginning at the Vernal Equinox. v. *Celestial Sphere.*

Zodiacal Aspects. Those measured in degrees along the Ecliptic. When used in connection with Primary Directions the Promittor's place is taken without latitude in contrast to the usual method used with mundane aspects wherein one takes cognizance of the longitudinal degree at which the aspect is complete.

Zodiacal Directions. Those formed in the Zodiac, by the progressed motion of Ascendant, Midheaven, Sun, and Moon, to aspects with the planets. These may be: Direct, in the order of the signs; or Converse, against the order of the signs.

Zodiacal metals: are those of the planetary Rulers:
Aries-Scorpio.............Iron
Taurus-Libra..............Copper
Gemini-Virgo..............Mercury
Cancer-Leo................Gold

Sagittarius-Pisces........Tin
Capricorn-Aquarius........Lead

Zodiacal Parallels. Any two points within the Zodiac that are of equal declination are said to be in zodiacal parallel with each other. If both are North or both South declination they were anciently termed antiscions. Some older authorities deemed that both were equally effective, but most modern authorities ignore the contra-antiscions and attribute astrological significance only to those between two bodies in parallel on the same side of the Equator. The zodiacal parallel may be formed by direction in the Primary System, or by progression in the Secondary System. To direct the Sun to an approximate parallel: In the ephemeris find the number of days subsequent to the birthdate, viz, the date on which the Sun attains the declination for the planet desired, this number of days equaling the interval in years at which the influence will become operative. Or, to be exact, subtract the Right Ascension of the Sun when it forms the parallel from the Sun's R.A. at birth, and reduce this arc of direction to time at the rate of 1º for a year and 5' for a month.

"Zodiacus Vitae." The Zodiac of Life. An old school book by Marcellus Palingenius Stellatus, which was extensively used in England in Shakespeare's time. The earliest edition extant is that in the British Museum, dated 1574, issued by the Stationers' Company in 1620. A modern edition with annotations by Foster Watson, M.A., Professor of Education in the University College of Wales, was published by Philip Wellby in 1908. In an Appendix to his work one reads this: "Palingenius understood at least as much as was current teaching among astrologers of his day in regard to the twelve divisions of the Houses of the Horoscope, and probably he knew something more.... The twelve signs of the zodiac were for him something more than mere pegs on which to hang an argument or elaborate a discourse.... Mystically considered, the purport of the twelve chapters of Palingenius will find their parallel in the twelve labors of Hercules, and thus will typify the evolution of the human soul through successive stages of mental and spiritual enlightenment."

www.ingramcontent.com/pod-product-compliance
Lightning Source LLC
Chambersburg PA
CBHW060603230426
43670CB00011B/1946